RELIGION: EMPIRICAL STUDIES

Treating 'religion' as a fully social, cultural, historical and material field of practice, this book presents a series of debates and positions on the nature and purpose of the 'Study of Religions', or 'Religious Studies'. Offering an introductory guide to this influential, and politically relevant, academic field, the contributors illustrate the diversity and theoretical viability of qualitative empirical methodologies in the study of religions. The historical and cultural circumstances attending the emergence, defence and future prospects of Religious Studies are documented, drawing on theoretical material and case studies prepared within the context of the British Association for the Study of Religions (BASR), and making frequent reference to wider European, North American and other international debates and critiques.

Religion: Empirical Studies

A Collection to Mark the 50th Anniversary
of the British Association for the Study of Religions

Edited by
STEVEN J. SUTCLIFFE

ASHGATE

Published by
Ashgate Publishing Limited
Gower House
Croft Road
Aldershot
Hants GU11 3HR
England

Ashgate Publishing Company
Suite 420
101 Cherry Street
Burlington, VT 05401-4405
USA

Ashgate website: http://www.ashgate.com

British Library Cataloguing in Publication Data
Religion: empirical studies
    1. Religion – Congresses   2. Religion – Methodology – Congresses
    I. Sutcliffe, Steven, 1961–
    200.1

Library of Congress Cataloging-in-Publication Data
Religion : empirical studies / edited by Steven Sutcliffe
       p. cm.
    Includes bibliographical references and index.
    ISBN 0-7546-4158-9 (alk. paper)
    1. Religion–Study and teaching. I. Sutcliffe, Steven, 1961–

BL41.R362 2004
200′.71–dc22   2004007475

ISBN 0 7546 4158 9

Printed on acid-free paper

Typeset by Tradespools, Frome, Somerset
Printed and bound in Great Britain by Antony Rowe Ltd, Chippenham, Wilts

Contents

List of Contributors

Miranda Aldhouse-Green is Professor of Archaeology and Head of the SCARAB (Study of Culture, Archaeology, Religion and Biogeography) Research Centre at the University of Wales, Newport. She is Vice-President of the Prehistoric Society, a Member of the Ancient Monuments Board for Wales and an Honorary Fellow of the Centre for Advanced Welsh and Celtic Studies at Aberystwyth. Her research interests concern the archaeology of ritual and religion in north-west Europe between c. 700 BC and 400 AD. Her publications include *Celtic Goddesses* (British Museum Press 1995), *Exploring the World of the Druids* (Thames and Hudson 1997) and *Dying for the Gods* (Tempus 2001). *An Archaeology of Images* (Routledge) and *The Quest for the Shaman in European Antiquity* (co-author: Thames and Hudson) are both forthcoming.

Elizabeth Amoah is Senior Lecturer and former Head of Department for the Study of Religion, University of Ghana at Lagos. She is a founding member of the Circle of Concerned African Women Theologians and also helps to run the Institute of African Women in Religion and Culture at Trinity Theological Seminary. Her publications include 'Women and Rituals in Akan Society' (*Dialogue and Alliance* **4**, 1990), *Where God Reigns: Reflections on Women in God's World* (editor: Sam Woode, 1997) and *Divine Empowerment of Women in Africa's Complex Realities: Papers from the Circle of Concerned African Women Theologians* (editor: Sam Woode 2001).

Peter Antes is Professor and Head of the Department for the History of Religions (Religionswissenschaft) at the University of Hannover, Germany. He was President of the German Association for the History of Religions from 1988–1993 and was elected IAHR president in 2000. He has published widely on Islam and methodology, including *Der Islam als politischer Faktor* (Niedersaechsische Landeszentrale fuer politische Bildung, 2001), 'The New Politics. History and History of Religions: The World after 11 September 2001' (*Diogenes* No. 50: International Council for Philosophy and Humanistic Studies/UNESCO) and 'Why should people study History of Religions?' in *Themes and Problems of the History of Religions in Contemporary Europe: Proceedings of the International Seminar, Messina, March 30–31, 2001,* (ed. G. S. Gasparro, Lionello Giordano 2002).

Chris Arthur, MA PhD (Edinburgh) is Senior Lecturer in Religious Studies at the University of Wales, Lampeter. He has also held Research Fellowships at the Universities of St Andrews and Edinburgh. His most recent publications include *Religion and the Media: an Introductory Reader* (editor: University of Wales Press, 1993), *The Globalization of Communications: Some Religious Implications* (WCC, 1998) and *Religious Pluralism: a Metaphorical Approach* (The Davies Group, 2000). Other publications include a collection of essays on religious education entitled *Biting the Bullet* (Saint Andrew Press, 1990), and *In the Hall of Mirrors* (Mowbray 1986), comprising lectures given at the University of St Andrews under the terms of the Gifford Bequest.

Brian Bocking is Professor of the Study of Religions at the School of Oriental and African Studies (SOAS), University of London. He took his BA in Religious Studies at Lancaster University in 1973 and his MA and PhD (on Chinese Madhyamika) at Leeds. He subsequently taught Religious Studies, especially Japanese Religions, at Stirling University and Tsukuba University, Japan. He was Head of the Study of Religions department at Bath Spa University College for twelve years before moving to SOAS in 1999. His publications include *Nagarjuna in China* (Edwin Mellen Press, 1995), *A Popular Dictionary of Shinto* (Curzon 1996) and *The Oracles of the Three Shrines: Windows on Japanese Religion* (Curzon 2000).

Marion Bowman is Senior Lecturer in Religious Studies at The Open University, President of The Folklore Society and Conference Organiser for the BASR. Between 1993 and 2002 she organised an annual conference on 'Contemporary and New Age Religions' and in 2003 co-organised the international 'Alternative Spirituality and New Age Studies' conference at the Open University. She organised the first EASR Conference in 2001, and an ESRC Research Seminar in European Ethnology in 2003. Her publications include *Healing and Religion* (editor: Hisarlik Press, 2000), *Beyond New Age: Exploring Alternative Spirituality* (co-editor: Edinburgh University Press, 2000) and 'Pagan Identities' (co-edited: *DISKUS* special issue, 2000).

George D. Chryssides studied at the University of Glasgow as an under-graduate and gained his doctorate from the University of Oxford. He has taught at several British Universities and is currently Head of Religious Studies at the University of Wolverhampton. He has published extensively on new religious movements: his books include *The Advent of Sun Myung Moon* (Macmillan, 1991), *Exploring New Religions* (Cassell, 1999) and *Historical Dictionary of New Religious Movements* (Scarecrow Press, 2001). He has also contributed to numerous international academic journals and edited collections. He is a member of the BASR Executive Committee and since 2002 has edited the BASR Bulletin.

James L. Cox is Reader in Religious Studies and Convenor of the Religious Studies Subject Group in the University of Edinburgh, and since 2003 has been President of the BASR. From 1993 to 1998, he directed the African Christianity Project in the Centre for the Study of Christianity in the Non-Western World at the University of Edinburgh. He previously taught at Westminster College, Oxford, the University of Zimbabwe and Alaska Pacific University. His many publications include *The Impact of Christian Missions on Indigenous Cultures* (Edwin Mellen, 1991), *Rational Ancestors: Scientific Rationality and African Indigenous Religions* (Cardiff Academic Press, 1998) and *Expressing the Sacred: An Introduction to the Phenomenology of Religion* (University of Zimbabwe, 3rd printing, 2000).

Armin W. Geertz is Professor in the History of Religions in the Department of the Study of Religion at the University of Aarhus, Denmark. Since 1993 he has been Director of the Research Network on New Religions (RENNER), and since 1998 he has been Chairman of the Advisory Committee on Religious Denominations for the Danish Government. He was co-founder and Chairman of the Danish Association for the History of Religions (1982–1994), Treasurer of the IAHR from 1990–1995, and since 1995 has been General Secretary of the IAHR. His numerous publications include *Hopi Indian Altar Iconography* (Brill 1987) and *The Invention of Prophecy: Continuity and Meaning in Hopi Indian Religion* (University of California Press, 1992).

Richard Gombrich has been Boden Professor of Sanskrit at Oxford University and a Fellow of Balliol College since 1976. He was educated at Oxford and Harvard Universities. He has published extensively on the history and anthropology of Buddhism, including *Precept and Practice: Traditional Buddhism in the rural highlands of Ceylon* (Clarendon Press, 1971), *Theravāda Buddhism: A Social History from ancient Benares to modern Colombo* (Routledge and Kegan Paul, 1988) and *How Buddhism Began: The Conditioned Genesis of the Early Teachings* (The Athlone Press, 1996). He has served as Secretary and then President of the Pali Text Society and is currently founding the Oxford Centre for Buddhist Studies.

Gerrie ter Haar is Professor of Religion, Human Rights and Social Change at the Institute of Social Studies, The Hague, Netherlands. Trained as a scholar of religion, she specialises in the study of Africa, but has also done field research in Europe and Asia. She is the author of *Halfway to Paradise: African Christians in Europe* (Cardiff Academic Press, 1998, republished by Acton Publishers, Nairobi, 2001) and co-author of *Worlds of Power: Religious Thought and Political Practice in Africa* (Hurst & Co., London, and Oxford University Press, New York, 2004); her edited and co-edited publications include *The Freedom to do God's Will: Religious Fundamentalism and Social*

Change (Routledge, London, 2003). She is deputy secretary-general of the IAHR.

Ria Kloppenborg, who died in 2003, was Senior Professor of History of Religions and Comparative Religion in the Department of History of Religions, Faculty of Theology, University of Utrecht, the Netherlands. Her many publications include *The Paccekabuddha: A Buddhist Ascetic* (Leiden, Brill, 1974), *Selected Studies on Ritual in the Indian Religions* (co-editor: Brill, 1983) and *Female Stereotypes in Religious Traditions* (co-editor: Brill 1995).

Kim Knott is Professor of Religious Studies at the University of Leeds and Director of the Community Religions Project. She has researched modern Hindu groups, the religions of minority ethnic groups in Britain and gender and destiny. Her publications include *My Sweet Lord: The Hare Krishna Movement* (Aquarian, 1986), *Hinduism in Leeds* (University of Leeds, 1986) and *Hinduism: A Very Short Introduction* (Oxford University Press, 1998). She is currently directing research on the role and representation of religious communities in British public life, democratic participation and urban regeneration, and is completing a book on *The Location of Religion: A Spatial Analysis*. She is a former president of the BASR and is membership secretary of the European Association for the Study of Religions.

Julia Leslie is Senior Lecturer in Hindu Studies, and Chair of the Centre for Gender and Religions Research, in the Department of the Study of Religions at the School of Oriental and African Studies, University of London. Her publications include *The Perfect Wife: the Orthodox Hindu Woman according to the Strīdharmapaddhati of Tryambakayajvan* (Oxford University Press 1989; Penguin 1995), *Authority and Meaning in Indian Religions: Hinduism and the Case of Vālmīki* (Ashgate 2003), *Rules and Remedies in Classical Indian Law* (editor: Brill 1991), *Roles and Rituals for Hindu Women* (editor: Pinter 1991; Motilal Banarsidass 1992) and *Invented Identities: the Interplay of Gender, Religion and Politics in India* (co-editor: Oxford University Press 2001).

Tariq Modood is Professor of Sociology, Politics and Public Policy and the founding Director of the Centre for the Study of Ethnicity and Citizenship at the University of Bristol. He is a joint founding editor of the journal *Ethnicities* (Sage) and his publications include (co-author) *Ethnic Minorities in Britain: Diversity and Disadvantage* (Policy Studies Institute, 1997), (editor) *Church, State and Religous Minorities* (Policy Studies Institute, 1997), *Multicultural Politics: Racism, Ethnicity and Muslims in Britain* (Minnesota University Press and Edinburgh University Press, 2004) and (joint editor) *Nationalism, Identity and Minority Rights* (Cambridge University Press, 2004).

Peggy Morgan is Lecturer in the Study of Religions at Mansfield College and a member of the University of Oxford's Faculty of Theology for which she teaches papers and convenes an interdisciplinary seminar in the study of religions. She was president of BASR from 2000–2003 and previously served as conference organiser and secretary. She is also a past chair of the Shap Working Party on World Religions in Education and a Governor of The Oxford Centre for Hindu Studies. From 1996–2002 she was Director of The Religious Experience Research Centre. Her publications include *Ethical Issues in Six Religious Traditions* (co-editor: Edinburgh University Press 1996) and *Six Religions in The Twenty First Century* (co-editor: Stanley Thornes 2000).

Steven J. Sutcliffe was recently Lecturer in Religious Studies at the University of Edinburgh and previously Research Fellow in Religion in Contemporary Scotland in the Department of Religious Studies, University of Stirling. He has published widely on 'New Age' religion, including *Beyond New Age: Exploring Alternative Spirituality* (co-editor: Edinburgh University Press, 2000), *Children of the New Age: A History of Spiritual Practices* (Routledge, 2003) and 'Studying "New Age": Reconfiguring the Field', a guest edited issue of *Culture and Religion* (2003). He is on the editorial boards of *Culture and Religion* and *Religion*.

Terence Thomas is former Senior Lecturer and Staff Tutor in the Open University in Wales and former Head of the Department of Religious Studies at The Open University. His publications include *Paul Tillich and World Religions* (Cardiff Academic Press, 1999), *The British: Their Religious Beliefs and Practices* (editor: Routledge 1988) and *Paul Tillich: The Encounter of Religions and Quasi-Religions* (editor: Edwin Mellen, 1989).

Foreword

Peggy Morgan

'The 1950s were the best time I have known for doing philosophy in an interdisciplinary setting', remarks Dorothy Emmet, one of the founding members of the British Section of the International Association for the History of Religions (IAHR) – later to become the British Association for the Study of Religions (BASR) – in her final book of reminiscences (Emmet 1996, p. 90). Despite its original name, BASR was never dominated by historians, but involved in its field of interest, alongside history, philosophy, anthropology, archaeology, sociology, philology, area and single religion studies, comparative studies, phenomenology and so on. It did, however, take over thirty years for the name to change and a good summary of the debate in progress is in *Bulletin* 44 (1984) by Karel Werner. Further responses from Steve Collins and Jan Knappert were published in *Bulletin* 45, with a reminder that this had been debated before, in 1975!

As is discussed in the introduction to this volume, terminology has changed over the years and is still fiercely debated. In 1904, the Manchester Chair of Comparative Religion was located in a Theology Faculty, which was a problem for J.G. Frazer who, according to Sharpe 'gave serious attention to the possibility of becoming the first Professor of Comparative Religion in the University of Manchester' but rejected the offer 'on the grounds that his views on "religion in general and Christianity in particular" would make it difficult for him to teach men preparing for the Christian ministry' (Sharpe 1986, pp. 88, 132–3).[1] This was not a problem for the Pali scholar T.W. Rhys Davids who became its first occupant. The adjective 'comparative' is now more specifically used by those who do comparative ethics or comparative theology; 'great' religions have become 'world' religions and then, more embracingly, 'religious traditions'. Other professional, discipline and single tradition associations whose interests overlap those of BASR have also emerged and grown. Examples of these are the British Association for Jewish Studies, United Kingdom Association of Buddhist Studies, The Shap Working Party on World Religions in Education and the British Sociological Association Sociology of Religion Study Group. These include many dual memberships with BASR and there is a friendly and supportive exchange of information.

International Congresses for the History of Religions had begun in 1900 in Paris. Britain hosted the third of these in Oxford in 1908 (Allen and Johnson 1908) and already had a strong tradition in the field through the work of scholars such as F.M. Müller, J.E. Carpenter, A.M. Fairbairn, T.W. Rhys Davids, E.B. Tylor and many others.[2] The IAHR was founded at a seventh congress in Amsterdam in 1950. Its journal *Numen* was launched in 1953 and in 1954 the British Section of the IAHR began at Exeter College, Oxford. The founding group of nine people included E.O. James, who was President for the next eighteen years until his death, and Geoffrey Parrinder, who at the time of writing is in his nineties and the last surviving founder member. Eleven other people sent their apologies, making an initial membership of twenty. At the 2003 AGM in Chester, substantial growth is indicated by a membership figure of 235.

BASR's international links have stayed strong, both through the networking of individuals such as Ninian Smart, Ursula King, Michael Pye and Rosalind Hackett, but also in events such as the 1975 IAHR Congress, held in Lancaster (Pye and Mckenzie 1980). BASR was also a key player in establishing a European Association for the Study of Religions (EASR) in 2001, hosting EASR's first gathering and AGM in Cambridge at a conference entitled 'Religion and Community'. Members of BASR are automatically members of both these asssociations. The BASR's constitution, which owes a great deal to Terence Thomas, as well as its lively Bulletin (every new editor brings new ideas) and its financial support (through IAHR's contingency fund) to enable those from poorer associations to attend the quinquennial international congresses, are seen as models for others to follow.

For many years after its foundation BASR seemed rather exclusive by contemporary standards. I had joined the gatherings as a visitor at the Cherwell Centre in Oxford many times and attended the 1975 Lancaster IAHR Congress, but when I became a member in 1982, people were still proposed and seconded by two existing members who spoke about the appropriateness of their nomination at the AGM. That changed soon afterwards, but the annual gatherings were still about 25–30 people only, usually in armchairs at the Cherwell Centre. It was always a very friendly group, interested in new faces and new ideas. Timothy Fitzgerald ('a fairly new member') wrote in *Bulletin* 44 in November 1984 that it was 'a slightly intimate, almost club-like atmo-sphere..., friendly and creative at a personal level'. Ian Calvert (retiring from ten years as treasurer) responded robustly to these comments in *Bulletin* 45 (March 1985), by defending the Association's standards of membership and pointing out that cuts in the subject area had affected conference attendance. Whatever was felt about size, in comparison, for example, with the American Academy of Religion, BASR gatherings were always a good place to meet and listen to key figures in the developing, though frequently threatened, field in the UK, including guests from abroad. People such as Geoffrey Parrinder, W.

Montgomery Watt, Ninian Smart, Cyril Williams, Frank Whaling, John Hinnells, W. Owen Cole, Ursula King, Michael Pye, Kim Knott, to name but a few, have been loyal supporters. The *Bulletin* began in 1972 under the editorship of Michael Pye and has gone from strength to strength as a record of conferences, publications, debate in the field and the state of the departments over the years. The *Bulletin* has also provided some lively debate, most recently in the exchange between Robert Segal and Frank Whaling (No. 100, November 2003) over the contribution to the field of the Harvard Centre and Wilfred Cantwell Smith, a loyal member of BASR.

BASR has represented to me a scholarly community which has provided a doorway into national and international scholarship in a field which has not diminished in interest or relevance in the nearly forty years that I have been involved. But it has been much more than that. I found as a young woman its senior scholars welcoming and affirming and that the atmosphere at meetings involved critique but not destructive confrontation or academic arrogance. This seems to have continued, with young scholars being funded and encouraged at BASR conferences to give reports of work in progress and short papers. I have often heard newcomers remark that thay have been made to feel very welcome and that we are an interesting and warm group of people whom they have enjoyed meeting. It has retained its atmosphere of a professional community of friendship when education has lost much of its warmth in these pressurised and insecure times. At fifty years, as the sample of Occasional Papers dating from 1991 in this volume indicates, the intellectual vitality and diversity of debate and educational relevance of its subject matter has not declined but looks set for further decades. It is intended during the fiftieth anniversary conference in Oxford in 2004 that the archives of the Association will be lodged in the Bodleian library as a resource for future researchers into the Association and individual members' contribution to the study of religions.

It has been my personal privilege to serve the Association for three years (2000–2003) as its Honorary President and before that as its conference organiser and secretary. I am delighted to see these occasional papers brought together into a volume which maps some important approaches and foci in the field and I thank Steven Sutcliffe on behalf of the Association for undertaking the task and adding his personal voice to the history of the field.

Notes

1 The incorporated quote is from a personal letter of Frazer's.

2 For material on these scholars and the subsequent history of the subject in the UK, see Sharpe (1986) and King (ed., 1990). Hulmes (2002) also provides interesting, if sometimes anecdotal, material.

Bibliography

Allen, P.S. and Johnson, J. de M. (eds), 1908. *Proceedings of the International Association for the History of Religions Congress, Oxford 1908*, Oxford: Oxford University Press.

Emmet, Dorothy 1996. *Philosophers and Friends*, London: Macmillan.

Hulmes, Edward 2002. *The Spalding Trust and The Union for The Study of The Great Religions*, Durham: The Memoir Club.

King, Ursula (ed.), 1990. *Turning Points in Religious Studies: Essays in Honour of Geoffrey Parrinder*, Edinburgh: T. & T. Clark.

Pye, Michael and McKenzie, Peter (eds), 1980. *History of Religions: IAHR Proceedings*, Leicester: University of Leicester Studies in Religions 11.

Sharpe, Eric 1986[1975]. *Comparative Religion: A History*, 2nd edn, London: Duckworth Werner, Karel 1984, 'Are We All Historians? A Renewed Plea for BASR', *BASR Bulletin* **44**, November, pp. 4–5.

Qualitative Empirical Methodologies: An Inductive Argument

Steven J. Sutcliffe

> The common ground on which students of religion *qua* students of religion meet is the realization that the awareness of the numinous or the experiences of transcendence (where these happen to exist in religions) are – whatever else they may be – undoubtedly empirical facts of human existence and history, to be studied like all human facts. (from a statement by R.J.Z. Werblowsky to the 1960 IAHR conference in Marburg, Germany, quoted in Schimmel 1960, p. 236)

> The study of religions refers to a field which is, in the common phrase, 'out there'. (Pye 2000, p. 217)

BASR, Methodological Diversity and the Politics of Representation

The chapters in this volume are fully revised versions of a selection of papers originally given by British, European and African scholars at conferences of the British Association for the Study of Religions (BASR) from the early 1990s to 2002. Formerly known as the British Association for the History of Religions (BAHR), the BASR is the sole autonomous professional academic association in the UK predicated upon the categories 'religion' and 'religions'. These chapters were first delivered orally at BASR conferences, most as annual lectures; all were later revised for publication in an ongoing 'Occasional Papers' series.[1] They represent a series of positions on appropriate theories, methods and subject matter within a field known somewhat confusingly in the UK first as 'comparative religion',[2] then (in the post-world war II period) often as 'world religions',[3] and more recently (usually with some rather different methodological nuances and emphases) as 'Religious Studies'[4] or 'Study of Religions'.[5] It is with the methodologies underpinning the latter pair that this volume deals, although contributors are not confined exclusively to such self-designated academic departments but come also, for example, from archaeology, ethnology, philology and sociology, and hence bring their own distinctive disciplinary methods into the equation. However, given the chapters' common production base in BASR conferences, the selection is designed to illustrate work broadly representative of some central theories, methods and subject matter in academic studies of 'religion' in the UK.[6] The chief concern of this introduction, then, is to map and contextualize some of this methodological diversity and then to explore the significance of what we might call a 'qualitative empiricism' in securing some (politically important) methodological common ground for the field as a whole.

On first inspection a very broad methodological outlook underpins official statements of the BASR, and this breadth and diversity certainly comes through in the contributions to the present volume. In brief statements in the BASR's *Bulletin* and on its website, the BASR is represented as the devolved British branch of the International Association for the History of Religions (IAHR) whose objective is 'the promotion of the academic study of religions through international interdisciplinary collaborations'. Criteria of membership are similarly inclusive, simply being described as 'open to scholars whose work has a bearing on the academic study of religions and who are normally resident in the United Kingdom'.[7]

The breadth of this stance of course accords with a well-known position on the pluralised, aspectual stance taken by the modern study of religion, summarized by Smart (1998, p. 18) as 'the study of religion as an aspect of human existence in a cross-cultural way and from a polymethodic or multidisciplinary perspective'.[8] This position understands the study of religions as a cluster of debates and conversations that emphasises methodological diversity and inclusivity. The sum is a multifaceted model of Religious Studies, analagous to an intellectual feast with an open invitation to table. This model in turn has encouraged a view of the study of religion as a 'field' akin to thematic or area studies (Gender Studies or American Studies, say) rather than a self-contained 'discipline', such as 'History of Religions' in the USA and *religionswissenschaft* or 'science of religions' in Europe, where a 'disciplinary' formation has been justified historically by an autonomous object of study with its own specialist methodology. In fact, both these approaches to the construction and regulation of an academic regime – 'field' and 'discipline' – have taken the lead at different times and in different places in the modern historiography of the study of religion, and indeed often co-existed. But the 'field' view has been generally dominant in the UK, in particular in association with the model developed at the Department of Religious Studies at Lancaster under the direction of Ninian Smart (1927–2001) and others from 1967. The success of the 'field' model in turn has had the effect, at least implicitly, of aligning Religious Studies with 'postmodern' stresses on diversity, heterogeneity and polyvocality rather than the closure-driven, totalizing 'metanarrative' (Lyotard 1984) of modernity, although – as Nye (2000) argues – Religious Studies has been hesitant to engage fully and directly with postmodern cultural theory.

A problem with the polymethodological model, however, has lain in determining who, if anyone, *cannot* be invited to table: who, if anyone, is to be *excluded* from the BASR (or indeed the IAHR) on methodological grounds. This has been perceived to be an issue on both discursive and institutional grounds: put simply, if we are to differentiate a *particular* body of scholars and hence develop and refine a set of cumulative explanatory discourses, not to mention an institutional and financial production base, we cannot have a completely 'open house'.

The demarcation issue is long-standing. One possibility for articulating a positive political identity has been to represent BASR as an inter-disciplinary partner able and willing to co-operate with peer discourses. Hence in April 1992 a joint conference was held at St. Mary's College, London, between BASR, the British Sociological Association Sociology of Religion Study Group and the Religion and Politics section of the Political Science Association.[9] But in practice, such co-operative ventures have been rare, if only for the reason that, historically, BASR is already constituted as an interdisciplinary field by default and therefore could (and does) include members who are already sociologists of religion or (more rarely, certainly) political scientists.

The historical touchstone of the debate has been the validity or otherwise of 'theology' within the range of polymethodic discourses sanctioned by the academic study of religions and – for present concerns – by BASR in particular. This has generated a lengthy literature *pro* and *contra* the relative validity of scientific and naturalistic analyses of religion over and against theological and confessional stances (either on behalf of particular religions, or of a generic 'religionism').[10] In practice this has tended to mean that overtly apologetic and evangelistic theologies have been relatively easily identified and, by tacit agreement, more or less effectively proscribed, while a degree of liberal and comparative theology, often implicit, has been tolerated and even assimilated into the field as a whole, as Fitzgerald (2000) argues. It is not hard to find concrete instances of the faultline in this debate. Some recent polymethodic compendia, such as Peter Connolly's *Approaches to the Study of Religion* (Connolly 1999; see Whaling 1999), or Mark Taylor's *Critical Terms for Religious Studies* (1998), blend theology fairly seamlessly into the polymethodological spectrum.

Other publications appear to exclude 'theology' rhetorically while giving it space in practice. A good example of such co-existence is *The Scottish Journal of Religious Studies* (*SJRS*). Edited by Glyn Richards in the Department of Religious Studies at Stirling, Scotland, between 1980 and 1996, *SJRS* represented an important UK intervention into the politics of defining the remit and function of 'Religious Studies'. According to Richards' inaugural editorial, the journal's aim was 'to promote a critical investigation of all aspects of the study of religion through the use of different methodologies while at the same time recognizing the importance of the interrelation between different religious traditions and their respective cultures' (Richards 1980). He updated this brief statement ten years later in Ursula King's (1990) survey of Religious

Studies in the UK, although he now adds explicitly that the *SJRS* editorial position represents 'the academic study of religion, *as distinct from* Christian theology' (Richards 1990; emphasis added); simultaneously he goes on to unpack the 'different methodologies' alluded to earlier, to include 'anthropological, sociological, philosophical, phenomenological, historical and comparative approaches' (*ibid*).

The first volume of *SJRS* (2 issues, 1980) featured papers by leading international scholars of the day, several of them BASR members (Ninian Smart, Trevor Ling and W. Montgomery Watt). But despite both the plurality of methodologies itemised in Richards' 1990 statement alongside the concern to demarcate a disciplinary field 'in its own right', 'distinct from Christian theology' (Richards 1980, 1990), the impression gained from scanning back issues of *SJRS* across its near-twenty-year career is of a preponderance of textual analyses, many with an overt or implicit comparative theological or interreligious dialogical and/or evaluative agenda. This is suggested also by the focus of early special issues of the journal under Richards' editorship, such as 'Mysticism' (vol. 3 no.1, 1982) and 'Truth in Religion' (vol. 5 no. 1, 1984), as well as of the bulk of book reviews throughout the journal's history, where Christian theology and philosophical studies are the dominant methodologies driving the items under review.

Of course, monolithic representations of 'Christian theology' (Richards 1990) as a sharply differentiated, taboo 'other', standing over against a purified 'Religious Studies', rather begs the question of what 'theology' is made to mean by its detractors in the academic study of religions; indeed, whether 'theology' has more often than not been set up as a straw man to knock down. Frank Whaling has raised this issue persistently (1984, 1999), focusing on ecumenical theologies of religions done by non-Western theologians in a global perspective by way of shifting the issue of the place of theology in the academic study of religions to (implicitly) postcolonial contexts and concerns, and hence away from dominant polarizations of naturalistic *versus* confessionalist discursive paradigms. In the light of Whaling's (and others'[11]) work, we might reflect on the possibility that a strongly constructed opposition between Religious Studies and Theology has been a problematic faultline to police, functioning to keep Religious Studies firmly in the shadow of Theology through its relentlessly negative self-defining, thereby taking up energies that might be more positively used in exploring specific new theories and methods or the broader institutional positioning of the field within a secularist academy. As Taylor (1998, p. 13) cautions: 'Insofar as religious studies defines itself as essentially antitheological, theology continues to set the terms for debate'. Similarly, Nye (2000, pp. 450–51) argues that this 'stand-off' mentality has had a negative impact on theoretical developments in the academic study of religions, insofar as many scholars have 'been so taken up with perpetuating and maintaining a discipline of religious studies for themselves vis-à-vis theology and theologians that they have failed to notice that the wider [theoretical] vista outside these narrow confines has been rapidly changing'.

In all this we must keep firmly in mind the material base of production of academic discourses if we are going to continue to enjoy an academic discourse on religion/s at all. In the UK the sticky demarcatory issue has been further compounded by the recent emergence of the disciplinary-administrative rubric of 'Theology and Religious Studies' (TRS), under which title college and university programmes for the study of religion are categorized for funding, staffing, student applications and other disciplinary-administrative purposes. In a detailed 'benchmarking statement' on the nature and remit of TRS, prepared by a working group of UK academics, we find continuing irresolution as to whether TRS is a subject 'area' or 'discipline'. Acknowledging the political ramifications of the debate, the statement remarks that the relation-ship between Theology and Religious Studies has been marked by 'hostilities' in other countries, but that in the UK it represents a 'lively ongoing debate ... which has enriched both academic traditions' (Theology and Religious Studies Benchmarking Group 2000, pp. 1–3). Notwithstanding the irenic tone of this statement, the net effect of operating under the chosen administrative rubric ('TRS') is that the academic study of religion/s in UK academic jurisdiction is made to function as an institutional subset of, or at best a 'junior' partner to, a Theology 'master' taxon, strikingly recalling S.G.F. Brandon's supposedly superceded characterization of 'comparative religion' as 'handmaid to Theology' (Brandon 1970, p. 1).[12] At a fairly superficial level, this means that students browsing the lists of degree courses in the UK typically will not find a separate section for 'Religious Studies' or 'the Study of Religion' but must search under 'higher order' rubrics of 'Theology' or 'Divinity'. At the same time – and ironically – although now increasingly encapsulated within Divinity faculties or tagged on to Theology departments, pluralist and comparativist 'RS' degree pathways often re-emerge as amongst the most popular components of an undergraduate 'TRS' degree – once, that is, the student has got her bearings within this classificatory hall of mirrors, an epistemological labour which in itself may well occupy a large part of the time and energy of an undergraduate degree. The sum, too often than not, is that the academic study of religions as a qualitative, reflexive, non-confessional and analytical enquiry into religion(s) has become effectively institutionally captive and contingent, rather than primary and formative.

Given this persistent ambivalence on the relationship between 'RS' and 'T' it is perhaps unsurprising that the historiography of Religious Studies is littered with the rhetoric of 'failure of nerve' (Wiebe 1984) and 'crisis' (McCutcheon 2003, pp. 54ff). This is no mere 'navel-gazing': in UK universities alone, the record suggests that the combination of wider economic pressures with a sensitive demarcation history periodically translates into closure of smaller autonomous 'Study of Religions' or 'Religious Studies' departments as and when certain winds (particularly economic, but also of intellectual fashion) blow chill. Despite the broad success of 'Religious Studies' as an export template for a polymethodic, liberal arts curriculum – particularly associated with the work of Ninian Smart (for example 1960, 1973, 1986), the Lancaster programme and its graduates – the long-term institutional security and development of the field in the UK, *qua* 'Religious Studies' or 'the Study of Religions', has been in the medium to long term rather less certain.[13] In reminding BASR membership of the history of 'downsizing' and threats of closure, Peggy Morgan (2003, p. 9) remarks that 'we are often in danger of thinking that cuts, closures and economic constraints are unique to our own times and contexts'. The occasion for her remarks was a wave of closures of programmes of 'Religious Studies' at a number of 'new' universities (formerly colleges or polytechnics) in the UK around the end of the 1990s, including Sunderland, Chichester, Middlesex and Derby. Making the point that this was, unfortunately, nothing new, Morgan reproduced a press release signed on behalf of the BAHR (as BASR was then known) nearly twenty years previously, in September 1981, by Ninian Smart and Michael Pye, which speaks of 'a serious crisis in the provision of facilities for study and training in the field of religion'. This was followed by a speech in the House of Lords by Viscount Combermere in February 1982 which notes with dismay that 'there are very few faculties of religious studies in the universities of this country' (both cited in Morgan 2003, pp. 9, 11).

When and where Religious Studies has survived and even flourished institutionally over the last thirty-five years, it would seem that a broadly 'phenomenological' methodology has served to maintain a more-or-less distinctive methodological base line or common ground, although this has not always been explicit.[14] What 'phenomenology' means, precisely, in its various use contexts is a moot point, but in the UK at least the term has acquired a reasonably steady set of connotations. In a nutshell, as Kim Knott (1995, p. 215, n.2) explains, 'in Britain, the discipline commonly known as *Religionswissenschaft* or the science of religion goes by the name of religious studies [and] generally signals the application of historical and/or phenomenological approaches'. A good index of how this field is taught and reproduced in practice is provided by Knott's own 'methodological autobiography', dictated in 1990, in which she reflects upon her early UK training:

> we were schooled very much in the tradition of understanding the material and *describing* it, but not explaining it in the sense of giving some overt outsider's interpretation of what was going on. The account that we were to present was *the believer's own account* uncontaminated by theoretical interpretations that did not come from that account. (Knott 1995, p. 202; emphasis added)

Knott's account of this approach, with its *epoche* or 'bracketing' of 'outsider' interpretations and its concern to validate 'insider' or emic interpretations, exemplifies a key strand in Euro-American phenomenological tradition. It is represented most strongly in the Norwegian scholar W. Brede Kristensen's famous statement 'there exists no other religious reality than the faith of the believer. If we really want to understand religion we must refer exclusively to the believer's testimony' (cited in Sharpe 1986: 228), or in Canadian scholar Wilfred Cantwell Smith's proposition that 'no statement about a religion is valid unless it can be acknowledged by that religion's believers' (Smith 1959: 42).[15] Knott is, of course, reflecting on her own student training in this passage, and in fact proceeds in the same paper to scrutinize and critique this 'received wisdom', in her particular case drawing on feminist methodologies of reflexivity and relationality. Other reassessments have followed; Knott's paper itself came out in Ursula King's *Religion and Gender* (King, ed. 1995), an important volume which tackled gender-blindness in both contemporary theorizing on religion and in the historical constitution of the field *qua* phenomenology or history of religions, questioning dominant representations of practitioners and communities in terms of implicit gender normativity and undifferentiated collective subjects. King's own paper on the position of women scholars within the IAHR (King 1995) chronicled the historical hegemony of male scholars within the field. In another strong critique, albeit from a rather different direction and this time from the USA, Russell McCutcheon (2001) charged the 'unreconstructed' phenomenologist of religion as functioning as 'caretaker' rather than 'critic' of religion, the point of studying religion being in his view to 'redescribe' phenomena in scholarly categories rather than simply collect, collate and endorse practitioners' testimonies.

And yet those keen to move 'beyond phenomenology' (Flood 1999) – and there are certainly different positions on this debate in the UK – should, arguably, be careful not to throw the baby out with the bathwater. With reference to the italicized elements in Knott's methodological autobiography above, a good case can be made for a scholar of religion's methodological toolkit to include, not as an optional extra but as central middle-order strategy, the attentive and detailed *description* of the phenomena packaged as 'religion' in any particular concrete instance, and, furthermore, for paying close attention to the 'believer's own account' as *part of* the explanatory process. That is, careful contextualized description of what the scholar has selected for attention under the rubric 'religion', including close attention to the subjectivities of the practitioners and/or the texts concerned, should be a basic methodological component in the study of religion/s insofar as this specialist field constructs 'religion' as a social and material arena of practice 'done' by embodied others. To put this another way: if it does *not* construct religion like this – that is, as an inquiry into a field that is, in Pye's terms (2000, p. 217), 'out there' in a shared social world – what exactly *is* distinctive about our field, and how can we defend its salience?

The Salience of Qualitative Empirical Methods

First, lest I be misunderstood as indicating by Pye's phrase 'out there' some quasi-mystical referent or *sui generis* quality for religion, let me confirm that I am simply using it as shorthand for a discursive and material field of practice 'done' by people in an everyday social and political world that exists quite independently of the scholar. The original context of Pye's remark is itself quite unambiguous on this score. Elsewhere I have argued for a similarly critical realist epistemology, arguing for a 'realistic' study of religion as a 'life-like, three-dimensional, materially viable' practice that should be tackled from a 'broad' methodological base 'open to all explanatory hypotheses which take empirical and behavioural dimensions seriously' (Sutcliffe 1998, pp. 269–70). Byrne (1999[1997]) arrives at a similarly 'empirical' position, this time from a more overtly cultural-symbolic approach based on Dilthey's notion of the place of *verstehen* in studies of the human world. Byrne concludes that 'religious studies is scientific to the extent that there really is a world of human meaning with religious facets awaiting exploration', and that the disciplinary coherence and integrity of the Study of Religions *qua* Study of Religions depends not on 'the details of natural scientific procedures' but simply in the requirement 'to establish that there is a publicly accessible object for it to study and publicly agreed ways, acceptable to folk holding different philosophies of life, for revealing the facets of that object' (*ibid*, p. 258).

I think that this kind of broad methodological base, which I call 'qualitative empirical', can indeed be detected beneath the diversity and inclusivity that has traditionally characterized the BASR's position, and I think that making it explicit could be a useful exercise in clarifying the parameters of the field. I want to begin this task by re-examining the term 'description', which has acquired negative connotations in some circles, particularly under the influence of the recent fervour for 'theory' (which I wholeheartedly endorse insofar as it is bound up with contextualized representations of fields of human practice/s 'out there'; a point I return to below). 'Description' itself as category and method, however, is not always fully attended to in recent otherwise sophisticated and conceptually reflexive volumes on theory and method in the study of religion/s. For example, 'description' merits no separate chapter in *Guide to the Study of Religion* (Braun and McCutcheon, eds, 2000), even though it gets to name (and hence 'discipline', in a Foucauldian sense) the entire first section of this large volume, including chapters on 'definition', 'classification', 'comparison' and 'interpretation' (although the *lacuna* is subsequently addressed by McCutcheon's 'redescription' programme, drawing on the work of J.Z. Smith [McCutcheon 2001, pp. *xiv–xv*]). The basic question here is not 'description' *per se* – since any act of writing by definition must and will 'describe' (Lat. *describere*/to write down) – but what *kind* of description of data we chose to make. To 'de-scribe' is implicitly to theorize; our choice of precisely which elements to pick out, and our use of language (or other media) to do so, already depends on subtle (and not-so-subtle!) theoretical presuppositions about what is significant in the world. In this sense renewed consideration of the function of description in the representation of 'religion' requires making the epistemological base of description more self-reflexive and transparent, which in turn, appropriately, leads us straight into the contemporary debate on the politics of representation between and within different cultural groups and practices.

Some clues on the theoretical salience of 'plain old description' surface in the present collection. For example, in Chapter One Marion Bowman robustly defends the ethnological value of description 'in the sense of accurate, judgment free reporting', since 'unless we check our analyses against what is actually happening in the field, we risk perpetuating false assumptions and blatant inaccuracies'. A similar attention to what Bowman calls 'what is actually happening in the field' is found in Kim Knott's account of the 'community religions' and 'religion in locality' research programmes at the University of Leeds (Knott 2000). Drawing for comparative illustration on fiction, particularly on a passage in *Angels and Insects* (1993) by A.S. Byatt describing the narrator's attempts to classify a Victorian naturalist's eclectic archive, but also on the 'sleuthing' method of Agatha Christie's famous detective, Miss Marples, in *Murder at the Vicarage* (1930), Knott summarizes the methodology of the Leeds programme thus:

> The intellectual process which is predominant … is one of inductive rather than deductive reasoning, inferring from the particular to the general, though there will be some shifting back and forth from the one to the other, and from the descriptive to the theoretical. (Knott. 2000, p. 93)

She suggests an analogy with Miss Marples' detective method:

> Practising her investigative skills and honing her moral sense in the local domain, she was then able to extend her powers of critical analysis to comparable situations further afield, finally drawing out general character-istics and offering explanatory models. (*ibid*)

This interplay between inductive and deductive reasoning, contextualized by material, behavioural and historical descriptions, constitutes a kind of methodological dialectic between theory building and data collection (some-what analogous to the 'grounded theory' of sociologists Glaser and Strauss 1967). Perhaps the key point of working inductively in the empirical sense outlined by both Knott and Bowman is to counteract an entrenched tendency in studies of religion, both naturalistic and theological, to idealize or normativize religion: that is, to subject particular historical instances of practice to abstracted typologies of various kinds. That is, we should be careful 'not to import, deductively, general notions of how religions *ought* to operate, what religious people *should* believe or do' (Knott 2000, p. 97; emphasis added). In contrast:

> Our interest is in what they *actually* think and do, and, issuing from this, what the implications of such data might be for ... challenging notions of what religions *are* and how they *operate*. (*ibid*, p. 97; emphasis added)

Hence the case for a central role in the academic study of religion/s for methodologies based in 'accurate, judgment free reporting' (Bowman) and shaped by an inductive-deductive theoretical dialectic 'inferring from the particular to the general' and 'shifting back and forth from the descriptive to the theoretical' (Knott). I will call methodologies based on such an approach 'empirical'.

Clearly 'empirical' is not a new term in the study of religion/s. Indeed, my use of it in part deliberately draws attention to the famous faultline in the history of the IAHR – the 1960 debate at Marburg, cited in the epigraph to this introduction – and therefore locates my argument in a familiar European strategy of demarcating the study of religion from more confessional and theological pursuits. However, I believe that the theoretical implications of the poststructuralist and postcolonial critical turns requires that 'empirical' can and should be relieved of its more positivistic associations. Hence in what follows I argue that *qualitative* empirical methodologies have largely informed the construction of 'religion' and 'religions' under the BASR rubric, and should continue to do so. Qualitative empirical methodologies are well placed to take account of practitioners' *subjectivities* (to rephrase phenomenologists' concern with believers' testimonies) as these are, in turn, articulated within diverse cultural 'webs of significance' (Geertz 1973, p. 5) as well as within powerful socio-economic systems. This would amount to taking due account, in empirical explanations, of practitioners' 'meaning-making' intentions and their practices directed to this end, while at the same time accounting for real historical and structural constraints on subjects' agency. In other words, subjectivities are to be taken seriously in a reflexively-constructed (as opposed to positivistic) academic study of religion/s, but they are not *in themselves* sufficient: they require social, cultural and historical contextualization if adequate analysis is to be achieved. In this way, by drawing on various methodologies based in intersubjective social inquiry (historical, textual, ethnographic and so on), qualitative empirical approaches construct 'religion' not as an ahistorical essence, Platonic universal, or scientific atom, but as a 'social formation' in Althusser's sense (Mack 2000;

McCutcheon 2001, chapter 2), embedded in and generated by particular cultural and political contexts and practices. I suggest that the chapters in this volume amply illustrate this 'qualitative empirical' tendency, albeit with different subjects, emphases and nuances.

The word 'empirical' has a complicated and uneven genealogy; Raymond Williams (1976, p. 98) cautions that it is amongst 'the most difficult ... in the language'. The Oxford English Dictionary (1961) states that, originally, an 'empiric' was

> a member of the sect among ancient physicians called *Empirici* who (in opposition to *Dogmatici* and *Methodici*) drew their rules of practice entirely from experience, to the exclusion of philosophical theory.

This particular lexical history helps to explain the foci on experimental observation and induction inscribed in the OED's first and fourth definitions of 'empirical': respectively, basing methods of practice 'on the results of observation and experiment, not on scientific theory'; and 'pertaining to, or derived from, experience ... a formula arrived at inductively, and not verified by deductive proof'.[16]

There are clearly close resonances in these definitions with the 'empirical' methodology I have outlined so far based on a qualitative, grounded, contextualized descriptivism. We can in fact envisage the terms 'empirical' and 'empiricism' on a spectrum from 'softer', more qualitative and intersubjective uses, to 'harder', more quantitative and neo-positivistic applications. In all cases social and cultural contextualizations remain paramount. If the approaches of Bowman and Knott incline towards the former pole, O'Sullivan et al. (1997, p. 104) illustrate a 'harder' position when they describe empiricism as 'an approach emphasizing the importance of observable, measurable and quantifiable evidence', one which 'seeks verification through controlled, repeatable but public discussion'. But perhaps the potential for polarization, and certainly for incommensurability, is overstated. While some in the humanities – including Religious Studies – may eschew the 'scientistic' flavour of this language, few would doubt the need for criteria of 'observable' evidence in accounts of human practice 'out there' (unless 'religion' is to become completely invisible or otherwise esoteric); and what are conferences and publications if not 'softer' cultural variations on the theme of what O'Sullivan et al. call 'controlled, repeatable ... public discussion'? In his characterization of empirical method, Michael Pye (2000, p. 217) puts it simply (and perhaps with a trace of irony):

> there are in fact data in the field which can be documented on the basis of sources open to more than one investigator and consequently studied in a publicly accessible manner.[17]

Further clarification on the accuracy and sharpness of 'reality purchase' sought by empirical approaches is provided in a useful discussion on sociological method by Woodland (1985), who distinguishes between several types of definition of 'empirical'. His first type is particularly relevant. By focusing on the notion of 'operationalization', Woodland distinguishes between 'inquiry ... operationalized and tested by ... social reality' on the one hand, and 'that which lacks operationalization and whose usefulness or validity is therefore still in question' (*ibid*, p. 65) on the other. In other words, for inquiry to be counted as 'empirical' involves the formulation of measurable or assessable concepts capable of being put into use and recognized as meaningful – that is, 'operationalized' – in some real life context or setting. This is in contrast to purely formal propositions, conceptual schemes or metaphysical controversies which have not been, and perhaps cannot be, so tested. 'Religion' itself is a case in point: indeed, I would suggest that whether or not we can operationalize our definitions of 'religion' – that is, make them empirically tenable or viable in the sense of differentiating 'religious' data from an immense variety of other cultural practices in real-life settings – is *the* key difference between the study of religion/s on the one hand, and theological (particularly metaphysical and confessional) approaches on the other, and this holds whether or not we nuance our approach towards the 'harder' social science pole or the 'softer' cultural studies end of the spectrum.

There can be pitfalls where empirical methodology becomes theoretically naive, or unbridled in application; hence Knott (2000, pp. 101–2) warns against a 'tendency towards anecdotalism, an inability to see beyond the particular ... and the problem of universalising from what is local'. There is also the 'anti-theoretical' connotation, mentioned earlier: Williams (1976, p. 100) points to a long tradition of such derogatory association, culminating in the rhetorically loaded use of 'empirical' to mean 'positive opposition or indifference to theory' (*ibid*). But it would be a serious mistake to use or equate empirical methods, at least in the sense outlined here, with these and other historical stereotypes. Anticipating and repudiating these issues, Knott (1995) makes clear that, for her, the 'empirical study of religion' is based on fieldwork, qualitative interviewing and critically reflexive scholarly engagement with a world of embodied practitioners, their cultures and institutions. In a related, explicitly anthropological move, Malory Nye (2003, p. 208) urges a methodological programme with 'strong emphasis on studies with an empirical basis' such as 'fieldwork, interviewing, surveying, archival research or textual analysis'. At the same time he makes clear that the 'empirical basis' of such methodologies is not an end in itself but exists to ground 'analysis of gender, ethncity and other social relations and categories' (*ibid*). These and other theoretically-alert accounts explicitly call into question simplistic accusations that empirical methods are inherently anti-theoretical and/or positivistic.

Perhaps enough has been said about the merits (and pitfalls) of 'empirical' to suggest that the demarcatory issue discussed earlier can now be effectively tackled by recourse to criteria of 'empirical' methodologies. Put simply, their presuppositions entail that where theology entails a normativizing, confessionalist and metaphysical self-construction,[18] such a knowledge practice is simply of a different conceptual and disciplinary order to the representation of the social and material *practice* of religion, across different (Smartian) 'dimensions' and in comparative cultural contexts, which demonstrably has dominated the study of religions' agenda in its quest to become an autonomous academic field in the modern era. Clearly the full empirical reality of religion includes the theologizing of (a range of) practitioners and their use and interpretation of (diverse) texts, and hence theologians may well have skills to offer the study of religions in particular instances by way of a second order deconstruction and explication of practitioners' rhetorical and confessionalist discourses. But there is a subtle yet crucial difference between the first order act of theologizing, and the second order act of representing its practice.

Perhaps better put – because more nuanced – we could say that theologians and other confessionalists may on occasion be invited to that polymethodic feast mentioned earlier, but in the role of *guests* who, respecting guesthood etiquette, share our meal but neither prepare it, nor plan the menu. In blunt terms this is because in many concrete instances in the empirical study of religion, theologians and other confessionalists and evangelists count as *practitioners of religion* who thereby constitute – for particular purposes in a particular disciplinary context – *our data* (McCutcheon 2001, Smith 1997). While this may and will on occasion be painful and awkward for our relationships with colleagues (and I would argue that academic life requires facing up to the substantial yet largely elided impact on its practitioners' theories and practices, of emotional subtexts and undercurrents) it need not cause intellectual offence insofar as (again, in a particular disciplinary context) we are attempting to construct a viable methodology for the human sciences and not – at least *qua* scholars of religion – to engage in interfaith dialogue, comparative theology or 'religionistic' solidarity.[19] A realistic model of human behaviour – and particularly of academic life – suggests that in the round of academe (as indeed in human life in general), we are each in turn datum and theorist for the other.[20]

In sum, I want to argue that it is a theoretically-nuanced 'empirical' orientation on the part of the study of religion/s that makes *the* difference between a largely confessional, normativizing or otherwise idealistic model of 'religion', and a fully social and cultural model, based on actual historical beliefs, practices and utterances, that can be tested, replicated and falsified across a spectrum of *qualitative* signifiers in terms of both empirical description and comparative theory. As I have said, this is not a new position to take by way of differentiating Religious Studies from Theology: indeed it comes, in part, as a primary datum of the field, part of the basic job description of Religious Studies scholars, and is well represented in the historiography of the study of religion/s, particularly in Europe in the post-world war II period. But restating the obvious is sometimes salutary; making manifest once again what has become merely latent and implicit can shift structural-institutional stasis. Furthermore, nuancing and qualifying empirical methodologies – in a direction that will enable them to accommodate in their representations emerging poststructuralist and postcolonial emphases on power, agency and difference – is a potentially productive direction in which to move (and one already taken by many contributors in the present volume, as well as others internationally). In the process we have the opportunity to disaggregate empirical methodologies from any lingering neo-positivism – whether real or imagined – by exploring their capacity for reflexivity and relationality in knowledge-making practices, and expanding their ability to represent practitioners' subjectivities as part of the overall explanatory process in the study of religions.

The bottom line for qualitative empirical methodologies is encapsulated in Nye's (2003, p. 208) remark that 'although there are many abstract and philosophical issues raised in the study of religion ... there needs to be some attempt to ground such issues in cultural practices in either contemporary or historical contexts'. Arguably the empirical descriptivism characteristic of British traditions of 'phenomenology' (for example Pye 1972, Parrinder 1984, Smart 1996) has, if only by default, maintained a generally social and material model of religion centre-stage in the lush marketplace of competing models, many of which are highly elusive and rarefied and therefore – however subtle on their own terms and ground – hardly conducive to empirical operationalization in the sense argued here (for example, the bulk of the contributions in Derrida and Vattimo 1998).

The term 'empirical', then, usefully indicates a certain set of minimum requirements for the task of accounting for a 'worldly' model of religion: a field of sociocultural practice 'which is, in the common phrase, out there', as Pye (2000, p. 217) stresses. To put this claim on the value of empirical knowledge practices in a broader intellectual context, one authoritative source on the history of science has written that, at minimum, 'few modern philosophers would want to deny the epistemic value of experience ... or the ideas that at least some terms in a theory must be partially empirically defined or that law-like statements are ultimately to be judged by their instances' (Bynum et al. 1981, p. 121). There is nothing obscure or 'scientistic' about such a meta-theoretical statement, the scholarly realization of which drives a range of human sciences. It should be no different for the academic study of religion.

A Review of the Chapters

The chapters are roughly divided into two parts to represent both methodological and substantivist currents in BASR scholarship: that is, comparative reflection on theory and method (Part One), and particular studies of traditions (Part Two). Grouping the chapters in this way is convenient rather than normative: there is obviously methodological engagement in Part Two – the 'particular studies' or 'single traditions' section – and vice versa. So the division I have adopted is pragmatic rather than prescriptive. The majority of authors are of course British-based, but African and European scholars represent one-third of the contributors, emphasizing the culturally inclusive 'reach' of scholarship pursued by BASR and thus undermining essentialist – that is, narrowly geopolitical or ethnocentric – constructions of a 'British' scholarly association.

Part One, entitled 'Category and Method', concerns some quite specific issues of category, theory and method in the study of religions. It comprises seven chapters. In the first, Marion Bowman defends a method of phenomenological fieldwork, arguing that it has particular value for accessing and representing 'folk' or 'vernacular' religion, an important aspect of practice that has tended to be downplayed or even ignored in the historiography of the study of religions which has often privileged an 'official' model of religion as the theological and liturgical practices of elites. Bowman goes on to explore folk and personal dimensions of practice through a case study of popular Catholicism in Newfoundland. In Chapter Two, Chris Arthur draws attention to a pervasive 'media-blindness' in Religious Studies, arguing that we have normalized a print-media approach to the representation of religion that is itself only one out of a range of possible media representations and therefore represents a peculiarly 'Protestant' methodological bias. A fuller range of media representations of religion/s should also include oral, visual and material object sources, any or all of which may well be more significant for practitioners in a given context than academic entextualized representations. Furthermore, Arthur examines ways in which media actively *shape* discourses and practices rather than just passively disseminating them. In Chapter Three, Peter Antes examines the construction and interpretation of 'experience' in religious and non-religious traditions, including Jewish, Christian and Muslim traditions, and Freudian and Jungian discourses. He argues that experiences – both religious and non-religious – are always actively 'made' by practitioners themselves, drawing for their interpretations upon the language and symbolic resources of their particular cultural and historical context. Experience is not closed but constrained: new and different experiences may subsequently be 'made' by practitioners, but always dependent upon the availability of sources in the historical-cultural context in question.

The next three chapters analyse the usage, and problematics, of particular well-worn terminologies in the academic study of religions: 'sacred', 'community' and 'diaspora'. In Chapter Four, Terence Thomas questions the widespread use of the terms 'sacred' and 'the sacred', basing his argument both on a close examination of recent textbooks and on the twentieth-century development of the concepts in the work of Otto, Tillich and Eliade. Thomas finds a paradigmatic expression of the raw – potentially deadly – power of 'the sacred' in the Hebrew bible; in contrast, he finds a progressively diluted sense of the concept in twentieth-century academic models, where its usage becomes bound up with exotic and orientalistic representations of 'religion' whilst also functioning as a symptom of a creeping theological agenda in the face of societal secularization. In Chapter Five, Kim Knott turns her attention to discourses on 'community' in relation to religion, beginning by mapping out a history of uses of this slippery term. She discusses a range of problematizations of the word 'community' in recent socio-cultural theory, always with an eye both for contiguous debates on the reification of the term 'religion' in Religious Studies, and for possibilities in cross-disciplinary theoretical fertilization. She steers her chapter towards a reflexive, 'applied' consideration: what do scholars of religion/s have to offer contemporary debates on multicultural citizenship? In Chapter Six, Gerrie ter Haar examines sub-Saharan African migration into Western Europe, with a special focus on religious identity formation among African Christian diaspora communities in the Netherlands. She uses the Jewish diaspora as a template and extrapolates three main elements of the diaspora experience: dispersion, identity and return. Although she finds the latter two elements politically problematic in the context of the (Dutch) state's regulatory agenda of identifying and hence ringfencing religious 'others' (that is, non-Europeans), she argues that 'diaspora' can both serve the specific cause of studying migrant African Christian communities as well as play a useful role as a generic comparative category.

To close Part One, Brian Bocking in Chapter Seven defends the enduring salience of a 'post-Smartian' phenomenological methodology, exemplifying its value through a case study of the subtle interfusion of Shinto/Buddhist iconography in Japan. He then moves to the institutional arena in which Religious Studies – amongst other subjects – operates in the UK, arguing that the current regime of Quality Assurance Agency (QAA) audits of academic departmental performance is effectively a 'phenomenological' methodology played back upon the phenomenologists; academics' discomfort under this regime becomes an opportunity, for Bocking, for reflexive ethical scrutiny of the impact of 'our' research practices on 'others'.

Part Two, entitled 'Case Studies', contains eight chapters built around empirical historical studies of particular traditions, including Buddhist, Celtic-Romano, Hindu, Hopi, Ghanian, Korean and Muslim examples, and ranging from close philological analyses to sociological contextualizations. In Chapter

Eight, Richard Gombrich builds a careful comparative survey of 'religious experience' as represented in William James' seminal book, *The Varieties of Religious Experience*, and the Pali canon of early Buddhist texts. Gombrich provides a detailed philological examination of Pali texts in order to argue that 'religious experience' is certainly an applicable category for Buddhism, but one that needs to be partly relocated from James' preoccupation with solitary, spectacular and discontinuous states, into a more sociologically-contextualized mode of interpretation where 'religious experience' is something taught and learnt, and hence actively transmitted, within traditions of practice. In Chapter Nine, Miranda Aldhouse-Green surveys the range of representations of women as goddesses in the Celtic and Romano-Celtic period across the British Isles and north-western europe, based on the iconographic and epigraphic evidence of archaeology. She finds representation of a 'female principle' to be widespread, complex and powerful, and she traces various forms in particular deities, cults and shrines, and in association with various animals. Her detailed survey concludes with an examination of different combinations of female dieties in the Celtic world, from single goddesses, to duotheistic representations and finally, triplism. In Chapter Ten, Julia Leslie analyses the contrastive roles of *satī* ('immolation') or widowhood for a woman upon the death of her husband, as prescribed in classical Sanskrit religious law. She examines these in the context of prescriptions for male renunciate paths, as discussed in two Sanskrit treatises. Developing an implicit parallel in the text between the classical ideal of male renunciation and the role options available to the widowed woman, Leslie argues that the career of 'widow-ascetic' in religious law had at least the potential to function as a positive religious path for women parallel to the life of a renouncer for men, although she notes that this interpretation is in considerable tension with historical practice.

In Chapter Eleven Ria Kloppenborg analyses the public debate between Christian missionaries and indigenous Buddhists at Pānadura in Sri Lanka in 1873 in the historical context of the emergence of both 'Buddhist modernism' and post-colonial interfaith 'encounters' and syncretisms. By setting the rhetorical and exegetical extravagances of the textual record against the historical aftermath of the debate – its immediate attraction for the Theosophists, Olcott and Blavatsky, and its longterm influence on Sri Lankan interreligious exchanges well into the contemporary period – Kloppenborg underscores the political ramifications of doctrinal debate in post-colonial contexts. In Chapter Twelve, Armin W. Geertz analyses Hopi Indian ritual practices – specifically the unexpectedly violent initiation of Hopi children – through the multiple theoretical lens of sociology, social psychology and cognitive theory. Drawing on the work of Durkheim and Mead concerning the dynamic social-psychological relationship between self and community, Geertz argues that Hopi religious ritual inculcates within initiates the voice of the 'generalised other' (in Mead's term) through which control is subsequently exercised over group ethos and conduct.

The final three chapters take up once more the issues of cultural encounter and/or contestation, and the political impact of religion (and its study), that have been a persistent sub-theme of the volume. In Chapter Thirteen, Elizabeth Amoah surveys religious innovations in African contexts, particularly in Ghana. She finds innovation and syncretism to be widespread and inevitable functions of religious plurality, not just in Ghana or the African continent, but by implication globally. She summarizes her views on some chief characteristics of traditional African religiosity before considering the mutual imbrication of local cultural traditions with post-1970s Christian charismatic movements, finding a mutual emphasis on the perceived benefits, for practitoners, of a pragmatic everyday spirituality. George D. Chryssides develops the theme of syncretism in Chapter Fourteen in the context of the emergence of a 'new Christian' movement, the Unification Church (UC), from its origins as an amalgam of South Korean folk shamanic practices and Christian colporteur missiology, to its brief internationalization as a 'new religious movement' in the 1970s and 1980s. During this period the movement was a prominent target of the 'anti-cult movement', and Chryssides explores the doctrinal tensions between Unificationist beliefs and Western conservative evangelical critiques. The UC's recent career as 'just' one religious movement amongst many has led to it re-emphasizing its (local) Korean shamanic roots, with a consequent reduction in its appeal in the (global) Anglo-American marketplace. In the final chapter, Tariq Modood examines the challenge to secular multiculturalism in the UK of a politics of difference based upon religious equality, specifically for Muslims. Modood argues that until the 'Rushdie affair' at the end of the 1980s, British Muslims had inherited from the United States a discourse of equality based upon 'race'. In the UK context, however, Muslims *qua* Muslims did not qualify as an 'ethnic' group and hence were deprived of a category of civic status and legal protection available to other politically constructed 'others' (Sikhs and Jews, for example) who did so qualify. Modood argues that strategies of Muslim self-definition must be understood in the context of the emergence of a wider politics of identity difference in the UK, in which the classic liberal model of merely 'tolerating' difference is challenged by a 'post-secularist' model asserting the value and right of public difference in 'religion' in general, and Muslim identity in particular.

Conclusion

There is, therefore, a three-fold purpose to this volume. First, it offers a selection of important explorations and analyses of religion as implicitly or explicitly an empirical phenomenon: that is, 'religion' is primarily treated not as a metaphysical domain, nor as a confessional adventure (there are plenty other professional associations and learned societies for these concerns), but as a fully social, cultural, historical and material field of practice. In this model of 'religion', the data cannot be assumed or taken for granted but must always be constructed empirically – through fieldwork, text-based analyses, surveys, interview – as a basic constituent of the research and teaching process. The value of the papers gathered here lies not only in substantiating this methodological orientation but in illustrating the nuance and diversity of accounts of religion pursued under these parameters within the BASR. Second, the volume serves as a modest 'British' contribution to the academic historiography of the study of religion.[21] In confining its scope to a selection of texts from the most recent period in the history of BASR, the present collection clearly does not offer the scope and detail of a specialist historical monograph. But it does share the concerns of a wider, reflexive historiographical 'turn', evident in certain sectors of Religious Studies, in taking seriously the history of the construction of the academic study of religion/s as an important reflexive datum. Third and finally, the volume is offered not in the spirit of an abstract, decontextualized 'history of ideas', but as a modest yet inescapably political intervention in the sociology of the UK academy at a particular historical moment. In this sense I hope that the papers function collectively to help question, re-articulate and re-group the presuppositions of a field that need once again to become explicit if maximum intellectual purchase, and appropriate institutional status and security, is to be maintained and developed. I assume that this is viable, desirable and sometimes urgent both for 'pure' academic purposes (the acquisition and dissemination of knowledge, and knowledge practices, relating to 'religion') and in more 'applied' settings (defining the remit and disclosing the politics of humanities methodologies within tertiary education, for example, or providing data and debating issues on religious identities, beliefs and practices in appropriate public policy deliberations).

In short, this volume is offered in the belief that a qualitative empiricism, such as is displayed across the range of contributions to this volume, is a condition of viable methodologies in the study of religion. Necessary, that is, but not in itself sufficient: as the chapters demonstrate, particular theoretical concerns must also come into play. But a common ground – the 'common ground on which students of religion *qua* students of religion meet' (Schimmel 1960, p. 236), no less – is given by our constructions of 'religion' as signifying an empirical reality: something *done* by people 'out there' in the world.

I am indebted to the writers of these various chapters for their good faith in allowing me to prise them gently and, appropriately enough, inductively from their original contexts of delivery and publication and to reposition them in the current volume, to illustrate both the diversity of BASR approaches and simultaneously to evince latent methodological common ground.

A Note on the Texts

I first proposed a version of the current volume at the BASR committee meeting in May 2001 when I was then *Bulletin* editor. The final selection of texts largely reflects my own choice of topics and subjects (informed by some committee feedback) and is designed to illustrate the diversity of approaches represented under the BASR umbrella in recent years in terms of specific methods, theories and topics, whilst also advancing an inductive argument on methodological common ground in the context of a longstanding debate on disciplinary identity (with attendant institutional pressures). Since more than a decade separates the dates of first publication of the chapters gathered here, a note on the editing process is required. The texts varied quite widely in terms of length and internal reference and annotation systems, and the degree to which they had already been revised and edited for publication following their original public delivery as oral addresses (in the context of very different conference themes). My rubric, therefore, has been that the present volume is itself a new context of presentation requiring a degree of editorial attention when and where appropriate, whilst reflecting as much as possible of the original historical context of the papers. In this sense the papers' (re-) presentation here is only the latest stage in the evolving redaction process familiar to philologists.

In most cases my interventions have been restricted to standard tasks: tidying up, correcting and standardizing references and bibliographies, omitting strong cases of the spoken voice and/or references to particular intra-conference debates or events, and standardizing format across the volume. This, however, has been complicated by the fact that the occasional papers themselves are the product of a series of editors with different emphases in presentation; some papers were presented in second languages; and a good proportion of the original files were no longer available and therefore had to be scanned onto disc. In two cases pertaining to evidently shorter texts, I sought minor up-dating by the authors in order to attain a semblance of parity across the volume as a whole. If some chapters are still unavoidably longer than others, I trust that this does not distract readers from the quality of discussion and debate displayed across the volume.

Acknowledgements

For suggestions and critical comments on earlier drafts I am grateful to James Cox, Mathew Guest, Kim Knott, Peggy Morgan and Terence Thomas. My additional thanks to Kim Knott for sourcing rare texts, and to Lynn Robertson at New College, University of Edinburgh, for scanning multiple printed copies onto disc. I would also like to thank the team at Ashgate – in particular senior commissioning editor Sarah Lloyd and editorial manager Ann Newell – for their very courteous help in producing the volume as a whole to a tight deadline.

Notes

1 First suggested at the BASR AGM in Oxford on 23 September 1989: see BASR *Bulletin* 59, November 1989, p. 5. Terence Thomas was founding editor of the series at the Open University in Wales in Cardiff from 1991 until 1996. A complete list of the (ongoing) series of BASR occasional papers can be found on the BASR website: http://basr.org.uk.

2 Early British statements under this rubric include Carpenter (1913) and James (1938); it was also the title of the first Chair in the field in the UK, at Manchester in 1904 (first held by T.W Rhys Davids). In the postwar period see *inter alia* Bouquet (1950[1942]), Zaehner (1958, chapter one), Parrinder (1962), Sharpe (1970), Brandon (ed., 1970) and Pye (1972).

3 It was generally under this rubric (which Smith [1998, p. 278] calls the 'most enduring device' in the scholarly classification of religions) that the study of religious diversity and 'other religions' was introduced into UK primary and secondary education: see *inter alia* Hilliard (1961), Parrinder (1965) and Herod (1970), and the (ongoing) work of the Shap Working Party on World Religions in Education, founded in 1969. The 'world religions' typology is not new – C.P. Tiele used it as early as 1884 (Smith 1998: 279) – and in expanded and contracted forms (that is, incorporating more or less 'members' of an originally quite exclusive 'club' or 'league') continues to be used – problematically, in my view – both explicitly and implicitly as a function of curriculum design (e.g. Beckerlegge, ed., 1998, Ridgeon, ed., 2003) and encyclopaedic authority (Bowker, ed., 1997) in UK secondary and tertiary education into the present period. For a critique of the category, see Fitzgerald (1990).

4 Whaling (ed., 1984), Thrower ed., (1986), King (ed., 1990).

5 Smart (1986[1968]), Lewis and Slater (1969), Holm (1977); to compound ambiguities in the overall title of the field, the first item is Smart's inaugural lecture as Professor of Religious Studies at Lancaster (in 1968), the second was first published as *World Religions* (in 1966), and the third came out in a series called 'Issues in Religious Studies'. A related 'nominalistic' taxonomy deals simply with 'religions', either in historical mode – e.g. Kellett (1962[1933]) and James (1956) – or in survey or encyclopaedic form – e.g. Gundry (1958) and Hinnells (ed., 1984). Smart (1960) began in this simple nominalistic category but on paperback publication, just a few years later, adopted the compound 'world religions' title (Smart 1966). Another taxonomic genealogy anthropomorphizes 'religions' by making the focus of classification their 'life' or 'death', as in 'living faiths' (Zaehner, ed., 1959) and 'living religions' (Hinnells, ed., 1997). The prolix co-mingling of these various rubrics in the British context is amply confirmed by these examples, many of which were written by stalwart BASR members (e.g. Beckerlegge, Brandon, Gundry, James, King, Lewis, Parrinder, Pye, Smart, Thrower, Whaling).

6 The object of our studies is also, historically, a moot point: are we studying religion, religion*s*, 'religioning' or 'religion' (cf. Idinopulos and Wilson 1998, Platvoet and Molendijk, eds, 1999, Nye 2000)? Qualitative empirical approaches can work equally effectively with the plural form (as in the titles of BASR, IAHR and the UK disciplinary rubric 'Study of Religions'), the singular form (so long as this is constructed nominalistically rather than ontologically) or Nye's recent verbal formulation, 'religioning', which reconceptualizes 'religion' as 'a process of doing', not 'a "thing" but an action': 'what people do, and how they talk about what they do' (Nye 2003, pp. 7, 18). 'Religions' appears to designate plural social formations and came into use in order to differentiate these as valid objects of study from the metaphysical or perennial 'essence' sometimes implicit in (disguised) uses of the singular noun 'religion'. However, there is the potential danger

that this plural form in fact reifies 'religions' by sharply differentiating a 'religious something' from everyday cultures and their actors, and hence smuggling in (once more!) a *sui generis* status for 'religion*s*' as autonomous social institutions. Conversely, metaphysical/ontological reduction need not be entailed by singular definitions of 'religion', insofar as they are constructed transparently and stipulatively, as is amply demonstrated by the content history of the North American journal *Method and Theory in the Study of Religion* (est. 1989).

7   All quotes from *BASR Bulletin No. 100, November 2003*, p. 4.

8   For a recent re-statement of this position in the UK, see Connolly (ed., 1999), a collection endorsed by Smart (1999, p. *ix*) in the foreword as 'the real portrait of Religious Studies'. Other significant collections based on this principle include Whaling (ed., 1983, 1985) and Hinnells (ed., forthcoming 2004); outwith the UK, see, *inter alia*, Waardenburg (ed., 1973). A current trend in the field, this time in the USA, is towards categorial handbooks: for example Taylor (ed., 1998) and Braun and McCutcheon (eds, 2000), although this is not a new approach (cf. Sharpe 1971).

9   See the brief review in BASR Bulletin 66, June 1992, pp. 2–3.

10   On the normativity of scientific methodologies within an IAHR frame of reference, see *inter alia* Werblowsky 1960, Schimmel 1960, Pye 1989 and 1991, Lincoln 1996, Wiebe 1999, Geertz 2000, McCutcheon 2001 and Wiegers 2002. An earlier period of debate on this bifurcation between scientific and theological method – the nineteenth and early twentieth centuries – is tackled in Molendijk and Pels (eds, 1998). Although I cannot develop the point here, the 'demarcation debate' should be understood 'meta-theoretically' (Flood 1999, pp. 2–8): that is, not as an obstacle to 'getting on with the job' but as an intrinsic datum in the field, derived from the cultural-ideological power of 'religion'.

11   Joy (2000) and Geertz (2000) provide accessible surveys of (and different responses to) emergent postcolonial agendas in the study of religions.

12   On the rationale behind the expansionist designs of some 'Theology' departments on the comparative syllabus of 'religion' studies, see Ford (1999, pp. 18–19), who considers that 'best practice' in the UK lies with 'those [departments] which try to combine theology and religious studies – or, even better, refuse to recognise any simple splitting of the field into two'. It is interesting to speculate whether the reversal of the order of names in the title of a recent volume, *A Companion to Religious Studies and Theology* (Bond et al., eds, 2003), might over time effect a corresponding shift in the dynamics of the subjects' relationship. Unfortunately the editors offer no discussion of the disciplinary reasoning behind either the volume's content or title, which rather suggests that moving from 'TRS' to 'RST' will merely re-arrange the furniture.

13   For a sample of historical and contemporary surveys of the development of Religious Studies in the UK up to the 1980s, see Sharpe (1980), Walls (1980), Smart (1988), King (ed., 1990), Thrower (1995) and Byrne (1998); for accounts of the history of BASR, see Gundry (1956, 1980) and King (1994). On more recent developments in the UK, see the series of reports in the BASR *Bulletin* on the contemporary state of British Departments (concerning staffing, syllabi, student numbers, etc.): e.g. *Bulletins* 50–55 (1986–1988) include reports on Aberdeen, the Open University, West Sussex (now Chichester) Institute of Higher Education, Sunderland, Bath College of Higher Education (now Bath Spa University College), Newcastle, Lampeter and Westminster College, Oxford. Sutcliffe (ed., 1998) contains a cross-section of methodological debate in the UK from the mid-1990s, largely by BASR members. For other recent discussions on the shape and preoccupations of the field in the UK, see the special issue of *Religion* 31/4 (October 2001), 'Tributes to Ninian Smart, 1927–2001'; Knott (1997) for a perspective from one prominent English 'TRS' department (Leeds); and Cox and Sutcliffe (forthcoming) on institutional trends in Scotland. The private archive of the BASR, including minutes of meetings (from 1954) and Bulletins (from 1972), will be housed at the Bodleian Library, Oxford, from 2004.

14   The history of phenomenology of religion in Europe and the USA is extremely complex: for overviews see, amongst others, Waardenburg (1973), Sharpe (1986, pp. 220–250) and James (1995). For expositions of *religionswissenschaft*/'science of religion' in Europe, see Smart (1973) and Honko

(ed., 1979); for a critical account of 'history of religions' in the USA and continental Europe, see Grottanelli and Lincoln (1998). For substantial historiographies across both rubrics, see King (1984) and Geertz and McCutcheon (2000).

15 Variations upon phenomenological strategy are discussed in the chapters by Marion Bowman, Brian Bocking and Elizabeth Amoah in the present volume.

16 Space constraints preclude discussion here of the question of the historical influence on qualitative empirical methods of the so-called 'British empiricist' philosophers, especially John Locke (1632–1704) and David Hume (1711–1776).

17 Pye (2000, pp. 215–218) includes 'empirical' in a quartet of 'elementary features of any theory of religion(s)' alongside 'rational', 'explanatory' and 'testable'.

18 I accept that 'theology' does not fit this picture everywhere, and that certain *theoretical* nuances in contemporary 'theology' in the UK (and elsewhere, of course) have blurred a sharp demarcation between 'T' and 'RS'; hence the note of caution. But *politically* and *historically* the argument stands.

19 See Morgan (1995) for a discussion of issues involved in the relationship between the study of religions and interfaith dialogue.

20 Which is, of course, to bring the perennial question of agency and structure into the workings of the academy itself. As Asad (1993, p. 4) puts it: 'Since everyone is in some degree or other an object for other people, as well as an object of others' narratives, no one is ever entirely the author of her life. People are never only active agents and subjects in their own history'.

21 See note 13 above for a sample of British historiographies. International historiography is slowly growing: see *inter alia* Sharpe (1986) and Molendijk and Pels (eds, 1998), and – for diverse institutional histories and contexts of category formation – see U. King (1995), Lease (ed., 1995), Chidester (1996), McCutcheon (1997), R. King (1999), Fitzgerald (2000), Thomas (2000) and Doležalová et al. (2001).

Bibliography

Asad, Talal 1993. *Genealogies of Religion: Discipline and Reasons of Power in Christianity and Islam*, Baltimore, MY: Johns Hopkins Press.

Beckerlegge, Gwilym (ed.) 1998. *The World Religions Reader*, London: Routledge.

Bond, Helen K., Kunin, Seth D. and Murphy, Francesca Aran (eds) 2003. *A Companion to Religious Studies and Theology*, Edinburgh: Edinburgh University Press.

Bouquet, A.C. 1950[1942]. *Comparative Religion: a Short Outline*, Harmondsworth: Penguin.

Bowker, John (ed.) 1997. *The Oxford Dictionary of World Religions*, Oxford: Oxford University Press.

Brandon, S.G.F. (ed.) 1970. *A Dictionary of Comparative Religion*, London: Wiedenfeld and Nicolson.

Braun, Willi and McCutcheon, Russell (eds) 2000. *Guide to the Study of Religion*, London: Cassell.

Bynum, W.J., Browne, E.J. and Porter, R. (eds) 1981. *Dictionary of the History of Science*, London: Macmillan.

Byrne, Peter 1998. 'The Foundations of the Study of Religion in the British Context', in A.L. Molendijk and P. Pels (eds), *Religion in the Making: the Emergence of the Sciences of Religion*, Leiden: Brill, pp. 45–65.

——— 1999[1997]. 'The Study of Religion: Neutral, Scientific, or Neither?', in R. McCutcheon (ed.), *The Insider/Outsider Problem in the Study of Religion: A Reader*, London: Cassell, pp. 248–259.

Carpenter, J. Estlin 1913. *Comparative Religion*, London: Home University Library of Modern Knowledge/Oxford University Press.

Chidester, David 1996. *Savage Systems: Colonialism and Comparative Religion in South Africa*, Charlottesville: University Press of Virginia.

Cox, James L. and Sutcliffe, Steven J. (forthcoming). 'Religious Studies in Scotland: A Persistent Tension with Divinity', *Religion*.

Derrida, Jacques and Vattimo, Gianni (ed.) 1998. *Religion*, Cambridge: Polity Press.

Doležalová, Iva, Martin, Luther and Papoušek, Dalibor (eds) 2001. *The Academic Study of Religion During the Cold War: East and West*, New York: Peter Lang.

Edgar, Andrew and Sedgwick, Peter (eds) 1999. *Key Concepts in Cultural Theory*, London: Routledge.

Fitzgerald, Timothy 2000. *The Ideology of Religious Studies*. New York: Oxford University Press.

―――― 1990. 'Hinduism and the World Religion fallacy', *Religion* **20**, pp. 101–118.

Flood, Gavin 1999. *Beyond Phenomenology: Rethinking the Study of Religion*, London: Cassell.

Ford, David 1999. *Theology: A Very Short Introduction*, Oxford: Oxford University Press.

Geertz, Armin W. 2000. 'Global Perspectives on Methodology in the Study of Religion', in A. Geertz and R. McCutcheon (eds, 2000), *Perspectives on Method and Theory in the Study of Religion*, Leiden: Brill, pp. 49–73.

Geertz, Armin W. and McCutcheon, R. (eds) 2000. 'The Role of Method and Theory in the IAHR', in A. Geertz and R. McCutcheon (eds, 2000), *Perspectives on Method and Theory in the Study of Religion*, Leiden: Brill, pp. 3–37.

Geertz, Clifford 1973. 'Thick Description: Towards an Interpretive Theory of Culture', in *The Interpretation of Culture*, London: Fontana.

Glaser, B. and Strauss, A. 1967. *The Discovery of Grounded Theory*, Chicago: Aldine.

Grottanelli, Cristiano and Lincoln, Bruce 1998[1984–5]. 'A Brief Note on (Future) Research in the History of Religions', *Method and Theory in the Study of Religion* **10** (3), pp. 311–325.

Gundry, D.W. 1956. 'The History of Religions in Britain'. *Numen* **III**, pp. 77–78.

―――― 1958. *Religions: A Preliminary Historical and Theological Study*, London: Macmillan.

―――― 1980. 'The Beginnings of the British Association for the History of Religions', *BASR Bulletin* **31** (November), pp. 7–9.

Herod, F.G. 1970. *World Religions*, London: Blond Educational.

Hilliard, F.H. 1961. *Teaching Children about World Religions*, London: George G. Harrap and Co.

Hinnells, John R. (ed.) 1970. *Comparative Religion in Education*, London: Oriel Press.

―――― 1984. *The Penguin Dictionary of Religions*, Harmondsworth: Penguin Books.

―――― 1997[1984]. *A New Handbook of Living Religions*, Blackwell: Oxford.

―――― forthcoming 2004. *The Routledge Companion to the Study of Religions*, London: Routledge.

Holm, Jean 1977. *The Study of Religions*, London: Sheldon Press.

Honko, L. (ed.) 1979. *Science of Religion: Studies in Methodology*, Den Haag: Mouton.

Idinopulos, T.A. and Wilson, B.C. (eds) 1998. *What is Religion? Origins, Definitions and Explanations*, Leiden: Brill.

James, G. 1995. *Interpreting Religion: the Phenomenological Approaches of De La Saussaye, Kristensen and Van Der Leeuw*, University Press of America.

James, E.O. 1938. *Comparative Religion*, London: Methuen and Co.

―――― 1956. *History of Religions* ['Teach Yourself Books' series], London: English Universities Press.

Joy, Morny 2000. 'Beyond a God's Eyeview: Alternative Perspectives in the Study of Religion', in A. Geertz and R. McCutcheon (eds, 2000), *Perspectives on Method and Theory in the Study of Religion*, Leiden: Brill, pp. 110–140.

Kellett, E.E. 1962[1933]. *A Short History of Religions*, Harmondsworth: Pelican.

King, Richard 1999. *Orientalism and Religion: Postcolonial Theory, India and 'The Mystic East'*, London: Routledge.

King, Ursula 1984. 'Historical and Phenomenological Approaches to the Study of Religion: some major developments and issues under debate since 1950', in F. Whaling (ed.), *Contemporary Approaches to the Study of Religion: Volume I, the Humanities*, Berlin: Mouton, pp. 29–164.

—— 1994. 'Celebrating Forty Years of the BASR', *Bulletin* **73** (November), pp. 13–16.

—— 1995, 'A Question of Identity: Women scholars and the Study of Religion', in U. King (ed.), *Religion and Gender*, Oxford: Blackwell, pp. 219–243.

King, Ursula (ed.) 1990. *Turning Points in Religious Studies*, Edinburgh: T. and T. Clark.

Knott, Kim 1995. 'Women Researching, Women Researched: Gender as an Issue in the Empirical Study of Religion', in U. King (ed.), *Religion and Gender*, Oxford: Blackwell, pp. 199–218.

—— 1997. 'Response to the *Lingua Franca* Article', *Bulletin of the Council of Societies for the Study of Religion* **26** (4), pp. 81–82.

—— 2000. 'Community and Locality in the Study of Religions', in T. Jensen and M. Rothstein (eds), *Secular Theories on Religion: Current Perspectives*, Copenhagen: Museum Tusculanum Press, pp. 87–105.

Lease, Gary (ed.) 1995. 'Pathologies in the Academic Study of Religion: North American Institutional Case Studies', *Method and Theory in the Study of Religion* **7** (4).

Lewis, H.D. and Slater, Robert L. 1969. *The Study of Religions*, Harmondsworth: Penguin/Pelican.

Lincoln, Bruce 1996. 'Theses on Method', *Method and Theory in the Study of Religion* 8/3, pp. 225–227.

Lyotard, Jean-Francois 1984[1979]. *The Postmodern Condition: A Report on Knowledge*, Manchester: Manchester University Press.

Mack, Burton L. 2000. 'Social Formation', in W. Braun and R. McCutcheon (eds), *Guide to the Study of Religion*, London: Cassell, pp. 283–296.

Markham, Ian S. (ed.) 2000[1996]. *A World Religions Reader*, 2nd edn, Oxford: Blackwell.

McCutcheon, Russell 1997. *Maufacturing Religion: the Discourse on* Sui Generis *Religion and the Politics of Nostalgia*, New York: Oxford University Press.

—— 2001. *Critics not Caretakers: Redescribing the Public Study of Religion*, New York: SUNY Press.

—— 2003. *The Discipline of Religion: Structure, Meaning, Rhetoric*, London: Routledge.

—— 2004. ' "Just Follow the Money": The Cold War, the Humanistic Study of Religion, and the Fallacy of Insufficient Cynicism', *Culture and Religion* 5/1.

Molendijk, A.L. and Pels, P. (eds) 1998. *Religion in the Making: The Emergence of the Sciences of Religion*, Leiden: Brill.

Morgan, Peggy 1995. 'The Study of Religions and Interfaith Encounter', *Numen* **42**, pp. 156–171.

—— 2003. 'Looking Forward to Looking Back: From Past Bulletins of BAHR/BASR 2', *BASR Bulletin* No. 99, pp. 9–12.

Nye, Malory 2000. 'Religion, post-Religionism and Religioning: Religious Studies and Contemporary Cultural Debates', *Method and Theory in the Study of Religion* 12, pp. 447–476.

—— 2003. *Religion: The Basics*, London: Routledge.

O'Sullivan, T., Hartley, J., Saunders, D., Montgomery, M. and Fiske, J., eds, 1997[1994]. *Key Concepts in Communication and Cultural Studies*, London: Routledge.

Parrinder, Geoffrey 1962. *Comparative Religion*, London: George Allen and Unwin.

—— 1965. *A Book of World Religions*, Amersham: Hulton Educational Publications.

—— 1984. 'Thematic Comparison', in F. Whaling (ed.), *The World's Religious Traditions*, Edinburgh: T. and T. Clark, pp. 240–256.

Platvoet, J.G. and Molendijk, A.L. (eds) 1999. *The Pragmatics of Defining Religion: Contexts, Concepts and Contests*, Leiden: Brill.

Pye, Michael 1972. *Comparative Religion: An Introduction through Source Materials*, Newton Abbot: David and Charles.

———— 1991. 'Religious Studies in Europe: Structures and Desiderata', in K. Klostermaier and L. Hurtado (eds), *Religious Studies: Issues, Prospects and Proposals*, Atlanta, Georgia: Scholars Press, pp. 39–55.

———— 2000. 'Westernism Unmasked', in T. Jensen and M. Rothstein (eds), *Secular Theories on Religion: Current Perspectives*, Copenhagen: Museum Tusculanum Press, pp. 211–230.

Pye, Michael (ed.) 1989. *Marburg Revisited: Institutions and Strategies in the Study of Religion*, Marburg: diagonal-Verlag.

Religion 31/4 (October) 2001. 'Tributes to Ninian Smart, 1927–2001'.

Richards, Glyn 1980. 'Editorial', *Scottish Journal of Religious Studies* (vol. 1 no. 1).

———— 1990. 'British Academic Journals in Religious Studies: the Scottish Journal of Religious Studies', in Ursula King (ed.), *Turning Points in Religious Studies. Essays in Honour of Geoffrey Parrinder*, Edinburgh: T. and T. Clark, p. 69.

Ridgeon, Lloyd (ed.) 2003. *Major World Religions: From their Origins to the Present*, London: Routledge.

Schimmel, Annemarie 1960. 'Summary of the Discussion', *Numen* 7, pp. 235–239.

Sharpe, Eric 1971. *Fifty Key Words: Comparative Religion*, Richmond VA: John Knox Press.

———— 1980. 'Comparative Religion at the University of Manchester 1904–1979', Manchester: The John Rylands University Library of Manchester.

———— 1983. *Understanding Religion*, London: Duckworth.

———— 1986 [1975]. *Comparative Religion: A History*, London: Duckworth.

Smart, Ninian 1960. *A Dialogue of Religions*, London: SCM.

———— 1966. *World Religions: A Dialogue*, Harmondsworth: Penguin/Pelican.

———— 1973. *The Science of Religion and the Sociology of Knowledge*, Princeton: Princeton University Press.

———— 1986. 'The Principles and the Meaning of the Study of Religion' (inaugural address, University of Lancaster, 1968), *Concept and Empathy: Essays in the Study of Religion*, London: Macmillan, pp. 194–206.

———— 1988. 'Religious Studies in the United Kingdom', *Religion* 18, pp. 1–9.

———— 1996. *Dimensions of the Sacred: An Anatomy of the World's Beliefs*, London: HaperCollins.

———— 1998. 'Methods in My Life', in J. Stone (ed.), *The Craft of Religious Studies*, Basingstoke: Macmillan/New York: St. Martin's Press, pp. 18–35.

———— 1999. 'Foreword'. In P. Connolly (ed.) *Approaches to the Study of Religion*, London: Cassell, pp. ix-xiv.

Smith, Jonathan Z. 1997. 'Are Theological and Religious Studies Compatible?', *Bulletin of the Council of Societies for the Study of Religion* 26/3: pp. 60–61.

———— 1998. 'Religion, Religions, Religious', in M. Taylor (ed.), *Critical Terms for Religious Studies*, Chicago: Chicago University Press, pp. 269–284.

Smith, Wilfred Cantwell 1959. 'Comparative Religion: Whither – and Why?', in M. Eliade and J. Kitagawa (eds), *The History of Religion: Essays in Methodology*, Chicago: University of Chicago Press, pp. 31–58.

Sutcliffe, Steven 1998. 'Studying Religions Realistically', *Method and Theory in the Study of Religion* **10** (3), pp. 266–274.

———— (ed.) 1998. 'Selected Proceedings from the Symposium on Methodology and the Study of Religions, Bath Spa University College, UK, November 16, 1996', *Method and Theory in the Study of Religion* **10** (3), pp. 241–310.

Taylor, Mark C. (ed.) 1998. *Critical Terms for Religious Studies*, Chicago: University of Chicago Press.

Theology and Religious Studies Benchmarking Group 2000: 'TRS Benchmark Statement', Gloucester: Quality Assurance Agency for Higher Education.

Thomas, Terence 2000. 'Political Motivations in the Development of the Academic Study of Religions in Britain', in A. Geertz and R. McCutcheon (eds, 2000), *Perspectives on Method and Theory in the Study of Religion*, Leiden: Brill, pp. 74–90.

Thrower, James (ed.) 1986. *Essays in Religious Studies for Andrew Walls*, Department of Religious Studies, University of Aberdeen.

Waardenburg, Jacques 1973. *Classical Approaches to the Study of Religion*, 2 vols. Den Haag: Mouton.

Walls, Andrew F. 1980. 'A Bag of Needments for the Road: Geoffrey Parrinder and the Study of Religion in Britain', *Religion* 10, pp. 141–149.

Werblowsky, R.J.Z. 1960. 'Marburg – and After?', *Numen* 7, pp. 215–220.

Whaling, Frank 1999. 'Theological Approaches', in P. Connolly (ed.), *Approaches to the Study of Religion*, London: Cassell, pp. 226–274.

Whaling, Frank (ed.) 1983. *Contemporary Approaches to the Study of Religion, Volume I: The Humanities*, Berlin: Mouton.

—— (ed.) 1984. *The World's Religious Traditions: Current Perspectives in Religious Studies*, Edinburgh: T. and T. Clark.

—— (ed.) 1985. *Contemporary Approaches to the Study of Religion, Volume II: The Social Sciences*, Berlin: Mouton.

Wiebe, Donald 1984. 'The Failure of Nerve in the Academic Study of Religion', *Studies in Religion* 13, pp. 401–422.

—— 1999. *The Politics of Religious Studies*, New York: St. Martin's Press.

Wiegers, Gerard A. (ed.) 2002. *Modern Societies and the Science of Religions*, Leiden: Brill.

Williams, Raymond 1976. *Keywords: A Vocabulary of Culture and Society*, Glasgow: Fontana.

Woodland, D.J.A. 1985. 'empirical; empiricism', in G. Duncan Mitchell (ed.), *A New Dictionary of Sociology*, London: Routledge and Kegan Paul, pp. 65–66.

Zaehner, R.C. 1958. *At Sundry Times: An Essay in the Comparison of Religions*, London: Faber and Faber.

—— (ed.) 1959. *The Concise Encyclopaedia of Living Faiths*, London: New Horizon Books/Hutchinson.

PART ONE
CATEGORY
AND
METHOD

CHAPTER 1

Phenomenology, Fieldwork and Folk Religion

Marion Bowman

Introduction: Defining 'Folk Religion'

This chapter was triggered by discussion of phenomenology of religion with Japanese students on the Comparative International Studies programme at Bath College of Higher Education (subsequently Bath Spa University College). When the time came for examination revision in Study of Religions, we dutifully went over various points concerning phenomenology – epoche, eidetic vision, Smart's dimensions and so on. I told the students they would have to be prepared to discuss the *pros* and *cons* of phenomenology, and this produced some interesting reactions. One student was perplexed, as she could only think of positive things to say of phenomenology. Another, however, put forward the old accusation that phenomenology was *merely* descriptive.

Descriptive – yes; *merely* descriptive – no. I am not for a moment suggesting that there is no need or place for analysis in the study of religious traditions. I am, however, suggesting that it is necessary to remember that description, in the sense of accurate, judgement-free reporting, is invaluable in the study of religions. Analysis without phenomenological fieldwork can be suspect at best, dangerous at worst. Unless we check our analyses against what is actually happening in the field, we risk perpetuating false assumptions and blatant inaccuracies.

The need I perceive for phenomenological fieldwork stems from my own particular area of interest, which is popular or folk religion, by which I mean what people actually do, say, think, believe in the name of religion. Another way of putting it might be to say that I am interested in the Little Tradition, but the Little Tradition does not exist in isolation from the Great Tradition and *vice versa*, so that is not how I would normally choose to put it. These are not terms with which I feel particularly comfortable. Having read Religious Studies at Lancaster University and Folklore at Memorial University of Newfoundland,[1] I am happier with the term folk religion. Don Yoder (1974a, p. 14) defines folk religion as 'the totality of all those views and practices of religion that exist among the people apart from and alongside the strictly theological and liturgical forms of the official religion'. Obviously, where appropriate, 'theological and liturgical' could be replaced by philosophical and ritual.

I am, of course, aware that the term 'folk religion' can and has been used in a variety of ways, and that is why I am careful to nail my colours very specifically to Yoder's mast. In his article 'The Folk Religion of the English People', for example, Edward Bailey (1989) comments on the use of the term folk religion among Church of England clergy since the 1970s, citing John Hapgood's 1983 definition of it as

> a general term for the unexpressed, inarticulate, but often deeply felt religion of ordinary folk who would not usually describe themselves as Church-going Christians yet feel themselves to have some sort of Christian allegiance.

While rejecting this as too narrow a view of what folk religion is, it is only fair to point out that Yoder's definition is itself based on the German term 'religiose Volkskunde', which he translates as 'the folk-cultural dimension of religion, or the religious dimension of folk culture' (1974a, p. 14). This term was originally coined in 1901 by a German Lutheran minister, Paul Drews, whose concern was to investigate religious folklife so that young ministers were better equipped to deal with rural congregations whose conception of Christianity was often radically different from the clergy's official version. In Drews' case, the term folk religion came from 'an attempt, within organised religion, to narrow the understanding gap between pulpit and pew' (Yoder 1974a, p. 3). There might still be a need to narrow the understanding gap between the Study of Religions and the religions studied.

I would like to suggest that accounts of religion which do not take into account folk religion risk telling less than the whole story, and that phenomenological fieldwork is often the only means of gathering such information. I have certainly found this to be the case in my own fieldwork experiences.

Three Components of Religion

Frequently, when scholars talk of religion they tend to mean 'official religion', usually perceived in terms of theology or philosophy and ritual, which is just one aspect of most people's religious experience. Believers live according to their own perceptions of the religious traditions to which they adhere, and if their beliefs and practices do not always accord with the official view they remain religious nevertheless; their faith does not become any less sincere or worthy of study. As Susan Tax Freeman (1978, p. 121) has pointed out:

That the personal system of faith may elevate the unsanctioned objects of belief to at least the same level as the sanctioned ones and draw them coherently together has either been ignored or is obliterated by the definitions of religion in use.

Ninian Smart (1977, p. 11) claims that 'to understand human history and human life it is necessary to understand religion'. It is tempting to suggest the corollary that to understand religion, it is necessary to understand the relationship between official, folk and individual beliefs and practices. In religion, as in so many aspects of human endeavour, theory and practice do not necessarily coincide, nor do people behave in exactly the same way. To study the *practice* as opposed to the *theory* of religion, 'ordinary' people's ideas and behaviour must be taken into account. It is thus helpful to view religion in terms of three basic components – the official, the folk and the individual. Official religion is concerned primarily with theology/philosophy and ritual, and is the aspect of religion which tends to receive most scholarly attention. Folk religion can be described as 'the totality of all those views and practices of religion that exist among the people apart from and alongside the strictly theological and liturgical forms of the official religion' (Yoder 1974a, p. 14), a vast but comparatively neglected field. The individual component is basically each person's understanding of religion and the part it plays in his or her life.

These components are rarely analysed, or indeed recognised, in relation to each other. Believers and observers have tended to be unaware of the extent to which these components are interrelated, and this can lead to inaccurate and/or misleading appraisals of religious phenomena. In order to comprehend religion in its broadest sense it is necessary to appreciate how official, folk and individual ideas and behaviour interact with each other.

There is a carefully cultivated 'solidity' about official religion, but it is not a well-defined, static entity. Theological notions can be developed, modified or abandoned. Previously condoned ideas or practices can be actively opposed, or just quietly dropped. However, a belief can continue to be acted upon, regardless of the fact that it is no longer officially approved. It slips from official to folk religion. Conversely, folk religious ideas and practices can gain approval and become official. The process works both ways. Folk religion thus 'exists in creative tension with official religion and involves a body of belief and practice that overlaps with that of official religion in both directions – the permitted forms overlapping inward into official religion, the unpermitted or unsanctioned forms remaining outside the strict edge of official religion'(Yoder 1974b, p. 1).

At the individual level, religion is a mixture of a received religious tradition and a personal belief system. In talking of the 'received' tradition, I am making the point that in many cases what the individual learns of religion does not come from purely orthodox sources. Relatives, contemporaries and others make their mark by example and by passing on their interpretations of religious matters, and it can be quite difficult for the individual to know what actually comprises 'official' religion. The personal belief system evolves from the received tradition, but it is affected by the individual's particular outlook, experience and suchlike. Even if a number of people were to receive a similar tradition, there would still be scope for individual interpretations of it, 'for each person's religion has to do with himself and his own autonomous needs' (Douglas 1973, p. 26). On occasion the ideas of an individual, such as Augustine or Aquinas in the Christian tradition, can radically affect official religion. A personal belief or practice can likewise pass into folk religion.

In diagrammatic form, the relationship between official, folk and individual religion might be expressed thus:

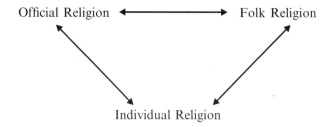

Official Religion ⟷ Folk Religion

Individual Religion

In drawing attention to the relationship between official and folk religion, and the lack of standardisation in people's received traditions and personal belief systems, I wish to make the point that there is considerable scope for variety and variation in religion.[2] Indeed, it seems almost inevitable. However, there is a tendency towards concentration on homogeneity in religion and minimisation of diversity. But there is no such thing as pure religion, whatever the religious tradition. Official, folk and individual components interact to produce what, for each person, constitutes religion. To understand religion in its broadest sense it is therefore necessary to take into account not just theology or philosophy and ritual, but the perceptions, beliefs and behaviour of those practising it. I am not, of course, suggesting that to say anything about any religion it is necessary to talk to everyone involved. I am, however, appealing for a realistic view of religion, and the recognition that folk religion, as defined by Yoder, is not an aberration, but an important and constant element of religion *per se*. In other words, folk religion should be a descriptive, not a pejorative term.

Case Study: Devotion to Saint Gerard Majella in Newfoundland

This brings us back to the value of phenomenology. The subject of my MA thesis was devotion to St Gerard Majella in Newfoundland. In brief, St Gerard was born in Muro, Southern Italy, in 1726; a remarkably pious child and exemplary adolescent who suffered from delicate health, he became a Redemptorist lay brother but died in 1755. He was not beatified until 1893 and was finally canonised in 1904. Although a seemingly incongruous role for a sickly male virgin who died young, he has been best known and most vigorously promoted in Newfoundland as Patron of Expectant Mothers. I first became aware of him because it seemed to me that a disproportionately high number of Newfoundlanders were named Gerard, and this impression was confirmed by others. A St John's judge, for example, claimed that 'every other young fellow hauled up' before him was a Gerard, while a female friend remarked that 'practically every second chap' in her community was a Gerard. The names were a reflection of the high level of devotion to St Gerard.

Much of what has been written of the saint system has either been by Catholic apologists or by theologians and historians complaining of 'abuses' of it at popular level.[3] As a result, we know comparatively little of how the saint system has operated in the lives of ordinary Catholics. The range of beliefs and practices associated with this type of devotion has received comparatively little attention. This is partly because religion has often been studied in terms of what people *should* do or think; whatever has not conformed to that has either been condemned or, more frequently, simply ignored.

There are also practical difficulties. It can at times be very hard to judge whether some aspect of religious belief is official, folk, or simply idiosyncratic; the boundaries between official, folk and individual religion are not well-defined and they can be virtually indistinguishable. Frequently folk ideas and behaviour are so much part of a religious tradition that participants and observers alike consider them normative. In addition, much of religious life takes place outside ritual settings and is not easily observable. Religion can be very a personal matter, and it is therefore necessary to consult those involved in religious activity to ascertain what is actually happening. Since the relationship between an individual and a holy or supernatural figure in whatever tradition is essentially a personal affair, the minutiae of devotion and the part it plays in the lives of individuals can only be discovered through consultation with devotees.

In the study of folk and individual beliefs and practices, the flesh on the bare bones of official religion, I believe that phenomenology provides an invaluable methodological basis. While what follows is probably now so familiar as to seem like a collection of clichés, let me nevertheless restate some of its underlying principles. Phenomenology of religion, Bleeker (1971, p. 16) claims, 'must begin by accepting as proper objects of study all phenomena that are professed to be religious'. As it 'attempts to describe religious behavior rather than explain it' (Bettis 1969, p. 3), debates as to the existence or reality of the focus of devotion are futile and inappropriate. As Smart (1973, p. 54) points out, 'God is real for Christians whether or not he exists.' We do well to remember that scepticism is every bit as biased an outlook as belief. The personal experience narratives of devotees of whatever persuasion provide evidence which must have the status of religious fact. As Kristensen cautioned, 'Let us never forget that there exists no other religious reality than the faith of the believer' (quoted in Sharpe 1986, p. 228). One can analyse and contextualise, certainly, but to condemn, dismiss or ignore the experiences of those living a religion is to diminish our understanding of the tradition, and to tamper with evidence in a way which we would consider improper in other disciplines.

When I first started interviewing Newfoundland women about their devotion to St Gerard, I quite expected some reticence as I was asking about deeply personal matters, but people were remarkably candid and forthcoming. Women generally seemed pleased to share their experiences with an interested listener, such as the one who started 'Oh yes, we had a miracle here a few years back' with the same aplomb and in much the same tone as describing what they had had for lunch. I mention this because it seems to me that frequently it is the investigators who are somewhat coy or uncomfortable about this sort of exchange rather than the informants, for whom it is all just part of their experience.

An extreme example of mundanity in connection with religious experience is contained in the Memorial University of Newfoundland Folklore and Language Archive (MUNFLA), collected c.1971:

> Mrs Elizabeth March. ... always chewed gum. One night about 18 years ago she put her wad of gum on her bureau and went to bed. The next morning when she went to take up the gum to chew [it] again the gum had changed into a small statue of the Blessed Virgin. (She was a Roman Catholic.) She was very surprised and told everyone about it. She also showed it to people. People who saw it and heard about it thought that this was a kind of reward for her having had to work hard all her life. (MUNFLA 71-9-32)

In similar vein, in March and April of 1990 the British media briefly showed interest in the appearance of aubergines (eggplants), which, when split lengthways, were said to reveal the Arabic script for 'Allah', or some verse from the Koran, picked out in the aubergine seeds (Bowman 1990). The BBC Radio 4 'Today' programme's report on 29 March 1990 featured both an Islamic scholar claiming that there is no place in Islam for miracles, and a person who had seen one of the aubergines declaring it a miracle. We should remember that much folk religious belief is empirical, so if people have seen an aubergine containing the holy name written in seeds, they are not going to accept from anyone that such things do not or cannot happen.

Putting this event in context, we might say that here was a community, to some extent socially disadvantaged, feeling marginalised and misunderstood (over the Salman Rushdie affair). Similarly, at times of social and religious tension in Europe, the Virgin Mary has appeared to some of the Catholic faithful. The ordinariness of the owners of the aubergines, like the recipients of visions of the Virgin in the Catholic tradition, makes the event all the more remarkable. The people involved are neither particularly holy, nor profession-ally religious – one reason why the officials of any religion frequently look askance at such happenings. But if you have complete faith in a supernatural figure, why should anything surprise you? Literally anything might be possible, and why would you doubt what you have experienced for yourself?

When I lived in Bahrain in 1980–1982, some young men playing football on wasteland fell through the ground into what was immediately declared to be the grave of a holy man. While scholars protested that there was no record of such a holy man, far less his grave, some people could smell sweet perfume emanating from the grave and people with various afflictions were cured after visits to it; it was also said that people who took earth away from the grave developed headaches. Lack of documentary evidence about the holy man seemed a pretty poor excuse for doubt in the face of such tangible experiences.

It should therefore be stressed that frequently, when phenomenological fieldwork is undertaken, it becomes obvious that people do not just pull ideas or practices that are beyond the pale of official religion out of nowhere. Efficacy and experience are important shapers of belief and behaviour. I discovered at an early stage that devotees of St Gerard knew remarkably little of the saint's biography (although many of them possessed booklets containing such information); what I was told repeatedly were stories of the saint's help to friends and relatives, or personal experience narratives. What mattered was that St Gerard *worked* – a criterion common to the faithful of most religious traditions.

When dealing with devotion to saints, a frequent complaint by apologists and scholars has concerned the 'misuse' of devotional objects such as medals and relics. Many Newfoundland women wore St Gerard medals, for example, to show they had placed themselves under the saint's protection, but there were occasions when the medal was clearly acting as more than a mere memorial or aid to contemplation. That people were in some circumstances prepared to go to considerable lengths to get a medal is demonstrated by the following incident, related by a woman in a remote Newfoundland outport:[4]

> Well, her first baby, you know, she had a lot of trouble and they come to my place to get the medal, ... her mother come to my place in the middle of the night, twelve o'clock in the night to get the medal. Yeah, and you know 'twas a rough night, see, in the winter, and she come and asked for the medal ... And she said, 'Don't think she [the midwife] is going to save her', so she come after the medal twelve o'clock in the night. And eh, she went in and put the medal on her, and the next morning they come out and said she was all right, she had a baby boy.

The fact that someone was prepared to venture out on a stormy night to obtain a medal indicates an assumption that the power of the saint could in some way be more effectively appropriated by the presence of his medal; conversely, the fact that the situation improved after the medal had been obtained could be taken as justification of that assumption.

There was much interesting material in this respect to be gained from popular devotional literature. Because this type of material tends not to be taken seriously by scholars, its influence at popular level can be under-estimated. In the case of devotion to St Gerard, for example, three magazines published by the Redemptorists – *Eikon, Mother of Perpetual Help* and *Madonna* – were particularly influential. Such literature demonstrates how religion has been presented to the masses, and although it might emerge from an official source, its concern with popularising its message and contents seem on occasion to override strictly theological considerations. *Madonna* magazine, for example, ran various articles on medals. Readers were reminded that 'the effects don't depend upon the medal itself, but upon the mercy of God who regards the prayers of the Church and the dispositions of the wearers of the medal' ('Medals In Your Life,' *Madonna*, 33/2, Feb. 1960, p. 27). Nevertheless, the contention that 'Medals in your life, if worn with faith and devotion, can obtain God's protection for you and endless Blessings' would appear to imply that medals could be sources of divine power, thus reinforcing folk religious practice.

The extent to which the intermingling of official, folk and individual beliefs and practices is a constant feature of religion should not be underestimated, as comparisons between pre-Reformation and contemporary Catholicism show. Ronald Finucane (1977, p. 68), for example, writes that: 'In practice the distinctions between what is now called "folk remedy", faith-healing and proper medical attention are inappropriate to the Middle Ages. The sick drew upon all at the same time or went from one to the other'. But such behaviour is not unique to the Middle Ages. One woman told me that her mother used to treat eye sties by crossing them with her wedding ring (an established folk-religious cure), crossing them with her picture of St Gerard (of whom she was particularly fond), and bathing them with boracic acid (a widely recognised folk remedy). Another woman said: 'You don't ask the impossible of St Gerard, you know, you go to the doctor too. ... but his help, his intercession along with your medical'. There is nothing peculiar about making use of what are seen as complementary resources at times of need.

Another rather typical contention is that 'an outstanding characteristic of the "barbarian" [*sic*] Christianity of the early Middle Ages was the belief in relics that worked wonders' (Finucane 1977, p. 25). Briefly, there are three different classes of relics: first class – remains of the saint's body; second class – objects with which the saint came into contact when alive; third class – objects which have been in contact with a first class relic. A *Madonna* article 'What Do You Know About Relics?' told readers that 'Of themselves relics do NOT possess any miraculous powers', but asserted that 'Miracle upon miracle attests to the power of the Saints, WHEN INVOKED THROUGH THEIR RELICS' (*Madonna*, 29/1, Jan. 1956, pp. 4–7).

I was told a number of personal experience narratives by mothers, a midwife and a Redemptorist father involving relics, of which the following is an example. The woman involved has particular devotion to St Gerard and possesses a third class relic of St Gerard.

> When I had me last one we was having trouble, and there was no doctor in the bay, so that's what I used, me relic of St Gerard, and I always says that's who helped me ... [The midwife] she said, 'I know you've got devotion to St Gerard,' she said, 'so pray to him.' And I said to her, I said, 'You pass over the relic,' I said, 'St Gerard will do whatever he can.' So that's what she done, she passed the relic and crossed me stomach, and next pain me daughter was born. Now, I never haemorrhaged one bit afterwards, but I was haemorrhaging before.

This perfectly normal woman is no 'barbarian'. She merely accepts the commonly held view that a saint can operate most effectively through his relic, and has had this view reinforced by her own experience.

We should remember that the difficulties of keeping abreast of what actually comprises official religion are considerable. In Newfoundland, for example, the only theology most people knew had come from the pulpit, from popular devotional literature, from nuns, from fellow Catholics – none of them necessarily reliable sources. A priest had told an informant, who was carrying his bag at the time, that helping a cleric earns 200 days indulgence. It was interesting to compare a young Redemptorist priest who actively squirmed when an older woman with great devotion to St Gerard tried to cross him and me with her St Gerard medal, with the older Redemptorist who had told me about a miracle he had helped effect with the aid of a relic of St Gerard, and who himself frequently crossed people with a St Gerard medal. To be more extreme, we might compare a Vatican II theologian with the nun who told me that her third class relic of St Gerard (a medal containing a tiny piece of cloth which had been touched to a first class relic) was 'more powerful' than a medal because it was 'a piece of the saint'. It should be remembered that whatever a professional religious person in whatever tradition tells a lay person, albeit a folk or purely idiosyncratic belief or practice, is liable to be believed and taken as official because of that person's status.

I drew attention earlier to the fact that beliefs and practices can slip from official to folk, and vice versa. In the Catholic tradition, an element of folk belief and behaviour is implicit in the official procedure for the creation of a saint. Similarly, I would like to conclude with a good example of something slipping from official to folk religion – devotion to St Christopher. St Christopher is commonly known in Newfoundland as 'patron of the cars', and when he comes up in conversation people tend to quip things like 'He

guarantees nothing over sixty, mind.' Most people simply do not mention the
fact that St Christopher has fallen from official favour. However, one man
explained the apparent contradiction:

> See, since the new liturgical calendar, there's been a lot of changes. St
> Christopher was erased. Everybody prays to him. They seemed to take him
> off the calendar. But actually, he was only taken off the liturgical calendar
> to make room for later saints, you know? As far as I'm concerned, he's still
> active.

One example of a fairly typical St Christopher narrative involving a variety of
aspects of folk belief was related to me in relation to a particular spot in
Newfoundland:

> You see this stretch of road here? Well, there was an accident here a whiles
> back. Car just didn't make that last bend there, just left the road, and went
> down on those rocks there, see? Driver should've been dead but he got out
> that car and walked back up the road. See, he had one of them little St
> Christophers, and he says himself, 'twas only the statue on his dashboard
> saved him.

Putting this into context, one could say that at a time when devotion to saints is
being played down in official circles, narratives affirming the efficacy of
devotional objects can be seen as a means of expressing and upholding
traditional folk piety (see Bowman 1981). However, without the phenomenological fieldwork, without recognising that this aspect of belief and practice is
a coherent part of what comprises religion for these people, we would have a
much less accurate picture of their religious life. If we were simply to condemn
or ignore such behaviour as unofficial, there would be nothing to put in context
and our understanding of popular religion would be the poorer for it.

I am thus suggesting that phenomenology, far from being *merely* descriptive,
is an important methodological tool if we are to attain a realistic view of
religion as it is lived, as opposed to some sanitised ideal of how it should be. I
am suggesting, furthermore, that religion can be viewed in terms of three basic
components: official religion (meaning what is accepted orthodoxy at any given
time, although this is subject to change), folk religion (that which is generally
accepted and transmitted belief and practice, regardless of the official view) and
individual religion (the product of the received tradition, plus personal beliefs
and interpretations). I have tried to show something of the interplay between
these categories, and the problems of distinguishing between them for both the
participant and the observer. The difficulties of keeping abreast of what
actually comprises official religion are considerable, and innumerable people's
religious ideas and behaviour contain a proportion of folk religion of which
they are unlikely to be aware. I think we can safely assume that the woman

who ventured out on a stormy night to obtain a St Gerard medal for her daughter is unlikely to have thought 'Expecting this to do any good is just folk religious and not officially sanctioned, but I'll give it a try anyway.' It was all part and parcel of what comprised religion for that person.

Yoder, you may recall, describes folk religion as 'the totality of all those views and practices of religion that exist among the people apart from and alongside the strictly theological and liturgical forms of the official religion'(1974a, p. 14). I would like to suggest that both believers and scholars tend to overestimate the strictly theological or philosophical content of most people's religious beliefs and practices, and consequently underestimate the extent and importance of folk religion. To dismiss folk religion as aberrant religion, or regard it as a deviation from the norm, is to misunderstand what is normative. To ignore it is to impoverish our understanding of religion.

Phenomenology of religion may be descriptive, but it is not *merely* descriptive. Accurate, judgement-free reporting is invaluable in the study of religions, and we undervalue it at our peril.

Afterword: From 'Folk' to 'Vernacular' Religion

I gave this paper in 1991 at the first BASR conference I attended. At its heart is a double plea for the recognition of fieldwork as an invaluable tool in the study of religion, and for the serious consideration and recognition of folk religion, which I characterised as 'religion as it lived'. While it seemed best to leave the paper in its original form as a historical record, I add here a comment on recent developments, and in particular on the concept of vernacular religion, the term I now tend to use in preference to folk religion.

I made no secret in this paper of Ninian Smart's influence, and his contention that religion is an enduring human phenomenon which can be studied and appreciated as a phenomenon, on its own terms, without making a judgement as to whether it is true or false. Individuals were asked, when studying religion, to 'bracket' their own belief or disbelief and concentrate on what was happening for the believer; attention was to be paid to believers' accounts of their religious life and experiences. As Sutcliffe points out in the Introduction to this volume, the validity, practicality and desirability of this approach have rightly all been questioned, debated and contested. However, what I find interesting in this context is that, as a student in Religious Studies at Lancaster in the mid-1970s, I went on no fieldtrips to places of worship; as undergraduates we were given little encouragement towards, and certainly no training for, fieldwork. Considering how much time many of us, more recently, have spent organising field trips to places of worship, or arranging placements enabling students to spend time in a huge variety of spiritual communities, students now seem to have rather more opportunity for 'reality testing' at earlier stages in their careers. The study of new religious movements and the movement over spatial and cultural boundaries of various 'world religions', increasing attention to internal diversity within religions and to the development of much non-aligned spirituality (which has no one authority figure, canon of literature or tradition at its core) have all made it increasingly obvious that a 'one model fits all' approach to the study of religion simply will not do, and that the pursuit of 'pure religion' will help little in recording or comprehending religion in the 21st century. Contemporary religious diversity and fluidity is forcing attention to detail, to the practice rather than simply the theory of religion.

The central category of the original paper, 'folk religion', remains a contested term, with different people using it in a variety of ways. It is clear that many Anglican clergy in England, for example, continue to use the term 'folk religion' in a fairly self-referential and somewhat idiosyncratic way. In his doctoral thesis 'Clergy Attitudes to Folk Religion in the Diocese of Bath and Wells', for example, Geoffrey Walker (2001) records that in answer to the question 'What aspects of Folk Religion do you encounter?', his respondents included earth-religion, school religion, Wicca, the cult of Princess Diana (after the August 1997 fatal car crash), road-accident shrines, eastern religions, New Age healing, horoscopes/astrology, palmistry, Freemasonry, crystals, 'self-religion', Tarot, Druidism, leylines, dowsing, aromatherapy, acupuncture, Anglo-Buddhism (*sic*), Spiritualism, corn dollies and wassailing! Conversely, without adopting the term folk religion, Peter McGrail's doctoral study of first communion in Liverpool (McGrail 2003) showed how local parish communities use the occasion as the focus of a celebration centred on, but going considerably beyond, a religious ceremony, and the tensions between parents and religious authority thus caused. As well as highlighting the 'religious dimension of folk culture' and 'the folk cultural dimension of religion' (Yoder 1974, p. 2), it revealed how the religious meaning of the event is presented, articulated and explained *differently* by various authority figures – priests, teachers, nuns – thus demonstrating the lack of homogeneity even at the 'official' level.

That folk religion is an area of research taken more seriously and is better developed, studied and understood in continental Europe, was amply demonstrated by the choice of topic for the 40th Anniversary Symposium of the Finnish Society for the Study of Religion, 2003: 'Method and Theory in the Study of Folk Religion'. In Scandinavia there has been longstanding and fruitful interaction between departments of Folklore and departments of Religious Studies in universities such as Turku in Finland and Bergen in Norway, Bergen's recent collaborative project 'Magic, Myth and Miracle in Modernity and Post-Modernity' being but one example. Similarly, in North America it is not uncommon to find scholars with an academic background in both Religious Studies and Folkloristics. As one such scholar, Leonard

Primiano (1995, p. 41), has commented: 'one of the hallmarks of the study of religion by folklorists has been their attempt to do justice to belief and lived experience'. Particular aspects of folklore studies which complement the study of religion and alternative spirituality include: the refusal to privilege written over oral forms; attention to different forms of narrative (from legend to personal experience narrative); attention to material culture and the use made of it, both formally and informally; the recognition that belief spills over into every aspect of behaviour; and an appreciation of the dynamic nature of 'tradition', which has been characterised by folklorist Henry Glassie (1995, p. 395) as 'the creation of the future out of the past'.

Nevertheless, the Finnish conference demonstrated that there is still much definitional debate and fluidity around 'folk religion'. At one level, it was argued, *all* religion involving people might be characterised as folk religion. Hakan Rydving from the University of Bergen put forward a series of possible conceptual relationships between 'religion' and 'folk religion' in the way these terms are sometimes used and/or understood. Some of these can be paraphrased as follows:

- Religion is to folk religion as theology is to religion.
- Religion is to folk religion as the religion of specialists is to the religion of laypersons.
- Religion is to folk religion as textual religion is to oral religion.
- Religion is to folk religion as ideas of what religion ought to be are to religion as it is.
- Religion is to folk religion as the religion of the elite is to the religion of the powerless.
- Religion is to folk religion as the religion of men is to the religion of women.
- Religion is to folk religion as religion as studied by history is to religion as studied by anthropology.

As I have argued elsewhere (see Sutcliffe and Bowman 2000; Bowman 2000), while 'folk' and 'popular' religion are terms that have been used in different ways, in UK Religious Studies more often than not it has simply been ignored – and ignoring a field of study is a way of demoting it, making value judgements as to what constitutes 'worthy' objects of study. So it has been and still remains important to question some of the implicit and explicit assumptions in the academy as to what constitutes 'real' or 'proper' belief, both in relation to vernacular religion and contemporary spirituality. Undoubtedly some of the neglect of popular belief has sprung from a rather 'literalist', text-oriented attitude that suspects or dismisses material culture, ritual or custom. Academic studies of religions, or religions as taught in schools and colleges, for example, sometimes tend to be rather 'bookish' versions of traditions.

While this may be seen as a necessary pedagogic device, the traditions and the students are done a great disservice if we give the impression that this skeletal form is all there is to it. The diversity within religious traditions, the role of folk religion and the individual 'spin' on religion are all there, and deserve to be acknowledged.

Returning to the triangular model I originally suggested of official, folk and individual traditions interacting with, influencing and being influenced by each other, I think the model still holds, for while Yoder's definition developed in a Christian milieu, it can be applied in any tradition in which there is a sense (emically or etically) of there being a hegemonic official or authentic 'version'. However, it could be argued that in the West, with the growth of more customised forms of spirituality and the relative decline in strength and social significance of official religion, it might be more appropriate to flip the triangle over to place the individual at the top and in the centre, being fed by and feeding upon a *variety* of official and folk traditions.

However, while 'folk religion' as a concept has currency (and academic respectability) in Europe and beyond, I have come to the conclusion that the term folk religion is best replaced by 'vernacular religion': 'religion as it is lived: as humans encounter, understand, interpret and practice it' (Primiano 1995, p. 44). The term 'vernacular' is perhaps most familiar in the context of 'vernacular architecture', which acknowledges and celebrates the existence of building variation and adaptation in relation to such factors as locality, availability of materials, the cultural origins of the makers and local aesthetics. As folklorist Henry Glassie points out: 'we call buildings vernacular to highlight the cultural and contingent nature of all building' (Glassie 2000, p. 17). That the comparison between architecture and religion is particularly apposite might be seen in architectural historian Dell Upton's comment that:

> Once introduced into the landscape, the identity of a building and the intentions of its makers are dissolved within confusing patterns of human perception, imagination, and use. Consequently, the meaning of a building is determined primarily by its viewers and users. This process of creation goes on long after the crew leaves the site; it never stops. Every structure contains several different buildings as imagined by different segments of its public. None of these is necessarily consistent with the others, nor do any of them bear any necessary relationship to the intention of designer, builder, or client. Yet so much of architectural history is directed toward identifying the pure form, the original condition, the architect's intention. How relatively unimportant these are! (Upton 1991, p. 197)

Primiano (1995, p. 44) describes vernacular religious theory as 'an inter-disciplinary approach to the study of the religious lives of individuals with special attention to the process of religious belief, the verbal, behavioral, and material expressions of religious belief, and the ultimate object of religious belief'. As an approach this is suited both to the study of more traditional forms of religion and to contemporary spirituality, as my longterm studies of Glastonbury demonstrate (Bowman 1993, 1999, 2000, 2003). Indeed, this approach is, I contend, of considerable usefulness in the study of religion *per se* and provides a means of 'studying religion realistically' (see Sutcliffe 1998). Just as the study of history in the 20th century witnessed a growing shift of emphasis away from the deeds and experiences of kings and generals to the lives, experiences and contributions of 'ordinary' people, there has been a growing scholarly interest in what people do, in the laity as well as the theologians, the 'ordinary' people as well as the religious *virtuosi*. I believe that trends both in contemporary religiosity itself as well as in the study of religions have been conspiring to force increasing numbers of Religious Studies scholars and students into ethnological modes of operating and making 'vernacular religion' – although certainly a term not yet broadly used – a valuable framework within which to work.

(First published as Occasional Paper No. 6, 1992)

Notes

1   See Bennett (1987, Chapter 1) for a good, brief survey of the history and present state of folklore studies.
2   Neither this variety, nor the reasons it occurs, are confined to religion: see Smith, 1981.
3   A notable exception is Christian (1972).
4   'Outport' is the Newfoundland term for a small coastal settlement; many outports are quite isolated, and some can still only be reached by sea.

Bibliography

Bailey, Edward 1989. 'The Folk Religion of the English people', in Paul Badham (ed.), *Religion, State and Society in Modern Britain*, Lampeter: Edwin Mellen Press, pp. 145–158.
Bennett, Gillian 1987. *Traditions of Belief*, Harmondsworth: Penguin.
Bettis, J.D. 1969. *Phenomenology of Religion*, New York and Evanston: Harper and Row.
Bleeker, C.J. 1971. 'Comparing the Religio-Historical and the Theological Method,' *Numen* **18**.
Bowman, M. 1981. ' "Twas only the statue on his dashboard saved him"': Narratives affirming the Efficacy of Devotional Objects', *Scandinavian Yearbook of Folklore* **37**, pp. 7–10.
——— 1990. 'Aubergines from Heaven: Folk Religion and Legitimation,' *Talking Folklore*, **9**, pp. 1–7.
——— 1993. 'Drawn to Glastonbury', in *Pilgrimage in Popular Culture*, Ian Reader and Tony Walter, eds, Basingstoke and London: Macmillan, pp. 29–62.
——— 1999. 'Faith, Fashion and Folk Religion in Glastonbury: Joseph of Arimathea's Legendary Luggage', Anders Gustavsson and Maria Santa Vieira Montez, (eds), *Folk Religion: Continuity and Change*, Universidade Nova de Lisboa, Portugal & Etnologiska Institutionen, Uppsala Universitet, pp. 25–32.

———— 2000. 'More of the same?: Christianity, Vernacular Religion and Alternative Spirituality in Glastonbury', in *Beyond New Age: Exploring Alternative Spirituality*, co-edited with Steven Sutcliffe, Edinburgh: Edinburgh University Press, pp. 83–104.

———— 2003. 'Ancient Avalon, New Jerusalem, Heart Chakra of Planet Earth: Localisation and Globalisation in Glastonbury', unpublished Keynote Lecture, 3rd European Association for the Study of Religion Conference, Bergen, Norway, May 2003.

Christian, William A. Jr. 1972, *Person and God in a Spanish Valley*, New York and London: Seminar Press.

Douglas, Mary 1973. *Natural Symbols*, Harmondsworth: Penguin.

Finucane, Ronald C. 1977. *Miracles and Pilgrims: Popular Beliefs in Medieval England*, Totowa, N.J.: Rowman and Littlefield.

Glassie, Henry 1995. 'Tradition', *Journal of American Folklore* **108**, pp. 395–412.

———— 2000. *Vernacular Architecture*, Bloomington: Indiana University Press.

McGrail, Simon Peter 2003. 'The Celebration of First Communion in Liverpool: a Lens to View the Structural Decline of the Roman Catholic Parish', unpublished PhD Thesis, University of Birmingham.

Primiano, Leonard Norman 1995. 'Vernacular Religion and the Search for Method in Religious Folklife', *Western Folklore* **54** (1), pp. 37–56.

Sharpe, Eric J. 1986. *Comparative religion: A History*, London: Duckworth.

Smart, Ninian 1973. *The Science of Religion and the Sociology of Knowledge*, Princeton: Princeton University Press.

———— 1977[1969]. *The Religious Experience of Mankind*, Glasgow: Fount Paperbacks.

Smith, Paul S. 1981. 'Communication and Performance: A Model of the Development of Variant Forms of Cultural Traditions', in A.E. Green and J.D.S. Widdowson (eds), *Language, Culture and Tradition*, Sheffield: The Institute of Dialect and Folklife Studies and the Centre for English Folk Cultural Tradition and Language, pp. 16–32.

Sutcliffe, Steven 1998. 'Studying Religions Realistically', *Method and Theory in the Study of Religion* **10** (3), pp. 266–274.

Sutcliffe, S. and Bowman, M. 2000. 'Introduction', in S. Sutcliffe and M. Bowman (eds), *Beyond New Age: Exploring Alternative Spirituality*, Edinburgh: Edinburgh University Press, pp. 1–13.

Tax Freeman, Susan 1978. 'Faith and Fashion in Spanish Religion: Notes on the Observance', *Peasant Studies*, **7** (2), pp. 101–123.

Upton, Dell 1991. 'Architectural History or Landscape History?', *Journal of Architectural Education* **44** (4), pp. 195–199.

Walker, Geoffrey 2001. 'Clergy Attitudes to Folk Religion in the Diocese of Bath and Wells', unpublished PhD Thesis, University of Bristol.

Yoder, Don 1974a. 'Toward a Definition of Folk Religion', *Western Folklore* **33** (1), pp. 2–15.

———— 1974b. 'Introduction', *Western Folklore* **33** (1).

CHAPTER 2

Media, Meaning and Method in the Study of Religion

Chris Arthur

Introduction

In his study of the Ituri Pygmies, Colin Turnbull describes the key role played in their religious life by the *molimo*, or sacred trumpet. This is used by the tribe's elders to 'waken the forest', on whose complex webs of life the Pygmies utterly depend. Eventually, having gained their trust, Turnbull is shown the *molimo*, which is treated with great reverence and secrecy. To his surprise, the Pygmies' most sacred object turns out to be a length of metal drainpipe (Turnbull 1961, pp. 72–73) . A similarly arresting example of how an unlikely object may be invested with religious meaning was reported in 1993 from San Francisco. A traffic bollard, dumped some years ago in that city's Golden Gate Park, had come to be regarded by many as a sacred object. Hundreds of worshippers, some from as far away as India, have travelled to San Francisco to pray, meditate and make offerings of flowers and incense in front of this latter-day *lingam*.[1] Such instances powerfully underline Mircea Eliade's (1958, p. 11) contention that 'we cannot be sure that there is *anything* that has not at some time in human history been transformed into a hierophany'. Eliade gives this generic name to the diverse evidence which shows how people have variously understood the sacred (rituals, myths, cosmogonies, symbols, sacred places, scriptures, ceremonial costumes, shamanic dances, and so on). Hierophanies are the raw material of religious studies.

Given that human religiousness expresses itself over such a staggering range of forms – everything from traffic bollards to the *Summa Theologiae* – it is, presumably, important for religious studies to try to cultivate a sensitivity to the *variety* of media through which its subject matter finds voice, otherwise we may end up uncritically assuming that religion admits of much neater definition and more clear-cut boundaries than is in fact the case. Yet there is a tendency in the subject towards what might be called 'media-blindness'. Such blindness not only fails to take into account the range of media involved in religious expression, but also ignores what Len Masterman (1985, p. 20) sees as the first principle of media studies, namely that 'media are symbolic systems which need to be actively *read*, and not unproblematic, self-explanatory reflections of reality'.

Masterman offers a simple illustration of the way in which this principle tends to be ignored. An art teacher holds up a painting of a horse in front of a class and asks what it is. The invariable reply is: 'it's a horse'. The teacher shakes his head and asks again. Eventually the distinction between a horse and its representation on canvas is established. The same point is made in Rene Magritte's famous painting of a pipe across which is written: *'ceci n'est pas une pipe'*.[2] Perhaps books about religion should bear similar disclaimers on their covers. By alerting us to their existence as media, this might help to avoid the intellectual solecism to which those who study religion are occasionally prone – judging Buddhists, Christians, Jews and Muslims against the blueprints found in books about them and finding the living representatives wanting.

I want to do three things in this chapter. First, draw attention to some work which challenges – I think effectively – the tendency in religious studies towards media-blindness; second, examine something of the impact of media on religious thinking; and third, suggest some arguments for adopting a more media-conscious approach to studying religion.

Part One

It is interesting to note that two of the three 'pointers to new directions' identified for the discipline in *Turning Points in Religious Studies* (King, ed. 1990), namely the arts and information technology, are very much media-related.[3] The third 'pointer', gender, also has some interesting conceptual links with the notion of 'media-blindness'. John Hinnells provides a useful general statement of the need to include non-verbal media in our efforts to understand religion. He begins by noting that mass literacy is 'a relatively recent and still mainly "western" phenomenon' (Hinnells 1990, p. 257), a claim borne out by comparative surveys of national adult literacy rates. It follows, therefore, that 'over the millennia the majority of the world's religious people have been illiterate' (*ibid*). As such, when the study of religion focuses on textual sources, it risks 'plugging in to a level of religion which most of the practitioners are not, or have not been engaged in' (*ibid*). To counteract the risk of such a partial view, Hinnells argues that, in addition to looking at written sources, the subject area must recognize in the arts a second significant form of religious expression. The arts, he says, do not just constitute the *earliest* means of religious communication 'but represent a major form of religious expression in modern times as well' (*ibid*). Marginalizing the arts, and Hinnells sees this as a common failing in religious studies, means 'excluding the possibility of an adequate appreciation of what it is that makes religion a living experience for the practitioner' (*ibid*, p. 271). Given the enormous diversity of hierophanies which constitute the raw material of our study, sampling those which manifest themselves in writing is, naturally, important. But it ought only to be part of a much more wide-ranging investigation.

Gregory Schopen's methodologically important paper, 'Archaeology and Protestant Presuppositions in the Study of Indian Buddhism' (1991), substantiates Hinnells' general warnings by pointing to specific examples where media-bias leads to the mis-representation of a religion. Schopen is concerned with exposing a double peculiarity. The way in which the history of Indian Buddhism has been studied by modern scholars is, he says, 'decidedly peculiar' (Schopen 1991, p. 1). But what is even *more* peculiar 'is that it has rarely been seen to be so' (*ibid*). The roots of these twin peculiarities lie in precisely the kind of media-blindness which Masterman identifies; the lesson which Schopen offers is analogous to the art teacher's efforts to get his class to recognize the difference between a horse and its representation in a painting. Schopen's paper reminds us that there are a *variety* of modes of religious expression to be considered and that religion as such ought not to be equated with any one of them.

Why is the study of Indian Buddhism 'peculiar'? Because, says Schopen, it operates a 'curious and unargued preference for a certain kind of source material' (*ibid*). There are two basic strands of media which cast light on this area. On the one hand there is archaeological material; on the other there are textual sources. Schopen identifies a clear scholarly preference for literary, rather than archaeological, material. Indeed, such is the strength of this preference, that 'textuality overrides actuality' (*ibid*, p. 11). Real Buddhism comes to be equated with textual Buddhism. And yet the literary material consists of heavily edited texts which are intended 'to inculcate an ideal', which record 'what a small atypical part of the Buddhist community wanted that community to believe or practise', whilst the archaeological material 'records or reflects at least a part of what Buddhists actually practised and believed' (*ibid*, pp. 2–3). 'Scholars of Indian Buddhism', says Schopen, 'have taken canonical monastic rules and formal literary descriptions of the monastic ideal preserved in very late manuscripts and treated them as if they were accurate reflections of the religious life and career of Buddhist monks in early India' (*ibid*, p. 5). This has led to serious misapprehensions, evident when archaeological evidence from the stupas at Bharut and Sanchi is considered. For example, we will reach very different conclusions about attitudes to private property and understandings of *karma* and transfer of merit according to whether we rely on archaeological or textual sources in drawing our picture of Indian Buddhism.

Having noted the peculiarity of simply allowing literary sources to assume primacy, a media-bias which he also detects in the study of early Christianity, Schopen attempts to account for it. The idea that religion is located in written sources is, he suggests, 'a decidedly non-neutral and narrowly limited

Protestant assumption' (*ibid*, p. 19). In other words, our picture of Indian Buddhism may reflect western theological values as much as it reflects the history and values of Indian Buddhism. By focusing too much on written sources, we may end up with a picture of Buddhism which is ill-suited to the variety of phenomena which make up this complex and media-diverse tradition.

An assumption about what religion is, whether expressed in terms of some explicit definition, or implicitly as a media-bias which leads us only to consider one type of material in our assessments of it, can have the effect of directing our inquiries away from the actual religiousness of those who constitute the living reality of a faith and towards abstract formulations whose claim to be representative of such faiths is open to question; hence Cantwell Smith's (1978) objection to the very concepts 'religion' and 'the religions'. As Margaret Miles has shown, what until recently was regarded as universal human history is, in fact, largely the history of an atypical, privileged minority, namely those who can read and write. If we want to democratize religious studies and ensure that our understanding of religions is fairly representative of the actual phenomena which make up the different faiths, then it is important not to adopt a mono-medium approach. There are, for example, many 'whose sense of self and relationship', as Miles (1985, p. 152) puts it, 'was informed by images rather than words'. Although she was referring to the situation in the pre-modern period, her observation also has considerable contemporary relevance. For instance, in his study of *Theology Through Film*, Neil Hurley (1970, p. 192) has noted the way in which we are 'literally barraged with images'. He talks about 'the saturation of visual communications' which we experience and estimates that the average New York commuter is exposed to some 5,000 images in the course of a weekday.

Miles' point about the way in which one type of medium is commonly read as universal human expression is, of course, very similar to the arguments of feminist critics of religious studies who see the discipline as only gradually awakening from a cognitive slumber in which male experience was assumed to be universal and normative. According to June O'Connor (1995, p. 48), 'the epistemological significance of feminist research in religion lies in its asking questions about how we know what we know, what the sources of our knowledge are and why we trust them'. O'Connor cites Daniel Maguire's contention that 'changes in *what* we know are normal; changes in *how* we know are revolutionary'.[4] On that criterion – which can, of course, be challenged – media critiques, like feminist critiques, have the potential to be revolutionary, because they focus on ways of knowing, rather than on the content of knowledge. (It is, perhaps, worth bringing to mind at this point Marshall McLuhan's famous warning that 'the "content" of a medium is like the juicy piece of meat carried by the burglar to distract the watchdog of the mind' [McLuhan 1987/1964, p. 18]. McLuhan felt – back in 1964 – that in trying to alert people to the significance of media he was in an analogous position to that of Louis Pasteur telling doctors about something invisible and unrecognized but with massive potential to affect the health of their patients. Correcting media and gender blindness in the study of religion involves addressing methodological afflictions which affect whole ways of seeing, rather than just specific blindspots which only miss easily itemizable parts of the religious scene. As such, they are likely to encounter strong resistance.)

Beyond the Written Word, William Graham's superb study of the oral dimension of written sacred texts, provides a further touchstone of support for anyone interested in highlighting the importance to religious studies of a sensitivity to different media. 'Too often lost to us', laments Graham (1987, p. *ix*) 'is the central place of the scriptural word recited, read aloud, chanted, sung, quoted in debate, memorized in childhood, meditated upon in murmur and full voice'. Our tendency to downplay, or altogether disregard, the oral aspect of scripture lies in our 'modern Western cultural biases' (*ibid*, p. *xi*). The 'ubiquity of printed copies of the Bible and most other sacred books, from the Qur'an to the Lotus Sutra' has, Graham believes, 'reinforced our notion of scripture as a concrete and often commonplace object belonging to the physical paraphernalia of religious life and practice' (*ibid*, pp. *ix–x*). The 'contemporary Western conception of books as silent written documents has skewed our perception of the special kind of book we call "scripture", especially as regards its important oral functions' (*ibid*, p. 8). Our media-blindness, in other words, in assuming that the written word is natural, normative and authoritative, has failed to see another important dimension at work. Graham argues convincingly that any concept of scripture that is going to be 'useful and meaningful for the study of religion must include recognition of its importance both as written and as spoken word' (*ibid*, p. 58).

In *The Meaning of Religion*, W. Brede Kristensen (1960, p. 13) famously argued that if we try to understand the religious data from a different viewpoint to that of the believers we 'negate the religious reality'. Looking at points raised by Hinnells, Schopen, Miles and Graham, it appears as if precisely such a negation may routinely happen because of a blindness to the significance of media, which in turn leads to an uncritical preference for writing in terms of where we locate religion, what we take religion to be, and where we direct our gaze in examining and attempting to understand it.

Part Two

The work of the four scholars I have mentioned so far alerts us to the existence of different media of religious expression and shows how our understanding of religion may be skewed if we over-emphasize one type. Walter Ong and Jack Goody are more concerned with the extent to which different media can actually *shape* our religiousness in the first place. Their work also goes a long way towards explaining why we tend so much to favour written sources above other media. To try to summarize the thinking of such prolific writers here would be misplaced. I want simply to touch on some of their ideas which serve to further strengthen the case for saying that religious studies needs to adopt a more media-conscious approach.

It is perilously easy to suppose that 'after a theology is thought out or put together, media simply circulate it' (Ong 1969, p. 462). Walter Ong's work challenges such a naive view by highlighting the cognitive consequences of introducing a *new* medium. According to Ong (1982, p. 78), 'more than any other invention writing has transformed human consciousness'. Without writing the literate mind 'simply could not think as it does' (*ibid*, p. 69). Not only does a medium such as writing influence the individual, it also affects societies. 'Oral communication unites people in groups. Writing and reading are solitary activities that throw the psyche back on itself' (*ibid*). Looking at differences between oral and literate cultures, Ong highlights the extent to which a medium facilitates and moulds thinking, rather than just neutrally carrying its ideas. For instance, oral societies must invest much time and energy in repetition, saying things over and over again to avoid forgetting. 'This need establishes a highly traditionalist or conservative set of mind that inhibits intellectual experimentation' (*ibid*, p. 41). In contrast, the text frees us from such conservative memory tasks, thus enabling the mind 'to turn itself to new speculation' (*ibid*, p. 46). Indeed for Ong, writing 'separates the knower from the known and thus sets up conditions for "objectivity" in the sense of personal disengagement or distancing' (*ibid*).

That this will have profound *religious* implications is clear. Some of these are spelt out by Jack Goody and Ian Watt, who suggest that in oral cultures a word like 'God' 'may hardly be conceived of as a separate entity, divorced from both the rest of the sentence and its social context. But, once given the physical reality of writing, it can take on a life of its own' (Goody and Watt 1968, p. 53). By objectifying words and by 'making their meaning available for much more prolonged and intensive scrutiny than is possible orally', writing 'encourages private thought' (*ibid*, p. 62). Goody sees religion as being profoundly influenced by writing. Religions associated with writing can become 'world' rather than just 'local' or 'national' faiths. The connection between such religions and literacy is well summed up by Goody (1986, p. 4) when he says, 'these alphabetic religions spread literacy and equally literacy spreads these religions'. Writing and religion, in other words, enjoy an intimate symbiotic relationship. Literacy not only facilitates the development of *world* rather than more local religions. It also gives rise to some of the characteristics of such religions, just as the absence of literacy helps to shape less encompassing traditions. Literate religions tend to be 'religions of conversion, not simply religions of birth' (*ibid*, p. 5). Their ethical framework is universalistic in scope and their teachings are not limited to particular times or places.

The way in which different media facilitate different senses of time and history is something often remarked on by scholars working in this area. For instance, William Graham (1987, p. 16) shows how 'literacy changes the way we understand the past and, therefore, ultimately the present'. It is easy to assume that something so fundamental to us as our sense of time is hard-wired into the psyche and operates independently of any external technology. But, to take the example John Staudenmaier (1993, p. 16) uses in his contribution to a media issue of the journal *Concilium*, 'public clocks long showed only one hand, the hour, but not the minute'. It was only in the eighteenth century that improved techniques allowed much greater accuracy. Staudenmaier argues that as 'instrument makers revolutionized the world of precision measurement and quantitative analysis', the religious impact of such a revolution was that 'religious and cultural leaders began to read the holy dark out of the Western canon' (*ibid*, p. 17). Just as 'factory masters tried to enforce precisely defined work rules, the church gradually turned to similarly detailed codes of law and doctrine' (*ibid*). Many of our ideas about history, time, precision, detail and order are, in other words, media dependent.

In a review article in *Numen*, Hans Kippenberg (1992, p. 107) identified what he terms 'a new area for development in the study of religions', where 'the literary forms used by the great religions' (*ibid*) would be examined. Whilst it is good to see an article appearing in a mainstream religious studies journal in which the significance of Jack Goody's work is acknowledged, it would be a shame to confine this new area for development to *literary* forms alone. We need, rather, to attend to *all* the varieties of media used to express religiousness. Indeed in much the same way that dentists use disclosing fluid to reveal the extent of placque, so some methodological equivalent is needed in religious studies so that the important media-dimension involved in this subject does not go unnoticed. Such disclosure is important, *not* so that we can remove something unwanted, as in the dental model, but simply so as we may be aware of its existence and its influence on our studies.

Part Three

I will conclude this chapter by suggesting very briefly six inter-related and often overlapping arguments which might be put forward to support the idea of a more media-conscious approach in religious studies.

First, as Hinnells, Schopen, Miles and Graham have suggested, a media-bias in favour of writing can act to shift our focus from actual lived religiousness to abstract statements of ideals. This brings back to mind Wilfred Cantwell Smith's objections to the very concept of 'religion' and his contention that 'fundamentally one has to do not with religions but with religious persons' (Smith 1978, p. 153). As Ninian Smart (1988, p. 443) likewise reminds us: 'ultimately *the* most important symbols communicating the essence of religion are the people involved'. Or, as Leonard Michaels (1990, p. *xiii*) puts it, 'individual speakers are the media of media'. We risk losing sight of the person as the most important medium of all, if we fail to take account of the full range of ways in which such individuals express their religiousness – drain pipes, traffic bollards, cave paintings, television, dance, popular film, architecture *and* writing.

Secondly, if as Ong, Goody and others have suggested, media are part and parcel of religious thinking, not simply inert means of conveying it, then if we want to access the full spectrum of such thought we ought not to confine our attention to any single medium. If major religious developments are related to the availability of different media, then to understand the history of religion we need a media-sensitive approach. For instance, the way in which religious evolution in India has recently 'entered a new phase' (Babb 1995, p. 1) due to the introduction of new media (mass produced colour posters, cassette tapes, film, TV and video) provides a good illustration of the way in which media facilitate religious development. This is something expertly explored by the various contributors to Babb and Wadley's *Media and the Transformation of Religion in South Asia* (1995). They variously show how new media 'have not only given religious symbols greater spatial mobility, but have significantly enhanced their social mobility as well' (*ibid*, p. 3) meaning that the religious vocabulary, so to speak, of millions of people has been altered, allowing them new resources of expression.

Thirdly, if, as is often claimed, religious experience is in some sense beyond words, then it would be unwise to be over-reliant on verbal media alone. Likewise, if we allow that inexpressibility in general tends to be an important feature built into many efforts to communicate religiously, then it would seem more appropriate to consider the full range of expressive attempts, rather than limiting ourselves to any one variety. Rudolf Otto's picture of religion, as a warp and woof of rational and non-rational elements, lends itself to supporting an approach which does not focus entirely on verbal sources. Otto was concerned that what he saw as the 'real innermost core' (1923, p. 6) of religion, namely the numinous, had been marginalized by our preoccupation with rationality, and he was keen to promote a more balanced approach. It is interesting to find in the work of Pierre Babin a very similar argument being applied specifically to the media of religious communication. Babin identifies two modes of communication. On the one hand there is the alphabetical, linear, conceptual; on the other the affective, symbolic, emotional. He is particularly concerned that modern Western Christianity has over-emphasized the first mode, adopting what he terms the 'Gutenberg attitude' (Babin 1991, p. 67) and that this risks ignoring the intuitively felt sense of the sacred which is resistant to such analytical forms. Babin advocates what he sees as a theologically therapeutic media middle way in which the rational and emotional sides of religion are kept in balance. So he argues for the strategic use of silence and images in religious communication to counterbalance the dominance of sound and word.

The fourth argument for supporting media-awareness in religious studies has to do with the impact of media change on religion. This is something which Thomas Boomershine has tried to map for the Judaeo-Christian tradition, identifying five important stages of media development, each creating its own particular religious contours: orality, writing, print, silent print and electronic media. Boomershine (1987, p. 275) argues that such changes are revolutionary because they transform the character of a community's experience of the sacred.

It is often said that we are currently experiencing a media revolution, involving a move from a typographic to a televisual epistemology. If this is indeed the case – and there are strong arguments for and against such a supposition – then the impact of the new media on religion must surely be of interest to religious studies. Many assessments of the impact of TV and film on modern religiousness are extremely pessimistic. These range from naive and strident Whitehousian tirades against the supposedly corrosive effects of on-screen sex, violence and profanity, to the much more sophisticated arguments of, say, William Fore (1987) or Neil Postman (1987). Fore sees TV usurping the traditional roles of religion, carrying an insistent and invasive worldview which is at odds with Christian values; Postman believes that, as a culture, we are at risk of 'amusing ourselves to death' – with religion, like everything else on TV, being reduced to entertainment. More tentative than Fore's or Postman's robust critiques is the worry voiced by Jorge Schement and Hester Stephenson (1996, p. 277) about the way in which what they term 'the religions of the Word are on the verge of being conquered by a new kind of orality, in which multi-media environments will frame the religious experience'. They pose the interesting question of whether the shift away from print culture which this involves 'to a new visual "virtual reality" culture' will 'undo the foundation from which Protestant Christianity grew' (*ibid*, p. 278). Others are more interested in identifying change, rather than in formulating critiques of its consequences. Thomas Martin (1981, pp. 54–55), for example, pointing to the new repertoires of insight afforded by slow motion photography (microscopic, telescopic and what he terms 'cosmic' photography), argues that 'human consciousness cannot be the same today as it was prior to the extension of its vision through film', and that 'neither can religious consciousness ever be the same'. One media-wrought change in religious consciousness, according to Gregor Goethals (1990), Quentin Schultze (1990) and others, is the extent to which TV and film constitute new and fecund reservoirs of myth, story and symbol which the religious imagination can draw on. But whatever our verdict on the desirability of the religious changes wrought by the new electronic media which are burgeoning all around us, the nature of their impact is surely an important and legitimate area of interest for religious studies to consider. Marshall McLuhan (1987[1964], p. 305) warned that 'the educational establishment, founded on print, does not yet admit of any other responsibilities'. Hopefully, several decades on, religious studies will not fall foul of this rebuke.

An appeal might also be made to McLuhan to introduce the fifth argument in favour of a more media-conscious discipline. In *Understanding Media*, he suggested that one day education would become recognized as 'civil defence against media fallout' (1987[1964], p. 305). Without advocating any kind of sweeping media condemnation, I think it is important to recognize that most people draw their information about many aspects of the world, including religion, from TV, newspapers, radio and so on, and that some of that information is misleading – or dangerously radioactive, to build on McLuhan's metaphor. For example, Akbar Ahmed (1992), Edward Said (1981), S.A. Schliefer (1993) and others have convincingly illustrated the highly unsatisfactory way in which Islam appears in the Western media. Religious studies as a discipline presumably has some kind of responsibility to be aware of such appearances and to do something to counteract them.

The sixth and final argument which I want to suggest for supporting media-conscious religious studies, stems from the religiousness of the mass media. This can be interpreted in two ways. First, as the expression of religious themes in the media; secondly, as the religiousness, or quasi-religiousness, of the media themselves. There has already been some interesting work done in terms of looking at the expression of religious themes in the media. Taking film, for example, we might point to Paul Shrader's *Transcendental Style in Film* (1972), which examines the way in which the sacred is expressed in the films of three directors, one Japanese, one French and one Danish. Shrader is concerned 'to track down a universal form, which is used by film makers in divergent cultures in order to express the Wholly Other' (1972, p. 111). Or we might turn to John May's identification of religious themes in modern American cinema. In their 'subtlety of allusion and richness of imagery and design', says May (1992, p. 75), 'the *Godfather* films stand among the finest achievements of the American religious imagination'. His study also includes *2001: a Space Odyssey*, *The Wizard of Oz* and *One Flew Over the Cuckoo's Nest* as serious religious 'texts'. Likewise in Martin and Ostwalt's *Screening the Sacred* (1995), religious themes are identified in *Star Trek*, *Alien*, *Platoon*, *Rocky* and so on. Or we might look at Patricia Erens' study of *The Jew in American Cinema* (1984) or Les and Barbara Keyser's (1984) examination of the image of Roman Catholicism in American films. Richard Niebuhr (1959, p. *ix*) once pointed out that 'religious currents have often flowed in other than obviously theological or ecclesiastical channels'. Unless we want to rule such currents off-limits, which would raise questions about the neutrality of the discipline, religious studies needs to be open to the expression of religion in what may strike some as rather unlikely places, such as popular films.

As well as looking at religious themes in the media, some commentators have suggested that the media are themselves religious or quasi-religious phenomena. Various arguments are offered to this effect in the work of, among others, Gregor Goethals (1990), Quentin Schultze (1990) and Michael Warren (1992). This should, perhaps, make us recall Thomas Luckmann's (1967, pp. 90–91) warnings that 'what are usually taken as symptoms of the decline of traditional Christianity may be symptoms of a more revolutionary change: the replacement of the institutional specialization of religion by a new social form of religion'. Perhaps we are sometimes at risk of mistaking change for decay. Might the Jeremiads of Postman and Fore be failing to appreciate 'symptoms of a revolutionary change', reading them as destructive of existing religion rather than as creative of new forms of faith? We come back, again, to the question of what religion is – where do we locate it, how do we define it?

Michael Warren's *Communications and Cultural Analysis: A Religious View* (1992) poses some particularly difficult questions about where we should look for someone's religiousness. Warren shows how religion and culture can act as signifying systems which posit vastly different values and goals. Today, he says, the electronically imagined world of the mass media is often in direct conflict with the religiously imagined world. Frequently, people's actual day-to-day allegiances, what guides and informs their lives, suggests a commitment to this electronically imagined world, rather than to whatever religion they happen to practise and profess. In such a situation, Warren (1992, p. 17) argues that one can gain access to the actual culture of religious groups only by carefully 'examining their life-structure rather than their explicit verbal claim'. Warren is largely pessimistic about the extent to which professed religion and actual way of life are likely to be satisfactorily aligned in concrete situations. The images controlling the imaginations of people who like to call themselves religious are, he believes, often 'the irreligious images of competition and even of violent domination' (*ibid*, p. 18). This raises all sorts of difficulties about how a theologically non-partisan study should handle those believers whose actual lives seem remote from their declared religiousness.

This is to suggest, very briefly, some of the ways in which media influence religious meaning and how method in religious studies might respond to this fact. I should, perhaps, have included here some mention of the ways in which the discipline itself might inculcate an openness to new forms of media in expressing the results of its work. And it would also have been interesting to have looked at how some of the criticisms directed at the way in which the mass media handle religion might be applied to the way in which religious studies handles religion. However, the medium of a short chapter imposes its own constraints; the further exploration of such matters must be located elsewhere.

(First published as Occasional Paper No. 15, 1996)

Notes

1 P. Reeves, 'Lo and Behold, a Bollard', *The Independent on Sunday*, 31/10/93.
2 For an illustration of 'Ceci n'est pas une pipe', see plate 206 in Torczyner (1977).
3 See King (ed. 1990), Part III, pp. 257–298: 'Pointers to New Directions'.
4 O'Connor (1995, p. 45), citing Daniel Maguire, 1986, *The Moral Revolution*, San Francisco: Harper & Row, p. 122.

Bibliography

Ahmed, Akbar S. 1992. *Postmodernism and Islam: Predicament and Promise*, London: Routledge.
Babb, Lawrence A. 1995. 'Introduction', in Lawrence A. Babb and Susan S. Wadley (eds), *Media and the Transformation of Religion in South Asia*, Philadelphia: University of Pennsylvania Press.
Babin, Pierre 1991. *The New Era in Religious Communication* (tr. by David Smith), Minneapolis: Fortress Press.
Boomershine, Thomas 1987. 'Religious Education and Media Change', *Religious Education* **82** (2).
Eliade, Mircea 1958. *Patterns in Comparative Religion*, London: Sheed and Ward.
Erens, Patricia 1984. *The Jew in American Cinema*, Bloomington: Indiana University Press.
Fore, William 1987. *Television and Religion: The Shaping of Faith, Values and Culture*, Minneapolis: Augsburg.
Goethals, Gregor 1990. *The Electronic Golden Calf: Images, Religion and the Making of Meaning*, Cambridge: Cowley.
Goody, Jack 1986. *The Logic of Writing and the Organization of Society*, Cambridge: Cambridge University Press.
Goody, Jack and Watt, Ian 1968. 'The Consequences of Literacy', in Jack Goody (ed.), *Literacy in Traditional Societies*, Cambridge: Cambridge University Press.
Graham, William 1987. *Beyond the Written Word: Oral aspects of Scripture in the History of Religion*, Cambridge: Cambridge University Press.
Hinnells, John R. 1990. 'Religion and the Arts', in Ursula King (ed.), *Turning Points in Religious Studies*, Edinburgh: T. & T. Clark.
Hurley, Neil P. 1970. *Theology Through Film*, New York: Harper & Row.
Keyser, Les and Keyser, Barbara 1984. *Hollywood and the Catholic Church: The Image of Roman Catholicism in American Movies*, Chicago: Loyola University Press.
King, Ursula (ed.) 1990. *Turning Points in Religious Studies*, Edinburgh: T. & T. Clark.
Kippenberg, Hans G. 1992. 'The Problem of Literacy in the History of Religions', *Numen* **39** (1).
Kristensen, W. Brede 1960. *The Meaning of Religion: Lectures in the Phenomenology of Religion* (tr. John B. Carman), The Hague: Nijhof.
Luckmann, Thomas 1967. *The Invisible Religion: the Problem of Religion in Modern Society*, New York: Macmillan.
Martin, Joel W. and Ostwalt, Conrad E. (eds) 1995. *Screening the Sacred: Religion, Myth, and Ideology in Popular American Film*, Boulder and Oxford: Westview Press.
Martin, Thomas 1981. *Images and the Imageless: A Study in Religious Consciousness and Film*, Lewisburg: Bucknell University Press.
Masterman, Len 1985. *Teaching the Media*, London: Comedia.

May, John R. 1992. 'The Godfather Films: Birth of a Don, Death of a Family', in John R. May (ed.), *Image and Likeness: Religious Visions in American Film Classics*, New York: Paulist Press.

McLuhan, Marshall 1987[1964]. *Understanding Media*, London: Ark.

Michaels, Leonard 1990. 'Prefatory Note', in L. Michaels and C. Ricks (eds), *The State of the Language*, London: Faber.

Miles, Margaret 1985. *Image as Insight: Visual understanding in western Christianity and secular culture*, Boston: Beacon Press.

Niebuhr, H. Richard 1959. *The Kingdom of God in America*, New York: Harper.

Ong, Walter J. 1969. 'Communications Media and the State of Theology', *Cross Currents* **19**.

———— 1982. *Orality and Literacy: The Technologising of the Word*, London: Methuen.

O'Connor, June 1995. 'The Epistemological Significance of Feminist Research in Religion', in Ursula King (ed.), *Religion and Gender*, Oxford: Blackwell.

Otto, Rudolf 1923. *The Idea of the Holy: An Inquiry into the non-rational Factor in the idea of the Divine and its Relation to the Rational* (tr. John W. Harvey), Oxford: Oxford University Press.

Postman, Neil 1987. *Amusing Ourselves to Death: Public Discourse in the Age of Show Business*, London: Methuen.

Said, Edward 1981. *Covering Islam: How the Media and the Experts determine how we see the Rest of the World*, London: Routledge & Kegan Paul.

Schement, Jorge and Stephenson, Hester 1996. 'Religion and the Information Society', in D.A. Stout and J. Buddenbaum (eds), *Religion and Mass Media: Audiences and Adaptations*, Thousand Oaks, CA: Sage.

Schleifer, S.A. 1993. 'An Islamic Perspective on the News', in C. Arthur, (ed.), *Religion and the Media, an Introductory Reader*, Cardiff: University of Wales Press, pp. 163–175.

Schopen, Gregory 1991. 'Archaeology and Protestant Presuppositions in the Study of Indian Buddhism', *History of Religions*, **31** (1).

Schultze, Quentin J. 1990. 'Secular Television as Popular Religion', in R. Abelman and S. Hoover (eds), *Religious Television: Controversies and Conclusions*, Norwood: Ablex, pp. 135–146.

Shrader, Paul 1972. *Transcendental Style in Film*, Berkeley: University of California Press.

Smart, Ninian 1988. 'Religion', in E. Barnouw (ed.), *International Encyclopedia of Communication*, New York: Oxford University Press.

Smith, Wilfred Cantwell 1978. *The Meaning and End of Religion*, London: SPCK.

Staudenmaier, John 1993. 'The Media: Technique and Culture', in J. Coleman and M. Tomka (eds), *Concilium* **6**/'Mass Media', London/New York: SCM/Orbis.

Torczyner, Harry 1977. *Magritte: Ideas and Images*, New York: Abrams.

Turnbull, Colin 1961. *The Forest People*, London: Jonathan Cape.

Warren, Michael 1992. *Communications and Cultural Analysis: A Religious View*, London: Bergin and Garvey.

CHAPTER 3

How to Study Religious Experience in the Traditions

Peter Antes

Introduction

Many historical traditions of humankind report that individuals as well as groups have seen their god(s) or goddess(es), that divine guidance was felt as the most important motivation for undertaking actions and that a dialogue was taking place between the divine and the human worlds. Human life, thus, was performed in continuous contact with the other world and all interpretations were given with reference to transcendent realities.

This, however, seems to be unknown to many Europeans and Americans at present. They say that they have never 'made' any religious experience of this kind and do not even understand how others can claim that they have 'made' religious experience.[1] The question thus arises whether this dichotomy is due to a total break between traditional forms of life and modern types of thinking, or whether it is produced by different patterns of interpretation concerning one and the same reality of life. If the first case proved to be true, it would lead to the conclusion that there are two different anthropologies: one relevant to the past and the other valid for some parts of the contemporary world. This seems to be a rather unlikely conclusion. The second hypothesis, that is that of different patterns of interpretation, seems much more convincing because it does not imply a total break in the anthropological conditions of humankind but refers only to the explanatory frame concerning the understanding of experience as such.

The purpose of this chapter is to follow the second hypothesis by setting out such a frame and discussing its theoretical implications. In a concluding remark two examples will be given in order to show how such an explanation can be useful for the study of religious experience in the traditions, so that further investigations can be carried out using this framework as a guide.

What is Religious Experience?

Unlike the first position referred to above, which says that the modern agnostic or atheist type of thinking represents a total break in the anthropological conditions of mankind with regard to former claims of religious experience, the hypothesis defended here is intended to make clear that religious experience is a specific category of human experience and should, consequently, be seen in the general explanatory frame of experience.

The study of religion has little to offer in this field. The reason for this is that the so-called classical phenomenology of religion was much more concerned with the contents of religious experience, that is 'the Holy' (cf. Rudolf Otto's famous book), than with the true nature of religious experience as it concerns the human being who 'makes' this experience. The only helpful explanation I have come across in this respect is Sundén's attempt to interpret religious experience in terms of role offers made by religions (Sundén 1975; 1982, pp. 33ff). Sundén's idea is to distinguish three different steps in the process of making experience. The first step, according to Sundén, is an initial situation. A good example of such an initial situation might be that an individual or group has to move from one place to another. Such a move in itself is not religious at all but may be interpreted in this way when the person starts (and this is the second step) to see the move – to take an example from the Judaeo-Christian tradition – as something which can be paralleled with Abraham's departure from Mesopotamia. The same applies to groups if they see their own move from one area to another as somehow being comparable to a significant event, for example the comparison with Muhammad's Hijra made by the Muslims who moved from India to Pakistan in order to live in an independent state of their own, following the end of British rule over the Indian sub-continent. The third and last step is the application of the prototype to the present situation (with its psychological implications) by assuming that the respective roles of Abraham and Muhammad will be imitated and repeated now, under the conditions of the present. The psychological consequences of such an identification process are obvious if one takes into consideration that the move could be either positive, as through identification with Abraham or Muhammad, or negative if identified with Jonah's unsuccessful attempt to flee from what God wanted him to do.

The great advantage of Sundén's concept is the clear distinction between the three different steps. The first step – that is, the concrete situation – is not religious at all. The second is religious in so far as it refers to religious behaviour in the traditions. But only if the first step is identified with the second step can we speak of religious experience in the third step, so that the 'making' of religious experience is finally due to the combination of the two preceding stages. I totally agree with Sundén in clearly distinguishing these three steps, but I disagree with him in the attempt to reduce religious experience to identification with role patterns alone. Unlike Sundén I propose here a much broader field of possible initial situations, including sensations of all kinds (auditory, visual, etc.) as well as moves and gestures (that is, roles in Sundén's understanding). Such a widening of the array of situations will, consequently, lead to a larger perception of identifiable patterns of interpretation so that the frame of experience in general and of religious experience in particular is open to all possible kinds of experience referred to both in religious texts of the traditions, and in 'profane' documents of the 'modern' world.

The theoretical framework proposed here for the study of religious experience now requires some clarifying remarks for each of the three steps to be taken into proper consideration.

Step 1: The Initial Situation

In the initial situation the emphasis is upon a starting event not yet interpreted. Not all the texts provide material for such a clear distinction of the three steps. Many texts just state that a religious experience was made, and describe in detail, for example, that ecstasy happened and what its manifestations were. They do not provide any item of information about the starting event. If so, these texts cannot be used for the type of study suggested here and have to be left aside. Only texts where such a beginning can clearly be depicted are relevant for attentive study in this context.

Yet from a theoretical point of view, our study is still not without problems, because the texts are written retrospectively, at a certain time and as a result of personal developments which lead to religious experience. This means that all texts are written retrospectively. Usually we do not have access to descriptions which were written during the ongoing process itself. The very first beginnings of the event are, therefore, in most of the cases, reported after further steps have taken place. Consequently, the argument is valid that later reports are neither purely descriptive nor truly objective but are shaped retrospectively according to the interpretation given to the event by the author. Though this cannot be denied, it seems, however, that many texts still preserve a reminiscence of the initial event and help to retrace some of the main constituents which appear before any interpretive or explanatory pattern of interpretation. Two examples of this will be given in my concluding remarks to prove that such an analysis can be successfully undertaken.

This also means that all texts are embedded in a historical setting. Concerning the historical argument, it is true that all texts which have been written down or embedded in their own time thus bear the traces of thinking which are typical of their time. This, however, holds true of every document of the past. With reference to some studies concerning Native Americans, Peter Burke (1988, pp. 26ff) reports that even dreams are marked by the historical conditions of the dreamers and, consequently, vary from generation to generation. The so-called classical phenomenology of religion, represented by scholars such as van der Leeuw, Otto, Heiler and Goldammer, paid no attention to the historical dimension of religious experience because the search for the true essence of religion hindered these scholars from taking historical changes sufficiently into account. The standard of present day research work in other disciplines does not allow the scholar of the study of religions to neglect the historical conditions of the text and thus requires of him or her a more attentive reading of the texts as concerns the specific, historical *Sitz im Leben*.

To clarify this point, dreams are indeed excellent examples. Pilgrims in ancient Greece, for example, went to Epidauros in order to find healing from their suffering. Many of them spent a certain time in the holy surroundings and slept in special rooms which were dedicated to dream revelations. It was thus expected that the suffering person would dream of how to get rid of his or her particular pains, and religious servants were trained to interpret the dreams which were rich in symbols or in vague indications, so that they were not immediately understandable to the dreamer. The expectations of both the dreamers and the religious servants in Epidauros, consequently, were that dreams were valid indicators for future acts to be taken. Dreams at that time were seen as looking towards the future and therefore as giving indications for the things to do. They were not understood as clarifications of the past.

In modern psychoanalysis, to the contrary, dreams are taken as unconscious stories which report events of the dreamer's past, and if such an analysis is undertaken in the Freudian way, the dream becomes, moreover, a hidden psychosexual story of the early childhood of the dreamer. It seems to me that these contradictory expectations will have an influence on the dreamer so that the progress of the dreams, and how they are expressed in words afterwards, is not independent of the presumptions of the dreamer. In both cases the dream loses its character as a series of rather incidental mental pictures and is taken instead as a consistent and intelligible message of either the past or of the future. The second instance – Freudian psychoanalysis – is not meant to be understood as being religious, whereas the first – within the frame of the religious organization of Epidauros – is interpreted as a healing revelation, that is, as a religious message. Here one might finally think of dreams as vocation visions by which the dreamer understands that he or she is sent to bring a special religious message to certain individuals or groups.

The example of dreams is only one of a whole range of expectations. Both religious and non-religious expectations obviously have a great influence on people's thinking and behaviour and this influence is even stronger if the expected interrelationship concerns not only a specific idea of the individual but also of the community as a whole. Here again, Freudian psychoanalysis is a striking example. Since German intellectuals started to analyse themselves, and in particular their dreams, by means of Freudian psychoanalysis, its interpretative vocabulary has become part of the normal reference system in everyday conversations to such an extent that even those who were in the beginning very hesitant in this respect have increasingly got used to the application of Freundian categories to their own life experience. And this has even become true for minor phenomena such as *lapsus linguae* or 'slips of the tongue' which nowadays is in most cases immediately interpreted in a Freudian way, thus suggesting that the word which was unintentionally said – that is the *lapsus linguae* – was intentionally present in the speaker's subconscious. Consequently, the reaction often is that the speaker or the listener – if not both – try to reveal the assumed subconscious thoughts of the speaker. A similar interpretation would not have happened in the past and is today only understandable on the basis of Freudian expectation which is due to a specific type of contemporary thinking. Generally speaking, the example makes clear the extent to which we are all children of our times, and therefore the historical dimension is of great importance for all studies of the traditions.

Finally, all texts bear traces of the author's own psychological development. In addition to the historical *Sitz im Leben* there is a very personal one, too. This has been clearly shown in the case of Martin Luther, for example. His search for a merciful God was not independent of great fears which were, first of all, a consequence of the very strict education to which he was submitted.[2] Theological speculation came second but played a role as a systematic expression of personal fears and hopes viewed through theological terms which were also accessible to many of Luther's contemporaries because they, too, shared with him much of this educational experience. The religious use of emotionally loaded words such as 'Father' in Christianity or 'Mother' in Hinduism is full of connotations taken from everyday life experience.

Tilman Moser, a contemporary German psychoanalyst, is a negative example of this close relationship between daily life and religious interpretation. In his confessions (Moser 1976)[3] he tries to show that from the very beginning he was told that God would observe him wherever he was and whatever he might do, so that he felt observed by his father and then even more so (when his father was absent, and he was alone) by God, who became for him a 'super-father' functioning as a policemen in heaven, a kind of Orwellian Big Brother watching him. Religious initiation and socialization in the religious community consequently pushed Moser increasingly in this suffocating direction so that he looks back to his own psychological development as if to a slowly increasing process of being poisoned with God. For years, he says, he was unable to experience intimacy with a woman because he constantly had in mind that they were never only two, but that God as a third party was permanently present to watch them and to judge their forbidden actions. If so, the presumption of God being present from the very first beginning in all situations is an obstacle to a neutral description of an initial situation such as is needed for the study of religious experience proposed here. A text such as

Moser's is too much loaded with the chosen pattern of interpretation so that the underlying initial event cannot be detected and studied separately.

Initial situations, consequently, can only be studied if they are clearly distinguishable as such. If so, we have to check whether the description is shaped with regard to a pattern of interpretation referred to retrospectively, and we must moreover pay attention to specific historical dimensions of expectations as well as to psychological factors due to the upbringing of the person whose experience is reported. My hypothesis is that, taking all these checks into account, there will still be many interesting descriptions which can be used for both case studies and comparative research work. The former would include, for instance, initial situations of Christian or Muslim mystics, while the latter would look at the broader field of religious mysticism (for example Buddhist, Muslim and Christian) or, even more widely, of experience in general. In this way we might compare initial situations of both religious and non-religious experience in order to see whether or not in both cases they are similar to each other, so that it may clearly be proved that the experience is *made* religious or non-religious with regard to the patterns of interpretation involved, and not through completely different initial situations.

Step 2: Patterns of Interpretation

The importance of patterns of interpretation has been underlined above so frequently that a close look at what they actually are is now imperative.

Tilman Moser's confessions are enlightening in this respect. He refers to his training sessions in group therapy and tells us that the trainer used to ask which types of impediment were felt by the trainees. In his case, Moser says, only one stereotyped but extremely binding sentence came to his mind: 'What would God [in German: *der liebe Gott*] say?' (Moser 1976, p. 17). In all his actions, this was the only question he had in mind and according to which, if the answer was positive, he felt free to do things, but if the answer happened to be negative, he felt embarrassed to even want these things. His thoughts and feelings were thus unilaterally concentrated on his religious world view and in total contrast to and in conflict with what he instinctively desired and wanted to do. God, thus, became the cruel superior to whom he was totally submitted, feeling himself weak and defenceless in front of this celestial superpower. Moser adds that his students today are unable to imagine the suffering and pain this idea of God had produced in him as well as in so many others. They, he says, do not even recognize Biblical stories if quoted in lectures without an explicit mention of the Biblical reference, and do not, consequently, suffer from their implication as Moser himself had done for such a long period of his life. Moser argues that to these young people, Biblical paradigms are even unknown as a matter of general knowledge (Moser 1976, pp. 21ff).

No wonder, I would add, that these young people do not 'make' any Christian experience; but they do 'make' experience, and this is interesting here. Their experience is often closely related to what, in Moser's therapy groups, the trainer expected when he asked the trainee about her or his subconscious impediments, except that a Freudian or Jungian pattern of interpretation was in use instead of a religious one. Hence Moser felt himself to be so strange and untypical of his therapy group, because neither of the expected types of problem was his real problem. What he was in fact suffering from was not accepted within the rules commonly admitted in those groups.

First, the Freudian pattern of interpretation. Freud never wrote a systematic book where all the elements of his theory were put together into a consistent and coherent corpus of theorization. Nevertheless it is possible to bring the puzzle pieces of his theory, scattered as they are all over his writings, into a mosaic. If we do this, it becomes obvious that his theory is mainly based on psychosexual development with regard to the Oedipus drama, on a specific theory concerning neurosis, on a particular trauma theory, on a dream theory, and on a *lapsus* theory. To this, finally, could also be added elements of his theory of the death instinct as well as of his theory concerning the origin of civilization as being related to the murder of the father in the primitive horde. Each of these elements is under discussion and, at least according to Zimmer (1990, pp. 408ff), should even be given up because of obvious error. My intention here is not to go along with all these arguments and to show how relevant they are to modern interdisciplinary work. I take instead the Oedipus complex as an example of theorizing in order to indicate that such an approach is purely theoretical and not descriptive at all.

If a boy at the age of three is fighting against his father and seeking to be near his mother, we used to speak of a manifestation of the Oedipus complex. In doing so, the interpreters have already reached the third step of the distinction suggested here. They see the boy's attitude, which is empirically nothing else but the fact of fighting against the father and seeking to be near to the mother, and have in mind a theoretical concept of Freud's reading of the Greek myth of Oedipus. They put the two together by identifying the former with the latter, saying that what happens in this particular historical case is the repetition of a basic human pattern in the psychosexual development of the boy. Through this pattern of interpretation the boy's behaviour becomes both meaningful to the surrounding persons and a matter of diagnosis for a psychoanalyst. There is no doubt that in former times the surrounding persons would have used other patterns of interpretation by saying, for instance, that an evil spirit is possessing the boy. In order to make this evil spirit flee from the boy's body, they would have beaten the boy or they would have practised exorcist rituals. Neither the evil spirit nor the Oedipus complex can empirically be proved to be true, but without any theoretical reference system of this kind it is impossible to give a meaningful interpretation of the boy's attitude.

On the basis of this example we therefore come to the conclusion that patterns of interpretation – be they religious or not – are needed in order to render concrete situations meaningful, and that these patterns are usually not produced by the person who makes the experience, but that they pre-exist and pre-figure the event and are part of this person's general knowledge or conviction. That is, only after we have been told that such a thing as the Oedipus complex exists are we able to identify situations with it so that we notice its manifestation in reality.

Second, consider the Jungian pattern of interpretation. C.G. Jung was among the first followers of Freud to contradict him theoretically because Jung – as is well known – was not willing to accept that all psychological conflicts are due only to sexual problems. He suggested instead a variety of possible features where sexual themes are not excluded but are only one possible line of thinking along with many others. The wider range of eventual interpretations Jung suggested was reached by making reference to archetypes which – here again – are remembered in dreams and pictures but can hardly be fully expressed in words. Jung is convinced that these archetypes form a common stratum of all humankind, preserved in all civilizations but only unconsciously handed down from generation to generation. It is done unconsciously because later, more obvious distinctions – mainly due to the differentiation of humankind into races – have wiped out the memory of this common ground of humankind. It would, therefore, be helpful to have a detailed study of Jung's concept of the 'race' as the dividing factor in humankind, but this study has still to be written.

What appears to be so attractive in Jung's theory is on the one hand that its interpretative range is not bound to sexuality only, and that on the other, his reference to archetypes opens new horizons for interpretation with regard to all civilizations of humankind. For example, in his introduction to the *Bardo Thodöl*, 'The Tibetan Book of the Dead', Jung interpreted the numerous colours and beings seen in the hereafter as manifestations of the archetypes, which thus are immediately accessible to him without any previous study of Tibetan thought or language. Hence neither distance in time (that is the historical dimension, referred to above) nor cultural differences are obstacles to the correct understanding and interpretation of what is going on. Religious experience is understood as based on the manifestation of archetypes which can systematically be learned and used in Jungian analysis and serve the cross-cultural encounter of humankind. Jung's concept of archetypes is as theoretical as Freud's Oedipus complex but unlike the former, the latter is not noticed as such in modern discussions. Hence there is still a need to emphasize that both concepts are not empirical but two myths which by their nature are therefore connected with the realm of religion.

Third, we come to the religious pattern of interpretation. Tilman Moser's question, 'What would God say?', makes clear that within this religious frame the first and decisive problem is to ask what God's vision of things is. The world is thus viewed through God's eyes and human behaviour is in this perspective understood as either good or sinful. Feelings of good conscience and of guilt are related to these interpretations and are very important for human welfare within this type of thinking. Unlike Sundén I do not reduce the religious frame to role patterns alone but take all types of religious thinking into account. God as well as the devil may play an active role in many people's lives whereas in others, fears of sins and guilt can have a likewise decisive influence on the believer. Here again, the psychological implications of the dogmas may vary from one context to the other. Muslims, for instance, do not obviously suffer psychologically when they refer to themselves as 'servants' or 'slaves' of God, their Lord, whereas Christians like Moser may feel completely weak and defenceless with regard to a similar statement. Consequently, religious as well as non-religious world views imply for some people positive chances of psychological development while for others they are the real reason for being ill.[4] One and the same Biblical reference to God's omnipresence may be a great help of divine assistance for one person or may lead, in Moser's case, to a total lack of privacy and intimacy for the other. The psychological consequences of certain dogmas are already part of the third step, which we now consider, where the identification of concrete life situations with the chosen pattern of interpretation takes place.

Step 3: The Identification of Life Situations with Patterns of Interpretation

The *making* of experience takes place when the chosen patterns of interpretation are identified with the initial event so that what happened becomes meaningful thanks to a broader reference system. It is this very moment that enables the person to say that he or she has 'made' a religious or a non-religious experience. If no identification process takes place, the event remains uninterpreted and therefore meaningless. The reference to a chosen pattern of interpretation, however, may suggest that the choice is arbitrary and consequently the experience is neither authentic nor open to new kinds of experience, so that finally the psychological implications are wrong and offer no real chances or obstacles for the person. All these arguments are serious and must be looked at closely.

First, is the choice of the pattern of interpretation arbitrary? From this theoretical point of view one may draw the conclusion that the array of possible choices is indefinite and the choice of one of these instead of others is purely arbitrary. One may even think that the person goes around with the initial event and tries to find an appropriate 'tool' for its interpretation by testing several offers on the free market of ideas. In reality things do not happen like this. Where religious experience is reported in the traditions, people are already well embedded in their religious system of interpretations so that this type of thinking comes automatically to their minds as evidence, as was the case with Moser's question, 'What would God say?'. And if we study mystical texts, the event is itself, in most cases, the result of long training in and initiation into this type of thinking, so that the event itself is not completely independent from the expectations of the religious world these people lived in. Hence interpretation is often made both preceding and following the event and so is not an arbitrary act without any previous instruction or training. But if this is so, then we must ask how authentic such an experience really is, and to what extent it is open to new kinds of experience.

We can initially approach the question of authenticity of religious experience by remarking that, wherever we read texts which speak of religious experience, one phenomenon is striking though rarely noticed. The deities who are seen, the voices which are heard and the worlds which are witnessed are other than everyday realities, but nevertheless recognizable on the basis of the traditional religious vocabulary the person had known before. Never has a Christian mystic said that the God who appeared to him or her was Krishna if he or she had never heard of Krishna before. And likewise we do not find in the Veda, the Upanishads or the Bhagavad Gita that Yahweh was seen and worshipped. If in Italy a glorious lady is seen, she is always Mary or another well known female saint, but in no case is she Kali or Durga while, on the contrary, among Hindus manifestations of Durga or Kali are common but those of Mary are unknown.

It is therefore not unreasonable to think that during the identification process itself, expectation plays a clarifying role. As soon as the idea is born that the light which is seen might be Mary, the seer usually looks at the manifestation more precisely in order to clearly distinguish her typical characteristics. Muslim handbooks of mysticism, for instance, are full of instructions for scrutiny to make sure that the manifestation is really that of a celestial person and not a misleading apparition of the devil's world or the domain of souls of baser instincts.

All this seems to suggest that a religious as well as a non-religious experience is always made within the frame which is already set by the type of thinking that the people in question are used to. But what about conversions? Do they not contradict what has been said? It does not seem so. When Saul on the road to Damascus was hit by a stroke of light and recognized in it Christ, whose followers he was going to persecute, this initial event was indeed interpreted by him as the appearance of one whom he already knew of before. His conversion was the turning point in the evidence which made him choose between Jesus Christ and his traditional Jewish religion. The conversion would only contradict what has been said if Saul had adopted Krishna, for instance, whom he had never heard of before.

Both conversion and continuation in one's traditional practice show that the experience a person *makes* is closely related to the pattern of interpretation which the person has learned or struggled with, so that the *made* experience is both authentic and related to a learnt reference system. The example of conversion shows, moreover, that this learnt reference system is not closed but open for changes within the range of already known possibilities of decision, although it seems not to be open to totally different types of interpretation patterns.

Finally, the chosen pattern of interpretation determines the boundaries of the eventual psychological consequences of the choice made. The choice of Abraham or Muhammad by migrating Jews and Muslims, as we said in the beginning of this paper, implies a positive connotation with regard to their geographical move, while an identification with Jonah would have produced negative expectations of success. Consequently, it seems normal that positive and negative psychological developments take place within each of the choices made, but do not go beyond these boundaries. Whether a person feels happy because of God's omnipresence, which is then seen as a guarantee of being well-looked-after and never being left alone, or whether he or she like Moser feels hopelessly exposed to the eyes of a severe Lord watching everything, depends on the person's internal psychological development. In both cases personal development is closely related to God's omnipresence as the cause for either happiness or depression.[5] The same is true, by the way, for those who do not believe in God. Here too, some may suffer terribly from being thrown into the world as mere products of a cosmic accident, while others feel free because they are not submitted to an almighty Lord.

This does not mean that the problems expressed are not real for the person, but it does show the extent to which the choice made is decisive for that person. Whoever finds life situations meaningful does so because of patterns of interpretation, be they religious or non-religious. It is, therefore, not a question of blaming the religious choice and praising the non-religious patterns instead, or vice versa, but the study of religious traditions has to demonstrate how these patterns are positively as well as negatively used, and to compare the religious use with the non-religious one. That is what my contribution in this chapter is intended to address.

I have tried to make clear that religious experience is in its very nature not different from non-religious experience. Both are *made* by each identifying a neutral initial event on the one side and an already known pattern of interpretation on the other. And it is this identification process which *makes* the experience. If the pattern is religious, it *makes* the experience religious and if not, it *makes* it non-religious. While the initial event is neutral, the choice of the pattern is not and will automatically lead to psychological consequences for the choosing person.

Just two examples may, as a concluding remark, illustrate the process in action. In Augustine's *Confessions* (VII, 10) the initial event is clearly stated: 'I saw ... light.' But this light was not comparable with ordinary light. It was much 'clearer' and 'embraced everything'. Augustine immediately characterized it as 'immutable light', adding, some lines later, that 'who knows the truth, knows it [that is, the light], and who knows it, knows eternity'. Here the interpretation pattern enters in and will finally lead to the declaration that it was God who was experienced by Augustine.

A similar description can be found in Ramakrishna's vision. Here again the initial event was a vision of light:

> In whatever direction I turned great luminous waves were rising. They bore down upon me with a loud roar, as if to swallow me up. In an instant they were upon me. They broke over me, they engulfed me. I was suffocated. I lost all *natural* consciousness. (Rolland 1960, p. 33)

Ramakrishna's interpretation of this reads: 'Round me rolled an ocean of ineffable joy. And in the depths of my being I was conscious of the presence of the divine mother' (*ibid*). Augustine recognized a male God in the light, while Ramakrishna saw his divine mother, Kali. Both, consequently, were loyal to their respective religious traditions. It would be interesting to compare this appearance of 'light' with Muslim texts, Buddhist sources and non-religious documents where similar initial events are reported. All this and much more has to be done. For reasons of space it could not be accomplished here, but it will be possible for it to be studied in the future if the frame proposed here is taken seriously and serves as a guideline for future investigations. And if so, there is no need any more to claim a break in anthropology with regard to religious experience and modern non-religious types of experience.

(First published as Occasional Paper No. 5, 1992)

Notes

1   The form 'to make (religious) experience' is deliberately used for reasons which, it is hoped, will become clear in the remainder of the chapter.

2   Cf. the comparative study of the upbringing of Luther, Calvin and Zwingli by Oskar Pfister (1944).

3   This is a booklet written in the form of a prayer addressed to God and thus intended to be both an imitation of and an opposition to Augustine's *Confessions*.

4   Cf. with regard to the latter, Kolbe (1990, pp. 62–74).

5   In the case of depression we used to speak of neurosis due to religion or to religious socialization. Cf. Siebenthal (1950), Solignac (1976) and Thomas (1986[1971]).

Bibliography

Burke, Peter 1988. *Städtische Kultur in Italien zwischen Hochrenaissance un Barock. Eine historische Anthropologie*, Berlin (German tranlsation of *The Historical Anthropology of Early Modern Italy*, Cambridge, 1987).

Kolbe, Christoph 1990. *Wenn Glaube krankt macht – Über den Zusammenhang von Glaubensvor-stellungen und psychischen Strukturen, in Krankheit und Heilung in den Religionen – Islam – Hinduismus – Christentum*, Herrenalber Protokolle. Schriftenreihe der Evangelischen Akademie, Baden, Nr.67.

Moser, Tilman 1976. *Gottesvergiftung*, Frankfurt.

Pfister, Oskar 1944. *Das Christentum und die Angst. Eine religionspsychologische, historische und religionshygienische Untersuchung*, Zürich.

Rolland, Romain 1960. *The Life of Ramakrishna* (6th edn), Calcutta.

Siebenthal, Wolf 1950. *Krankheit als Folge der Sünde. Eine medizinhistorische Untersuchung*, (*Heilkunde und Geisteliwelt*, 2), Hannover.

Solignac, Pierre 1976. *La Névrose Chrétienne*, Paris.

Sundén, Hjalmar 1975. *Gott erfahren. Das Rollenangebot der Religionen*, Gütersloh.

——1982, *Religionspsychologie* (German trans.), Stuttgart.

Thomas, K. 1986[1971]. 'Ekklesiogene Neurosen', in *Lexikon der Psychologie*, ed. W. Arnold et al., Vol. 1, 1971, p. 457 (6th new edn), Freiburg-Basel-Wein.

Zimmer, Dieter E. 1990. *Tiefenschwindel. Die endlose und die beendbare Psychoandlyse*, Reinbek bei Hamburg (new and enlarged pbk. edn).

CHAPTER 4

'The Sacred' as a Viable Concept in the Contemporary Study of Religions

Terence Thomas

Introduction: 'Sacred' Power in the Hebrew Bible

If I were a cynic, which I am not, I would say that the body of the contemporary study of religions is suffering from a rash called 'the sacred', a rash that gives me a sort of itch and it is an itch that I cannot refrain from scratching. In a time when many people are wont to lament the state of the world they inhabit, especially their little part of it, and the cry frequently goes up, 'Nothing is sacred any more', I wish to say 'Wrong, everything is "sacred" these days'.

There is nothing that gives me greater pleasure than to read works in the study of religions of the nineteenth century. I am constantly amazed at the knowledge that was available to our predecessors and freely published in such works as *The Penny Cyclopaedia* (1833 onwards) under the auspices of the Society for the Diffusion of Useful Knowledge. While preparing this paper I wondered at my delight in the nineteenth century, compared with much that I read of contemporary studies, and came to the conclusion that one of the things that contributes to that delight is the virtual total absence of the term 'sacred' let alone the neologism 'the sacred'. I have to wonder if the term 'sacred' and especially the term 'the sacred' can be applied to the wide range of phenomena that are addressed in the contemporary study of religions.

We have been made aware of the definition of religion given by Emile Durkheim, which involves the distinction between the sacred and the profane in defining what religion is. However, there are strong arguments against such a simplified definition irrespective of whether the term 'sacred' can be applied universally in the way suggested by Durkheim. Some sociologists have veered in the direction of ascribing the description 'religion' to virtually every aspect of human behaviour, so much so that Peter Berger, in criticising Thomas Luckmann for this approach, asks what does it gain the human to describe everything as religious, if the human then has to demonstrate what the difference is between, shall we say, celebrating the Christian Eucharist and conducting a scientific experiment. The same strictures can be advanced against the prodigal use of the term 'sacred' when it is applied to everything from what went on in the Holy of Holies in the Temple in Jerusalem to the daily rituals of the London Stock Exchange. In saying that, we should remind ourselves that what went on in the Holy of Holies was not in itself sacred, only that the actions were directed to the Almighty God who alone was (and in this context still is) sacred, or to use the more usual English term 'holy', a term which effectively acts as a synonym for sacred.

It is necessary to remind ourselves that the term 'sacred' for most of its history, by which I mean before Rudolf Otto got to work on it, has stood for that which the Hebrew considered to belong to God alone and by extension to things that belonged to God or were imbued with sacred power because of their direct association with God. Whenever I teach students about the notion of what is sacred, I have used the example of the fate that befell Abinadab's son Uzzah. The story goes like this:

> David ... went with the whole army to Balath-judah to fetch the Ark of God which bears the name of the Lord of Hosts, who is enthroned upon the cherubim. They mounted the Ark of God on a new cart and conveyed it from the house of Abinadab on the hill, with Uzzah and Ahio, sons of Abinadab, guiding the cart. They took it with the Ark of God upon it from Abinadab's house on the hill, with Ahio walking in front. David and all Israel danced for joy before the Lord without restraint to the sound of singing, of harps and lutes, of tambourines and castanets and cymbals. But when they came to a certain threshing-floor, the oxen stumbled, and Uzzah reached out to the Ark of God and took hold of it. The Lord was angry with Uzzah and struck him down there for his rash act. So he died there beside the Ark of God. David was vexed because the Lord's anger had broken out upon Uzzah, and he called the place Perez-uzzah, the name it still bears. David was afraid of the Lord that day and said, 'How can I harbour the Ark of the Lord after this?' He felt he could not take the Ark of the Lord with him to the City of David, but turned aside and carried it to the house of Obededom the Gittite. (2 Samuel 6:1–10)

It hardly needs anyone to interpret this story. One commentator says: 'In the popular mind [Uzzah's] death was attributed to his violation of the sacrosanct character of the ark.' (*Interpreter's Dictionary of the Bible*, Vol. 4, p. 741.) The Westminster Study Bible rather surprisingly to my mind says: 'How Uzzah died is not said, but his death is attributed to the almost magical powers of the Ark.' Whatever be the cause of death the occasion is clear: Uzzah touched something imbued with sacred power, that is the power of God, and it proved fatal. We do not have to believe that the Ark actually had power to kill. All we have to realise is the power the Ark had in the minds and imagination of those who were close to it.

Scholars have claimed to identify a number of interpretations of the Ark in the scriptural documents. They include: '(a) as the extension or embodiment of the presence of Yahweh, a counterpart of the divine soul; (b) as a war palladium of Israel's amphictyony in the days before the monarchy; (c) as a container, whether of a fetish stone from a sacred place like Sinai,... or of the two tables of the Decalogue; (d) as a portable throne for the invisible presence of Yahweh.' (*Interpreter's Dictionary of the Bible*, Vol. 1, p. 223.) In at least two of these contexts the Ark derives its terrifying power from its close association with Yahweh. Indeed close association is a rather weak description: we need to see it as the physical embodiment, an icon, of Yahweh.

The terrifying picture presented by Uzzah's death has always appeared to me as paradigmatic of the notions of power, terror, awe and mystery which are employed by Rudolf Otto in his attempt to illustrate his re-discovery of what is sacred. It is surprising at first that Otto does not make use of such a narrative. Then we discover that, for Otto, it is far too 'primitive', too bound up with a crude notion of God. He illustrates this by comparing someone who listens to hurdy-gurdies and bagpipes in their young days and then graduates or matures, as he says, to finer music. It is the finer music that Otto wants to talk about. That is why his illustrations are taken from Bach and Mendelssohn and such aesthetic/emotional roots (Otto 1936, pp. 72, 73, 75). *Mysterium tremendum atque fascinans* is interpreted as awe, terror and creature feeling – but not too awe-ful, not too terrifying, not too creature-feelingly. However, I would argue that when we wish to talk about 'the sacred' we should remember Uzzah. It is not a pretty sight, not refined, not aesthetic, not emotionally fulfilling, not expressed by feeling, whether a 'feel-good' feeling or not, just raw, sacred energy hurled forth by a wrathful (ideogrammatically speaking, of course, out of respect for Otto) God and it is what gives meaning to the term 'sacred'. We use the term in derived or adjunct ways at our semantic and cultural peril.

'The Sacred' in Contemporary Approaches to the Study of Religion

Earlier I referred jokingly to the fact that 'the sacred' appears as a rash in the contemporary study of religions. I have already mentioned Otto in the enthroning of 'the sacred' in this way. It must be acknowledged that Otto made an important contribution to an understanding of 'the sacred', particularly within the context of the study, teaching and preaching of the Judaeo-Christian traditions. In a later essay we find that Otto's aim was to clarify the notion of 'the holy' for Christian theological purposes. 'Our line of inquiry in *The Idea of the Holy*,' he writes, 'was directed towards Christian theology and not towards religious history or the psychology of religion. We sought, by means of an investigation of the Holy,... to prepare ourselves for a better and more definite understanding of the experience of God revealed in the Bible and especially in the New Testament.' (Otto 1931, p. 30.) We do not need reminding that many have seriously questioned whether his application of the same concept to traditions other than the Judaeo-Christian was valid or meaningful. And it was Otto himself who suggested a wider constituency for the application of the sacred. But we must ask: Is it allowed to a western Christian theologian – and Otto was, first and last, such a theologian – to say that 'the "void" of the eastern, like the "nothing" of the western, mystic is a numinous [by which he means "holy"] ideogram of the "wholly other" '? (Otto 1923, p. 30.) The answer, from Otto's perspective, was obviously, 'Yes'. And many others have followed him, as we shall see. Otto has had an incredible influence on the study of religions in the west and even finds his way into Radhakrishnan's commentary on the *Bhagavad Gita*.

A considerable number of works offering an introduction to the study of religions in recent years clearly show the influence of Otto. I have chosen three purely at random. They are works that I have come across in book shops or in conferences. There is no particular reason for choosing them other than I have happened upon them. They do not represent a scientifically observed cross-section of books on the study of religions but I suspect that they are, to a considerable extent, typical of a genre much used in the expansion of the study of religions in higher education in the UK and in other English language areas of the world. The works I wish to refer to are James C. Livingston (1989), *Anatomy of the Sacred: An Introduction to Religion*, William E. Paden (1992), *Interpreting the Sacred: Ways of Viewing Religion* and James L. Cox (1992), *Expressing the Sacred: an Introduction to the Phenomenology of Religion*.

We hardly need to look further than the titles of these works to demonstrate that each one defines religion in terms of the sacred. Note that each author refers to religion in the singular, not to religions in the plural: that is, each title explicitly equates 'religion' as such with the sacred. Livingston points to the diversity of ways of understanding religion, but says: 'Despite this problem, [of attempting general definitions of religion] most scholars today agree that religion is a system of activities and beliefs directed toward that which is perceived to be sacred or of ultimate value or power. Such things – be they spiritual beings, cosmic laws, natural places, persons, ideals, or ideologies – are thereby set apart as sacred or of ultimate significance' (Livingston 1989, p. 47.) The reference to 'ultimate significance' brings to mind Paul Tillich's notion of 'ultimate concern' and is a reference to what Livingston describes as 'a more reflective, philosophical stage of religion than those that engage the interest of Durkheim or Eliade'. Nevertheless, Livingston still maintains that in all the instances in which humans have 'sought ultimate security and meaning' – and the instances range from the monkey in north India to divine kings, the Chinese Tao, the Indian Brahman, the Buddhist Nirvana, and the God of Western monotheism – 'what is sacred is ultimate and what is ultimate is sacred' (*ibid*, p. 65). He goes on to ratify his statements about religion and the sacred with a series of studies all exhibiting facets of religions interpreted with reference to the sacred, so-called.

Paden also points to the diversity of ways of understanding what religion is. Much of his basic material on the study of religions is to be found in his earlier work, *Religious Worlds*. There he says that: 'The premise of the study of religion is that its subject matter constitutes a special kind of phenomena, a special kind of experience, a special kind of system positing its own world. In this, religion is like the arts, which also are not reducible to sociology and which also create their own frame of reference.' He then goes on to say that: 'religious behaviour is in any case that which is founded on the distinction of sacred and profane experience. The nonreligious person, conversely, is the one for whom there is nothing sacred or holy.' (Paden 1988, pp. 48–49.) I do not think Paul Tillich would agree with Paden but I happen to think that in this matter Paden adopts the right approach to the religious and non-religious.

Paden elaborates on this earlier work in his later book where he again addresses matters relating to the study of religion (singular). Paden is committed to a comparativist approach to the study of religion, in the tradition, it would seem, of Mircea Eliade, who is also referred to as a comparativist in contrast to Durkheim and Jung. For the comparativist 'religion is about the sacred', for the sociologist 'it is about society', and for the psychologist 'it is about the psyche'. He then writes:

> What does it mean to say that religion is a system of language and practices which organizes the world around what is deemed sacred?
>
> In this context the sacred refers to those focal objects which to the insider seem endowed with superhuman power and authority. Depending on the culture, it could be a scripture, a great person or high religious leader, a god, an ancestor, an institution like the Catholic Church, an aspect of nature such as a mountain or river, a path of discipline taught by a Buddha, or a sacred rite. [Note the tautology here: the sacred refers to a sacred (*sic*) rite.] These objects, words, beings and observances are charged with a power that governs, inspires, and obliges the life of participants. Any object can become a vehicle of sacred power. Any religion is a system of ways of experiencing the sacred, that is, objects which convey superhuman meaning. (Paden 1992, pp. 71–72)

What he writes appears to confirm the impression given by the title of his work: that religion (singular and comprehensive) is to be understood exclusively in terms of the sacred, so-called.

James Cox, in the title of his work, clearly commits himself to a phenomenological approach to the study of religion (again, singular). His work is a commendably careful and detailed exposition such as a phenomenological study entails. Although the title of the work suggests otherwise, Cox does not immediately come down on the side of the definition of religion in terms of the sacred. In a detailed section he examines critically attempts in the past to define religion, admits to the unattainability of a precise definition, but nevertheless offers his own working definition which is: 'Religion is a varied, symbolic expression of that which people (the I-We) appropriately respond to as being of unrestricted value for them.' (Cox 1992, p. 15.) The key term in this definition is 'unrestricted value'. There is no mention here of 'the sacred'. However, when Cox gets down to detailed examination of 'the phenomena' of religion, these are addressed in terms of sacred myth, sacred persons, etc. Furthermore, later in the work, 'the sacred' appears to parallel and even overtake the term 'unrestricted value' as the key term. In one instance we have a diagram which illustrates the 'Paradigmatic Model' for studying religion. The final stage of this model is described thus: 'Defining the unrestricted value/the sacred' (*ibid*, p. 117). This suggests that the terms 'unrestricted value' and 'the sacred' are co-terminous.

There is one more example that shows even more clearly that the defining term is really 'the sacred'. In another diagram Cox offers us an excellent breakdown of the phenomenological method. This model outlines a common pattern of approach to the study of three (or three hundred) hypothetical different religions. The ninth stage in the model, applicable to each religion in turn, is called 'Defining the unrestricted value'. Then we come to a crunch stage, stage ten, whereby for all three religions the observer/phenomenologist is invited to engage in the task of 'affirming the sacred as the structure of religious consciousness' (*ibid*, p. 158). This affirmation of the sacred is explained as follows: 'From a believer's point of view, the observer identifies an indefinable and unnameable mystery standing behind all religious traditions comprising the structure of religious consciousness.' (*ibid*, p. 159.) I emphasise that whereas the stages of analysis based on observation of x number of religions allows for variety in the collection of data up to and including the ninth stage, the next stage, stage ten, is the application of a single criterion to every religion irrespective of the variety of data observed. This sequence is, of course, in tune with the phenomenologist's trade, confirmed by the next stage which is 'achieving the eidetic intuition: the meaning of religion'. Intuition is something I shall return to presently.

It seems fairly clear to me that in that statement Cox justifies the title of his work in a way that his detailed approach to the definition of religion does not. But which is dominant: religion understood in terms of that which is of 'unrestricted value', or understood in terms of 'the sacred', so-called? It does seem to me that the answer is the latter. Once again religion is defined in terms of 'the sacred', so-called.

I have tried in this section of the chapter to exemplify some of the issues regarding the use of the term 'the sacred' in the contemporary study of religions. I believe I have demonstrated that there is a strong tendency to uniform acceptance of 'the sacred' as a term that defines or delineates religion, and by inference religions, and is the accepted way, for many of our colleagues, of studying religions and introducing their students to the study of religions. If I am correct in my conclusions then I think we should look carefully at this tendency and try to understand where the impulse for this approach comes from. To do that I will look at two exponents of different approaches to the study of religions (although on examination we may well find that they are not that different).

Paul Tillich and Mircea Eliade and 'The Sacred'

Paul Tillich and Mircea Eliade were men of roughly the same generation, though Tillich was the older by some twenty years. Both men had to make changes to their lives which were roughly similar. Tillich left Germany in his forties, Eliade had to leave Romania just before he was forty. Tillich arrived in America and proceeded to make a name for himself over a wider area than previously; Eliade did likewise. Both wrote and published important works in languages from which they had to be translated into English in order for them to reach a wider readership and give them wider fame. Both men achieved a leadership in their respective fields and a reputation which has outlived them. They shared a seminar on the history of religions in Chicago shortly before Tillich's death. There are many possible comparisons to be made between them but there are contrasts too.

By vocation we have an interesting contrast between Tillich and Eliade. Tillich was first and last a theologian. He might have been a philosopher as well and he might have engaged in what he considered to be the history of religion, too. And there are obvious occasions when he engages with what he understands as the sociology of religion. But these other disciplines were finally subservient to his vocation as a theologian. Eliade, by contrast, proclaimed himself to be a historian of religions, and a 'scientific' historian of religions at that. The terms 'historian' and 'scientific' recur again and again in his writings, most especially in his private four-volume *Journal* (1977–1990). Yet there are many who would question this self description. At least they would find it difficult to understand in what sense Eliade engaged in 'scientific' – by which he meant *wissenschaftliche* – study. There may not be a clearly defined vocation of 'historian of religions' but there cannot be the same lack of clarity when we consider the term 'scientific'. There may be differences of interpretation, but not such a broad disagreement.

In Eliade's case the matter becomes quite problematic. Eliade followed a hidden agenda of sorts. He seldom if ever admitted publicly what his agenda was. In the privacy of his journal he reveals that in the work entitled *Patterns in Comparative Religion* (1958) he has a 'secret message', namely 'the "theology" in the history of religions as I decipher and interpret it' (Eliade 1989a, p. 74). So much for being a *historian* of religions.

The Influence of Rudolf Otto on Tillich and Eliade

Tillich and Eliade both speak of the significance of Rudolf Otto and the publication of *Das Heilige* for the study of religion in general and in particular for their own work. As is well known, Otto had two aims in his work: to save the term 'holy' from its exclusively moral connotations, and, having done so, to analyse and describe what he understood as the holy in human religious experience in all its varieties. In order to rescue the meaning of the holy, he proposed the use of the term 'numinous', from the Latin *numen*, on the analogy of omen and ominous. (Actually the word 'numinous' in English goes back to 1647. In 1650 it is used to describe divine actions.) He defined the numinous experience in terms of *mysterium tremendum atque fascinans*. The numinous or the holy is also conceived of as being 'wholly other'. Finally:

> It follows from what has been said that the 'holy' in the fullest sense of the word is a combined, complex category, the combining elements being its rational and non-rational components. But in *both* ... it is a purely *a priori* category. (Otto 1936, p. 116)

The assertion that the holy is an *a priori* category is the basis also for the position that religion is to be explained purely in terms of religion itself, and is not to be explained, or explained away, by reference to any other way of understanding religion.

Tillich knew Otto personally and they spent time together in Marburg in 1924–1925 (Tillich 1967, p. 129). However, Otto's influence on Tillich goes back a few years earlier to the publication of *Das Heilige*. More than once Tillich referred to the impact of reading Otto's work. The telling of the story each time is significantly located in the midst of battle – 'im felde', at 'the front' (Tillich 1923, p. 184) – in the Rote Erde camp in Champagne (Tillich 1925, p. 179). Reading the book was 'an unforgettable event' which made a 'powerful impression' upon Tillich. 'Some peculiarities in the writing, and a completely unknown publisher, took me aback at first. But then began an astonishment, an inward fascination, a passionate agreement, such as one was no longer accustomed to when reading theological books' (*ibid.*). Tillich often looked back romantically from a long way off and exaggerated episodes in his life. These accounts, however, were written within six and eight years of the first reading of Otto's book. It is significant that Otto and his seminal work is still present in one of Tillich's last public statements, the posthumous *My Search for Absolutes* (Tillich 1967).

In his 'Autobiographical Reflections' (1982a), Tillich proceeds from the memory of his early life in a confessional Lutheran school and in the beautiful Gothic church in which his father was pastor, and where he received an experience of the 'holy' given as 'an indestructible good and as the foundation' of all his religious and theological work, to his reading of *Das Heilige*:

> I understood it immediately in the light of these early experiences, and took it into my thinking as a constitutive element. It determined my method in the philosophy of religion, wherein I started with the experiences of the holy and advanced to the idea of God, and not the reverse way. Equally important existentially as well as theologically, were the mystical, sacramental and aesthetic implications of the idea of the holy, whereby the ethical and logical elements of religion were derived from the experience of the presence of the divine, and not conversely. (Tillich 1982a, p. 6)

Otto does not feature prominently in Tillich's *Systematic Theology*, except at one significant point, namely in the section in Volume 1 dealing with 'God and the idea of the holy' (Tillich 1978, p. 215). The very use of these words points to the English translation of Otto's work, and Tillich uses Otto here as a launch pad for further thinking on the reality of God.

Eliade, too, found in Otto a seminal thinker. Reflecting on the popularity of *Das Heilige* Eliade concludes that it is due to:

> the novelty and originality of the perspective taken by the author. Instead of studying the *ideas* of God and of religion, Rudolf Otto set to work to analyse the modalities of *religious experience*. Gifted with great psychological discrimination and fortified by training both as a theologian and as a historian of religions, he succeeded in isolating the content and the specific character of that experience. (Eliade 1977, p. 123)

It is not clear what standing Eliade gives to psychology in Otto as opposed to history of religions compared with Tillich, who firmly rejected the idea that Otto's work should be classed as psychology of religion and declared him to be a phenomenologist (Tillich 1925, p. 182). Whatever be the case, Eliade goes on, following a brief statement of Otto's 'penetrating analysis', to suggest that we should retain this observation: 'that the sacred always manifests itself as a power of quite another order than that of the forces of nature'. While the human language employed by Otto expresses 'naively' truths about the 'wholly other', Eliade goes on, 'we know that this terminology is analogical, and simply due to the inability of man [*sic*] to express what is *ganz andere*; language is obliged to try to suggest whatever surpasses natural experience in terms that are borrowed from that experience.' (Eliade 1977, pp. 123–124.)

Hence the importance of Otto for both Tillich and Eliade lies in Otto's perception of religion and the divine as located in 'the holy' or 'the sacred'. Tillich and Eliade centred on Otto because Otto centred on the holy.

The Holy or the Sacred in Otto, Tillich and Eliade

The holy was a constant feature of Tillich's writing from the 1920s until his final years. One of the clearest statements by Tillich of the nature of the holy occurs in one of his late lectures.

> Every religious experience is an experience of the holy, of the sacred, and in the very nature of the holy lies the answer to our quest for a concept of religion which is all-embracing. All religions are related to something which they consider to be holy ... The holy is that which is separated. It is not part of the ordinarily encountered world, but it can be encountered within this world. It appears in it as that which is quite other than it. (Tillich 1989, p. 10)

Tillich then proceeds to give a fairly conventional description of the holy along the lines presented by Otto. In another lecture of the late period Tillich states very clearly what he considers to be the universality of the holy:

> There is no religion in which the presence of the holy as encountered in objects and persons ... is not the background and the foundation, and the religion in which this disappears has become either a philosophical system or a moral law and has ceased to be religion. (Tillich 1982b, p. 63)

Here we have very clearly stated that religion is to be defined by the holy: wherever the holy is manifested, there is religion established. It does not matter, apparently, what the historical or cultural differences might be: a religion is always a manifestation of the holy. This is very much as Otto would have it. Tillich was very impressed by Otto's travels to see religions in their habitat and accepted that if Otto had seen these religions in their habitat and had concluded that they all manifested the holy in essentially the same way, if not identically, then it must be right that the manifestation of the holy – and hence religion – is universal. It should be noted also that even without Tillich's knowledge of Otto's travels, the holy as a universal phenomenon was for Tillich an *a priori* in itself.

For Eliade, religion itself is defined by reference to the sacred. This term is so basic that each major section in *Patterns in Comparative Religion* (Eliade 1958), for example, is described in these terms: 'The Sacredness of the Sky', 'Sacred Stones', 'Sacred Places', 'Sacred Time'. In *No Souvenirs*, the second volume of his complete *Journal* (but the first to be published), Eliade writes:

Religion 'begins' when and where there is a total revelation of reality; a revelation which is at once that of the sacred – of that which supremely is, of what is neither illusory nor evanescent – and of man's [*sic*] relationship to the sacred, a relationship which is multiple, changing, sometimes ambivalent, but which always places man at the very heart of the real ... On the one hand, the sacred is, supremely, the other than man – the transpersonal, the transcendent – and on the other hand the sacred is the exemplary in the sense that it establishes patterns to be followed. By being transcendent and exemplary it compels the religious man to come out of personal situations, to surpass the contingent and the particular and to comply with general values, with the universal. (Eliade 1977, p. 20)

The sacred is therefore basic to Eliade's understanding of religion; indeed it is fundamental to his understanding of reality. Anything which lies outside the sacred is illusory. Like Tillich and Otto, Eliade finds the sacred everywhere and like Otto he decides to adopt his own vocabulary through which to speak of the sacred. The sacred is manifested in 'hierophanies' as a general category and as 'kratophanies' because the hierophanies are usually manifested in terms of 'power'. As Eliade puts it: 'the history of religions – from the most elementary to the most developed – is constituted by a number of important hierophanies, manifestations of sacred realities' (*ibid.* p. 124). Eliade goes on to point to the universality of hierophanies:

If we admit that all manifestations of the sacred are equivalent as such, in that the humblest hierophany and the most terrifying theophany present the same structure and are to be explained by the same dialectic of the sacred, we then realise that there is no essential discontinuity in the religious life of mankind [*sic*]. To look more closely at a single example: the hierophany that is attributed to a stone, compared with the supreme theophany, the Incarnation ... There are, of course, great differences between the innumerable hierophanies; but one should never lose sight of the fact that their structure and dialectic are always the same. *(ibid*, pp. 125–126)

We have now built up an interesting picture concerning the thought processes of a self-confessed 'historian of religions'. Eliade bases his understanding of religion completely on the sacred: on hierophanies. Hierophanies occur in different historical and locational contexts but essentially they are continuous in their nature and meaning. This one might expect given Eliade's perception of the sacred, based as it is on Otto. What I did not address in Otto's case was that he considered the incarnation of Jesus the Christ to be the supreme form of the sacred. Now we find the same view recurring in Eliade. The way the matter is expressed by Eliade is strongly reminiscent of the old evolutionary approach to religion, in which a development from lower to higher forms is claimed. In fact Eliade sees a strong development in the history of religion in the pre-historic shift from pastoral to agricultural modes of economic support. He also sees a significant development in the religion of the Hebrews (sustained by a distorted version of Hebrew religious history) wherein blood sacrifice is held to have given way to a prophetic form of religion. (What do we make of Eliade's reading of the history of this religion up until the destruction of the temple in Jerusalem and the loss of the altar there, which effectively put an end to sacrifice long after the prophets had had their day?) Finally he sees a hierophany in a stone, but the supreme theophany in the Christian incarnation. So much for an outmoded evolutionary approach long ago discredited by the ethnologists of whom Eliade is so scornful. For Eliade, the history of religions is not merely an exercise in theology, it is an exercise in Judaeo-Christian theology.

All this I am sure would have pleased Tillich because, apart from the evolutionary tendency (although Tillich himself more than once used the term *hoch religionen*, high religions), this is the kind of theological conclusion that Tillich himself would have appreciated. Therefore there is a strong reason for Tillich and Eliade to collaborate in a seminar. They had so much in common. They are both devoted to a theological history of religions, a category of studies recognised by Joseph Kitagawa (1959), for instance, but which some scholars, like Ugo Bianchi, would rule out as an incorrect description, regarding it rather as 'a Theology of Religions, as a branch of theology, that is, as theological reflections on the fact of the existence of other religions' (Bianchi 1975, p. 183). This would definitely be the case with Tillich, and one must draw the assumption that it was so for Eliade too, except that he hardly paid any attention to religions which belong in history, let alone that are living today.

Tillich and Eliade coincide in a broad way across the range of their religious or theological perceptions. They both base their ideas of religion on the manifestation of the holy or the sacred. Both come from a Christian background, the former a Lutheran, the latter a Romanian Orthodox. We do not have to make excuses for Tillich's activity as a theologian, nor for the fact that he sees the history of religion through a Christian prism. Tillich may be criticised for deciding, on no sound evidence, that all religion and revelation is based on the manifestation of the same Holy in each historical and cultural setting, but it is somewhat understandable in a theologian of Tillich's kind. Indeed, that is the history of this kind of theology based partly on Otto, himself a Christian theologian, and, as some would claim, basing his own 'discovery' of the holy on the work of Nathan Söderblom, also a theologian. Eliade does not admit to being a theologian but he does confess to having a theological agenda in the privacy of his *Journal*. In this sense he is the corollary, or obverse, of Tillich. But for a self-confessed 'scientific historian of religions' to engage in such a theological exercise demands some explanation.

I have referred to Tillich and Eliade because I think that they are paradigmatic examples of those who take the line that religion is to be understood with reference to the sacred or the holy. They are in Ugo Bianchi's language 'intuitionists', to return to James Cox's reference to 'eidetic intuition'. Bianchi criticises what he calls:

phenomenology of an irrationalistic intuitionist type which relies too much on intuitions, however efficacious these may be, like that of the 'holy', or of an 'ultimate' which is said to underly [*sic*] all religious manifestations and, in the final analysis, is their meaning. (Bianchi 1975, p. 20)

This would describe Tillich's position, but as Bianchi goes on to talk of 'hierophanies' and of 'religious value ... identified with the primordial and a-historical' it is fairly obvious that it is Eliade, primarily, whom he has in his sights. What Bianchi associates with 'intuitionism' – and he applies the term, as we have seen, to phenomenology – I would extend to theology. Tillich himself reckoned to be using phenomenology and he saw Otto as a phenomenologist too. Bianchi obviously includes Eliade among the phenomenologists. Otto and Tillich had theological aims and so did Eliade. This approach to the universalising of the sacred, that is to the definition of religion in terms of the sacred, is therefore fundamentally theological whether directly theological, as in the work of Tillich, or comparative theological, as in Eliade's work, and should be recognised as such in the study of religions.

The Use of the Term 'The Sacred' in the Study of Religions: Three Considerations

I have argued so far that the use of the term 'sacred' is theological. As such it is appropriate to use the term in theological works or works with a theological motivation, especially if they relate to the Judaeo-Christian traditions or works constructed from a Comparative Theological perspective where the normative bases are the Judaeo-Christian traditions. I further suggest that works which are based on an intuitionist approach to the religious data, even if they are not self-avowedly theological, are in fact theological in their import and meaning. There can be no prohibition on the creation of such works, provided that they are clearly identified for what they are and are not put forward as pretending to be something they are not.

There are some other considerations which we would do well to address by way of suggesting alternative approaches to the academic study of religions which some of us would consider more appropriate to be conducted under the aegis of a descriptive, non-normative, non-evaluative agenda. This is the kind of academic study of religions that should be conducted in institutions claiming to be objective and non-evaluative in their aims and in receipt of public funds gathered in a secular state which, though maintaining a religious establishment of sorts in the UK, in most other ways has abjured the religious dimension in the pursuit of public life, and where the practice of religion, of various choices, is a voluntary form of behaviour.

The first consideration concerns the history of the attempted rehabilitation of 'the sacred'. Many scholars writing about the modern study of religions refer to its practice as a consequence of an Enlightenment view of history and of humanism, both tendencies giving to us an interest in acquiring information about the various religions of the world which were increasingly becoming known in the West in the seventeenth and eighteenth centuries. There is also another factor relating to the Enlightenment, namely that it is as a result of Enlightenment thinking that the demystification and desacralisation of the universe is advanced and heightened. I believe that this movement pre-dates the Enlightenment itself and is evident not only as a result of the Renaissance but also as a result of the Protestant Reformation. Implicit in this movement through the banishing of priesthood, the re-interpretation of the Mass, the overturning of altars and the destruction of icons, the desacralisation of the universe also begins to take place.

The work of Otto and Tillich, in placing such emphasis on 'the holy' or 'the sacred' is therefore an attempt to re-sacralise the universe. I believe this is implicit in all that Otto does for Protestant Christian theology, and it was definitely what attracted Tillich to Otto. One of Tillich's constant themes is the construction of a *coincidentia oppositorum*, the two poles of which were 'the Protestant principle' (the critical or prophetic principle) and 'the Catholic substance'. The latter would give wholeness to Christian theology and Christian life if it is wedded to the Protestant principle. In the lectures of his final period on the encounter between Christianity and other religions, Tillich sets out a typology of religions always based on the sacramental type which represents 'the holy as given' in comparison with 'the holy as demand' (that is, the prophetic type).

We get an interesting insight into this aspect of Tillich's thought in an entry in Eliade's *Journal* at the time of their joint seminar. Eliade was expounding to Tillich the notion of the *deus otiosus*, the absent God. Tillich responded, according to Eliade, with the thought that:

> the theology of the Enlightenment represents a deistic form of the withdrawal of God from the world. As for American Protestant theology of the last fifty years, Tillich considers it 'Unitarian in Christ'. God is reduced to the second person of the Trinity. The demoniac elements of Yahweh disappear. God becomes moral law. (Eliade 1989a, p. 210)

That, it seems to me, is a reference to the desacralisation which I have been referring to. Tillich found in Otto the antidote to the theological weakness of Protestantism and determined to include the sacred, as interpreted by Otto, in his theology.

Ursula King has referred to Eliade's work in a similar vein:

his own hermeneutic exercise seems to take Eliade always back to the same point – to the repeated emphasis on an eternal return to the beginnings and to the unsubstantiated claim that the sacred is a part of the structure of man's consciousness and not part of the history of that consciousness. Furthermore, the manifestations of the sacred are best exemplified by religious phenomena from archaic and exotic cultures whereas modern man is 'fallen', a victim of the ultimate desacralization of the cosmos, … incapable of any important religious creation except that of complete secularization which implies the total identification of the sacred with the profane. (King 1981, p. 565)

This is a very clear statement of what I have suggested is the history of desacralisation in the West and the attempted re-sacralisation of the universe by Eliade, which mirrors the work of Otto and Tillich in drawing its inspiration from the same concerns and remedies.

I draw from this scenario the conclusion that the use of the term 'the sacred', not only as a defining term for 'religion' as such but for the defining of religious phenomena too, is not merely a theological use but represents an attempt by theologians or religionists to bring about a change in human perception of the world in which we live. This agenda is a propagatory one suitable for religionists, missionaries, preachers and religious functionaries and for academics of all kinds in their personal lives, but not appropriate for the university classroom.

The second consideration concerns the ethnocentric nature of the use of the term 'the sacred'. Academics like Joseph Kitagawa and Charles Long, both of the 'Chicago School' (incidentally largely nurtured by Eliade), have addressed the historical fact that the academic study of religions is, like desacralisation, a product of the Western Enlightenment. I will not address Kitagawa's concerns on the implications of this basis for Eastern religionists as the object of the Western study of religions. Here is what Long says on the matter:

The study of the Other as a science is a modern preoccupation of the West. The origins of these disciplines are in the Western Enlightenment. This orientation correlates the notion of reason to the idea of the human … This orientation is the background for the human sciences – a science in which the human constitutes both the object and the interpreter of the science … In the history of religions, at least from its origins, two heuristic norms, one emphasizing the similarity and the other the dissimilarity, dominate. Philology and written languages … constitute one side; the other from the side of that which is dissimilar is that of the primitives – they are not like us, being without written languages and noncivilized. The science of religion proposes to encompass both these modes within a common order of intelligibility through recourse to a deeper and more primordial order: the sacred, religious experience, and so forth. But however this deeper order is articulated, the objects of interpretation are still constituted as Others.

But this constitution of the Others as objects of interpretation is more than simply a procedure of investigation, for it represents the constitution of the interpreter – the desire to make sense of the meaning of the Others in one's personal and cultural life. From this point of view there is confusion or conflation of what is Other in the culture and history of the interpreter with the reality of the Others who are the object of interpretation. This is a central problem in the study of religion as a science of religion. The pretensions of the Enlightenment heritage explain the reason that this science has not been accomplished but is nevertheless always anticipated. (Long 1985, pp. 99–100)

Long's overall agenda does not coincide with mine but in this passage he expresses something that I think is of profound importance in the study of religions: namely, our interpretation of the Other(s).

Long does not refer to Edward Said but I find the mark of Said on Long's language. I do not know who first gave value to the term 'the Other' (capital 'O'), but in *Orientalism* (1978) Edward Said mounts a passionate attack on the way in which the Orient (for Said's purposes predominantly what we call the Middle East, although he does not exclude the far Orient) has been represented in the Western mind and mode of thought. Said labels this 'Orientalism'. In this, as in what I said previously, the dominant force behind the West's interpretation of the Orient is the Enlightenment. But for Said the Western view of the Orient is anything but enlightened. His work is too detailed, complicated and repetitious to do more here than briefly state his thesis.

I will quote very briefly from Said to give a flavour of what he says. 'My real argument', he writes, 'is that Orientalism is – and does not simply represent – a considerable dimension of modern political-intellectual culture, and as such has less to do with the Orient than it does with "our" world' (Said 1978, p. 12). In other words, Orientalism says very little about the Orient as such, but a great deal about 'us': those of us who write about the Orient. He is very accurate in this statement if we refer to the dominant mode of studying the major religions of 'the East' over the past century and a half. For instance he makes the very telling point that 'the Orient studied was a textual universe by and large; the impact of the Orient was made through books and manuscripts' (*ibid*, p. 52). Said makes the further point that: 'Even the rapport between an Orientalist and the Orient was textual, so much so that it is reported of some of the early-nineteenth century German Orientalists that their first view of an eight-armed Indian statue cured them completely of their Oriental taste' (*ibid*, p. 52).

Said engages in much detailed analysis of Orientalism with copious references and quotations. Of particular aptness is a quotation in a section in which Said analyses and compares the two Islamists, H.A.R. Gibb and Louis Massignon. While Gibb admired much of Massignon's work, writes Said, he 'finally drew back from' the way Massignon pursued what Gibb calls:

themes that in some way linked the spiritual life of Muslims and Catholics [and enabled him to find] a congenial element in the veneration of Fatima, and consequently a special field of interest in the study of Shi'ite thought in many manifestations, or again in the community of Abrahamanic origins and such themes as the Seven Sleepers ... [T]hese [links] are composed ... in two registers. One was at the ordinary level of objective scholarship, seeking to elucidate the nature of the given phenomenon by a masterly use of the established tools of academic research. The other was at a level on which objective data and understanding were absorbed and transformed by an individual intuition of spiritual dimensions. It was not always easy to draw a dividing line between the former and the transfiguration that resulted from the outpouring of the riches of his own personality. (H.A.R. Gibb, 'Louis Massignon (1882–1962)', *Journal of the Royal Asiatic Society* 1962, pp. 120–121, cited in Said 1978, p. 265)

It is pertinent to note that word 'intuition' again and its use in creating a world which does not conform with the hard objective data achieved by the 'established tools of academic research'.

I suggest that the Orientalist methods described by Said are the very same methods being employed in certain forms of the study of religions in imposing on the religions of 'the Others' the categories which belong to our own understanding of religion. I do not merely refer to the textually based studies of the F. Max Müller type, although Eliade's studies are almost entirely based on texts too, but also to the imposition of the category of 'the sacred' on religions and aspects of religions that do not, from within themselves, admit to this kind of categorisation. In this respect Long has rightly identified what has happened and still happens in much of what goes under the name of the history or science of religions. Said's concept of Orientalism is very much a product of the imperial posturing of western powers during the nineteenth century. Indeed, Said argues that Orientalism was and in some cases still is an arm of the Western powers who formerly, and now, try to exert a western hegemony over the states of the Orient. It could be argued that employing the term 'the sacred' as a generic term for religion, religions and aspects of religions is a subtle form of theological imperialism exercised by Western scholars on the Eastern and archaic Others.

My third and final consideration concerns the study of religions defined by the 'exotic'. A severe problem in the application of the notion of 'the sacred' to religion(s) and aspects of religions is that, if this were taken seriously, much of what appears in reality under the name of religion could not be studied at all or we would be deprived of the terminology with which to study religions as they are. The problem in applying the term 'the sacred' in the way in which I have portrayed it is that religion is defined on the basis of the exotic. I remind you again of the fate of Uzzah and the paradigmatic nature of that event, with which this chapter began. We cannot be limited in our study of religions on the basis that our basic categories are defined by the exotic rather than by the routine.

I illustrate this aspect of the topic by reference to a publication which had religious pilgrimages as the object of studies. In *Contesting the Sacred* (1991) – a title that I could have given to this chapter – the editors John Eade and Michael J. Sallnow challenge the views of Eliade and Victor Turner (seen as being influenced by Eliade) on the basis of closely analysed field studies and research, as opposed to what Eade and Sallnow see as approaches based on intuition or 'rarefied generalization' in Eliade and Turner. According to the editors, the contributors to the volume implicitly or explicitly contest the Eliadean notion of 'the sacred centre' manifest in 'the power of a miraculous shrine ... seen to derive solely from its inherent capacity to exert a devotional magnetism over pilgrims ... and to exude of itself potent meanings and significances for its worshippers'; to be seen 'so to speak, as *sui generis*: its power ... internally generated and its meanings ... largely predetermined' (Eade and Sallnow 1991, p. 9). On the contrary, the existence and operation of a shrine is in fact the expression of 'a diversity of perceptions and meanings which the pilgrims themselves bring to the shrine and impose upon it' (*ibid*, p. 10). Summing up the volume's challenge, the editors claim that its various researches demonstrate:

> that it is the meanings and ideas which officials, pilgrims, and locals invest in the shrine – meanings and ideas which are determinately shaped by their political and religious, national and regional, ethnic and class backgrounds – which help to give the shrine its religious capital, though this investment might well be in a variety of theological currencies. The power of the shrine, therefore, derives in large part from its character almost as a religious void, a ritual space capable of accommodating diverse meanings and practices – though of course the shrine staff might attempt, with varying degrees of success, to impose a single, official discourse ... The sacred centre, then, in this perspective, appears as a vessel into which pilgrims devoutly pour their hopes, prayers and aspirations. And in a perfect illustration of the classic Marxist model of fetishization and alienation, the shrine then appears to its devotees as if it were itself dispensing the divine power and healing balm they seek. (*ibid*, pp. 15–16)

This gives a much more routine account of pilgrimages and pilgrimage centres, and, quite frankly, from observations of religion generally it is no more than I would expect. This kind of study could be repeated over and over again and the same results would generally be achieved. Not only is the term 'sacred' to be used with economy in its rightful context rather than be liberally sprinkled over any number of allegedly holy events, persons and locations, even within its rightful context the term needs to be used with foresight and reflection lest its coinage be debased.

Conclusion

One of my motivations for engaging with the subject of this chapter is my awareness of the kind of religion from which I have emerged in West Wales. Whenever I think of the Eliadean categories of 'sacred this' and 'sacred that' I ask myself, 'How could I ever begin to study the religious environment in which I grew up and which I have observed in my native domain generally if I were restricted to these categories of "the sacred"?' If the answer is that I could not – and I am convinced that this is the answer – then a serious question is posed against these categories. They might, and I stress *might*, be useful in the study of religious exotica, a very narrowly based area of observation and discourse. They are not useful, and indeed I consider them a hindrance, to the study of most religious situations as they exist in the lives of real people and real situations. If we limit ourselves to the general scene, to the macrocosm, we could still do without 'the sacred' as our nineteenth-century forebears did. If we concentrate on microcosms then the notion of 'the sacred' is a positive hindrance if we are to be faithful to the content of our observations. This is the view taken by W. Baetke of Leipzig (and others of that university such as Kurt Rudolph), as reported by Ugo Bianchi. Baetke, according to Bianchi, objected to Otto's interpretations on the grounds that 'the history of religions is not primarily concerned with religious men and their "experience" but with religions and with the communities which diffuse them, the religious experience of the individual being fundamentally conditioned by the religion of the community to which he belongs' (Bianchi 1975, p. 173). Bianchi continues:

> What Baetke asserts is that 'the history of religions does not find in the initial stage a religious *Urerlebnis* (a primordial experience), a numinous "emotion", or the "onrush" of a "primordial numinous" feeling, but instead everywhere and above all finds institutional religions fully developed, and men who belong to this or that historical religion', and so all the feelings and experiences to which Otto [and by extension Eliade] refers always presuppose historical (that is, concrete and institutional) religion, and the 'holy', as it is concretely expressed in a religious tradition, is a phenomenon which precedes the religious man who becomes aware of it. (*ibid* p. 174)

This analysis, I suggest, demonstrates what the religions that are our object of study are really like and how our study and research of religions should be carried out. The objective, scientific, academic study of religions and of aspects of religions, unless it specifically refers to traditions and events and contexts in which the sacred is an ineradicable factor, calls for the use of 'the sacred' only in appropriate contexts and the abandonment of its use as a generic term, both in order to avoid regression to theology, out of which our discipline is held to have emerged and from which it is held to have achieved its independence, and to advance progression to a system based on academic integrity, academic rigour and academic independence.

(First published as Occasional Paper No. 13, 1995)

Bibliography

Bianchi, Ugo 1975. *The History of Religions*, Leiden: Brill.

Cox, James L. 1992. *Expressing the Sacred: an Introduction to the Phenomenology of Religion*, Harare: University of Zimbabwe Publications.

Eade, John and Sallnow, Michael J. (eds) 1991. *Contesting the Sacred: the Anthropology of Christian Pilgrimage*, London: Routledge.

Eliade, Mircea 1977. *Myths, Dreams and Mysteries*, Glasgow: Fontana.

——— 1958. *Patterns in Comparative Religion*, London and New York.

——— 1989–1990. *Journal, Vol. I* (1990a); *Vol. II* (1989a; orig. pub. in 1977 as *No Souvenirs*); *Vol. III* (1989b); *Vol. IV* (1990b), Chicago: Chicago University Press.

King, Ursula 1981. 'A Hermeneutic Circle of Religious Ideas', in *Religious Studies* **17**, pp. 565–569.

Kitagawa, Joseph 1959. 'The History of Religions in America', in M. Eliade and J. Kitagawa (eds), *The History of Religions*, Chicago and London: Chicago University Press pp. 1–30.

Livingston, James C. 1989. *Anatomy of the Sacred: An Introduction to Religion*, New York: Macmillan.

Long, Charles 1985. 'A Look at the Chicago Tradition in the History of Religions: Retrospect and Future', in Joseph M. Kitagawa (ed.), *The History of Religions* pp. 87–104.

Otto, Rudolf 1931. *Religious Essays: A Supplement to 'The Idea of the Holy'*; tr. Brian Lunn, Oxford: Oxford University Press.

——— 1936. *The Idea of the Holy*, tr. John W. Harvey, (orig. pub. 1917 as *Das Helige*; first English trans. 1923), Oxford: Oxford University Press.

Paden, William E. 1988. *Religious Worlds: the Comparative Study of Religion*, Boston: Beacon Press.

——— 1992. *Interpreting the Sacred: Ways of Viewing Religion*, Boston: Beacon Press.

Said, Edward 1978. *Orientalism*, (1991 edn.), Harmondsworth: Penguin.

Thomas, Terence 1999. *Paul Tillich and World Religions*, Cardiff: Cardiff Academic Press.

Tillich, Paul 1923. *Die Kategorie des "Heiligen" bei Rudolf Otto*, in *Gesammelte Werke*, Band XII, Stuttgart: Evangelische Verlagswerk, S. 184–186.

———1925. *Der Religionsphilosoph Rudolf Otto*, in *Gesammelte Werke*, Band XII, Stuttgart: Evangelische Verlagswerk, S. pp. 179–183.

——— 1967. *My Search for Absolutes*, New York: Simon & Schuster.

——— 1978. *Systematic Theology*, Vol 1, London.

——— 1982a. *The Theology of Paul Tillich*, ed. Charles W. Kegley, The Pilgrim Press, New York. (Rev. edn. of the 1952 publication, ed. Kegley and Bretall, New York: Macmillan).

——— 1982b. Recordings of lectures delivered by Tillich and transcribed and contained in the Appendix to D.A.T. Thomas, *Paul Tillich and World Religions: A Study of Paul Tillich's Thought on Inter-Religious Encounter and Dialogue*, thesis presented for the award of a Ph.D. of the University of Nottingham (revised version published as Thomas 1999).

——— 1989. *The Encounter of Religions and Quasi-Religions*, ed. Terence Thomas, Lewiston/ Queenston/Lampeter: Edwin Mellen Press.

CHAPTER 5

The Sense and Nonsense of 'Community': A Consideration of Contemporary Debates about Community and Culture by a Scholar of Religion

Kim Knott

'Community' is a dishonest word ... It is invariably a party to pious fraud.
(Ignatieff 1992)[1]

Thus postmodernity, the age of contingency *für sich*, of self-conscious contingency, is for the thinking person also the age of community: of the lust for community, search for community, invention of community, imagining community. (Bauman 1992, p. 134)

A fraud, yet something we lust after? What riddle is this? Categorically different intentions lie behind the use of the term 'community' by these two commentators on the 1990s. Michael Ignatieff was referring to the use of the term in public discourse in relation to ethnic minorities at the time of *The Satanic Verses* controversy. But he was also signalling the capacity of the term to be taken up and used to mask real social relations. His comment suggests, first, that those groups identified as 'communities' may not, in fact, be so, and, secondly, that the term may be used falsely to infer coherence and unity. Ignatieff points to the problematic nature of the term. The quotation from Zygmunt Bauman's *Intimations of Postmodernity* does not refer to the *use* of the term but to what the word promises in an age of reflexive contingency, to the hopes and expectations caught up in 'community'. To Bauman, and a number of other social theorists, the principal characteristic of the postmodern or late-modern condition is the drive for community, in all its ambiguity, for 'contingency with roots, freedom with certainty' (*ibid*, p. 135).[2] Our time, as Michel Maffesoli (1996) has claimed, is 'the time of the tribes'.[3]

Both of these striking claims are significant for the study of contemporary religion in the West. Together they signal the fertility of a focus on religion and community, but sound a note of caution in pursuing it.[4] It is a deceptively simple theme that requires our full critical attention and must be approached with vigilance and sophistication, using the newly sharpened tools of our own field of enquiry in relation to the object of our deliberations – religion – and to the theories and methods best suited to its investigation,[5] but also in open engagement with scholars in other disciplines in which debates about the meaning and use of 'community' are further advanced than they are in religious studies.[6] For my part, I can do very little here. What I will not do – and I am aware of the risk in this – is say anything at all about the way in which religions themselves have developed social forms and have articulated ideas about community. Keith Ward has tackled this subject in his recent book on religion and community (Ward 2000) and the SHAP Working Party on World Religions took it as the theme for its 2001 journal.[7] The task I have set myself is expressed in the subtitle of this chapter: to come at contemporary debates about community and culture as a scholar of religions. Religion, thereby, gets rather short shrift, as I have seen my task as introducing some of the critical discussion about 'community' which is taking place in sociology and social anthropology, and which is akin to our own debates about the reification of 'religion', its ideological usage, its fluidity and situated nature.

What follows is in three sections, the first setting the context and raising some issues, the second discussing the problematisation of the term in social studies and the third addressing the debate on 'community' as a sign of the times and the meaning of this for religion and spirituality. An afterword concludes the chapter.

Part One: The Sense and Nonsense of 'Community'

It is certainly timely for me to look hard at the concept of 'community' and its relationship to religion. The year 2001 saw the 25th anniversary of the Community Religions Project, formed in 1976 by Michael Pye, Ursula King, and William Weaver as a research group within the Department of Theology and Religious Studies at the University of Leeds, and of which I am currently the Director. Its original purposes were 'to carry out and publish research into the religious communities of Leeds and neighbouring cities, and to relate such research to associated matters such as community relations, inter-religious understanding, religious education, and teaching programmes within the University' (Pye 1976, p. 1). I thought it might be instructive to look back at the founding documents from 1976 and 1977 to see how they might illuminate discussion of religion and community. I was not entirely surprised to find that they did so hardly at all. Rather, it was the *absence* of any definition of 'religious communities' which was illuminating. The term was evidently so 'taken-for-granted' that it was not deemed necessary to define it. Why was this the case? In short, I would suggest that in the mid-1970s, the notion of 'community' in British public discourse (whether related to class, religion or ethnicity) was used uncritically as a safe and respectful term to indicate groups of others. At that time we had the national Community Relations Commission and local Community Relations Councils.[8] We had had a plethora of studies on working class communities (such as those by Young and Wilmott 1957, and Hoggart 1957) and on race and community (such as Rex and Moore 1967). The sociologists Bell and Newby had published *Community Studies* in 1971, a critical study of the sociology of community which challenged the assumption of a link between locality and community, followed by their edited reader *The Sociology of Community*, in 1974.[9] The journal of the Community Relations Commission, *New Community*, was established in 1971, the title supporting the idea that the site of community studies had shifted from rural village or urban working class locations to Britain's new minorities, settlers from the Caribbean and the Indian sub-continent in particular. From that time on in British public discourse, as Baumann (1996, p. 15) has suggested, community became 'a polite term for "ethnic minority"'.

So, in the fields of British public policy and social studies in the 1970s, the term 'community' was much in evidence, though its meaning and use were only gradually gaining critical attention. At that time also, little was made of the role or significance of religion, or culture more generally, as a factor in community life. Even in the new studies of race and ethnicity, religion was mentioned only briefly, its importance for the groups involved noted, but with little attention paid to the meaning and practice of religion, its ideological power, its symbolic significance or sociological role.[10] And this brings us back to the Community Religions Project. Whilst its founding members were silent on the meaning of 'community', they knew what they were after when it came to religion – the discovery and investigation of what was 'near at hand' rather than many miles away or centuries ago, the culture shock of being exposed to living religions, and the possibility of engaging with other agencies and academic disciplines with an interest in Leeds and neighbouring cities and in issues of community relations and education (Pye 1976, 1977).

Whether or not the Community Religions Project succeeded in fulfilling its intentions is not relevant here. What is noteworthy is the unreflective grounding of the early work in 'community studies'. In some of the studies undertaken by members of the CRP, the term 'community' was defined and discussed, in others it was used unselfconsciously to signal all people notionally associated with the same (world) religion in a given region, city or neighbourhood. In most – precisely because they were ethnographically rich – the complex social and religious subdivisions (caste, sect, etc.) which cut through and across 'the Muslim community' or 'Hindu community', for example, were identified and investigated, but the term 'community' itself continued more often than not to be used.[11] Why? Because it continued to have a place in common parlance, in public discourse at both a local and national

level, and among the people who were the subjects of study – local Sikhs,
Pakistani Muslims, Polish Catholics, etc. As we shall see later, the dynamics of
this are worthy of greater investigation.

> It was when I suddenly realised that no-one ever used 'community' in a
> hostile sense that I saw how dangerous it was ... Community can be the
> warmly persuasive word to describe an existing set of relationships, or the
> warmly persuasive word to describe an alternative set of relationships ...
> What is most important, perhaps, is that unlike all other types of social
> organisation (state, nation, society, etc) it seems never to be used
> unfavourably .... (Williams 1976, p. 66)

This was Raymond Williams's response to the term 'community' in the year of
the Community Religions Project's foundation. He voiced a suspicion about
the term which is no less relevant today than it was in the 1970s. Despite his
caution, the term continued – and continues – to be used extensively and
largely uncritically by many. In fact, in contemporary Britain we are obsessed
with 'community' – we mourn its loss, celebrate it, idealise it, long for it,
develop policy to encourage it, categorise our society according to it, give
power to those who represent it or claim to build it, and package and
commodify it.[12] We are the very proof of Zygmunt Bauman's prophetic 1992
claim.[13]

We love communities, particularly religious – or 'faith' – communities,
because we think they offer the key to social solidarity and improved local
relationships (particularly race relations), to sources of ethics and ethical
continuity down the generations, to a sense of belonging that will issue forth in
greater social responsibility and social action, and to the local monitoring and
policing of behaviour. In New Labour philosophy, community is linked to
notions of *partnership* (between public, private and voluntary sectors) and
regeneration, the balance of *rights* and *responsibilities*, and *citizenship* and
voluntary action.[14] These are all contemporary political key words. The
political drive to build community and get communities working is the new
social engineering. If it works, it will be economical and will improve crime
statistics, education levels, and social cohesion, and will produce more
responsible citizens – or so it is thought. A great deal rests on this notion of
'community'.

Our obsession is clearly illustrated by Robin Richardson, writing about his
involvement in the Commission on the Future of Multi-Ethnic Britain in *Living
Community* (SHAP 2001).[15] The Commission saw Britain as 'a community of
communities', a phrase much pilloried by the press.[16] Richardson himself cites
a cartoon in the London *Evening Standard* – no doubt appealing to our
European colleagues – of two Roman centurions looking out from their ship to
the white cliffs of Dover, one of them saying 'Apparently, they're not Britons.
They're just a multi-ethnic community of communities' (Richardson 2001,

p. 55). The full phrase, 'a community of communities and citizens', as Richardson points out, stresses

> that everyone is an individual with their own rights as well as embedded in a community. The Commission stressed also that communities overlap with each other, that they are interdependent, and are continually developing and influencing each other. All people in Britain belong to more than one community, and accordingly may experience conflicting loyalties within their own hearts and minds. (*ibid*, p. 53)

Thus the Commission accepted the naivety of asserting community without also recognising the diversity inherent within communities, their inter-relatedness and potential divisiveness, and their contribution to the formation of complex identities (Runnymede Trust 2000, pp. 27–28). 'A fixed idea of community understates the degree of differentiation within the new communities' (p. 28). This signals some sophistication (only to be expected given the identity of the Chair and the Commission's members), despite the rhetoric of community. The features that the Commission then identified as intrinsic to community (*ibid*, pp. 50–51; see also Richardson 2001, pp. 53–54) further demonstrate this: belongingness, dignity and identity are cited repeatedly, with gratitude (of members to their communities) and responsibility also being mentioned. Criticism and conflicts of interest and power are conceded as aspects of community life. The two other features listed are boundaries (sometimes hard and fast, sometimes fluid), and the symbols and ceremonies which bind a community together and 'which mean the same to all members' (Runnymede Trust 2000, p. 51) – something we, as scholars of religion, might wish to debate.

Above all, the Commission's report affirms the centrality of the notion ('concept' seems too strong a word for so loose a term) of 'community' to contemporary public debate about the nature of British society. And religion is right at the heart of this, often providing the *raison d'être* for community, being the source of its symbols and customs, bound in with its stories and memories, the focus of the 'faith' which is intrinsic to it, and the source of its ethos and moral teachings.[17] Religion is rarely mentioned explicitly – more often it is 'faith' – but the communities are commonly identified with reference to 'World Religions' – a process whose genealogy may be traced back to the work of categorisation set in train by colonial administrators of the 19th century in India if not earlier.[18]

Sense or nonsense? Does the very looseness of the word 'community' with all its many applications to locality, faith, ethnicity, politics, education, sexuality and so on make it nonsensical, or only barely sensical – having reference to no more than 'shared interests'? Is it just a vain hope, nostalgia in the face of contemporary uncertainty and fragmentation? It can certainly be deconstructed; it can even be abandoned and replaced, as we shall see in the next section. However, it would be misguided to suggest that the term is without sense, for it 'makes sense' to people in so far as it conveys the very things that Raymond Williams and others have worried about – nostalgia, warmth, something to be longed for, an ideal. It is a sensuous word, in no way merely a neutral social scientific term.[19] In its use it can carry desires, transmit a sense of respect for others, mask difference, include or exclude, among other things.

What it does not do is offer any necessary analytical precision. Academic users of the term may offer operational definitions of it, but to sustain a single, uncompromised use of it would, I suggest, be virtually impossible.[20]

Part Two: The Term 'Community', its Reification, Destabilisation and Replacement

The purpose of this section is to explore the ways in which the term has been problematised. Starting with Gerd Baumann's study of Southall, *Contesting Culture*, which examined both popular and social scientific uses of the term 'community', I shall then touch briefly on the two debates of multiculturalism and globalisation in which social anthropologists and sociologists have considered the application, relevance and limitations of the term. Religion, as an aspect of culture, often the dominant one, is caught up in both debates.

Baumann, whose intention was not to discuss 'religious communities' in Southall *per se*, organises his book with reference to several of them precisely because this was how Southallians identified themselves and referred to one another. On the basis of six years ethnographic familiarity with the area, he examines the way in which the five principal groupings made sense of themselves and jostled for ideological advantage with reference to conceptions of community and culture. Summarising his observations, he writes that

> Sometimes, Sikh Southallians would subdivide their *community* into *communities* of caste, although at other times they would insist that Sikhism entailed a denial of caste altogether. Many Hindu Southallians, though certainly not all, could endorse a Hindu culture that encompassed not only sections of the Sikh *community*, but other *cultures* too ... Irish Southallians were sure that they formed part of an Irish *culture*, but denied the existence of an Irish *community*; English Southallians were unsure how to apply either term to themselves or their neighbours, unless their neighbours were 'coloured', that is, 'people of ethnicity' as certified by the dominant discourse. Afro-Caribbean Southallians spoke of a *community* that had, as yet, not 'found its own *culture*'. (Baumann 1996, p. 6)[21]

He distinguishes between a dominant discourse and demotic discourses in relation to the two terms. The dominant discourse in Southall and beyond 'reifies culture and traces it to ethnicity, and reifies ethnicity and postulates "communities" of "culture" based on purportedly ethnic categorizations' (*ibid*, p. 20). Although Southallians participated in this dominant discourse as and when it suited them, they developed their own alternative, demotic discourses which separated *culture* and *community*, and which turned the latter into 'a creative project' (*ibid*, p. 190). '*Communities* are processually constructed rather than found as the ready-made social correlates of consistent and bounded cultures' (*ibid*, p. 191).[22] Different groups of Southallians 'remapped' their *communities* according to where they were and to whom they were speaking, that is, to both context and relationship (*ibid*, p. 31).

For several of the *communities* in Southall, religious identity, including religious narratives of origin, religio-political positioning, socio-religious symbols, and reifications of communal religious history and teachings, were central; for others, they were less so. Nevertheless, religion remained the most significant marker of identity among Southallians.

For scholars of religion, an important aspect of Baumann's work is his separation of culture and community.[23] Some Southallians he spoke to suggested that their *communities* were divided internally by *culture*, others that several *communities* shared some cultural practices.[24] This overturns the point made in the report of the Commission on the Future of Multi-Ethnic Britain to which I referred earlier: not all members of a so-called community buy into the same understanding of customs and symbols, and, indeed customs and symbols are not necessarily owned by one group alone.[25] Intriguingly, however, although it was evident that there was no necessary relationship between community and culture in the Southall case, most Southallians, whilst willing to use 'community' fluidly, to break and remake it, and to employ demotic notions of it, continued to employ a reified notion of 'culture' (generally predicated on religion) (Baumann 1996, pp. 196–197). Even local critics of particular cultures (such as Southall Black Sisters) did not challenge their solidity.[26]

The construction of community and its relationship to identity were central to debates about race, ethnicity, religion, and multiculturalism in Britain well before Baumann published his study of Southall.[27] John Eade, in his 1989 book, *The Politics of Community*, on the Bangladeshis of East London, cited the work of Verity Saifullah Khan and Pnina Werbner on Pakistanis in Britain as significant in understanding the relationship between ethnic community building and the political process. Saifullah Khan, in the mid-1970s, identified the role of community leaders in constructing 'the community' in engagement with outsiders such as state agencies, the media and academics; Werbner, a decade later, focused rather on the competing interests of voluntary associations within ethnic minority communities, noting that those leaders who came to the fore in constructing community were the ones most able to manipulate cultural symbols effectively (ironically, those closest to the margins and most willing and able to work with outsiders). Eade himself suggested that communities only became constituted as a result of political activity. He argued that a term such as 'the Bangladeshi community' could only be understood 'in the context of particular debates and practices operating within the political arena' (*ibid*, p. 185). I take it that he was distinguishing between the ideological reification and construction of community (as in Baumann) and the practical development and construction of community, the latter occurring locally, perhaps spasmodically, within and through particular events and meetings: calling 'community' into being through the activities and statements of insiders and outsiders.

More recently, Ayse Caglar (1997) has considered what uses of culture and community are at work in the adoption of hybrid or hyphenated identities. Might such identities – such as British Muslim, or young, gay, British African-Caribbean Christian – actually help us to unfreeze the reified notions of culture which seem to beset popular and scholarly discourse on multiculturalism?[28] They certainly challenge notions of cultural integration and separation – by signalling multicultural competence – but, she asks, 'are they not still rooted in the old idea of culture?' They continue 'to rest upon an original separation' of culture based on ethnicity (*ibid*, p. 175), with communities representing the institutionalisation of such cultures (*ibid*, p. 179). Talk of hybridity, then, binds rather than frees the debate about individuals and groups to the problematic concepts of culture, community and ethnicity. Cultures are seen as incommensurable (*ibid*, p. 175). Rather, as Caglar insists, 'there is no community defined *a priori* that constitutes the pregiven object of our investigations' (*ibid*, p. 180). Like Eade and Baumann, she calls for a situational method which will avoid the need to define collectivities in advance.[29]

Here, then, is just one field in which 'community' – as a social institution and a reified concept – has been criticised and destabilised. (Had I time, in addition to multiculturalism I might equally have demonstrated this process at work in debates about gender, power and community, virtual communities, nationalism and community, congregation and community, or diaspora and transnational communities.[30]) However, it is the sociologists of globalisation, for whom culture and community have again been key foci, who have begun to provide an alternative terminology.

In a major empirical study of the globalisation process at work, *Living the Global City* (Eade ed., 1997), Eade, Albrow and Dürrschmidt, among others (following globalisation theorists such as Appadurai, Giddens, Robertson and Featherstone) unravel the history of the sociological use of 'community' from 19th century economic and social theorists (Tönnies among them), through the work of Park and the Chicago School, and the British community studies of the 1950s, to the anthropological studies of ethnic minorities in the 1970s and 1980s.[31] The definitional problems associated with the term do not seem to have been resolved, they say. Rather, it is with the move to imagined and diasporic communities in the work of scholars of nationalism (Anderson), globalisation (Appadurai) and hybridity (Bhabha and Gilroy) that a growing sophistication has begun to emerge.[32]

To quote Albrow (1997, p. 23):

> The shift to seeing the imagined community as the guiding principle for lived social relations represents an important step towards the disembedding of community, for it opens the possibility of representing the absent and distant as being integral to the local.

This possibility, however, has required the identification of new terms to express the new social formations brought about by globalisation, terms such as 'flows', 'scapes', 'spheres', and 'milieux'. The motivation for identifying such terms comes from the process, identified by Giddens (1990) as 'disembedding', whereby modern technology has enabled people to maintain social relationships – or community – across the globe. This has opened up new social possibilities for religions and new religious movements (not a neutral process by any means, say our authors, citing the emergence of global 'fundamentalist' movements: Eade et al. 1997, pp. 23–24). From Appadurai, the suffix 'scape' is favoured (he refers to media-scapes and ethno-scapes, among others) to reflect 'the fluidity of social formations under conditions of global cultural flow' (*ibid*, p. 38). Albrow deploys the term 'socio-scapes' to indicate the many overlapping social visions operating within the London Borough of Wandsworth which defy any conception of local community and extend beyond its boundaries to encompass cultural configurations criss-crossing the globe.[33] In the same volume Dürrschmidt (1997, pp. 57, 61) prefers the term 'milieu' to 'community' which, he suggests, retains the sense of relative stability and situatedness without the demands of 'the local'. Milieux co-exist within a place, but are not limited by it. Rather, they are the sites of micro-globalisation processes.

Several ideas have emerged from the discussion so far which have a potential bearing on the study of religions:

- The term 'community' has been decoupled from 'locality'.
- The term 'community' has been decoupled – by subjects themselves, if not in the dominant discourse – from 'culture'.
- Both locality and culture remain potential starting points for an investigation of community – though there are others, such as consumption – but with the proviso that a direct relationship between locality and community, or culture and community, is not assumed.
- Where communities are referred to in public discourse, they are generally reified, often related in a fixed way to particular cultures, often assumed

to have traditions, boundaries, symbols, rules of inclusion and exclusion, etc.

• Actual communities and their boundaries are constituted situationally through symbol (Cohen 1985), practice (Eade 1989) and discourse (Baumann 1996). People negotiate communities into being.

• The social scientific study of communities has shifted to a consideration of imagined communities, scapes and milieux as scholars have responded to processes of social and cultural disembedding in late-modernity. (This runs counter to the still-prevalent popular notion of the embeddedness of people in communities and communities in places: see Richardson 2001.)

Part Three: Contemporary Sociality, the Sacred and Memory

What can be discerned about the Western spiritual condition and the vitality of religious bodies from this discussion about the contemporary nature of community and current uses of the term? To what extent is the anxiety over the loss of community and the equally urgent lust after community a sign either of the persistence of the sacred or the re-enchantment of society? Is the search for community that was witnessed in Part One itself a spiritual quest?

On the one hand, this is evidently a religious matter. Contemporary religious bodies must themselves have an interest in considering what this longing for community means, and in providing for it.[34] On the other hand, this is most certainly a matter for the sociologist of religion. And, given Durkheim's understanding of the intrinsic relationship between religion and society, and his broad acceptance of Tönnies' analysis of community, it is not surprising that it is particularly those working within the Durkheimian sociological tradition who have felt the need to investigate this contemporary desire for belonging, and its spiritual meaning and significance.

Within Britain and beyond the future direction and relevance of religion and the sacred have been debated by sociologists and public commentators in the academic press and media. The focus of the debate has, of course, been secularisation, the retreat of religious institutions, religious explanations and symbols from public life. Alongside this debate, often independently, but sometimes related, has been the public bemoaning of the demise of community. At those times when the sacred has re-emerged in abundance, for example with the Toronto Blessing or the death of Princess Diana, sociologists have variously seen this as evidence *for* or *against* the onwards march of secularisation. These events might merely represent the last gasps of a dying tradition or a trace memory of something from the past; alternatively, they might be evidence of the vitality and promise of contemporary spirituality. These same events – with others such as demonstrations about the cancellation of debt or anti-capitalism, and the rise of online social networks – are equally provided as evidence for, either, the demise of real communities and their replacement with single-issue interest groups, or the burgeoning of alternative forms of sociality.

Mellor and Shilling in their book on religion, community and modernity, *Re-forming the Body* (1997), have more sympathy with the latter view, as, in their opinion, 'it would be wrong to associate recent laments for the loss of community with the absence of structured relational forms' (1997, p. 165). Community need not only be equated with such forms; and, indeed, the lament for it may have little to do with their presence or absence in contemporary society.[35] Mellor and Shilling describe modernity as 'Janus-faced' with regard to its social configurations, retaining, on the one hand, the *banal associations* of the Protestant contract mentality – of which goal-oriented, rational organisations are typical – and *sensual solidarities*.[36] These are consumption-oriented rather than production-oriented, and are affective, offering the effervescence of being together with others, and, at their extreme, are transcendent in character. Mellor and Shilling deny that they represent a return to traditional community in its *Gemeinschaft* type (an expression of instinct, habit and spontaneity). Rather, they are self-aware, fleeting, evolving and dissolving, affinity-based, fulfilling only part of the identity and needs of those who are attracted to them.

These *sensual solidarities* (Mellor and Shilling 1997), *emotional communities* (Davie 1996, from Hervieu-Léger), *aesthetic communities* (Bauman [after Kant] 1992, pp. 137–138), or *neo-tribes* (Maffesoli 1996 [1988]) are conditioned by the contingent nature of late-modernity. They are not communities of fate, but personal, chosen communities.[37] They are not tightly-structured, or local, neither do they regulate their membership; rather, they are 'formed ... by [a] multitude of individual acts of self-identification' (Bauman 1992, p. 136, following Maffesoli). They are, according to Bauman, at their most powerful when they remain in the domain of hope – beyond that they become fragmented and dissipated as their adherents fail to find consensus (*ibid*, pp. 137–138).

For Maffesoli (1996, p. 25), the 'social divine' emerges in the sharing of simple and routine gestures, 'the habitus or custom [serving] to concretize or actualize the ethical dimensions of any sociality'. Neo-tribes exhibit shared sentiments (the aesthetic aspect), a collective bond (the ethical aspect), and a habitus or 'way of being with others' (custom). However, in distinguishing neo-tribal custom from religious ritual, Maffesoli holds back from equating neo-tribal sociality with religious communities as such. In fact, he asserts that *God*, the *Mind* and the *Individual* (all capitalised and reified) 'step aside' for this reorienting of society (*ibid*, p. 74).

It is this very problem of discerning the difference between modern meaning systems with a religious character and those without that occupies Danièle Hervieu-Léger in *Religion as a Chain of Memory* (2000, [1993]).[38] Resisting the old secular/religious distinction based on the absence or presence of the transcendent, she identifies modernity as a time which 'pluralizes ways of producing meaning and causes their increased dissociation', and sacredness as 'one of the possible methods of organizing collective meaning' (*ibid*, p. 106).[39] The experience of the sacred, which may be witnessed in relation to sport, popular music, etc., does not automatically issue forth in religious beliefs, practices or communities, however.[40] The sacred and the religious may be dissociated. Religion – or 'the religious' as she prefers it – offers a different way of organising meaning, '[one] based upon identification with a chain or line of belief' (*ibid*, p. 107). Hervieu-Léger contends that it is this lineage of belief which links together members of a believing community, and it is that community which then draws in past, present and future members, who then legitimise their beliefs on the basis of this memorised tradition (Davie 1996, p. 110). Her interest then turns to how religious and other sacred communities are faring in late-modernity: she cites the problem of collective amnesia (breaks in the chain of memory), and the contemporary significance of ephemeral 'small memories' (a *bricolage* of memories from various traditions, including invented memories) which may become the basis for new groupings. She refers to these as 'elective fraternities', describing them as 'both willed and ideal', as voluntary, and as offering 'real solidarity, transparency of thought and communication, and common values and memories' (*ibid*, p. 150). It is only when the fraternity feels the need to legitimate itself, to extend itself beyond its immediate experiences, and 'to acquire a representation of itself that can incorporate the idea of its own continuity' (*ibid*, p. 152) that it takes on a religious character. The rise of fraternities – including those that become religious – occurs, according to Hervieu-Léger, in inverse proportion to the demise of primary communities as a result of the modern condition of uncertainty and isolation (*ibid*, p. 150). So, to Hervieu-Léger, as to Bauman, Mellor and Shilling, and Maffesoli, the nature and practice of community has been transformed in the later stages of modernity. It is Hervieu-Léger, however, who provides the most thorough analysis of the nature of the social formations which ensue, and offers a method for differentiating religious from other expressions and experiences of sacredness.

From a Durkheimian perspective, the mutuality of the social and the sacred continues to invite scholars of religion to uncover the particular customs or rituals, symbols, ideas or beliefs emerging in the new social arrangements of this age of contingency, as Bauman calls it. Or we may prefer to start at the other pole, where the religious, its effects and expressions, serves as 'a clue to society and its ordering' (Jenkins 1999, p. 13).[41] From this perspective, how does a particular social formation emerge around a religious text, a religious event, a religious site? What is the nature of the social formation that is called into being by the practices and activities associated with that text, event, site? Following Hervieu-Léger, does that social formation or 'community' participate in or develop a chain of memories which will sustain it? What does it tell us about our times?

The methodological question to which this discussion repeatedly draws us, however, is this: is it not possible for us to work as scholars of religion without assuming either 'community' or, indeed, 'religion' as 'the pregiven object of our investigations'? For in making such assumptions we may participate in shoring up preconceived, often dominant, notions of one or the other, thus contributing to their reification and manufacture.[42]

Afterword

But are we not forced into such a methodological trap by the very nature of our discipline? No, we are not, because we are fortunate to participate in a field of study with open borders, multiple perspectives and methods. What alternatives do we have, then, if we are to avoid such pitfalls?[43] Drawing on the ideas of several anthropologists whose work I have already introduced in this discussion, let me pose three suggestions. One offers a different object of investigation as a starting point for an examination of culture and society; the second offers a methodological strategy; the third an ethical approach. They are all situational, and may be used separately or in relationship to one another.

The first suggestion is to follow the advice of Ayse Caglar, whose question (1997, p. 180) about the inadequacy of community as a pregiven object of investigation I borrowed above. She invites us to take person-object relationships, or consumption, as our starting point for uncovering patterns of individual and collective self-definition (see footnote 29). What might we learn about social expressions of meaning and order from people's use of various commodities and objects?

Secondly, we might apply the interpretative approach adopted by Timothy Jenkins in his study of the Kingswood Whit Walk in Bristol. For him (Jenkins 1999, p. 83), an appropriate methodological strategy is to undertake a description of local particularity which reproduces or imitates the procedure it seeks to describe:

> There is no 'social structure' in Kingswood, no coherent way of life that one can learn to see. Rather, there are local strategies employed to make sense of life, including how one makes sense of and to outsiders ... In this perspective, social life, like social anthropology, is a process of interpretation. (*ibid*, pp. 83–84)

Uncovering these local strategies for coping with reality, and giving voice to them through a process of mutual construal (participant understandings interwoven with the gaze of the outsider) is more difficult than it sounds. It requires a painstaking inductive approach, that is, one which neither starts with 'community' or 'religion' nor ends up by deducing them (through a process of comparison or generalisation) from an account of local particularity.[44] Jenkins acknowledges, however, the necessity of some degree of engagement with 'the accounts already given of ... "societies" or "cultures", both academic and popular', as these play a part in the process of local sense-making.[45]

Thirdly, for an ethical approach to the problem we might return to the (personal) example of Gerd Baumann, this time in his 1999 book, *The Multicultural Riddle*. Baumann, we recall, discussed the uses of culture and community, and their separation, in his ethnographic study of multi-ethnic Southall (Baumann 1996). In his later book, whilst conceding with Jenkins that reified notions of community and culture are part of the very society we study, he offers the salutary warning that, 'by reifying cultural identity one risks playing along with cultural essentialists, and one risks condoning the policing of cultural purity by elitist elites' (Baumann 1999, p. 138). This forces him – and us, as scholars of religion – to ask the question, 'What do I do to become a useful multicultural citizen, and how do I break with the reifications with which the multicultural dreamscape has been land mined?' (*ibid*, p. 140). His answer comes in two forms: in a final chapter on the practice of multicultural thinking, and in a personal footnote. It is in the latter that we may find his ethical approach to the avoidance of adopting pregiven notions of community and religion:

> The best practice to develop multirelational, multicultural thinking is easy: Try to unreify all accepted reifications by finding crosscutting cleavages. Whenever the reifying discourse talks about citizens or aliens, purple or green ethnics, believers or atheists, ask about rich or poor citizens, powerful or manipulated ethnics, married or sexual-minority believers. Who are the minorities within majorities, who are the unseen majorities right across minorities? Combine every method of questioning to every possible category around you, for the permutations are endless when it comes to questioning reifications. (*ibid*, p. 141)

So, is it possible to study the religious (Hervieu-Léger) without being trapped into an acceptance of the pregiven categories of 'community' and 'religion' and thus into their reification and manipulation? There is no doubt that it is difficult to avoid such a trap, but not impossible, as these three strategies have suggested. Evidence of the success of a combination of two of these (the interpretive method and the ethical approach) may be found in *Beyond Hindu and Muslim*, a compelling study by Peter Gottschalk (2000) of the multiple identities discernible in the narratives employed by villagers in the Arampur area of northern India. Gottschalk challenges the adequacy of communal identifiers – Hindu and Muslim – to describe the reality of social relations in

India: 'My own work asserts that villagers share identities other than those of "Hindu" and "Muslim". These include affiliations with class, caste, family, devotion, gender, and territory.' (Gottschalk 2000, p. 8.)[46] His analysis of narratives then reveals how group identities form around a variety of shared interests in addition to religious identification.[47] In fact, the latter masks cross-cutting identities:

> To what degree can Sufi shrine veneration be accurately described as "Islamic" when so many non-Muslims participate and so many Muslims disparage such activities? When I identify Shastri Brahm's temple as "Hindu," don't I establish expectations as to whom its clientèle includes and does not include? ... It becomes all too easy ... to simplify the portrayal of a religious tradition [and community] to the point that social contexts shared with members of other traditions [and communities] disappear. (Gottschalk 2000, p. 178)

But is it really necessary to go to such lengths to resist reifying and giving primacy to religions and the communities associated with them? I have come to think that it really is important to do so in order that we may avoid contributing to the hardening of cultural boundaries and the ideological encapsulation of communities, which, in turn, may set individuals and groups against one another and may silence marginal and subaltern voices. We are obliged to understand the embeddedness of scholarly activity in citizenship, the imperative of scholarly accountability, and the importance of thinking critically and responsibly about the social and political consequences of our work on religion.

The importance of an ethical and engaged scholarship came into sharp focus following the tragic events of 11 September 2001, and their destabilising aftermath. News broke of the attacks in the United States on the World Trade Center and the Pentagon as we were actually gathered at the BASR/EASR conference to deliberate on the theme of 'religion and community' (see note 42). The incidents were too terrible, our information too unreliable, and the shock too great for us to make a considered response during the conference itself. But it was not long before 'Islamic extremism' emerged in the media as a probable explanation for the terror. Globally, we witnessed the hardening of cultural boundaries, the re-emergence of communities of culture, and the construction of competing moral high grounds through the ideological use of terms such as good and evil, civilisation, fundamentalism, freedom, crusade. We seemed all too quickly locked into the false alternatives of Islam versus the West.[48] This rhetorical oversimplification of the issues then created further fear and mistrust, negated shared grief and common interests, and fuelled extreme hatred on all sides. It also masked the real and complex issues – historical, economic, social, political, as well as religious – that lay behind the original attack and the various responses to it.

Like *The Satanic Verses* controversy of the early 1990s, the public accounts of this event and the consequent war in Afghanistan offer scholars the opportunity to analyse the representation of religion, its contemporary ideological role, and centrality in debates about community. Will we rise to the challenge and help students and members of the wider public to question the rhetorical and oppositional characterisation of *Islam* and *the Muslim community, fundamentalism, the West* and *liberalism*, or will our work further entrench boundaries and reify dominant traditions? We have a choice. At the very least, we should give serious thought to the consequences of the construction we place on events in our research and writing for the public understanding of religion and its role in social and political affairs.

(First published as Occasional Paper No. 22, 2002)

Notes

1   I am indebted to Gerd Baumann (1996, p. 14) for this reference.

2   Sociologists have held differing opinions about the use of the terms 'modernity', 'late-modernity' and 'postmodernity', and modernism and postmodernism. For a short discussion, see 'Modernity', by Krishan Kumar, and 'Modernism and postmodernism' by Tom Pinkney in Outhwaite and Bottomore (1993).

3   This phrase is the English translation of the title of Maffesoli's 1988 book, *Les Temps de Tribus: Le declin de l'individualisme dans les sociétés de masse* (Paris, Klincksieck).

4   However, some recent books that set out the terms of the contemporary study of religions have ignored 'community' e.g. Taylor (1998), Braun and McCutcheon (2000).

5   For examples, see McCutcheon (1997), Flood (1999), Fitzgerald (2000) and articles in the North American journal *Method and Theory in the Study of Religion*.

6   Particularly the disciplines of sociology, political studies, and anthropology. Some notable works in these fields which give special attention to 'community' include Anderson (1983), Cohen (1985), Etzioni (1995), Baumann (1996), Mellor and Shilling (1997), Rheingold (2000), Bauman (2001), Putnam (2001) and the works of Eade (1989, 1997).

7   Ward discusses the attitudes held by religions about community, and presents a set of ideal types of community associated with different religions (2000). Religions, he writes, 'are a major means of inculcating a sense of community, so important to human flourishing' (2001:17).

8   The Community Relations Commission was established in the late 1960s. After the Race Relations Act of 1976, it was succeeded by the Commission for Racial Equality. At a local government level, Councils for Community Relations were formed. These were succeeded by Race Equality Councils as the political mood shifted from the problematisation of community relations to that of racial justice, and from paternalism to positive action.

9   It was these books that introduced a more critical note into the study of community. As well as discussing definitions and theories of community, and analysing previous American and European studies, Bell and Newby (1971, 1974) identified community study as a method. They criticised community studies for their subjectivity, descriptiveness, lack of enumeration, and incomparability. Following Stacey (1969) and Elias and Scotson (1965), they stressed the importance of institutional interrelationships, and the issues of power and conflict in the study of communities.

10   In the 1969 report on British race relations, *Colour and Citizenship* (Rose and associates 1969), religion and other aspects of the culture of minority communities were largely ignored, though the response of British churches to 'the newcomers' was considered. Rex and Moore's study of Sparkbrook (1967) was notable for taking religious congregations and organisations seriously in depicting relationships in this 'zone of transition'. Neither was religion treated as a significant variable in articles selected for the first year's issues of *New Community* (1971–2). However, in the special issue on ethnic minorities in Britain in Volume 1:5 (1972), we see religion being identified with community in the case of the Sikh *Jats* and Ismailis (though in neither case was religious belief or practice discussed in any depth).

11   Several works published in the monograph series (est. 1986) of the Community Religions Project (CRP) are worthy of note here. Barton (1986, p. 10) wrote that 'It is not meaningless to speak of "the Bengali community", but it is a community defined by nothing more precise than very broad ethnic, religious and geographical factors... So the community in Bradford is new and quite different from the long-established village communities in which most of the migrants were born'. Knott (1986, p. 53) discussed the meanings of the term, commenting that, 'The Council for Community Relations, local "dialogue" groups..., and the press refer to Sikhs, Hindus and Muslims as "religious communities". However, although the term "community" is used in a spirit of polite goodwill, it is, to some degree, inappropriate and inaccurate as a description of the South Asian groups concerned'. Kalsi (1992) utilised the term 'community' in relation to the Sikhs of Leeds and Bradford, but discussed in detail the many social and religious subdivisions – of caste and sect – which cut across them and rendered them problematic. Geaves (1996) critically assessed both 'community' and '*ummah*' in relation to South Asian Muslims in Britain, asking in what sense, if at all, it was possible to refer to 'the Muslim community'.

12   In an article in *The Observer*, Peter Wilby wrote of contemporary British political rhetoric, '...the word "community" is repeated constantly: we have "active community", "renewal of community", "core values of community", "fragile web of community", "idea of communitiy"...' (Wilby 2000). Evidence that this is more than rhetoric, however, may be seen in various Government policies and initiatives introduced between 1997 and 2001, such as the New Deal for Communities, Community Investment Tax, Active Community Unit, Neighbourhood Renewal Fund, Experience Corps, Sure Start, and regeneration partnerships (with local faith communities).

13   However, it is social commentators in the United States who have most thoroughly depicted and charted the demise of community (e.g. Etzioni 1995; Putnam 2001). British sociologists have differed on the extent to which Britain merely follows in American footsteps.

14   'Equal worth, responsibility, community – these values are fundamental to my political creed', said Prime Minister Tony Blair in a speech to the Christian Socialist Movement in March 2001. In that speech, he made reference to these ideas in the context of discussing faith in politics and the relationship between faith communities, their organisations, and government at both a local and national level (Blair 2001). Blair's socio-political values are derived in part from his engagement with the ideas of American sociologist Amitai Etzioni, author of *The Spirit of Community: Rights, Responsibilities and the Communitarian Agenda*, first published in 1993. In the 1995 edition of his book, Etzioni included a 'Preface to the British Edition' in which he stated, 'To argue that the contemporary United Kingdom need not be concerned with the development of strong communities for fear that they turn out to be domineering – say, run by right-wing religious groups – is like arguing that we should forego heating in the winter because a hot summer may follow. The West is in the cold season of excessive individualism and yearns for the warmth of community to allow human relations to blossom' (1995, p. *x*). Key aspects of communitarianism are the raising up of responsibilities in the context of a rights-based society, and a focus on the moral voice. For a clear statement of this agenda, see Etzioni (1995, pp. 1–2).

15   The Commission on the Future of Multi-Ethnic Britain was set up in 1998 by the Runnymede Trust, an independent think-tank, with Bhikhu Parekh as Chair. The report of the Commission (Runnymede Trust 2000) was edited by Robin Richardson.

16   The report of the Commission begins with a preface by Parekh which describes Britain as 'both a community of citizens and a community of communities, both a liberal and a multicultural society' (Runnymede Trust 2000: p. *ix*).

17   Chapter 17 of the Commission's report deals with religion and belief (Runnymede Trust 2000, pp. 235–249).

18   This identification is discussed by, for example, Morris (1968), Pandey (1990), Appadurai (1993), van der Veer (1994), King (1999) and Ballard (1999). Gottschalk (2000, p. 19) questions whether colonialism is a sufficient explanation for religious categorisation and communalism.

19   Bauman (2001, p. 1): 'Words have meanings: some words, however, also have a "feel"'. The word "community" is one of them'.

20   In 1955, the American sociologist G.A. Hillery cited ninety-four separate definitions of community. These are discussed by Bell and Newby (1971).

21   Baumann italicises the terms 'community' and 'culture' when referring to Southallians' own use of these terms (as opposed to scholarly uses). I have continued this practice in my discussion of his ideas.

22   Baumann's analysis builds on the anthropological approach articulated succinctly by Cohen (1985). Cohen did not utilise the term 'imagined communities' (which we identify with the work of Benedict Anderson on nationalism), but he wrote in similar terms, stressing the ideological construction of such social formations: 'Our argument has been ... that community is largely in the mind' (*ibid*, p. 114). Communities, to Cohen, were matters of feeling and thinking, reflexively created through the symbolic construction of boundaries.

23   For further discussion of the relationship between culture and community see the debate about multiculturalism, especially Sahgal and Yuval-Davis ('Introduction', 1992), Modood and Werbner (1997), Baumann (1999), Parekh (2000) and Bauman (2001).

24   An example of the former was those Muslims who were aware that their 'local community of believers was divided into a variety of contending cultures' (Baumann 1996, p. 189), whilst an example of the latter was those 'communities' of both Hindus and Sikhs of Punjabi heritage who shared certain cultural interests relating to food, music, or devotion to *sants*.

25   Parekh (2000) had more opportunity to evaluate the complexities of the relationship between culture (including religion) and community than the Commission did in its report. He conceded, for example, that cultures are dynamic, and that 'every culture is internally varied, speaks in several voices, and its range of interpretive possibility is often indeterminate' (*ibid*, p. 144). However, at other points in his discussion, he wrote of cultures as if they were both intrinsically linked to communities and monolithic (*viz* the notion of a community having a 'shared culture'): 'a cultural community has two dimensions, cultural and communal. It has a content in the form of a particular culture, and a communal basis in the form of a group of men and women who share that culture' (*ibid*, p. 154); 'although culture and society are inseparable in the sense that there is neither a society without a culture nor a culture which is not associated with some society, the two have different focus and orientation' (*ibid*, p. 146). This underlines the difficulty we all face in our attempt to avoid reifying, solidifying and homogenising these terms (community and culture) and the groups, beliefs and practices to which they refer.

26   See Southall Black Sisters (1990), and Sahgal and Yuval-Davis (1992, especially the Introduction and Sahgal's essay on 'Secular spaces'). The use of terms such as 'fundamentalist' and 'orthodox' to describe the cultures of those within British religio-ethnic communities is suggestive of an inadequately nuanced conception of 'culture' in its religious form (e.g. *ibid*. pp. 3–7, 8–11, 179–183). There is a suggestion that it is only secular spaces which provide a place from which religious culture can be viewed. What is absent is the idea that there are many linked and overlapping cultures (as well as communities) associated with 'the Muslim community' and other such 'communities', and that these may provide differing cultural viewpoints and spaces. See Dwyer (1999) for a discussion of these issues in relation to questions of identity among young British Muslim women.

27   In my own work in the late 1980s, for example, I sought to get beneath the overarching conceptions of ethnic and religious community to the strategies of conflict and cooperation which constituted them (Knott 1988).

28   Baumann (1999) is insistent on the need to understand and critique the process of cultural essentialisation that has been at the heart of multiculturalism, but without giving up on the project itself: 'Multiculturalism is not the old concept of culture multiplied by the number of groups that exist, but a new, and internally plural, praxis of culture applied to oneself and to others' (*ibid*, p. *vii*).

29   In fact, she presses for an alternative methodological approach to the study of identity, focused on commodities and consumption, which places person-object relationships rather than communities at the forefront of our studies (Caglar 1997, pp. 180–183; see also Bauman 1992, pp. 222–225 and Urry 1995, Part III).

30   Gender, power and community: see Sahgal and Yuval-Davis (1992); Jeffery and Basu (1998), particularly articles by Ritu Menon and Tanika Sarkar; Dwyer (1999). Virtual communities: see Rheingold (2000) and the bibliography therein. Nationalism and community: Anderson (1983), Ignatieff (1993). Congregation and community: see Vertovec (1992), Nye (1993) and Becker (1999). Diaspora and transnational communities: see Vertovec and Cohen (1999) and the website of the ESRC Transnational Communities Programme (www.transcomm.ox.ac.uk). 'Diaspora' is perhaps the earliest and most long-standing term for a form of 'imagined community'. For a useful discussion of the distinction between transnational community and diaspora, see Vertovec (2000).

31   See also the account of the history of the sociology of community from Tönnies to the globalisation theorists in Featherstone (1995, chapter 7).

32   See the bibliography (Eade et al. 1997, pp. 181–189) for references to these and other works.

33   At the 2000 IAHR Congress, Rachel Dwyer spoke of the 'religio-scape', borrowing Appadurai's suffix to account for the global formation of the Swaminarayan Hindu Mission.

34   For example, in a recent paper Jacqui Stewart (2001), a British Christian theologian, challenges current Christian embodiments, practices and language of community in the light of contemporary social theory.

35   Bauman (2001, p. 3) refers to this lament as 'paradise lost or a paradise still hoped to be found. "Community" stands for the kind of world which is not, regrettably, available to us'. To Bauman, the desire for community is the search for 'safety in an insecure world' (2001; book subtitle).

36   See Mellor and Shilling (1997, chapter six), for a full discussion of these two types.

37   A juxtaposition utilised by Ray Pahl in a radio discussion on community (BBC Radio 4, September 2001).

38   Hervieu-Léger wrote earlier about 'emotional' communities in her 1990 book, *De l'émotion en religion: renouveaux et traditions*, with Françoise Champion.

39   Most sociological conceptions of religion, she suggests, have focused on either an exclusive or an inclusive definition of the sacred, which has led on the one hand to an unhelpful intellectual division between religious and other social groups, hence to the juxtaposition of religion and sociology, and on the other to an openness which has made comparative analysis problematic. Hervieu-Léger (2000) discusses these definitional problems in Part I as a precursor to offering her own analytical method in Parts II and III of her book.

40   Hervieu-Léger's argument on this point goes beyond the idea of sporting and musical occasions as religious surrogates or analogies. Using examples of a British football match (from Marc Augé) and the Hillsborough tragedy (from Grace Davie), she explains that such sacred experiences may demonstrate the potential for becoming religious whilst remaining in the domain of the secular (2000, pp. 102–106).

41   Despite the title of his book (*Religion in English Everyday Life*) Timothy Jenkins (1999, pp. 12–14) resists the terms religion and religious, preferring to write about 'the human aspiration to flourish' or 'the desire to be human in a particular form'.

42   When I delivered the first, oral version of this chapter as a keynote address at the BASR/ EASR conference in Cambridge in 2001, this may have seemed a sudden, even irresponsible, place to end. But where better to stop a keynote address than with a question? My afterword offers aspects of an answer.

43   I am not suggesting that I have always been aware of such pitfalls myself, or, even that, if and when I have been, I have succeeded in avoiding them. Critics of my work in the special issue on British Hindu communalism in *Ethnic and Racial Studies* (2000) have claimed that I have contributed to the formation of a dominant ideology of Hinduism. Admittedly, in preparing *Hinduism: A Very Short Introduction* (Knott 1998) I found it extremely difficult to write about the religious traditions which cluster under the heading of Hinduism without reifying it. My approach was to argue for the complexity and multiplicity of Hinduisms in India and beyond, and for the critique of Hinduism from the margins.

44   For a further discussion of this methodological strategy, see Knott (2000).

45   cf. Baumann's (1996) treatment of Southallians' use of dominant and demotic discourses.

46   See Gottschalk (2000, chapter 1: 'Multiple identities, singular representations') for a discussion of the history of religious representation in India.

47   His ideas are informed by Paul Ricoeur's theory that shared interests are expressed through common narratives (Gottschalk 2000, pp. 5–6). This theory is also pursued for the study of religions by Flood (1999).

48   This communalising process was witnessed in Europe in the indiscriminate attacks on Muslim women wearing *hijab* by white youths, and reached a peak on 28 October 2001 when eighteen Pakistani Christians were killed by Islamic extremists in a church in Pakistan in a revenge attack for American military action in Afghanistan.

Bibliography

Albrow, Martin 1997. 'Travelling beyond local cultures: Socioscapes in a global city', in J. Eade, (ed.), *Living the Global City: Globalization as Local Process*, London: Routledge, pp. 37–55.

Anderson, Benedict 1983. *Imagined Communities: Reflections on the Origin and Spread of Nationalism*, London: Verso.

Appadurai, Arjun 1993. 'Number in the colonial imagination', in C. Breckenridge and Peter van der Veer, *Orientalism and the Post-Colonial Predicament*, Philadelphia: Philadelphia Press, pp. 314–339.

Ballard, Roger 1999. '*Panth, kismet, dharm te quam*: Four dimensions in Punjabi religion', in Pritam Singh and Shinder Thandi, (eds), *Religion and Globalisation: The Punjabi Experience*, Delhi: Oxford University Press, pp. 7–37.

Barton, Stephen 1986. *The Bengali Muslims of Bradford: A study of their observance of Islam with special reference to the function of the mosque and the work of the imam*, Community Religions Project Monograph Series, University of Leeds, Community Religions Project.

Bauman, Zygmunt 1992. *Intimations of Postmodernity*, London and New York: Routledge.

———— 2001. *Community: Seeking Safety in an Insecure World*, Cambridge: Polity.

Baumann, Gerd 1996. *Contesting Culture: Discourses of Identity in Multi-Ethnic London*, Cambridge: Cambridge University Press.

———— 1999. *The Multicultural Riddle: Rethinking National, Ethnic, and Religious Identities*, London: Routledge.

Becker, Penny Edgell 1999. *Congregations in Conflict: Cultural Models of Local Religious Life*, Cambridge: Cambridge University Press.

Bell, Colin and Newby, Howard 1971. *Community Studies*, London: George Allen and Unwin.

———— (eds) 1974. *The Sociology of Community: A Selection of Readings*, London: Frank Cass.

Blair, Tony 2001. 'Faith in politics', speech by Tony Blair to the Christian Socialist Movement, London, www.labour.org.uk (29 March 2001).

Braun, Willi and McCutcheon, Russell (eds) 2000. *A Guide to the Study of Religion*, London: Cassell.

Caglar, Ayse 1997. 'Hyphenated identities and the limits of culture', in Tariq Modood and Pnina Werbner (eds), *The Politics of Multiculturalism in the New Europe*, London: Zed Books, pp. 169–185.

Cohen, Anthony P. 1985. *The Symbolic Construction of Community*, Chichester: Ellis Horwood, and London and New York: Tavistock.

Community Religions Project, *Monographs, Research Papers* and *Working Papers*, 1976–2001, Leeds: University of Leeds.

Davie, Grace 1996. 'Religion and modernity: the work of Danièle Hervieu-Léger', in Kieran Flanagan and Peter C. Jupp, (eds), *Postmodernity, Sociology and Religion*, London: Macmillan, pp. 101–117.

Dürrschmidt, Jörg 1997. 'The delinking of locale and milieu: On the situatedness of extended milieux in a global environment', in J. Eade (ed.), *Living the Global City: Globalization as Local Process*, London: Routledge, pp. 56–72.

Dwyer, C. 1999. 'Contradictions of community: questions of identity for young British Muslim women', *Environment and Planning*, 31, pp. 53–68.

Eade, John 1989. *The Politics of Community: The Bangladeshi Community in East London*, Aldershot: Avebury.

——— (ed.) 1997. *Living the Global City: Globalization as Local Process*, London: Routledge.

Elias, Norbert and Scotson, J.L. 1965. *The Established and the Outsider*, London: Frank Cass.

ESRC Transnational Communities Programme, www.transcomm.ox.ac.uk (October 2001).

Etzioni, A. 1995. *The Spirit of Community*, London, Fontana [first published 1993].

Featherstone, Michael 1995. *Undoing Culture: Globalization, Postmodernism and Identity*, London: Sage.

Fitzgerald, Timothy 2000. *The Ideology of Religious Studies*, New York, Oxford: Oxford University Press.

Flood, Gavin 1999. *Beyond Phenomenology: Rethinking the Study of Religion*, London: Cassell.

Geaves, Ron 1996. *Sectarian Influences Within Islam in Britain with reference to the Concepts of 'Ummah' and 'Community'*, Community Religions Project Monograph Series, University of Leeds, Community Religions Project.

Giddens, Anthony 1990. *The Consequences of Modernity*, Cambridge: Polity.

Gottschalk, Peter 2000. *Beyond Hindu and Muslim: Multiple Identity in Narratives from Village India*, Oxford, New York: Oxford University Press.

Hillery Jr. G.A. 1955. 'Definitions of community: areas of agreement', *Rural Sociology*, 20.

Hoggart, Richard 1957. *The Uses of Literacy*, London: Chatto and Windus.

Hervieu-Léger, Danièle 2000. *Religion as a Chain of Memory*, Cambridge: Polity [1993].

Ignatieff, Michael 1992. 'Why "community" is a dishonest word', *The Observer*, 3 May, editorial page.

——— 1993. *Blood and Belonging: Journeys into the New Nationalism*, London: Vintage.

Jeffery, Patricia and Amrita Basu, (eds) 1998. *Appropriating Gender: Women's Activism and Politicized Religion in South Asia*, London: Routledge.

Jenkins, Timothy 1999. *Religion in English Everyday Life: An Ethnographic Approach*, New York and London: Berghahn Books.

Kalsi, Sewa Singh 1992. *The Evolution of a Sikh Community in Britain*, Community Religions Project Monograph Series, University of Leeds, Community Religions Project.

King, Richard 1999. *Orientalism and Religion: Postcolonial Theory, India and the Mystic East*, London: Routledge.

Knott, Kim 1984. 'Community religions at the University of Leeds', *Community Religions Project Research Papers (NS)*, 1, Leeds: University of Leeds.

—— 1986. *Hinduism in Leeds: A Study of Religious Practice in the Indian Hindu Community and in Hindu-Related Groups*, Community Religions Project Monograph Series, University of Leeds, Community Religions Project.

—— 1988. 'Strategies of survival among South Asian religions in Britain: parallel developments, conflict and cooperation', Chuo Academic Research Institute, *Conflict and Cooperation Between Contemporary Religious Groups*, Tokyo, Chuo Academic Research Institute, pp. 95–128.

—— 1998. *Hinduism: A Very Short Introduction*, Oxford: Oxford University Press.

—— 2000. 'Community and locality in the study of religions', in T. Jensen and M. Rothstein, *Secular Theories in the Study of Religions*, Copenhagen, Denmark: Museum Tusculanum Press.

Maffesoli, Michel 1996. *The Time of the Tribes: The Decline of Individualism in Mass Society*, London: Sage [1988].

McCutcheon, Russell 1997. *Manufacturing Religion: The Discourse on Sui Generis Religion and the Politics of Nostalgia*, New York and Oxford: Oxford University Press.

Mellor, Philip and Shilling, Chris 1997. *Re-Forming the Body: Religion, Community and Modernity*, London: Sage.

Modood, Tariq and Werbner, Pnina (eds) 1997. *The Politics of Multiculturalism in the New Europe*, London: Zed Books.

Morris, H.S. 1968. *The Indians in Uganda*, London: Weidenfeld and Nicholson.

Nye, Malory 1993. 'Temple congregations and communities: Hindu constructions in Edinburgh', *New Community*, 19, pp. 201–215.

Outhwaite, William and Bottomore, Tom 1993. *The Blackwell Dictionary of Twentieth Century Social Thought*, Oxford: Blackwell.

Pandey, Gyanendra 1990. *The Construction of Communalism in Colonial North India*, Delhi: Oxford University Press.

Parekh, Bhikhu 2000. *Rethinking Multiculturalism: Cultural Diversity and Political Theory*, London: Macmillan.

Putnam, Robert D. 2001. *Bowling Alone: The Collapse and Revival of American Community*, Touchstone.

Pye, Michael 1976. [Untitled], *Community Religions Project Working Paper*, 1, Leeds: University of Leeds.

—— 1977. 'A paper presented at the Senior Seminar, 16 March 1977', *Community Religions Project Working Paper*, 3, Leeds: University of Leeds.

Rex, John and Moore, Robert 1967. *Race, Community and Conflict: A Study of Sparkbrook*, London: Oxford University Press.

Rheingold, Howard 2000. *The Virtual Community: Homesteading on the Electronic Frontier*, revised edition, Cambridge MA, and London: The MIT Press [1993].

Richardson, Robin 2001. 'Multi-ethnic Britain: A community of communities and citizens', SHAP Working Party on World Religions in Education, *Living Community*, London: SHAP, pp. 53–55.

Rose, E.J.B. and associates 1969. *Colour and Citizenship: A Report on British Race Relations*, Oxford: Institute for Race Relations.

Runnymede Trust 2000. *The Future of Multi-Ethnic Britain: Report of the Commission*, London: Profile Books.

Sahgal, Gita and Yuval-Davis, Nira (eds) 1992. *Refusing Holy Orders: Women and Fundamentalism in Britain*, London: Virago.

SHAP Working Party on World Religions in Education, 2001. *Living Community*, London: SHAP.

Southall Black Sisters 1990. *Against the Grain: A Celebration of Survival and Struggle*, London: Southall Black Sisters.

Stacey, Margaret 1969. 'The myth of community studies', *British Journal of Sociology*, 20:2, pp. 134–147.

Stewart, Jacqui 2001. 'Sheep and goats: a theological and sociological critique of the concept of community', paper presented at the Norwich Cathedral Institute, summer 2001 (submitted to *Political Theology*).

Taylor, Mark C. (ed.) 1998. *Critical Terms for Religious Studies*, Chicago and London: University of Chicago Press.

ter Haar, Gerrie (ed.) 1998. *Strangers and Sojourners: Religious Communities in Diaspora*, Leuven: Peeters.

Urry, John 1995. *Consuming Places*, London: Routledge.

van der Veer 1994. *Religious Nationalism: Hindus and Muslims in India*, Berkeley: University of California Press.

Vertovec, Steven 1992. 'Community and congregation in London Hindu temples: divergent trends', *New Community*, 18, pp. 251–264.

——— 2000. 'Religion and diaspora', a paper presented at the conference on *New Landscapes of Religion in the West*, School of Geography, University of Oxford, and forthcoming in Peter Antes, Armin W. Geertz and Randi Warne (eds), *New Approaches to the Study of Religion*, Berlin and New York: Verlag de Gruyter.

Vertovec, Steven and Cohen, Robin (eds) 1999. *Migration, Diasporas and Transnationalism*, Aldershot: Ashgate.

Ward, Keith 2000. *Religion and Community*, Oxford: Oxford University Press.

——— 2001. 'Religion and community', SHAP Working Party on World Religions in Education, *Living Community*, London: SHAP, pp. 15–17.

Wilby, Peter 2000. 'Blair's warm blanket looks threadbare', *The Observer*, 11 June 2000.

Williams, Raymond 1976 *Keywords: A Vocabulary of Culture and Society*, London: Fontana/Croom Helm.

Young, Michael and Willmott, Peter 1957. *Family and Kinship in East London*, Harmondsworth: Penguin.

CHAPTER 6

Chosen People: The Concept of Diaspora in the Modern World

Gerrie ter Haar

Introduction

People from all over Africa have settled in all parts of Western Europe in substantial numbers over the past thirty years.[1] In many cases, it is the political and economic situation in Africa which forces people to move outside their country to look for work and security. From the little we know it is clear that the circumstances of migration are a vital factor in shaping the religious life of those concerned.[2]

Many African migrants in Europe belong to one of the two major religious traditions, Islam or Christianity. In both cases we lack substantial information on the religious dimension of their life in Europe. We may feel reasonably well informed about Muslims in Europe more generally (for example Shadid and van Koningsveld eds, 1996), including those from North Africa, but we have little specific information on the religious life of Muslim communities in Europe which originate in sub-Saharan Africa. One may think of the large Somali communities in various countries of Europe, including the Netherlands; of the Malian and Senegalese communities in France, or East African Muslim communities in Greece. The same is true for African Christian communities in Europe, including the Ethiopian community representing the ancient Coptic tradition, or the Kimbanguist Church representing the independent church tradition in sub-Saharan Africa. The most striking developments are presently found in the large number of pentecostal and evangelical congregations which have recently been established mostly by West Africans. In the United Kingdom such developments have a longer history than in most of continental Europe. In Britain, Nigerians in particular have been founding new and independent churches since the mid-1960s (Killingray 1994, p. 19), while on the European continent the foundation of new congregations has been a development of only the last few years which can be largely ascribed to Christian believers from Ghana (ter Haar 1995b).

The growth of African Christian communities on the European continent is one of the most striking developments in the recent religious life of Western

Europe. Examples are Germany, Italy, Belgium and Holland, to mention some front-runners. This is certainly true of the Netherlands, where African-initiated churches now exist in many cities. The majority are in Amsterdam, where there are almost forty such churches, mostly in one particular district, the Bijlmermeer, which is known as a home of migrant communities (ter Haar 1996). Many of these new churches have been established in the empty spaces under the multi-storey car parks that are situated under the tower blocks in the district. While previously invisible and unheard of, the world came to know about them after a tragic accident one Sunday in October 1992 when a cargo plane crashed into some of these towerblocks.

Any analysis of these new religious developments should be seen in the light of the global process of migration, which defines the lives of many Africans in Europe. International migration provokes strong political response in most countries of Europe today. One of the most disturbing aspects of European immigration policy is its tendency towards the exclusion of black people. This has already led to the European Union being described as 'fortress Europe' (Dunkwu 1993), a stronghold for whites to defend against the 'surging' crowd from Africa.[3] The religious response of Africans to this situation is often ignored or minimised by Western observers, if not dismissed altogether. Alternatively, the role of religion in the life of African migrants is reduced to an exotic aspect of life that may seem colourful against the background of Western secular life. Or again, their religious expression is simply related to a 'traditional' background in Africa. None of these approaches take as its starting-point the religious life of Africans in Europe, which to many migrants is a central feature of their existence.

It is against this background that I want to look at the concept of diaspora as it is often used today in either a popular sense or among academics with regard to religious minority groups. In doing so I will focus on the African diaspora communities, notably the Christian ones, taking the Netherlands as my example. Terminology is important. All writers, to some extent, use a vocabulary which reflects their own cultural attributes and ideology, and it is important to be aware of this (ter Haar 1995c). It is interesting, for example, to see that the common notion of 'scattering' which is connected to the diaspora concept refers to members of a religious community who are living among a *different* faith community, such as in the case of Muslims or Hindus living in a European country shaped by Christian tradition and culture. The application of that same idea to Christians coming from Africa, as is happening today, has serious consequences for their situation in the West. It obscures the fact that African Christians living in Europe are not adherents of some strange unknown religion, but are *Christians*. The general connotation is for people described as being 'in diaspora' to be basically unhappy and pitiful, because they find themselves in a place where they neither belong nor desire to be. As a minority group, they are commonly believed to link up with their 'own' people at home, that is in their original homelands, and thus retain what is believed to be their 'own' identity, than to link up with the majority in their new homelands. This appears to be also the case even if in the migrants' own opinion they share at least a common faith, as African Christians do. For ideological and sociological reasons, therefore, it is important to look into the meanings of the diaspora concept as we use it to refer to religious minority groups (see also Baumann 1995).

The Concept of Diaspora

The concept of diaspora has been marked by the indelible experience of exile as part of Jewish history. It originally referred to Jews living outside Judea, as they had been doing since the sixth century BCE after the city of Jerusalem had been conquered by the armies of the Babylonian empire.[4] The word 'diaspora' was subsequently coined by the makers of the Greek translation of the Hebrew Bible, the so-called Septuagint, to designate a specific group of people who find themselves in a state of being scattered. It appears, however, that some connotations which have become attached to the word 'diaspora' are modern. Tromp (1995, pp. 2–3) has pointed out that it is often taken for granted that the Jews who lived outside Judea experienced their migrant status as undesirable, and that Jerusalem became the symbol of their happiness and their longing to live in the land of their God. These Jews, he argues, are generally understood to have felt homeless and uprooted in antiquity. Their environment, believed to be fundamentally hostile to the Jewish way of life, would on the one hand have allured them because of the social and economic advantages assimilation seemed to offer, but on the other hand repelled them because of the threat to their proper, traditional identity represented by cutural assimilation.

According to Tromp, this is a very misleading picture, which is also incompatible with the self-perception of the Jews living outside Judea. He shows how in the Old Testament the word 'diaspora' is used in such a way as to bring out the omnipotence, righteousness and mercy of God, as the one who graciously gathers the dispersed. All emphasis is on the acts of God, and the term, therefore, tells us very little about the dispersed themselves and how they experienced their situation (*ibid*, p. 11). The term 'diaspora' is primarily used to praise God who has the power to gather the scattered, and not to describe the pitiful situation of people living abroad. Moreover, the ancient Jews in the diaspora were not at all in a deplorable situation, as Tromp shows on the basis of some historical examples. The life of Jewish minorities in some of the main urban centres in the Hellenistic and Roman empires demonstrates not only how Jews living outside Judea were firmly settled in the lands and cities where they lived, but also how, in spite of being Jews, they were socially and legally accepted by the non-Jewish inhabitants. Tromp's conclusion is that these Jews had no particular longing for Jerusalem, which was to them a foreign city, in the same way as Judea was to them a foreign country, but that they regarded the very places where they were living as their home.

This, of course, has some consequence for the question of identity. What constituted a Jewish identity in these circumstances? One important aspect is that Jews in the so-called diaspora were not easily recognisable as such. An outsider could not distinguish a Jew from a non-Jew unless the Jew made himself known as such. As Tromp points out, they were not racially distinct, they did not wear special clothes, they often had quite ordinary names and they all spoke ordinary Greek (*ibid*, p. 18). In other words, Jews living outside Judea could only be designated as Jews on the basis of their *self-definition*. A problem enters where others – in this case, non-Jews – come to define Jewish identity, such as was the case in ancient Alexandria. When the Romans conquered the city in 30 BCE the position of the Jewish minority changed drastically. The Roman administration introduced a poll-tax, from which the Greek citizens of Alexandria were exempt. This, in turn, required the inhabitants of the city to prove their Greek descent, which set in motion a process of ethnic labelling with political implications. The Jews, who before had had no reason to hide their Jewishness, felt suddenly degraded to second-class citizens. They therefore resisted the new measure and demanded – as Jews – to be acknowledged as legitimate citizens of the city, equal to the original Greeks. From then there is a development in Jewish writings which insists on keeping the Jewish law, in contrast to a number of non-Jewish writings attacking the Jewish way of life. In short, as Tromp concludes, the new Roman polity created an ethnic strife which caused Jews to stress their otherness, now that they had been confronted with their distinction from the non-Jews which had formerly been taken for granted (*ibid*, p. 19). Due to new policy, it was no longer possible to be Greek and Jew at the same time. As a result, the Jews began to defend an exclusive collective Jewish identity which had, in fact, been forced upon them; a process which initiated an increasing estrangement between Jews and non-Jews and led to violence (*ibid*, p. 20).

The African Diaspora

The Jewish example is very instructive because of its bearing on the situation of Africans today living outside the African continent. The use of the term 'diaspora' in reference to peoples of African origin clearly draws on the Jewish experience, tailoring it specifically to the situation of Africans scattered outside the African continent. Its use in this context is rather new. Although its origins may be traced to the nineteenth century,[5] it came into fashion around the 1960s, notably among African-American scholars or referring to the African-

American population, and is also referred to at times as the 'black' diaspora. Historical research in the United States has shown that there is a relationship between the use and development of the term 'African diaspora', the dismantling of the European colonial empires and the emergence of independent nations in Africa. Before that era, the idea may be traced to the works of some nineteenth-century historians and other writers who applied the Biblical concept of the diaspora. It is often argued that the concept of the *African* diaspora can be traced to the Bible, notably to the text of Psalms 68:31 which speaks of Ethiopia stretching out her hands unto God which – we may note in passing – is also the text underlying the emergence of the first independent churches in Africa at the turn of the twentieth century, in South Africa, known as 'Ethiopian churches' (Sundkler 1961). Another relevant Biblical reference in this context is the story in the Acts of the Apostles (Ch. 8: 26–39) which relates the encounter between the Ethiopian eunuch and Queen Candace.

In the 1950s and 1960s the African diaspora emerged as an explicit concept in the English-speaking world; it found a counterpart in the French-speaking world around the same time in the development of the concept of *négritude*, advanced by the former President of Senegal, Léopold Sédar Senghor. From the 1960s onwards the term 'African diaspora' has become a well-known concept, although often used in an unscholarly manner. George Shepperson, for example, a British expert on the African diaspora, points to the fact that the historical distinction between diaspora and exile in the Jewish tradition is often overlooked. 'Exile' always implies forced or involuntary dispersion, whereas 'diaspora' includes some element of voluntary migration. To overlook that difference, in his view, would connect the study of the 'African diaspora' exclusively to the study of enforced dispersal, that is to slavery (Shepperson 1993). But the term 'African diaspora', as it is often used today, is problematic for a number of reasons, mostly because the concept has been shaped by the American context and since it is not clear what precisely we mean by it in the context of Europe. In the United States, the term is commonly used to refer to all citizens of African descent, that is black Americans, many of whom today consciously refer to themselves as African-Americans. They share a collective memory of the transatlantic slave trade which forcibly expelled millions of Africans from the continent of their birth.[6] The intrinsic connection of the African diaspora with the history of the slave trade constitutes the essential characteristic of the diaspora concept in both North and South America. African diaspora studies are a standard feature of the academic syllabus in North America and are generally considered in the light of this specific history. In 1979, Howard University in Washington established the First African Diaspora Studies Institute (FADSI), bringing together for the first time scholars from Africa, the Americas, and Europe to discuss various aspects of researching and teaching African diaspora studies (Harris 1982, p. 4).

Discussion of the applicability of the term diaspora, therefore, has been taking place in the United States for some considerable time. Although there seems to be a broad consensus regarding the use of the term, there is also a clear awareness that this may encourage irrelevant comparisons with the Jewish diaspora of the modern era. Therefore, the suggestion to use the term in a purely *descriptive* manner to describe 'the historical phenomenon of the dispersion and settlement of Africans abroad' (Harris 1982, pp. 4–5) not only suits the scholar of religion but also does justice to the original event that gave rise to the phenomenon, that is the slave trade. What is required, however, is to analyse the phenomenon and try to explain its meaning. Within the broadly defined framework of the dispersion and settlement of Africans abroad it remains important to consider the specific features of the African diaspora in America and distinguish them from the situation pertaining to Europe. If we follow the definition provided by FADSI, the African diaspora embodies:

> the voluntary and forced dispersion of Africans at different periods in history and in several directions; the emergence of a cultural identity abroad without losing the African base, whether spiritually or physically; the psychological or physical return to the homeland, Africa'. (Harris 1982, p. 5)

We see that the term 'African diaspora' here contains three key elements: *dispersion*, *identity*, and *return*. It may be useful to see how far these elements are relevant to the specific conditions of Africans in Europe. I propose to examine this more closely by taking the Netherlands as my example.[7]

Dispersion

The dispersion of Africans on a more or less large scale has taken place since medieval times when large numbers of Africans were captured and taken to the Middle East and Asia for forced labour by intruding people. The dispersion to the Americas started after the voyages of Columbus, as a result of the ensuing spread of knowledge about the Americas to a European public. This led to a form of globalisation – an encounter of two worlds – of which the African diaspora was an important by-product (Conniff and Davis 1994, p. 306). It became a central aspect during the slave trade of later centuries when the 'African diaspora' proved vital in the shaping of the Americas. Since then the African diaspora has expanded in all directions and recently also made its impact on the European continent. The migration of Africans to Europe is generally a modern phenomenon which – although not totally unrelated – does not arise directly from the history of the slave trade, but is born of circumstances inherent in the conditions of a globalised world. Labour migration is one important aspect of that, as a result of which Africans can be found everywhere in the industrialised world.

Today, we find Africans scattered over most countries of the European Union, while in some countries, notably the United Kingdom and France, one may speak of a tradition of African or, in a wider sense, black presence (Killingray 1994). The question whether their dispersion has been forced or voluntary goes beyond the descriptive level and depends to a large extent on the individual's subjective view in defining the matter. In present circumstances subjective views risk being influenced by the public debate on migration which has taken a new turn since the emergence of the European Union as a political entity. As a result, European governments have introduced refined categories designed to distinguish one type of migrant from another and to separate what they consider legitimate immigrants from those they see as illegitimate ones. An inflated vocabulary is one of the clearest expressions of this. In the Netherlands, a whole new vocabulary has been invented to distinguish between various types of refugees with a view to reducing the number of legal immigrants.

Definitions are rarely static, but it is nevertheless striking how rapidly the content of terms related to the process of migration is changing and adapted to the political needs of the day. What these labels have in common is the fact that they all refer to people who for one reason or another have felt obliged to leave their country and settle elsewhere. That is, they are all migrants, people on the move, in many cases individual travellers who have effectively removed the distinction between forced or voluntary dispersion which proved so significant in the American context. The reasons for the presence of Africans in Europe today are largely dictated by the state of affairs in the home countries. With the exception of Britain and France, the major former colonial powers in Africa, the great majority of Africans in Europe today have migrated because of some form of upheaval in their own country, of a nature which often makes it difficult to separate economic from political causes.

The circumstances of dispersion in Europe, therefore, are quite different from the conditions in America. The history of forced dispersion through the slave trade has marked the common psyche of African-Americans in a way which is not unlike the holocaust experience of Jewish history. The slave owners tried to erase all aspects of African culture, including religion, and to undermine every aspect of African identity. The slave experience which has been so vital to the development of a specific African identity in the Americas is virtually absent among African communities in Europe (although in the case of the Netherlands it is an irony that it is mostly Ghanaians who have settled there, thus by their very presence confronting the Netherlands with its own disreputable role in the seventeenth- and eighteenth-century slave trade in the former Gold Coast: Postma 1990). An exception has to be made, to some extent, for Britain, where the awareness of the slave past continues to live among African-American descendants.

Identity

The element of *identity* invariably proves the most important one in the diaspora context, whether for internal or external reasons. In anthropological terms, identity is a social concept about groups of people who think of themselves, or are thought of by others, as alike in some significant way (Moore 1994, p. 130). More generally, identity is taken as indicating a distinguishing character of a person or a group of persons, in this case suggesting a specific set of characteristics which may be ascribed to Africans in the diaspora and which can be seen as differentiating them from the society in which they live. Here, the emphasis is on cultural identity in which religion has an obvious part, and it is on the religious aspect that I will concentrate.

In the American context the development of an African identity has become highly important for descendants of the African diaspora due to the concerted efforts mentioned before to disrupt the African person. Since culture is an important aspect of identity, cultural issues figure high on the agenda of the African diaspora in America. This is also demonstrated by the new forms of religion which have emerged in the Americas as the result of a conscious interaction between belief systems of the past and present. One may think of religions such as umbanda and candomblé, which are very popular in Brazil, the voodoo religion of Haiti, or the winti religion of Surinam which also exists today in the Netherlands. Further examples include the many adherents of Yoruba religion in the United States, as well as many other cults which have their roots in the religious traditions of West Africa particularly. The link with the slave past is central to the emergence and development of the great variety of African-American religions and to the content of religious beliefs and practices of many African-Americans. An interesting example in this respect is the umbanda religion in Brazil, whose deities reflect the different cultural influences in the history of the country.

In contrast to the Americas, the presence of significant numbers of Africans in Europe is a relative novelty. It is because of these growing numbers that in the last decade so many African congregations have been formed in continental Europe, a trend which we saw has been noticeable in Britain for much longer. Due to the specific background of this latest diaspora trend, and unlike the situation in the Americas at the time of the slave trade, most Africans in Europe did not bring their African traditional religions with them (which is not to deny the existence of cultural links with African traditions), but rather, as a belief system, they brought with them their 'new' religions, Islam or Christianity. We are rather ill-informed about African Islam in Europe but it seems that African Muslims have not formed their own congregations in the same way as African Christian congregations have done. In France and Italy, for example, Muslims from Senegal have formed networks through the Mouride brotherhood, but these, in spite of their religious functions, seem more comparable to, for example, Ghanaians' cultural associations (Schmidt di Friedberg 1996). In the Netherlands, on the other hand, African Muslims tend to pray at one of the mosques which are frequented by Muslims from Turkey and Morocco or from Surinam, or practise their religion in private.

In the case of the African-initiated churches in Europe, it is not the history of the slave trade which exerts a pervasive influence on the lives of their members but rather the history of the colonial past. The history of Christian mission and church formation in Africa is inextricably bound up with the history of colonial domination and, among other factors, is the root cause of the emergence of independent churches in Africa.[8] From the very beginning African churches have struggled to escape from Western domination, particularly in the form of the so-called African independent churches, but increasingly also within the framework of the so-called mainline churches. The latter's concern with 'inculturation' – that is, finding ways of making the gospel relevant to a specific cultural context and thus allowing for the expression of an 'African identity' in religion – is a significant sign in this respect.[9]

The question thus emerges of how relevant the issue of African identity is to African Christians in Europe. With specific reference to the situation in the Netherlands, I have argued before that the discussion regarding the need for African Christians in Europe to develop their own identity as *African* Christians is being led by their European counterparts and serves European rather than African interests in at least some cases (ter Haar 1995a). African Christians in the Netherlands, for example, identify themselves first as Christians and only secondly as Africans or African Christians. That is, in their own view, their public adherence to Christianity constitutes the most important element of their identity. Yet, there is a general tendency in the Netherlands to separate African Christians from their Dutch counterparts by insisting on their perceived African identity, while ignoring their shared Christian identity. It is a pattern which fits in well with the Dutch social system of developing specific group identities and which, in the past, provided some of the intellectual basis for the system of apartheid. It would be interesting to compare the Dutch attitude with the situation in other parts of Europe, where different social mechanisms exist for the integration of foreigners.

Britain provides an interesting example in this regard. Gerd Baumann (1996), who has done research among South Asian migrants in Southall in London, has remarked on the interest of the state in negotiating identity. He demonstrates, with particular reference to the case of the Sikhs, how the British state uses a religious definition of identity for purely secular, administrative purposes. Although the people thus categorised may not have been consulted in regard to their own collective labelling, they can turn their new official identity to advantage by using it as a basis to negotiate their own interests with the state. One obvious example is the allocation of money for community welfare. When this happens, an originally religious identity becomes a political one as well, and the political component may in due time surpass the religious aspect in importance. This 'ethnicization' of religious diversity, Baumann shows, has the opposite effect of what is intended, namely integration and incorporation into the existing political system. The end result is likely to be the marginalisation of religious minority groups as specific ethnic communities within the boundaries of the secular state (G. Baumann 1995).

With similar effect intellectuals of all sorts tend to ascribe an ethnic identity to African Christians in Europe (M. Baumann 1995, p. 1). Academic specialists tend to emphasise migrants' African roots, thus contributing to segregation of Africans and non-Africans in this part of the world. In a different way, this is also furthered by the public insistence on Africans' right to develop their own – meaning 'African' – identity. This is not to say that Africans do not have such a right, but that the necessity to promote this should not be imposed by others. One result is, in the Dutch case, that while African Christians are trying to enter the mainstream of Western Christian culture by identifying themselves primarily as Christians, non-Africans ensure that they stay 'beyond the pale' by imposing on them a requirement to develop what *they* perceive to be central to their identity, namely their 'Africanness', as this is believed to express itself traditionally. One may wonder how much this is also symptomatic of a fundamental racial prejudice in the form of a belief on the part of some Europeans in the incompatability of being genuinely Christian and genuinely African at the same time.[10] A symptom of the same line of thought can be found in the common reference to African-initiated congregations in Europe as 'African churches', implying some form of Christianity which is only suitable for African Christians. A logical next step would be to suggest that African Christianity is a different religion altogether.

African Christians in the Netherlands are well aware that the emphasis on their perceived otherness will work against them in that it will contribute to their isolation in society rather than allowing them to link up with main-stream – that is Western – Christianity. For the same reason they are opposed to the label 'African churches' which is generally bestowed on them (for example Himmans-Arday 1996, p. 2). Instead, they refer to themselves as 'international churches', thereby expressing their wish to be open to all Christian believers, irrespective of race and colour. The insistence of many non-Africans on the existence of a specific 'African identity', whether this is inspired by religious orthodoxy or by intellectual liberalism, is in effect a continuation of the old colonial and early missionary discourse and praxis regarding the perceived 'otherness' of Africans (Hinga 1994). It also reminds one of the experiences of the Jews in Alexandria who – due to outside pressure

– were forced to develop a specific identity of their own which up to then they had not felt a need to do as they were content simply to be Jews among non-Jews. Similarly, I would like to argue that Africans in the Netherlands are happy to be Africans among non-Africans, that is the Dutch, without turning their African-ness into a major issue. For African migrants in Europe, their African identity is in principle as much a matter of course as a Jewish identity was for the Jews in the Hellenistic cities (Tromp 1995, p. 20); in both cases this originally had nothing to do with a deliberate choice. I would want to draw the parallel even further. Just as the ancient Jews felt no reason to assert their identity outside Judea as long as they were socially and politically accepted, but also had no reason to renounce their identity, since non-Jews accepted their way of life, in the same way African believers in Europe would have no reason to either emphasise or hide their identity if they were simply accepted as fellow-citizens of Europe, who to some extent have their own way of life.

Not only should the definition of one's identity result from a process of negotiation in which at least the people concerned participate, but I also believe that the development of a collective identity can take place only if one's personal identity, that is, the integrity of the individual, has been secured. Obviously, the mechanisms for that are influenced by the size of a particular minority group vis-à-vis the majority population, which marks another difference between the American and European diaspora situation. Africans in Europe are in a minority position, with little or no power as a group. For many of them, their religion helps them to achieve a type of security and inner strength which may well encourage them in future to reconsider their self-identity specifically in terms of being *African* Christians or Muslims. Alternatively, the experience of exclusion, inspired by racism or other excluding mechanisms, may have a similar effect. This is the case, for example, in Britain where, due to the circumstances of an entirely different context, African and Afro-Caribbean church leaders tend to insist on their African identity in the experience of their faith.[11]

Return

The element of *return* is the last key element in defining the concept of the African diaspora. The question here is to determine whether a longing to return to the 'homeland' pertains to the situation of Africans in Europe. In this case, too, I would argue that we are dealing with a fundamentally different situation, resulting from the different historical context in which the diaspora has been constituted. The post-war history of migration in Europe has taught us not only that physical return on a permanent basis frequently does not take place, not even among first-generation migrants, but that in the second and third generation also the psychological importance of return largely disappears. The belief that African migrants will return to their homelands as soon as they can possibly do so is contradicted by the realities of today. Of course, cases of individual returnees are known, for example in situations where stability returns to the 'home country' and a new future seems possible. In most cases, however, and in spite of the difficulties facing them, the future for Africans in Europe looks less dim than if they were to return to their home countries, particularly if they have succeeded in finding employment, and since many of them have started to raise families and are able to provide their children with better prospects. Although the link with the homeland is not likely to disappear, this has little to do with the longing for the country of the past as might be seen in America, where all existing links with homeland Africa were cut off by the slave trade.

If we examine the African congregations in Europe, to judge from my research in the Netherlands the element of return in the earlier defined sense is absent. Members of congregations are using their religious imagination to designate a legitimate space for themselves in the West by comparing their own experiences to those of the Israelites. They refer to Biblical examples which show that God does not respect borders and that his children today are as free as the children of Israel. Biblical models instil in them the faith that, with the help of God, borders will only prove temporary obstacles. In a different way, stories such as that of Ruth and Naomi, who left the land of Moab to find work and shelter in Bethlehem, inspire further faith among the believers. Throughout history, the imagery of the Bible has been a major inspiration for Africans in the diaspora, not least because of its perceived references to Africa.[12] The importance of the Bible in the lives of African Christian congregations, in Europe as in Africa itself, cannot easily be overestimated. While outside observers often tend to consider their attachment to the literal text of the Bible simply as a sign of 'fundamentalism' – another highly ideologised concept which seems to have almost completely lost its descriptive meaning – for African Christians themselves this constitutes a constant source of inspiration which helps them succeed in their struggle for life. Conversely, however, the idea of return to the homeland which is implicit in the diaspora concept is helpful in strengthening the belief among Europeans that one day these people will 'go home' – a politically convenient thought.

African Christians in Europe, as far as I can see, do not look back to the African past while spiritually and physically preparing for their return. On the contrary, they strike me as forward-looking people who use all their material and spiritual resources to secure for themselves a better future in Europe. They have lived in Africa, many in parts of the continent other than their place of origin due to the situation in their home country. It is relevant to recall, in this context, that Africa is the continent which not only contains more refugees than any other continent, but also has a long tradition of migrant labour within the continent.[13] Since Western Europe is one of the most stable parts of the world politically and economically, Africans, like migrants from other parts of the world, will continue to come looking for work, and their religious belief helps them greatly in their endeavour. In other words, at the present time, their promised land is not Africa, but Europe, and – similar to my suggestions on the concept of identity as a key factor in the diaspora complex – the belief in a return of African migrants to Africa appears to exist chiefly on the part of non-Africans.

Conclusion

If, then, as I have argued, at least two of the three major elements of what constitutes the 'African diaspora' in the light of the American experience (namely identity and return) are of doubtful application, can we still apply the term 'diaspora' in the context of Europe? In discussing the ancient Jewish diaspora, Tromp comes to the final conclusion that we had better abandon the term altogether as inappropriate, both on moral and empirical grounds. As he demonstrates, the popular connotations of the diaspora concept are not conducive to human dignity, while there is no empirical indication that these 'diaspora' Jews were intrinsically unhappy. The same applies to African Christians in Europe for whom the exclusive orientation towards Africa which is implied in the concept of 'African diaspora' would make their life in Europe by definition imperfect, in the same way as this was believed to be true for Jews living outside Judea because they should be, or at least long to be, in Judea (Tromp 1995, p. 21). Ancient Jews and modern Africans, in both cases, ought to have a feeling of alienation and to look at themselves as strangers in their actual place of living.

Yet, in spite of the problems involved, I think we can use the concept of diaspora in our work, quite apart from the fact that it would virtually be impossible to get rid of the term now that we have lived with it for so long. We can use it in an academically acceptable and responsible way as long as we are aware of the metaphorical meaning of the term, and if we are prepared to use it in a descriptive manner as a dynamic concept subject to historical change. We will then be able to approach the subject in a scholarly and broadly comparative manner in a way suggested by Shepperson (1993, p. 47). First of all we can identify and investigate the specific areas to which dispersed Africans have gone and in which their descendants are living. In the present case, this means taking the European context – and not the African one – as our starting point. Secondly, we can study the interaction between the centres and the peripheries of the African diaspora in Europe at all possible levels, introducing the link with the home country only as a secondary consideration. Finally, we can stop the 'ghettoizing' of African history (Curtin 1995), and attempt to integrate these studies into the overall history of humanity, which is at the same time a plea for taking African history, including African religious history, seriously.

These three successive steps can also be taken in studying specifically the religious aspect of the African diaspora in Europe, in conformity with the two pillars of the empirical study of religion: objective description and analysis. If this were to happen, a scholarly contribution would be made which – in the process – would rid the concept of diaspora of certain connotations and make it suitable for application in the broader comparative study of religion (M. Baumann 1995). The importance of the religious dimension in the study of so-called diaspora communities is easily overlooked by scholars from a more secular background in favour of ethnicity and ethnic adherence, which can easily lead to the political construction of ethnic religions.

In the case of African religious communities in Europe the tendency towards the 'ethnicisation' of religion poses a number of other questions to do with race relations which cannot be discussed here. But the observation that the preservation and perpetuation of religious identity can become a core issue in the diaspora can be fully shared for African Christians in Europe, whose independent churches single them out as 'chosen people'. In their own view, they have been chosen by God for a new purpose in Europe. Ironically, Europe does indeed regard them as 'different'.

(First published as Occasional Paper No. 15, 1996)

Notes

1   Throughout this chapter 'Africa' is read as 'sub-Saharan Africa', i.e. excluding Morocco, Algeria, Tunisia, Libya, and Egypt. According to the last available statistics, in 1993 the total number of African migrants registered in the then fifteen member states of the European Union was 831,547 (Eurostat, *Migration Statistics 1995*). This does not include an unknown number of undocumented migrants.

2   For the UK this becomes clear from the works, amongst others, of Gerloff (1992) and Kalilombe (1995); examples from the Netherlands are Amoako-Adusei (1991) and ter Haar (1995a).

3   Muus (1995, p. 121–125) has drawn attention to the problematic way in which migration processes are often described, invoking a specific image drawn from metaphors of water rather than giving an accurate description of migration.

4   The following argument is taken from Tromp (1995).

5   Some historical precedents are Edward Blyden, William Du Bois, and Marcus Garvey.

6   According to Postma's (1990) authoritative account, a total of some ten million Africans were carried as slaves to the 'new world'.

7   I am aware of the differences in situation in the various countries of Europe as defined by the differences in history and culture and therefore limit myself in this case to the Netherlands. For more specific information on the African diaspora situation in the Netherlands, see ter Haar (1994).

8 There is a large academic literature on the history of African independent churches, particularly with regard to southern Africa. Among the most prolific writers in this field are G.C. Oosthuizen and M.L. Daneel.

9 The subject of inculturation has been very popular, particularly in Roman Catholic circles: for example, the discussions on the issue at the African Synod in Rome in April 1994.

10 This is a point which has often been made by the former Archbishop of Lusaka, Mgr. Emmanuel Milingo, who was removed from office after a dispute concerning his healing ministry: see ter Haar (1992).

11 See for example *Building bridges between African independent churches and the historic mission churches*, a report of the proceedings of a consultation organised by the Centre for Black and White Christian Partnership (Birmingham, UK) and the Organisation of African Instituted Churches (Nairobi, Kenya) at Nairobi in November 1995.

12 Cf. Shepperson (1993, pp. 46–47) who stresses the importance of scholarly work on the Bible and Africa for the study of the African diaspora.

13 Although we lack reliable statistics on migration trends in sub-Saharan Africa, it is estimated that some 35 million Africans, or 8 per cent of the total population, live outside their own country (Muus 1995, p. 36).

Bibliography

Amoako-Adusei, J. 1991. *'Working in the boulevard of broken dreams': the activities of the R.C. chaplaincy for Africans. A short report*. Amsterdam: Brakkenstein.

Baumann, G. 1995. 'Religious migrants in secular Britain? The secular state as agent of religious encorporation', *Etnofoor*, **7** (2) pp. 31–46.

———— 1996. *Contesting culture: discourses of identity in multi-ethnic London*, Cambridge: Cambridge University Press.

Baumann, M. 1995. 'Conceptualizing diaspora: the preservation of religious identity in foreign parts, exemplified by Hindu communities outside India', *Temenos* **31** pp. 19–35.

Conniff, M.L. and Davis, T.J. (eds) 1994. *Africans in the Americas: a History of the Black Diaspora*, New York: St. Martin's Press.

Curtin, P.D. 1995. 'Ghettoizing African history', *ASA News*, Oct./Dec. 1995, pp. 6–7.

Dunkwu, P. 1993. 'Communities of resistance in fortress Europe', in L. Back and A. Nayak (eds), *Invisible Europeans?: Black People in the 'new Europe'*, Birmingham: AFFOR, pp. 129–136.

Gerloff, R.I.H. 1992. *A plea for British Black Theologies: the black church movement in Britain in its transatlantic cultural and theological interaction with special reference to the Pentecostal Oneness (Apostolic) and Sabbatarian movements*, Frankfurt AM.: Peter Lang.

ter Haar, G. 1992. *Spirit of Africa: the Healing Ministry of Archbishop Milingo of Zambia*, London: Hurst & Co.

———— 1994. 'Afrikaanse kerken in Nederland', in *Religieuze Bewegingen in Nederland*, **28** pp. 1–35.

———— 1995a. 'Ritual as communication: a study of African Christian communities in the Bijlmer district of Amsterdam', in J.G. Platvoet and K. van der Toorn (eds), *Pluralism and identity: studies in ritual behaviour*, Leiden: Brill, pp. 115–142.

———— 1995b. 'Strangers in the promised land: African Christians in Europe', *Exchange* **24** (1), pp. 1–33.

———— 1995c. 'African independent churches: the ideological implications of continuity and change', in A. Houtepen (ed.), *The living tradition: towards an ecumenical hermeneutics of the Christian tradition*, Zoetermeer: Meinema, pp. 159–170.

———— 1996. 'Engelstalige Afrikaanse christenen in de regio Amsterdam', in J.A.B. Jongeneel, R. Budiman and J.J. Visser (eds), *Gemeenschapsvorming van Aziatische, Afrikaanse en Midden-en*

Zuid-Amerikaanse christenen in Nederland: een geschiedenis in wording, Zoetermeer: Boekencentrum, pp. 174–213.

Harris, J.E. (ed.) 1982. *Global dimensions of the African Diaspora*, Washington: Howard University Press (reprinted 1993).

Himmans-Arday, D. 1996. *And the truth shall set you free*, London: Janus Publishing Company.

Hinga, T. 1994. 'Inculturation and the otherness of Africans: some reflections', in P. Turkson and F. Wijsen (eds), *Inculturation: abide by the otherness of Africa and the Africans*, Kampen; Kok, pp. 10–18.

Kalilombe, P.A. 1995. 'Black Christianity and its missionary outreach', paper presented at the Ethnic and Racial Studies Conference on 'Ethnic Minorities and Religions', London School of Economics and Political Science.

Killingray, D. (ed.) 1994. *Africans in Britain*, London: Frank Cass.

Moore, S. Falk 1994. *Anthropology and Africa: changing perspectives on a changing scene*, Charlottesville and London: University Press of Virginia.

Muus, P. 1995. *De wereld in beweging: internationale migratie, mensen rechten en ontwikkeling*, Utrecht: Jan van Arkel.

Postma, J.M. 1990. *The Dutch in the Atlantic slave trade 1600–1815*, Cambridge: Cambridge University Press.

Schmidt di Friedberg, O. 1996, 'West African Islam in Italy: the Senegalese Mouride brotherhood as an economic and cultural network', in W.A.R. Shadid and P.S. van Koningsveld (eds), *Political participation and identities of Muslims in non-Muslim states*, Kampen: Kok Pharos, 1996, pp. 71–82.

Shadid, W.A.R. and van Koningsveld, P.S. (eds) 1996. *Muslims in the margin: political responses to the presence of Islam in Western Europe*, Kampen: Kok Pharos.

Shepperson, G. 1993[1982]. 'African diaspora: concept and context', in J.E. Harris (ed.), *Global dimensions of the African diaspora*, Washington: Howard University Press, pp. 41–49.

Sundkler, B.G.M 1961[1948]. *Bantu prophets in South Africa*, London: Oxford University Press.

Tromp, J. 1995. 'The ancient Jewish diaspora: some linguistic and sociological observations', paper presented at the conference on 'Religious communities in the diaspora', held at the University of Leiden, 8 December, 1995.

CHAPTER 7

Study of Religions: The New Queen of the Sciences?

Brian Bocking

Introduction: On Phenomenological Methodology

My topic in this chapter is the significance of the Study of Religions as a modern academic discipline. In my inaugural lecture 'Religious Intelligence and the Study of Religions', given in April 2000 as Professor of the Study of Religions at the School of Oriental and African Studies (SOAS), University of London, I described for the benefit of non-specialists such matters as the phenomenological method in the study of religions, 'methodological agnosticism' and what I saw as the gradual maturation or evolution, or unfolding, or unravelling, of the discipline of Religious Studies, particularly in this country over the last thirty years or so; in other words, since I first encountered it as an undergraduate at Lancaster University in the early 1970s. This autobiographical reference was not accidental; one of the more obvious developments in the Study of Religions under the influence of postmodernism over the past few years has been the trend towards acknowledging the subjectivity of the scholar. We recognise now that we are agents in the construction of knowledge, not standard bearers of pure objectivity; that each of us has been formed by events and each of us has his or her own agenda.[1]

Recapitulating Ninian Smart's six or seven dimensions of religion (Smart 1997) and sketching in the pros and cons of the related approach known as 'methodological agnosticism' will seem at best unnecessary and at worst irrelevant for a readership more or less familiar with Religious Studies. Nevertheless a key point about methodological agnosticism often bears repeating, namely that while methodological agnosticism does not imply personal agnosticism, nor indeed any other type of personal religious belief, the interface between the personal and the professional in the matter of constructions of reality (academic, religious, etc.) is a difficult area and an important and persistent issue for everyone engaged in the social sciences or humanities. In practice, methodological agnosticism must be a practised professional stance, a skill or habit of mind which one develops only through repeated use. It programmatically maintains that the truth-claims of the believer (which may be unverifiable or non-empirical[2]) should take centre stage. This of course is a very important presumption when it comes to looking at the motivations and likely future actions of religious people and groups. It is the presumption that religious beliefs and values *per se* are very important in people's lives and that the academic is not in a position to dismiss them, or indeed to endorse them. So there is an enduring issue here about the voice of the academic commentator and the voice of the religious believer being kept separate. The method I was initiated into at Lancaster and thereafter adopted as my professional stance involved the idea that one explains a religion by relating the different dimensions; in the Smartian sense, the connected and interdependent elements of the constructed reality in which religious believers participate. According to this approach, a satisfactory account of a religious world is derived by giving an account of the relationships of all the various aspects of that world to each other.

The general thrust of my inaugural lecture at SOAS was that the Lancaster-style phenomenology of religion, understood both as a method of understanding religions and as an approach which takes seriously the perspective of religious subjects and communities, is a valid attempt to understand particular historical instances of religious belief and practice by understanding the connections and interrelationships between the various dimensions, and still has a lot going for it. I argued that it can, in fact, underpin the future of the subject for some time to come. I distinguished this pursuit from, on the one hand cultural studies, and on the other hand theology, each of which has its own particular world of meaning different in large part from that of the study of religions. In saying that the phenomenology of religion in this rather traditional sense could underpin the future of the subject, I acknowledge that there is a considerable body of literature and anecdote that characterises, indeed sometimes caricatures, the phenomonological method as outdated and implausible, or reduces it, as one of my colleagues used to say, to the history and geography of religions: a purely descriptive exercise. And I readily acknowledge that the approach and the methods of the phenomenology of religion were, as we can see with the benefit of hindsight, very much of their time.[3]

The phenomenology of religion as practised thirty years ago at Lancaster and for some time after that did not anticipate feminist theory; it didn't try to understand gender.[4] It was in many respects paternalist. It did not – and I suspect even now generally does not – benefit from the full range of postmodernist perspectives, though it rather splendidly challenged Eurocentrism well in advance of most other subjects. It did not do as much as we now think it could have done to advance the view that reliable knowledge of an 'other' requires essentially a dialogue between presumed equals, rather than the patient investigation of what amounted to a religious 'object' by an academic 'subject'. It failed, too, to address in any significant way the profound, if ultimately imponderable (and arguably futile), question of where 'religion' ends and 'culture' or 'society' begins. Anyone who promotes the idea of the phenomenology of religion as a methodology for today should indeed feel chastened by the criticisms which can quite easily be aimed at this approach.

Nevertheless, the phenomenology of religion as an approach and a method had then, and retains now, in my view, certain virtues, chief amongst which is its programmatic reluctance to propose any theory of religion which makes it impossible for the religious believer to go on believing, or the religious practitioner to go on practising. There is a question here about whether the study of religions is a purely theoretical or an applied science. Is the scholar simply trying to understand religions (and the question then arises of why?) or, as in most of the sciences, is one trying to understand in order to bring about some change; in order to develop something? If the latter, then we have to ask what are the implications of our explanations and understandings of religion?

There is an ethical issue here, because if what we do has implications and consequences, we need to ask whether they are beneficial or destructive. The International Association for the History of Religions (IAHR) conference in Durban in August 2000 began with two memorable inaugural addresses, one by the South African Deputy Minister of Education, the other by the Chair of the Human Rights Commission. Normally at conferences on religion the invited dignitaries venture some sentiments about the common search for truth and values and wish us all well. On this occasion the Deputy Minister delivered a lecture which would have impressed any audience on the shifts in policy and perspectives of the IAHR over the hundred years since its inception, arguing – for his lecture had a serious political purpose – that scholars of religion were now, and should now, be taking the perspective that religion is a *social* force; that there are pressing issues to do with the social impact and influence of religion of which we need to be aware. In other words, it was argued, we cannot go into the ivory tower, study religion and think that this has no effect. The Chair of the Human Rights Commission gave an equally compelling discourse on religion and human rights, citing legal cases brought to address difficult areas in which human rights and religious rights or freedoms came into conflict and where the state was obliged to adjudicate between these two principles. These important contributions to the IAHR's deliberations at Durban underlined the fact that the study of religions needs to be understood, at least in part, as an applied science with implications and effects.

With this in mind, I would like to identify what I believe to be two necessary characteristics of the study of religions as an academic discipline. The first I call a *working assumption* and the second an *attitude* of mind.

The *working assumption* is that religion is here to stay. My colleague Alexander Piatagorsky has observed that 'both Weber and Durkheim were so preoccupied with the problem of how modern societies would manage without religion, that they simply overlooked the fact that they could not' (Piatagorsky

1999, p. 33, n.19). This seems to me a very important observation for anyone involved in the study of religions. It may seem to run counter to our own enculturation if we live in the kind of society which thinks of itself as increasingly secularised, but if we look around us in the contemporary world there is an obvious truth here. Societies, let us declare, cannot manage without *some* kind of religion and for all practical purposes they never will. This is something a Study of Religions Department should talk about. The assumption that we can, either individually or collectively, think our way out of being religious is perhaps a rather obvious trap for theorists of religion, but it is a trap into which many capable theorists have fallen and continue to fall. The assumption, for example, that religion is some kind of disease and the academic theorist is the doctor ignores the high incidence of iatrogenic diseases in modern systems of medicine. And since, when this medical model is adopted, religious belief is generally characterised as a mental rather than physical illness, the Foucauldian question must always be raised of who in this doctor-patient relationship is mad and who is sane, not to mention who is there to cure the physician. It is, I would submit, one of the central tasks of the study of religions to account for religiosity without discounting religiosity, and this the phenomenology of religion can, I think, succeed in doing.

The *attitude* required is one of epistemological humility; that is to say, as far as our academic study is concerned we are not certain about whether a religion's truth-claims are valid or not. This links with the previous assumption that religion is here to stay and that we cannot, as a matter of fact, second-guess the direction and characteristics of a continually evolving religiosity. I interpret this as a matter of maintaining a professional detachment in the task of understanding and explaining religion. I cannot say that I have attained such epistemological humility in my own work and in my own reflection on religions (an example of which is discussed below) but then if I did claim to have attained humility, self-evidently I would not have done so.

It follows that we need to understand and explain religion in a way which enables people who comprehend and accept our explanation to continue being religious. Does my explanation of a particular religious phenomenon allow a religious person to understand it, agree with it and continue being religious? Most theories of religion, of course, do not do this. Most theories of religion embody the irony that once you have understood the explanation you can no longer believe and practise in the way that you used to. An example might be evolutionary sociobiology, whose explanation for the origin and persistence of religion is that religious faith has offered an evolutionary advantage. Having grasped this truth, if truth it be, there is a dilemma: should one continue to be religious in order to retain an evolutionary advantage, or should one cease being religious, having seen through the previously hidden reason for religion, thereby losing whatever evolutionary advantage religion might possess? The argument that it does not matter because the evolutionary advantage now lies with the sociobiologist is a bold and premature claim. But either way it is too late, because once the bio-evolutionary explanation of religion is accepted, one cannot ever be religious *simpliciter* in the same way as before.[5]

Case Study: The Iconography of Shinto and Buddhism

To illustrate some of the points addressed so far, I would like to refer briefly to my own recent study of some aspects of the iconography of Shinto and Buddhism embodied in a type of scroll known as 'The Oracles of the Three Shrines' (Bocking 2000). I would like to discuss just one of the findings of my research and to tease out the 'phenomenological' assumptions inherent in my approach. I say 'inherent' because I do not think that my approach in this research was *consciously* phenomenological. I have never been very good at marrying theory with practice: as an undergraduate at Lancaster we studied a course on theory and we studied religions, and I just could not see the connection. What happened to me was that I 'picked up' an approach – I won't say that it was 'caught not taught' because it was, of course, taught, but I think I absorbed a method without consciously realising what was going on. So when I approached the study of this scroll there was undoubtedly an attitude of 'warm science' or 'detached empathy' on my part of which I was hardly aware.

A major part of the research deals with the figure of the Shinto 'sun goddess' Amaterasu, who in modern illustrations (that is, from the 1860s to the present) almost invariably appears as a young woman or girl with long dark hair, illuminated from behind by the rays of the rising sun, dressed in a pure white robe and adorned with the Japanese 'imperial regalia' of mirror, sword and jewels. A study of this image as we trace it back over several centuries shows that the origin of the standing female goddess is in fact a Buddhist boy divinity named Uho Doji. He is also shown standing, but instead of the three imperial regalia he holds in one hand a traditional bodhisattva's staff (this later becomes Amaterasu's sword) and in the other hand not the modern circular mirror, but the Indian *cintamani* or wish-fulfilling gem. His robe is decorated with the wheel of the dharma and the modern motif of the radiant sun has evidently arisen from his conventional Buddhist halo. The small, five-storey *stupa* on the bodhisattva's head in some images emphasises that this is an eminently 'Buddhist' figure. By looking at successive examples of the scroll, especially those produced during the mid-nineteenth century when radical changes took place in Japanese religion and society, we can clearly see the transformation from male to female, and from 'Buddhist' to 'Shinto', taking place.

If one were to go to the Shinto authorities in Japan today and point out that the template for the modern image of Amaterasu (an image which now expresses a 'pure Shinto' aesthetic following the forced 'dissociation' of Buddhas from Shinto *kami* by government decree in the late nineteenth century) is in fact a Buddhist divinity, a bodhisattva, this might be seen as a hostile reductionism and an attack upon modern Shinto's conception of itself as an indigenous and purely Japanese tradition, separate from and untained by Buddhism. In fact at an early stage in my research I felt that I had discovered something which could only undermine modern Shinto's self-understanding; namely that the pedigree of Amaterasu's modern image is undeniably Buddhist. It would have been relatively easy to exploit my findings by adding my voice to the chorus of disapproval of Shinto that existed among Western scholars, as well as many in Japan, after 1945.[6]

However, my argument, as it has developed, is rather different, because the modern image of Amaterasu is seldom if ever found in isolation. It is sold as a scroll-picture, and the scroll usually finds its place in a catalogue or display of scrolls, the majority of which are either obviously Buddhist or secular fine art scrolls. As everybody knows, ordinary people in Japan (and this includes most educated people as well) participate in both 'Shinto' and 'Buddhist' beliefs and practices at various times of the year or on various occasions in their lives. Japanese people do not as a rule think of Shinto as a separate 'religion' and arguably never have done so at any point in Japanese history (Breen and Teeuwen 2000).[7] The 'discovery' therefore that the modern icon of Amaterasu is 'basically' a Buddhist image actually takes us closer to understanding how Japanese people both in the past and in the present have tended to view such images. We scholars have constructed an idea of Shinto – taking our lead from a nineteenth-century Westernising, modernising Japanese government – as something separate from Buddhism. We keep asking the unhelpful question 'how is Shinto different from Buddhism?' when the truth is that if we look at the real phenomena, the *realia*, of the iconography of Shinto/Buddhism we can see how the two images of Uho Doji and Amaterasu in fact constitute two sides of the same coin, or, to use a rather more subtle metaphor, two sides of a Möbius strip, a ribbon which has in effect only one side though appearing as two. My academic analysis of the image, which seemed at first glance to undermine Shinto's self-interpretation, in fact reveals that the image has greater religious depth than might appear. When we understand that the modern 'Shinto' image hides and thereby reveals another 'Buddhist' image, we actually understand more about the way in which Shinto and Buddhism in Japan simultaneously conceal and indicate each other, and this interrelation-ship in the area of iconography becomes a further example of the way in which the two traditions are intuitively understood as interdependent by ordinary Japanese people; an understanding which is expressed in ritual practice far more than in expressions of belief.

Queen of the Sciences?

Returning now to the title of this chapter – 'the Queen of the Sciences' – I use it because the phrase 'Queen of the Sciences' actually occurs in the 'benchmarking statement' for Theology and Religious Studies in UK institutions of Higher Education recently published by the UK's Quality Assurance Agency for Higher Education (QAA). The benchmarking statement has been developed by a group of colleagues in support of the efforts of the QAA to assess, and perchance enhance, the quality of what we do in the Study of Religions (Theology and Religious Studies Benchmarking Group 2000). In successive drafts of this document it is pointed out that Theology used to be referred to as the Queen of the Sciences; a statement undoubtedly true, though one learned colleague has suggested to me that from its inception the phrase had ironical overtones.[8] This set me thinking that if Theology is no longer the queen of the sciences, and if there were a reigning queen, what science would currently be that queen? It seemed to me to be worth considering the proposition that the Study of Religions now occupies the throne so long ago vacated by Theology.

Of course we need to know what 'queen' means (and it can mean quite a lot of things) and what 'science' means (*ditto*). I suppose the two poles of the interpretation of 'new queen of the sciences' are (1) a science which newly lords it over all the other sciences, and (2) the newest and least accepted bride and never-to-be equal of the king, the king in this case being something quite different from Study of Religions; probably something venerable, stately and set in its ways, like mechanical engineering or constitutional history.

As a matter of fact, despite the promise of my title, I do not think Study of Religions is the new queen of the sciences; not in either of these senses in any case. Of course the very conception of a 'queen of the sciences' now sounds distinctly odd. Academic fashions do bring certain disciplines to centre stage at different times – one can think of the heyday of economics, sociology, psychology and so on – but none of us is really seeking a new monarch among the disciplines. To think of the Study of Religions even as a 'discipline' hardly fits the case. It would be quite wrong of me to suggest that the study of religions is not embroiled in a crisis of disciplinary identity. Every other subject worth its salt is, certainly in the arts and social sciences. The old 'disciplinary' boundaries now survive perhaps only in the minds of education quality controllers and funding bodies administering limited resources, which is why academics have to fight for resources using the same terms.

The notion, in this demotic and reflexive age, that knowledge and interpretations of complex phenomena should be institutionally 'disciplined' and 'bounded', somehow contained in 'departments' (replace 'Department of the Study of Religions with 'Compartment of the Study of Religions' to see the point) is an idea whose time, one feels, has gone. We need departments but we do not want them as such. My own institution, SOAS in London, is itself an interesting example of an institution in which departments have to exist for administrative reasons but where the extent of crossover between departments is such as to render the intellectual boundaries between them virtually meaningless, to the extent that a very necessary additional cross-hatching structure of formal 'Centres' (for Africa, for Japanese Religions, for Islamic Studies, for South Asia, for China, etc.) has evolved to ensure that members of different departments with interests in common have a recognised arena for discussion and research. All Study of Religions staff belong to at least one such Centre as well as to the Study of Religions department, and at least half of our undergraduate students in the study of religions are taking joint degrees with another discipline or language. It is an irony that academics outside the study of religions are likely to have a less inclusive and more etiolated conception of what 'religion' comprises than anyone within our subject could ever do. No doubt this works in both directions – we probably have our stereotypes of how colleagues in other disciplines spend their time – but certainly people outside the study of religions often have a remarkably sparse understanding of what goes on within the subject and certainly do not think of it as the all-embracing multidisciplinary exercise we know it to be.

I do however think that the study of religions can – temporarily and perhaps accidentally – claim to be the queen of the sciences in a third and quite different sense, because a methodology which currently holds undisputed sway over all academic disciplines, in the UK at least, is one of the central methods used in the study of religions. I refer here to that pragmatic area of academia which in the UK is concerned with implementing the Quality Assurance process. The particular form taken by the current round of QAA inspections of Religious Studies departments may constitute in some respects a passing fad, but the conditions of our existence as providers of Higher Education in the early twenty-first century will no doubt continue to be governed by some variation of this detailed and time-consuming exercise in professional accountability. For the present, the QAA and similar quasi-governmental bodies can exercise an extraordinary degree of influence over all academic disciplines and, as it happens, the method the QAA is currently using to assess Higher Education departments across all subjects is virtually identical to the central method of investigation or analysis used within the phenomenology of religion.

While other subjects may think that the QAA's methodology is relevant only to the assessment of academic departments, the Study of Religions in the UK finds itself in the curious position of being researched by one of the principal methodologies it itself uses to research religions. Academics are not used to being researched, least of all by their own methods, but it is increasingly the case that we are being studied not only by those whom we study, and who as a result of the spread of educational opportunity are statistically more and more likely to be literate, articulate and to have an academic (and/or media or internet) voice of their own, but also by our peers, in exercises of professional accountability such as the current round of QAA reviews. For most of us this is still a relatively unusual, and probably uncomfortable, experience.

The present method of QAA assessment takes as its starting point a detailed 'Self-Assessment Document', produced by the department itself, in which we describe what we aim to do and how, and how well, we think we do it. Following a one-week review visit by a Panel comprising several academics from other religion departments, the Review Panel awards numbered grades reflecting their view of the accuracy (that is honesty) of our self-assessment document. The quality of our educational provision is therefore judged against criteria devised by ourselves, not by the QAA. This is quite different from the proposed new 'benchmarking' approach which the QAA plans to implement in the coming years and which establishes goals for student achievement across all departments of Theology and/or Religious Studies, described in written 'benchmarks and standards' documents.[9]

As it happens, the approach and methodology adopted by QAA to research and review academic departments throughout the UK is virtually identical to the methodology and approach to the study of religions pioneered by Ninian Smart and his colleagues at Lancaster from the late 1960s. According to this method a religion is described and explained by elucidation of the relationships between its various dimensions (ritual, doctrinal, mythological, etc.). Most readers will be familiar with some version of Ninian Smart's model of the six or seven 'dimensions' of religion (Smart 1997), either as an example of how religion is to be studied or how it is not to be studied, depending upon methodological preferences. QAA similarly has its six-dimensional model of Higher Education provision, whose six 'aspects' are entitled 'Student Progression and Achievement', 'Quality Management and Enhancement', 'Student Support and Guidance', etc. These aspects are studied not just as separate categories but explicitly in relation to each other.

My point however is not simply that there are six (or so) dimensions in Ninian Smart's model of religion and six aspects in the QAA's model of Higher Education, an observation as banal as it is accurate, but that the *approach* adopted by QAA to subject review is that of methodological agnosticism. QAA effectively says to the department: 'we have no opinion about what *should* be going on here; tell us about *your* departmental world, about your aims and aspirations, about your students' opinions and achievements'. QAA effectively treats us as a phenomenologist treats members of a religion: 'tell us about your beliefs, your practices, whatever they may be; when do you do that, why do you think you do this, what do you value about that?' The QAA review team listens patiently, engages in structured dialogues, cross-checks what is said against the departmental texts provided, looks at student work and listens to student opinion and so on, and arrives at a judgement of *how closely their (QAA's) perception of the department, based on their research, matches our account of the department expressed in our self-assessment document.* We are being assessed on honesty about ourselves, not against some presumed gold standard of university education. This approach makes good sense in the study of religions; if in the course of our research we play back to the believers our understanding of what they are doing and thinking and they say 'yes, that's correct, you have understood how we feel, how we think, why we do what we do', then we may consider that we have achieved a degree of accuracy in our understanding. If they say 'we now understand *more* about ourselves as a result of your research', so much the better. If our account of the religion is unrecognisable to the believers; if we are, as it were, tone-deaf to the music of their religion, our account can hardly be worth much.

This means that *cognitively* we should have little or no argument with the methodology adopted by the QAA, and in fact I feel reasonably happy about it. Of course *affectively* is quite another matter; like a Victorian anthropologist (and unlike the phenomenologist of religion) the QAA seeks to locate each department on some notional scale of educational evolution, awarding points out of 24 (the pinnacle of perfection); fewer points might at some future date mean less funding. And of course we are being researched, and this can be extremely uncomfortable (a fact which might surprise those used to being the researcher, not the researched). People react very differently to the experience. Nevertheless the QAA gives us a unique opportunity not just to observe but to experience the very phenomenological method, which many of us have employed, or criticised, being used upon us in earnest by our peers.

This of course raises a number of interesting issues. There is the ethical question: is what is being done to us (which, note, we may be quite happy, as peer reviewers, to do to others) legitimate and fair? Does it respect what we do and does it arrive at an understanding of what we do with which we are happy, or are we being traduced by the account which emerges? We can perhaps notice and acknowledge our own subaltern strategies; knowing that we are being researched, what do we do that we would not do if we were not being researched? To what extent, and with what degree of success, are we stage-managing the research visit?[10] Reflection on these matters may give us insights into the possible effects of the researcher on the (passive?) object of religious research. Who researches whom? Does the 'insider' in the department have a better understanding of the department than the QAA reviewer who comes and looks at things from the outside? Maybe the 'outsider' comes to know and understand more about us than we knew about ourselves. This is knowledge and understanding which we can reflexively incorporate without being diminished. Many other issues of comparison between researching religions and being researched as departments arise and present themselves to us in an unusually direct way. We may particularly wonder about those new religious movements which are subjected to more or less constant scrutiny by the media and other bodies less scrupulous in their methods than the QAA. How does research by one's peers, employed by a body such as the QAA which operates to strict published criteria to which it must adhere, compare with research on a religious movement undertaken by the press, or even by a scholar who, whilst broadly well-intentioned, perhaps adheres to no criteria beyond the general principle of 'academic freedom' and the necessity to preserve or even advance his or her academic career?

As required by QAA, we have articulated in our Self-Assesssment Document a departmental world-view, describing how our departmental rituals, beliefs, doctrines, symbols and staff work together in progress towards the somewhat chimeric goals of academic knowledge and understanding, empathy, insight, employability and so forth. The QAA methodology therefore provokes a critical self-awareness, but ultimately it leaves intact a department's own 'world-view'. Or does it? This is something we can discover only after the event. Is it at all possible, even where those who are researched set the agenda by an initial self-assessment and are judged only according to the honesty of that self-understanding, that the experience of being researched does not change the department? If so, what type of change takes place?

Given that the QAA methodology described here is evidence-based, that it is, like the best phenomenology of religion admirably dialogical, that the researchers involved are our professional peers who are required to suspend for the duration of the visit their own opinions (*epoche*?) about our idiosyncratic departmental conception of what the study of religions is, what exactly is wrong with this methodology and this approach? If methodological agnosticism and the phenomenological method are outdated or implausible as so many claim, what exactly is it that this method, which is being applied to ourselves more or less by ourselves, misses in its examination of the inner life and outer manifestations of a real-life Study of Religions department?

(First published as Occasional Paper No. 21, 2000)

Notes

1   On this topic see, for example, Flood (1999).

2   This is a difficult category – what may be non-empirical to one person may not be non-empirical to another. A religious experience which is not repeated and indeed not witnessed and a physical experience which is not repeated and not witnessed can have the same status when it comes to the narrative which represents these events.

3   For recent extended discussions of the problems of phenomenology of religion see Flood (1999) and Fitzgerald (2000).

4   I know this because I was there.

5   Wilson (1998) poses the dilemma from a sociobiological perspective thus: '[I]f history and science have taught us anything, it is that passion and desire are not the same as truth. The human mind evolved to believe in the gods. It did not evolve to believe in biology. Acceptance of the supernatural conveyed a great advantage throughout prehistory, when the brain was evolving. Thus it is in sharp contrast to biology, which was developed as a product of the modern age and is

not underwritten by genetic algorithms. The uncomfortable truth is that the two beliefs are not factually compatible. As a result those who hunger for both intellectual and religious truth will never acquire both in full measure.'

6   Such disapproval was reflected in a pointed neglect of Shinto as a serious topic of study in the field of Japanese religions and a focus instead on Buddhism (mainly Zen) and Japanese New Religions. Michael Pye's 1981 article 'Diversions in the Interpretation of Shinto' was a notable exception. Helen Hardacre's generally excellent *Shinto and the State, 1868–1988* was suspicious of modern Shinto. Shinto studies have recently been revitalised by the groundbreaking work of Toshio Kuroda and subsequent debates, on which see the 'Introduction' in Breen and Teeuwen (2000).

7   In an unpublished paper on 'Shinto as a Japanese New Religion', presented at Oxford Brookes University and LSE, I point out that 1946 was the first year in which Shinto was recognised in Japan as a *religion* (under the new USA-style Constitution).

8   I do not know the origin of the phrase 'queen of the sciences'. A brief internet search on the phrase reveals that it is a title which is currently being claimed (without irony) each for their own subject by writers in disciplines as various as Physics, Astronomy, Paleontology, Mathematics – and Theology.

9   There was a marked contrast between the QAA methodology described here and the methodology which the QAA (in 2000) was planning to adopt for the next round of departmental inspections. The new approach, based on 'benchmarks' and 'standards' which would apply to all departments in a broad field (in our case all Theology and/or Religious Studies Departments, regardless of history, size, scope and philosophy) conspicuously failed to recognise that different academic departments constitute different worlds of meaning and practice, ultimately irreducible to each other. However carefully phrased the benchmarks might be, the proposed new methodology conspicuously lacked the vital element of 'methodological agnosticism' built into the original approach and it was therefore fundamentally unethical – it ignored ethos. Like many academic colleagues I believed that we should resist this new and un-phenomenological methodology, and in fact QAA was stripped of its department-level powers of inspection not long after this chapter was first written, and now carries out only institution-level audits of quality assurance procedures.

10   Richard Gombrich pointed out in a lecture given in Japan that the Self-Assessment Document for Oxford's Oriental Studies QAA inspection was written by his daughter, a master of parody (which is not, or at least not yet, an Oxford degree). The document was praised by the visiting QAA review team and (allegedly) subsequently recycled by Cambridge. The moral of this story for us should be that religions can pull the wool over the eyes of sincere researchers with at least equal facility. Damanhur is a good example; for years the residents of this spiritual community in Northern Italy presented a fairly conventional surface image to visitors, including academic researchers, while secretly the members were hollowing out by hand the adjacent mountain to create a vast underground temple: a story now told at http://www.damanhur.org/temple/html/history.htm.

Bibliography

Bocking, Brian 2000. *The Oracles of the Three Shrines: Windows on Japanese Religion*, London: Curzon Press.

Breen, John and Teeuwen, Mark 2000. *Shinto in History*, London: Curzon Press.

Fitzgerald, Timothy 2000. *The Ideology of Religious Studies*, Oxford: Oxford University Press.

Flood, Gavin 1999. *Beyond Phenomenology: Rethinking the Study of Religion*, London: Cassell.

Hardacre, Helen 1989. *Shinto and the State, 1868–1988*, Princeton: Princeton University Press.

Piatagorsky, Alexander 1999. *Freemasonry*. London: Harvill Press.

Pye, Michael 1981. 'Diversions in the Interpretation of Shinto', *Religion* **11** (1), pp. 61–74.

Smart, Ninian 1997 [1996]. *Dimensions of the Sacred*, London: Fontana.
Theology and Religious Studies Benchmarking Group 2000. *TRS Benchmark Statement*, Gloucester: Quality Assurance Agency for Higher Education.
Wilson, Edward O. 1998. *Consilience: The Unity of Knowledge*, New York: Alfred A. Knopf.

PART TWO
CASE STUDIES

CHAPTER 8

Religious Experience in Early Buddhism?

Richard Gombrich

Introduction: William James, Religious Experience and early Buddhism

In this chapter I propose to examine on the one hand the overlapping concepts of religious experience and of mystical experience, and on the other hand the religious and/or mystical experiences of the Buddha and his immediate followers, in so far as these are accessible to us through the early Pali texts; and I hope that the two sides of my examination may shed some light on each other.

When we attempt to study religious experience, the founder and patron saint of our studies must surely be William James, and I take his great book, *The Varieties of Religious Experience* (James 1985), as the basis of my exposition of that topic. When I began thinking what to say about religious experience in general before applying it to the Buddha, I had a few ideas which seemed to be worth communicating. When I picked up that book, I found most of them in it. On this occasion I have been particularly struck by how well James agrees with the Buddha, as I understand him – even though James, writing a century ago, was naturally not very well informed about Buddhism.[1]

The first similarity that strikes me between the views of William James and the Buddha is set out in a letter that James wrote about his aim in writing his book: 'The problem I have set myself is a hard one: first, to defend ... "experience" against philosophy as being the real backbone of the world's religious life ...' (Marty 1985, p. *xix*). With this we may compare, for example, the Buddha's answer to the monk Mālunkya-putta, who wanted him to solve such metaphysical problems as whether the world was eternal. The Buddha replied that anyone who refused to lead the religious life till those questions were answered would be like a man wounded by an arrow who refused to have it removed till he knew the name and caste of the man who had shot it; his teaching was merely the practical way to release from misery (MN sutta 63). Most of the long sermon which tradition places first in the canonical compilation of the Buddha's sermons, the Brahma-jāla Sutta (DN sutta i), is in effect an expansion of the same position.[2]

A second important similarity between William James and the Buddha lies in the emphasis on results as the criterion by which to judge experiences. 'By their fruits ye shall know them, not by their roots,' writes James (1985, p. 20), and calls this an 'empiricist criterion'. Regardless of their neurological origin, says James, for the value of 'religious opinions', 'immediate luminousness, ... philosophical reasonableness, and moral helpfulness are the only available criteria' (*ibid*, p. 18). In his famous sermon to the Kālāmas (AN I, 188–193) the Buddha urges them to test whatever they are told on the touchstone of their own experience. I would prefer to call this pragmatic rather than empiricist, but that is not important. What is important is the congruence between this view of religion and the general epistemological stance with which I agree. James himself says: 'Scientific theories are organically conditioned just as much as religious emotions are' (*ibid*, p. 14); that is a slight exaggeration, but the main point is valid. Karl Popper has argued that the origin of any hypothesis can tell us nothing about its validity; that can only be determined by testing it against observable reality. The Buddha was not so directly concerned with epistemology in the abstract, but in effect said the same: that the only test of a religious teaching that counts is whether it works.

James devotes his second lecture to what he calls 'Circumscription of the Topic': what are to count as 'religious experiences'? Here again, I venture to suggest a similarity between James, the Buddha, and Karl Popper. James writes: 'It would indeed be foolish to set up an abstract definition of religion's essence, and then proceed to defend that definition against all comers, yet this need not prevent me from taking my own narrow view of what religion shall consist in for the purpose of these lectures ... and proclaiming arbitrarily that when I say "religion" I mean that.' Of course I can supply no similar quotation from the Buddha, but his insistence that his precise words were of no importance, it was the general meaning that counted, and that his teaching could be translated into any language (unlike the sacred brahminical Sanskrit texts), carries the same message. Karl Popper likewise has shown the fatuity of seeking for definitions: that words are tools and do not themselves convey (or conceal) truths.

I have always emphatically espoused this position myself (Gombrich 1996, pp. 1–2). I have likewise always taken an emic rather than an etic position, preferring to let informants speak for themselves. But if we are to provide analysis as well as description, we cannot in the end avoid, after doing our best to report the concepts and categories of our informants, applying to them our own concepts and categories; in no other way is discussion among us possible, let alone meaningful comparison of our data.

If there is no general agreement among us on what is meant by the term 'religious experience', that does not mean that we have to abandon it; I even hope to show that considering the problem may have heuristic value, or at least clarify our thoughts. For it is obvious that while we disagree about what religious experience is, there are an infinite number of things we can agree to be not religion, not experiences, and not religious experiences. We can also agree that the conversion of St. Paul on the road to Damascus was a religious experience, and that William James collected many other valid examples. So our disagreement amounts to no more than saying that there is a large grey area and there are all sorts of contentious and borderline cases. And investigating those might turn out to be interesting.

As academics, we are trained to be sensitive to such problems. But for many people in Britain the meaning of the term 'religious experience' does not seem to be all that problematic. For example, neither Michael Argyle (1997) nor the Religious Experience Research Centre (formerly at Oxford, now in Lampeter) seem to find definition a problem, for they deal with social surveys in which people are asked about their religious experiences, and the informants themselves seem (on the data provided) to have no trouble in understanding what is meant. Evidently the title of James' third lecture, 'The Reality of the Unseen', plays a central role in their understanding.

The American philosopher W.T. Stace, after inspecting a wide range of data from around the world (in the spirit of James), constructed a table of eight 'Features of Religious Experience' which he had deduced to be valid across cultures (reproduced in Argyle 1997, Table 2).[3] Two things strike me about the table. Firstly, that to my understanding it might more aptly have been headed 'mystical' rather than 'religious' experiences. Secondly, that most of the features listed may characterise experiences which the subject may not consider religious. For example, I have myself experienced the loss of sense of self, but it never occurred to me to think of it as religious. On ineffability I shall (I hope not paradoxically) have a great deal to say. But let me now return to James, for whom many religious experiences – indeed, the majority of those with which he deals – are not mystical.

James draws a distinction between two types of religion: 'At the outset we are struck by one great partition which divides the religious field. On the one side lies institutional, on the other personal religion' (James 1985, p. 28). As one might expect of a man whose personal and cultural background was Protestant, the latter is not merely the focus of James' interests, but for him is primary in every sense: institutionalised religion could not exist without it. 'Religion, therefore, as I now ask you arbitrarily to take it, shall mean for us the feelings, acts, and experiences of individual men in their solitude, as far as they apprehend themselves to stand in relation to whatever they may consider divine.' (*ibid*, p. 31.) James thinks that without the private experience there would be no religion. Religion as it is studied by social scientists is in the public sphere, a patterned, systematised phenomenon. It may be practised or believed by anyone, whether they have themselves had a religious experience or not.

James' narrow definition of religion leads him into an apparent circularity. He argues (*ibid*, p. 27) that 'religious sentiment' is 'a collective name for the many sentiments which religious objects may arouse,' so that 'it probably contains nothing whatever of a psychologically specific nature. There is religious fear, religious love, religious awe, religious joy, and so forth. But religious love is only man's natural emotion of love directed to a religious object,' while religious awe 'comes over us at the thought of our supernatural relations.' James is clearly aware that it is unsatisfactory to define religious feelings as feelings directed towards what is religious. The subject of the feelings, he is saying, is having a religious experience if the object of his experience is religious. The circularity might be avoided by saying that religious objects were so by virtue of their having become 'religious' in what for James is the secondary sense: if they had become associated with institutionalised, public religion. That would help with the logical difficulty. But it would leave one with far too broad a definition. 'I hate going to church,' for example, would become an expression of religious sentiment.

James tries to find another way out of his difficulty by drawing into his definition 'whatever they may consider divine' (*ibid*, p. 31). He has to do some special pleading here. 'There are systems of thought which the world usually calls religious, and yet which do not positively assume a God. Buddhism is in this case ... Modern transcendental idealism, Emersonianism, for instance, also seems to let God evaporate into abstract Ideality. Not a deity *in concreto*, not a superhuman person, but the immanent divinity in things, the essentially spiritual structure of the universe, is the object of the transcendentalist cult' (*ibid*, pp. 31–2.) This recalls another form of Indian religion, the monism of the classical Upaniṣads.

For James, therefore, an experience is religious if its referent so defines it. He goes on, however, to consider once again the character of the subjective experience. 'Religion, whatever it is, is a man's total reaction upon life' (*ibid*, p. 35.) But not every 'total reaction upon life' can be called religious. 'There are trifling, sneering attitudes even towards the whole of life; and in some men these attitudes are final and systematic' (*ibid*, pp. 35–6). 'There must be something solemn, serious, and tender about any attitude which we denominate religious. If glad, it must not grin or snicker; if sad, it must not scream or curse. It is precisely as being solemn experiences that I wish to interest you in religious experiences' (*ibid*, p. 38). He goes on to make a further point: that religious experience gives an 'added dimension of emotion' (*ibid*, p. 48). 'Religious feeling is ... an absolute addition to the Subject's range of life. It gives him a new sphere of power' (*ibid*). As a generalisation this may be rather too highly coloured. But James is surely right to say that we call an experience religious only if it seems to us to be significant. In fact I would go a step further and say that we find such an experience transformative, that we feel ourselves to be a different person after having it, even if that feeling may rapidly wear off. Again, however, I am not saying that we interpret all transformative experiences as religious – very far from it. Life and literature are full of experiences which have transformed people's lives for better or for worse, filling them with loving bliss or the desire for revenge. It is sometimes said that religious experiences are discontinuous from previous experience: that they are felt to arrive suddenly, 'out of the blue', and not as the result of normal recognised causal processes. No doubt this is generally true of religious experiences in the sense used by Stace and Argyle. But we shall see that to consider as 'religious' only experiences which arrive in this manner does not do justice to the data.

I thus feel happier with James' circumscription of his topic when he focuses on the quality of a religious experience than when he is trying to define its referent or contents. Indeed, it comes naturally to me, as a student of Indian religions, to wonder whether in discussing religious experience it is necessary to consider the referents of the experience – whether one needs to consider both subject and object. Of course, most thoughts have an external referent, and to communicate at all (which as humans we normally do through language) we need to refer to the public sphere, to those experiences which we can assume that we share with others. But what James may possibly have missed is that the very privacy of the experience he is out to explore as the quintessence of religion will make it extremely hard to communicate.

In this, religious experience is like all private experience. Communication about it is a hit and miss affair and depends for its success largely on whether the communicator can appeal to shared experience in the audience. Philosophers have for centuries toyed with the problem that we cannot communicate to a human blind from birth what it is to experience light. Communication about our experience of the external world is imperfect, but can better rely on shared experience of a common referent than can communication about our internal states. By 'internal states' I mean both physical and mental states. If I try to communicate to my doctor the feeling of pain in my leg, words are unlikely to convey it; but the doctor does not need to know just what I feel like. With him, communication is purely pragmatic: it is enough if he can find out what for instance, makes the pain worse, so that he can then work out what to do about it. If I describe an emotion, I can only do so by appealing to common experience. I can try to tell my sweetheart what my love for her is like, but if she has never experienced a similar sentiment I shall fail. In fact, I am likely to experience much anxiety about whether her sentiments do match my own. In a culture which is less romantically inclined than ours, this may matter little; there, the aim of my communication to her may be primarily pragmatic: if I can convince her and her parents of the strength and durability of my feelings I may secure the desired result. But whether she – or anyone else – has ever experienced just what I experience in my love, I shall never know. However, that is not peculiar to an emotion like love: to a greater or lesser extent it must be true of all experience. I shall never know whether you experience red exactly as I do; I shall only know it well enough for pragmatic purposes. When you drive through a red light I can deduce that you may be red-green colour-blind.

The less we can rely on common experience in our attempt to communicate, the more important becomes our skill as communicators. Any normal person can give a fairly adequate account of the external world. For experiences with internal referents, however, we need poets, painters, musicians. It is perhaps above all the musicians who can convey, at least to other people who are both musical and familiar with the conventions of the musical idiom used in the musicians' culture, the experiences which words cannot reach.

For James, however, the experiences which words cannot reach are a special sub-category of religious experience: mystical experience. I do not find it easy to grasp exactly what he means by a mystical experience, but it seems that for him it differs from other religious experience in having no external referent: the mystic is looking inwards. The person who has a religious experience by feeling an unseen presence is not, I think, having an experience with a public referent, but for James he is different from the mystic in feeling the referent of his experience to be outside himself. James says (*ibid*, pp. 380–81) that mystical states have four main characteristics: ineffability, noetic quality, transiency, and passivity. The latter two are 'less sharply marked' and I propose to ignore them. This is what James writes about ineffability:

> The handiest of the marks by which I classify a state of mind as mystical is negative. The subject of it immediately says that it defies expression, that no adequate report of its contents can be given in words. It follows from this that its quality must be directly experienced; it cannot be imparted or transferred to others. In this peculiarity mystical states are more like states of feeling than like states of intellect. No one can make clear to another who has never had a certain feeling, in what the quality or worth of it consists. One must have musical ears to know the value of a symphony; one must have been in love one's self to understand a lover's state of mind. Lacking the heart or ear, we cannot interpret the musician or the lover justly, and are even likely to consider him weak-minded or absurd. The mystic finds that most of us accord to his experiences an equally incompetent treatment. (*ibid*)

Though mystical experiences, on this account, are feelings rather than thoughts ('states of intellect'), James goes on to write of their 'noetic quality', by which he means that 'mystical states seem to those who experience them to be also states of knowledge. They are states of insight into depths of truth unplumbed by the discursive intellect' (*ibid*, p. 380), 'and as a rule they carry with them a curious sense of authority for after-time' (*ibid*, p. 381). Though they are felt to be states of knowledge, it follows from their ineffability that what is known cannot be articulated in words. I shall suggest that on this last point the Buddha might have disagreed with James.

James' stress on the personal, psychological character of religious experience has here led him into a confusion. All experiences, in so far as they are private, are ineffable. But when we try to talk about them – in other words, interpret them to ourselves and others – we use language, which is irreducibly social. So the experience enters the public sphere at one remove. Defining an experience as religious is already a social act because it uses the word 'religious', the meaning of which is socially constructed. Similarly, a mystical experience is (to follow James as closely as possible) distinctive not in being ineffable but in being talked of (almost paradoxically) as ineffable. Why this should be I have already suggested.

I must emphasise that I am not reducing religious or mystical experience to a language game, nor am I content to accept that you have had a religious experience just because you use those words to me, perhaps in jest or to mislead me. I do think that there must be at least some kind of generic resemblance among the experiences to which these expressions refer. So our examination of James, despite the confusion between an experience and its interpretation, has not been a waste of time.

Experience in Buddhism

According both to William James and to the general western understanding, the Buddha's Enlightenment was a mystical experience. But that is not at all how Buddhists see it. When I began to study Theravāda Buddhism, both from books and in the field, I found that there is nothing in that tradition or culture corresponding to James' idea of the mystical. Neither Pali nor Sinhala contains any word for 'mystical' or 'mysticism' or anything remotely like it. When I interviewed a famous Theravādin monk in Sinhala and he wanted to speak of mysticism, he had recourse to the English word.

What the Buddha achieved is expressed in various ways. He saw the truth; he destroyed passion, hatred and delusion; he saw things as they really are. This last expression, which occurs often in the Pali canon and tradition, is particularly significant: the Buddha saw reality – and described it. He saw the *dhamma*, a word which refers both to his teaching and to the content of that teaching; it is the truth, expounded in a list of truths (*dhammā* in the plural), true propositions which can be found in the texts. What makes his experience of importance to us is the truth that he discovered and taught; had it been ineffable, he could not have done that.

What is, of course, ineffable is the emotional quality of the experience that the Buddha enjoyed at his enlightenment (and was indeed held to enjoy for the rest of his life). This is described negatively as the absence of passion (sometimes greed), hatred and delusion. This experience is more difficult to describe than other experiences because it is not an experience that most people have ever had. Indeed, at the time when the Buddha had it there was no one else in the world who had, which is why he at first despaired of being able to explain himself to anyone and was disinclined to preach. Luckily he was persuaded, according to the story, to change his mind, so that in due course, as a result of following his preaching, other people had the experience too.

The experience at which Buddhists aim is called either *bodhi* (which is usually translated 'enlightenment' but literally means 'awakening'), which stresses its cognitive aspect, or *nirvana*. *Nirvana* is a metaphor. Its precise reference was forgotten after a while in the Buddhist tradition, but not for reasons connected with ineffability. *Nirvana* means blowing out. The Buddha preached that we are all 'on fire' with three fires, the fires of passion, hatred and delusion, and that our salvation consists in extinguishing those fires. The three fires are an allusion to the three fires which it was the duty of the brahmin householder to maintain and in which he was obliged to sacrifice daily. When Buddhism expanded beyond its original milieu in north India, where evidently brahmins formed an important part of the Buddha's audience, the structure of this metaphor was forgotten.

Extinguishing the fire of illusion is exactly the same thing for Buddhists as 'seeing things as they are': a common phrase in the early scriptures. This means clarity of vision, bringing everything into focus, knowing and being able to articulate everything that really needs to be known. While this runs counter to the 'ineffability' of mysticism as James conceives it, it does take us back to his remark that religion is a 'total reaction upon life'. This 'total reaction' does not mean dealing with everything in any detail; on the contrary, it means putting most things aside as unimportant. It deals with life by telling us what is important and what to think or feel about that.

What did the Buddha consider important? We cannot know as a certain historical fact what he said as soon as he had attained enlightenment, or what he put in his first sermon; but the tradition is in no doubt about the contents of the first sermon. He began by commending a style of life which he called the 'middle way', a way between self-indulgence and mortification of the flesh; he commended it because it enabled one to see the truth. The truth was expressed as fourfold. The first truth is just the single word *dukkha*, most often translated into English as suffering. The other three truths are the arising of suffering, the extinction of suffering, and the path leading to the extinction of suffering. Obviously these are not themselves 'truths', as they are not statements: the terms are mnemonics, or shorthand.

It has been reasonably objected by the west that life is not all suffering. Luckily we see that living beings are also sometimes happy and comfortable. The translation 'suffering' gave Buddhism an undeserved reputation in the West for pessimism. I therefore prefer the translation 'dissatisfaction'. We end up being dissatisfied even with the best of comforts, says Buddhism, because they are transient and repeatedly end in death. Only when we no longer have death looming ahead of us can we be truly satisfied.

The Buddha had a transformative experience, his enlightenment, which enabled him to tell us what the true quality of all our other experience is like. He could realise this because he (at first uniquely) realised its opposite: he could grasp the nature of normal human experience because he had something with which to contrast it. This did not render him inarticulate; quite the opposite. On the other hand, it gave him certainty that he had found out what was most important in life and how to deal with it. In this interpretation of his experience and insights, the Buddha was deeply influenced by brahminical religious texts, notably the *Bṛhadāraṇyaka Upaniṣad*. The early *Upaniṣads* argue that salvation (freedom from rebirth and from the suffering that that entails) is to be achieved by realisation that the essence of every individual living being and the essence of the universe are ultimately the same (though there are various interpretations of just what that means). What they have in common is that they are existence, consciousness and bliss – and nothing else. Existence is a plenum and so lacks nothing. Since suffering is always the lack of something, this plenum cannot lack and so cannot suffer. So man in his true nature is a part or aspect of what cannot include suffering. The salvific experience, moreover, merges subject and object into a blissful unity.

While the Buddha rejected some central features of *Upaniṣadic* metaphysics, there is obviously a close analogy between his experience of *nirvana*, the end of *dukkha*, and the Upaniṣadic account of salvation. However, he seems to have interpreted his experience differently (see below). I have argued in *How Buddhism Began* (1996; in this I follow Hamilton 1996) that the Buddha's argument with the details of *Upaniṣadic* metaphysics is of secondary importance; that what really matters is his insistence that experience is the primary concern; I call this 'How, not What' (Gombrich 1996). I have already mentioned the Buddha's sermon to the Kalāmās, in which he tells them not to accept any doctrine on authority alone; they are to test what religious teachers say on the touchstone of their own experience. This will, of course, show them that the Buddha is preaching the truth; but that is not the main point: the point is that to follow his advice will lead to *nirvana*, salvation. The truth of his teaching is to be experienced. This emphasis on experience is just what William James called 'the real backbone of the world's religious life' (*vide supra*). For it does not apply to the final goal of religion alone, but to the entire religious life which the Buddha prescribes. This has been beautifully captured in a modern ethnographic work about Buddhist monks. In the final, climactic chapter of *The Forest Monks of Sri Lanka*, Michael Carrithers (1983, pp. 280–81), meditating on the life of one of his informants, writes:

> The hallmark of the daily schedule, as of insight, is the principle of psychological pragmatism, of practicality. In giving oneself up to strict observance of the daily round, one effectively gives up both remorse and anxiety ... [T]he monk's way of life is more than merely a means to an end:

it is very nearly the end in itself. And indeed one never gets the idea from the canon and commentaries that a monk who attains release might then hang up his robes and do something else: the goal is wholly within the ambit of the monk's life.

The Buddha's entire teaching is not about changing the world but about changing our experience of it. Indeed, it is not even clear whether he thought in the final analysis that there was a world as we would say 'objectively', outside our experience, though the Theravādin systematisation of his teaching, the *abhidhamma*, certainly thought so. However, it would both negate my message and defeat my purpose to pursue this ontological problem. The Buddha's message is about how we should train and develop ourselves so as to lead less dissatisfied lives.[4] Spiritual progress, in the Buddhist formulation, has three components: morality, concentration, understanding (*sīla, samādhi, paññā*). Each is a pre-requisite for the next, though none is perfectible alone. The normal western expectation, I suppose, would be to look for religious experience primarily under the rubric of concentration. But I want to argue that for the Buddha all three have an equal title to be called religious experience. And I want to argue further that this is not idiosyncratic but a helpful way of looking at the whole topic.

The Buddha had an experience which concerned the very nature of experience: one could even call it a meta-experience. He saw that normal experience is vitiated by the transience of all worldly phenomena, a transience which renders them unsatisfying in the last resort. Our experience of their transience can only successfully be handled, he argued, by coming to terms with it: we should not want permanence, for ourselves or our loved ones, because we are not going to get it. We need of course to understand this fundamental fact if we are going to stop our vain desires. So we have both to control our emotions and to train our intellect. In other words, we have to adapt our entire mentality to reality, the reality of what life is like, including the fact that we all must die.

Morality, concentration and understanding correspond rather well to James' three criteria for judging religious opinions: immediate luminousness, philosophical reasonableness and moral helpfulness. Moral helpfulness corresponds to *sīla* and reasonableness to *paññā*, or at least to the content of that understanding. The experiential component in that set of criteria is the luminousness; this aptly describes the quality of the prized experience of salvific understanding. It is meditation which Buddhism prescribes as the training for that experience.

Meditation is so clearly an area of private experience where words are likely to prove inadequate; nevertheless we require a brief, necessarily superficial, look at the kinds of mental training and activity the early texts seem to be referring to. The most general word for meditation is *bhāvanā*, which means 'development'; this is a training of the mind. At a very early stage, before the canonical collection of texts was closed, this had been systematised into two sections, in some contexts called concentration and understanding, in others calming (*samatha*) and insight (*vipassanā*). 'Calming' is supposed to discipline the emotions, 'insight' to sharpen the understanding until one sees the world as the Buddha saw it. In this doctrinal system, 'calming' is in the last resort a training for 'insight'; in the canon it is probably considered to be indispensable, but later a minority tradition appears to have argued that for some people, salvific insight might be achieved without that kind of meditation (Gombrich 1996, Chapter 4, esp. pp. 123–7). The pair 'calming' and 'insight' seems to be a formulation which to some extent took over from another pair: 'awareness' (*sati*) and 'concentration' (*samādhi*). The latter two are the seventh and eighth components of the noble eightfold path which tradition considers the Buddha to have enunciated in his first sermon; they thus look like the culmination of that path, whatever later tradition may say about it. Similarly, the full description of how one reaches enlightenment found in the *Sāmaññaphala Sutta*, 'The Text on the Fruits of Renunciation' (DN sutta ii), has the renunciate first training himself in awareness at every moment before it has him sit down to practise what we would regard as meditation proper.

The systematised tradition aligns awareness with insight, but that falsifies the early texts. The other most famous canonical text on meditation in the canon, besides the *Sāmaññaphala Sutta*, is the *Mahā Sati-paṭṭhāna Sutta* (DN sutta *xxii*), 'The Text on Establishing Awareness'. Here awareness is to be directed to four kinds of things: bodies (one's own and other people's), feelings (as of pleasure and pain), states of mind, and finally to seeing the world in Buddhist terms as fleeting, unsatisfactory and devoid of essence. It is only this last of the four kinds of awareness that corresponds to the insight of the developed system.

As soon as we thus venture to deconstruct the systematised and homogenised account of the commentaries, we find it riddled with inconsistencies. And I make so bold as to say that this goes even for systematised accounts within the canon. The kind of awareness with which the renunciate begins to train his mind in the *Sāmaññaphala Sutta* is simply awareness of his own body. It is only after practising meditation in the narrow sense and achieving the four levels of concentration known as *jhāna* that the renunciate becomes fully aware of all his and other people's mental states. This achievement, in fact, immediately precedes the 'three knowledges' which constitute the culminating salvific experience.[5] In the *Sāmaññaphala Sutta* the term 'awareness' applies only to the awareness of one's body; the awareness of mental states is referred to as recognising them for what they are.

Close scrutiny of the four *jhāna*, the four levels of concentration, reveals something I find even more puzzling and discordant within the systematised account. According to that account, all achievement in calming or in concentration – whichever term you choose to use – is measured by these *jhāna*, and they are interpreted as a straightforward progression, the first being the lowest and the fourth the highest state. (It is irrelevant here that the scholastic tradition sometimes splits up the first into two, giving five *jhāna* in all.) The *Sāmaññaphala Sutta* gives the classic description of the *jhāna*; so far as I know there is no account of them that lacks the feature I am about to discuss.

One can achieve the first *jhāna* only after ridding oneself of all sensual desires and other immoral states of mind. One then calms one's body and concentrates one's mind so that one feels delight, but one is still thinking, in the normal sense of the term. In the second *jhāna* one intensifies the concentration to such an extent that what is translated 'discursive thought' disappears altogether and the mind is said to be 'one-pointed' (*cetaso ekodi-bhāva*). Everyone who discusses this assumes that this condition is what is referred to in the brahminical yoga system as 'cessation of the operation of thought' (*citta-vṛtti-nirodha*).[6] Certainly I would argue that if the mind is 'one-pointed' there is no thought, for a thought consists in making a connection. The description of the third *jhāna*, which can be attained only on the basis of having attained the second, strikes a different note. On the emotional level, the meditator moves from delight to equanimity. One-pointedness of mind is no longer mentioned; instead he is said to be 'aware and cognisant' (*sato sampajāno*). In the fourth *jhāna* equanimity and awareness are simply carried to their highest pitch, metaphorically described as 'purity' (*upekhā-sati-pārisuddhi*).

Although this is controversial, it seems to me that the third and fourth *jhanas* are thus quite unlike the second. One might be 'aware and cognisant' without being aware of anything in particular: the terms 'aware and cognisant' could perhaps be describing a state of receptivity, of potential rather actual thought. But I find this an unsatisfying argument. One has to ask whether a real meditator would or would not notice a flashing light or a loud noise in his vicinity. The natural explanation of the text, in my view, is that in the third and fourth *jhāna* he would, but in the second he would not. If that is correct, this description of the *jhāna* describes (and prescribes) two quite different cognitive states, and the later tradition has falsified the *jhāna* by classifying them as the quintessence of the concentrated, calming kind of meditation, ignoring the other – and indeed higher – element.

Buddhist Mental Training

We need to take a fresh look at the kinds of mental training that the Buddha prescribes, using our own vocabulary rather than that of the commentator Buddhaghosa. Here I can do so only very summarily: since I myself have no experience of meditation, I broach this topic with extreme diffidence.

First, it seems to me that on the whole the Buddha is not talking about what we nowadays call altered states of consciousness. These do however come up at two points. The states known as the 'formless *jhāna*', which are sometimes classified as coming after and above the four *jhāna* already mentioned, are surely such altered states: they are the plane of the infinity of space, the plane of the infinity of consciousness, the plane of the infinity of nothingness and the plane of neither apperception nor its absence. According to tradition, the Buddha had been taught to attain these states by his teachers, but found them insufficient, and added to the eight *jhāna* a ninth state, the extinction of apperception and feeling. These are states of what Mircea Eliade called 'enstasis'. Unlike the four *jhāna*, the higher enstatic states do not constitute an essential part of the path to enlightenment. Altered states of consciousness also crop up in descriptions of the supernormal powers (*iddhi*) that are available to someone who has achieved the four *jhāna*, powers such as flying and clairaudience. These are described by comparative religionists as shamanic; they are ecstatic as against enstatic. The Buddha accepts these experiences as facts but says that they are of no spiritual value.

What is it then that the Buddha recommends that we do with our minds? What are we to experience? In the first place, he states that morality, and in particular self-restraint, is a pre-requisite for spiritual progress. To consider what comes next, we must recall the cultural context of early Buddhism. There was no writing, so no reading. Educational institutions in any modern sense did not exist. A few brahmins learnt sacred texts by heart, and a tiny number of those even learnt to discuss their contents, but these were quite exceptional in society at large. It is easy for us to forget that schooling does not just teach us specific facts or skills; it teaches us while we are still children to be sensitive to people and things around us and to be able to concentrate on a task or a problem. In the Buddha's social environment there were of course skilled craftsmen, trained to concentrate on their work; and it is notable how they appear in the *Sāmaññaphala Sutta* in similes for the meditator as he acquires control over his mind. But even such people were in a small minority. And the Buddha aimed his message at people of all classes and both genders, even if we do find a disproportionate number of brahmins among his disciples. I suggest, therefore, that we today tend to over-interpret what was meant at one level by awareness and concentration. This over-interpretation began, no doubt, with the professional monks who systematised the Buddha's teachings. I am not denying that in order to achieve enlightenment, awareness and concentration have to be cultivated to a very high pitch. But what the Buddha was prescribing as mental training must initially have been what we more or less take for granted in an educated person.

Another mental faculty which the Buddha encouraged people to cultivate was the imagination, use of which is prescribed in various meditation exercises. For example, the monk is encouraged to visualise his body as composed of thirty-two listed components, all described in unattractive terms. For the similar exercise of observing the disintegration of a corpse, monks are encouraged to visit actual charnel grounds; but they are also encouraged to apply to their own bodies what can be observed on such a visit, to imagine how their own corpses will rot away. A different use of the imagination comes into play with the standard meditative technique known as the *kasina*. In this technique one concentrates on a visual phenomenon, such as a coloured clay disc, until one can see it without actually looking at it. This is not an after-image but an eidetic memory. One then extends this image by stages until it covers the whole world (*kasina* means 'whole'). Two other instances of the use of the imagination are worthy of attention. The *Mahāsamaya Sutta* (DN xx) begins by recounting how, while the Buddha is staying in a forest with attendant monks, a vast number of gods arrive to see him. He tells the monks he will teach them the gods' names:

> Then the Teacher spoke to his disciples, who delighted in his teaching: 'Troops of gods have arrived; be aware of them, O monks.' On hearing the Buddha's teaching they exerted themselves, and there appeared to them a true vision of non-humans [literally, 'knowledge, sight of non-humans']. Some saw a hundred, some a thousand ... some an infinity, filling space in all directions. (DN II, 256, 2–7)

Centuries later, with the rise of tantra, such visions of gods were systematically prescribed and accorded religious value. In the Pali canon I find no indication that this particular ability is to be cultivated, but it looks as if, like the shamanic powers of the meditative adept, some degree of it was taken for granted.

Visualising gods may not have been considered a valuable accomplishment, and indeed in his terms the Buddha might not have classified it as a 'religious experience'. It would be more difficult to exclude from that category the ability to visualise the Buddha himself. The Buddha seems to have discouraged such a personality cult, as when he said, 'He who sees the *Dhamma* sees me' (SN III, 120.) However, the old monk Pingiya complains of failing eyesight (Snip 1120), but says of the Buddha: 'I cannot stay away from him even for a moment ... I see him with my mind as if with my eye, being vigilant day and night ... I pass the night revering him. For that very reason I think that I am not staying away from him ... In whatever direction the one of great wisdom goes, in that very direction I bow down ... I constantly go on a mental journey, for my mind is joined to him' (Snip 1140–43; trans. Norman, slightly adapted). Here we find visualisation combined with the most familiar of religious sentiments, devotion.

Though devotion is not an emotion that the Buddha asked his followers to cultivate, no survey of the kinds of experience gathered under the rubric of meditation in early Buddhism would be complete without mention of the four ways of living with Brahman, also known as the 'boundless' (*appamāṇa*) states. The meditator is told gradually to suffuse the entire world with kindness, with compassion, with empathetic joy, and with equanimity. I have argued (Gombrich 1996) that originally this form of meditation was taught by the Buddha to be salvific. The tradition accords it great spiritual value but denies that it can by itself produce enlightenment.

This leads me to the last use of the mind I wish to mention: reasoning. The reason why the four boundless states were somewhat demoted (if you accept my view), or could never alone lead to enlightenment (to accept orthodoxy), is that they omit the use of the intellect to understand what the Buddha preached and so 'see things as they are'. I think it needs no lengthy argument to state that the Buddha's teaching was an intellectual *tour de force* and that Buddhism in all its forms admires the use of the intellect. Monks and nuns, as well as the more educated laity, have been taught to apply their intelligence so as to change their experiences, just as cognitive therapy does today.

My list of ways in which early Buddhism recommends the harnessing of the emotions, the imagination and the intellect to religious experience is surely not exhaustive. However, rather than pursue this topic further I feel it will be more productive to turn to another part of the Pali canon. What I have dealt with so far has been mainly a composite picture of how the Buddha himself envisaged religious experience, or, more accurately, what others reconstructed as his sayings on the subject. However, the canon also offers us more direct evidence of religious experience, the kind of first-person testimony informing William James' book. The Theravādin canon contains a collection of Pali poems written in the first person by monks and nuns, the *Thera-gāthā* and the *Therī-gāthā* respectively. Most of these poems are very short. All give some account of the author's experiences, although not always obviously or directly. A few of them make no reference to Buddhist (or other) moral or religious doctrine; for example: 'Coloured like the dark blue clouds, delightful with cool streams of pure water, carpeted with cochineal insects, those rocks give me joy' (Thag 13). However, Buddhists regard all these poems as authentic records of what we would call religious or spiritual experiences, and to deny their claim would seem to me to be wholly arbitrary. Let us take a brief look at what the authors say about themselves – or, for our comparative context, what they do not say.

First, while many of the authors claim explicitly, by their use of some Buddhist doctrinal expression, to have attained enlightenment, many others do not. Yet one would not easily notice the difference between the two categories. I anticipated this point when I quoted Carrithers (1983) earlier: the monk he describes is – so far as one can tell – leading a life in a remote jungle area in modern Sri Lanka which replicates the milieu evoked by the poems of the Buddhist elders which we can read in the canon.

The second noteworthy feature of these records is that nobody says that what they have experienced is beyond words, ineffable. The Buddha has supplied them with a vocabulary, a set of concepts, with which they can and do express their feelings. The general tone of these feelings is not dramatic or heroic, even though it is not uncommon for an elder to describe himself as 'victorious' (for example Thag 5–8 inclusive). What does come across, both explicitly and implicitly, is that by well-directed effort the author has had experiences which are the opposite of those of normal life, experiences which give him a sense of liberation. The elements which constantly recur are those summed up in the triad morality, concentration and understanding; and, pervading all three, words denoting self-control, vigilance and awareness (primarily of oneself). Let me cite just three typical verses, taken almost at random from the first few pages of the *Theragāthā*:

> Strong through understanding, behaving with moral restraint (*sīlava-tūpapanno*), concentrated, delighting in meditation (*jhāna*), aware, eating just what is necessary, one should await one's time in this world, all passion gone. (Thag 12)

This verse contains all the three terms *sīla, samādhi, paññā*:

> For a sage who is attentive, vigilant, training himself in the paths of sagehood, venerable, calm, always possessed of mindfulness, griefs do not come into existence. (Thag 68; trans Norman)
> Expert in imagination (*citta-nimittassa kovido*), recognising the flavour of solitude, meditating, wise, aware, one may achieve the bliss without carnality. (Thag 85)

The phrase I have translated 'expert in imagination' probably refers to skill in manipulating eidetic images like the *kasiṇa*. From other texts we know what 'understanding' refers to. But in these poems there is not much about the content of what is understood; it is spelled out, if at all, mostly in doctrinal formulae. More than the content of the understanding, it is its flavour that matters: it carries James' 'noetic quality', with its sensation of certainty. Indeed, freedom from doubt is quite often mentioned (for example Thag 5). I hesitate to follow James in calling it 'self-authenticating', for it has been authenticated by the Buddha; but it is clearly solemn and transformative.

What has been conquered? Sensuality, all kinds of moral and mental weakness. But also, crucially, fear. 'I fear no danger. Our teacher is expert in the deathless. Monks go by that path on which no fear remains' (Thag 21.) 'The immediate cause of fear, no doubt, is living alone in the jungle; but the ultimate fear is of death. The Buddha overcame Māra, death personified, by meeting him halfway. One is reminded of James' wise remark: 'Religion thus makes easy and felicitous what in any case is necessary' (James 1985, p. 51.)

Comparative Sociology of Religious Experience

Let me put the above data on early Buddhism into a comparative context by making use of Bryan Wilson's (1996) essay on the sociology of religious experience. Wilson demonstrates that James' ambitious programme cannot in fact be fulfilled: we cannot fully understand religious experience if we attend only to 'individual men in their solitude' without any regard for social context. For though all experience is private, and by that token and to that degree ineffable, our mere articulation of that experience is social because it uses a particular language, which is a social phenomenon, and our interpretation of what we have experienced is conditioned by society. As Wilson puts it in his opening paragraph:

> The usual idea of a religious experience is conceived in largely individual terms. It is generally seen as an uninduced, unanticipated and most probably sudden sense of some force, power, or mood which transcends everyday comprehension, and which is beyond ordinary empirical explanation. Where an explanation of such phenomena is attempted, the tendency is to seek to understand them in essentially psychological terms. What I wish to suggest is that, although this is the common understanding of what is implied by the term 'religious experience', in fact by no means all such experience is of a purely psychological kind. Many people, who would not claim to have encountered such a numinous sense of a force or a presence, would certainly claim to have acquired new religious insight by quite different means and in what would usually be quite different circumstances. These are people who have been introduced into a context – a congregation or a community – in which a special religious awakening is not only expected but which may even be canvassed. Its very form, sequence and effect, and even the occasion of its occurring, may indeed be well understood in advance. Although it is not involuntary, and is almost (to employ a metaphor) a ready-made experience, such a religious sensation is none the less valid for all that, and its effects, since it occurs in a much more structured context, may indeed be very much more influential and enduring. (Wilson 1996, p. 1)

Wilson focuses on conversion as typical of what most people would regard as a religious experience, but he argues

> that the religious experience that leads to, or accompanies, conversion is not necessarily of the type that conforms to the recorded account of Paul's conversion on the road to Damascus ... [T]hat narrative assumes that conversion must be sudden, dramatic, emotional, and the result of the operation of an external agency operating on the convert. It is seen as a single life-changing event, the effects of which are expected to last the entire span of an individual's lifetime. As a consequence of the experience, it is assumed that there will be a total transformation in the attitudes, dispositions and behaviour of the individual. (*ibid*, p. 5)

However, as Wilson continues:

> Religious experience need not be confined to this one intense manifestation
> of emotional turmoil. Sects differ in the extent to which emotional
> expression is regarded as necessary, desirable, permissive or prohibited. By
> no means all sects expect would-be converts to undergo the sense of being
> born-again. For many – Jehovah's Witnesses, Christadelphians, most
> conspicuously among them – religious experience is couched in intellectual
> terms. What candidates for admission must show is that they have studied
> and learned and understood a range of doctrinal propositions: their
> religious experience has been a steady, cumulative learning process,
> undertaken often with the help of sect elders, until candidates have
> mastered certain central tenets which qualify them for membership. The
> candidates have to learn quite consciously what they must do, and how
> they must henceforth comport themselves, since their experience must be
> sustained and their intellectual grasp of what the sect teaches must be
> constantly nourished by recurrent and continuous exposure to basic texts.
> (*ibid*, p. 5)

Wilson goes on to contrast the emotional type of conversion sought at revival
meetings with the slow process of becoming, for example, a Jehovah's Witness.
Common to both cases is that the future convert knows what is expected; this is
as true of those who attend the revival meetings as of those who attend regular
Bible classes. On the other hand:

> It follows, from the differences in the way in which conversion is conceived
> and experienced between different sectarian groups, that sectarians of
> diverse kinds will both account for their experiences and will recount those
> experiences, in distinctive terms – terms indeed that would be neither
> appropriate nor recognizable to sectarians of a different persuasion.
> Equally, the points chosen for emphasis in the consequential significance of
> conversion also differ. (*ibid*, p. 6)

To rectify the bias in James' too personalised and hence too emotionalistic
presentation, we need to consider the gradualist approach to conversion:

> Among Witnesses there is nothing approaching the 'road to Damascus'
> syndrome: indeed, to claim conversion in the terms suitable to Pentecost-
> alism would create the powerful suspicion that the speaker was totally
> deluded. For Witnesses, salvation depends on an understanding of the
> Bible and ·on persistent application to it through the media of the
> Watchtower Society's publications. There is no moment when this
> conversion experience is marked by a qualitatively different sense of
> things. Rather there is a slow, accretive growth of understanding in [*sic*] the
> way in which things fit together, until the convert becomes the recruit and
> decides that he must now undergo baptism as a mark of his commitment.
> The experience is intellectual rather than emotional, and to recount the

conversion is really to take the auditor through the stages of learning that have brought the outsider to his present allegiance.

When Witnesses talk about their conversion they, too, tell a 'before and after' story but that story is not one in which God or the Holy Spirit wrought a transformation in a sinner, but the story of how an individual achieved a new sense of things, and came to understand God's purposes in the world. Their tales are more articulate and invoke neither mystical imagery nor a repertoire of emotive recollections. (*ibid*, p. 7)

Wilson then quotes at some length a Witness's account of his own conversion, which ends with the words, 'I feel a better person than I was – no violent temper, which I had. I'm not me any more!' Wilson comments:

The religious experience of the Witness is not a sudden instance of illumination but rather a steady application in intellectual understanding and moral apprehension. It is not the less a religious experience for being protracted and cumulative: indeed, in terms of consequences, it is perhaps of more profound and persisting importance. Because there is no one occasion on which the Witness recognizes a life-transforming experience, he does not (unlike the Pentecostalist) seek to re-live the moment at which the Spirit is supposed to have struck. (*ibid*, p. 8)

It would be redundant to expatiate on the similarities that suggest themselves between the experiences of Wilson's Witnesses and the Theravāda Buddhist elders. In both the religious experience is something worked for, clearly envisaged, and not necessarily dramatic or sudden. For the participants, the difference between the monotheistic and the non-theistic belief framework is of course of great importance. For comparativists, it may be no less important to point out that the moment of conversion for the Witness, occurring as part of a long process, is primarily a social event: others tell him when he is ready. How does the Buddhist monk know when he has attained *nirvana*? Sometimes, no doubt, his teacher tells him, when he has reported particular thoughts or feelings. But the Buddhists probably lack a precise functional analogue to the community of a Christian sect, and this would explain why whether an individual has or has not reached the religious goal – the analogue of conversion – will in many cases remain vague; in other cases the individual is entitled by his *certitudo salutis* to speak out. It may not be too far-fetched to suggest that those who thus spoke out were those who had had the more dramatic, emotional type of experience. (In this case 'emotional' refers to cooling, not heightening, the emotions.) Foremost among those, obviously, was the Buddha himself. But even the Buddha had, according to the received account, been living in the jungle seeking enlightenment for six years. He had consorted with other ascetics who were following a similar lifestyle and pursuing the same quest for liberation from the dissatisfactions of normal worldly life. He was not the only one in that milieu to have religious experiences. Far from it: he studied with teachers who had routinised their attainment. What was distinctive about his final achievement was the intellectual discovery which embraced both the path and the goal of such a liberation.

Throughout the history of Buddhism there has been a certain tension between the quest for altered states of consciousness and rationalism, the effort to understand the way things really are; and most forms of Buddhism have a place for both. This tension can already be found in the canon. There are rather diverse accounts of what *nirvana* consists of, and no doubt divergent opinions among the compilers of the canon. Primarily these are differences of emphasis or perspective, but there may, if one honestly looks behind the commentarial homogenisation, be real disagreements. The Buddha knew of the *Upaniṣads* and their goal: an experience of loss of self through the sensation of merging into the essence of the universe. His own experience of loss of self may or may not have been a similarly monistic experience; on that there seems to be disagreement. Certainly, however, his teaching articulated it in a way which took issue with the *Upaniṣadic* interpretation. There are many ways of losing the self; even Wilson's Jehovah's Witness, from an utterly different background, says, 'I'm not me any more'. In the Buddha's case it is clear that the loss of self has both an emotional and an intellectual component, expressed respectively as the extinction of the fires of passion and hatred, and of the fire of delusion. The emotional component is the abolition of selfishness, as in the repeated canonical expression, 'This is not mine'; the intellectual component is the abolition of the idea that one has a self (in the *Upaniṣadic* sense), as in the paired expression, 'This is not I'.

The traditional account of the Buddha's spiritual progress tells the same story. During his search for liberation he studied meditation with other teachers, who taught him what the Buddhists came to call the 'calming' meditation to discipline the emotions, up to a high level of the 'formless *jhāna*'. But these altered states of consciousness did not bring him liberation, for all were impermanent. What he added to these, what tradition regards as the distinctively Buddhist achievement, was the set of realisations which came to be classified as insight (*vipassanā*), tantamount to 'seeing things as they are'.

In fact the situation was slightly more complicated than that. For the same tradition holds that the Buddha learnt from his teachers only as far as the penultimate level of 'calming', 'the plane of neither apperception nor its absence'; he added the final 'extinction of apperception and feeling' himself. So it looks as if there may have been a rival account of what the Buddha achieved, which made his crowning accomplishment an altered state of consciousness, an enstatic state. However, if this interpretation ever existed, it was decisively defeated. That the extinction of apperception and feeling is or was the same as *nirvana* is firmly denied by orthodoxy. The later tradition holds that a person who has attained that state of what we would call 'trance' cannot survive in it for more than seven days. Thus it is impermanent, which in turn means that it is not *nirvana* but belongs to *saṃsāra*, the phenomenal world. This recalls Wilson's contrast between the revivalist and the Witness. The revivalist's conversion experience is emotional and dramatic; then, however, its effects are liable to wear off, and revivalists often gather to repeat their ecstatic experiences. The Witness reaches his more intellectual experience methodically and it is an irreversible process. Buddhists likewise believe that once one has attained *nirvana* one cannot 'relapse', whereas the attainment of 'calming' states is more like a skill which one can practise when one wishes.

It seems likely that a famous Buddhist controversy centred on the same issue. In late eighth-century Tibet the ruler organised a debate between a Chinese Buddhist monk who claimed that enlightenment came suddenly and outside the sequence of causation, and an Indian monk who said that it was acquired gradually, by methodical preparation. The latter won. If I am right, Buddhists in India and in the Theravāda tradition have always tended to favour the 'gradualist' tradition, both because the effects of that kind of spiritual attainment are longer-lasting and because their Buddhism has a large cognitive content, an intellectual and rational emphasis, which to the more mystically inclined seems of little relevance.

I said earlier that 'mysticism' is the religious experience which is interpreted as being indescribable in ordinary language; that its hallmark is apophatic. This phenomenon was known at the very beginning of the Buddhist tradition but the tradition soon came to downplay it. That the Buddha felt the quality of his enlightenment to be ineffable is shown, I would argue, by the title he gave himself, according to Pali canonical texts: *Tathāgata*. It has two parts: *tathā*, which means 'thus', and *gata*, which commonly means 'gone'. Thus the word is often translated as 'Thus-gone'. The Buddhist tradition has made various fanciful attempts to etymologise the term. The word *gata* when it occurs as the second member of a compound of this type often loses its primary meaning and means simply 'being'. For example, *citragatā nārī* is not 'the woman who has gone into the picture' but simply 'the woman in the picture' (Coulson 1976, p. 111). So the Buddha is referring to himself as 'the one who is like that'. In my opinion, this is tantamount to saying that he can find no words to describe his state; he can only point to it. Moreover, though the epithet *Tathāgata* most commonly refers to a Buddha, and in later texts does so exclusively, in the Pali canon it can refer to any enlightened person (MN I, 140). Similarly, the epithet *tādi*, derived from Sanskrit *tādṛś*, also originally meant just 'such' or 'like that', though the commentators read other meanings into it. This word too could in the Pali texts be applied to any enlightened person (Thag 68). The word had a colourful history, for through phonetic change it was reconstituted, or should I say reinterpreted, in the Sanskrit of Mahayana Buddhists as *trāyin*, 'saving', and so became an epithet of Buddhas and Bodhisattvas, denoting their compassion.

The fact that the Buddhist tradition lost the original meanings of *tathāgata* and *tādi* bears witness, I suggest, to the anti-mystical (or at least non-mystical) stance of that tradition. The Buddha could not describe the quality of his experience because it was a unique private experience with no publicly available referent, but this in no way implies that the truths he discovered or the way to direct oneself or others towards a similar experience were inexpressible.

There is another canonical fragment which points in the same direction. There is a famous verse in the brahminical *Taittirīya Upaniṣad*:

> Before they reach it, words turn back, together with the mind;
> One who knows that bliss of brahman, he is never afraid.

This describes the salvific experience according to the Vedānta, in which the individual self is felt to merge into brahman, the only true reality. It is not well known that there is a short poem in the Pali canon (SN I, 15) which begins by asking 'From what do words turn back?' The answer (by implication) is *nibbāna*. But again, the tradition has apparently misinterpreted the question. The Pali word here used for 'words' is *sarā* (from Sanskrit *svara*); but the commentator seems to have interpreted it as a homonym which means 'streams' and assumed a reference to another metaphor, that of rivers merging into the ocean (see *Muṇḍaka Upaniṣad* 3, 2, 8). The Pali commentators were, it appears, no mystics.

It would seem, therefore, that the fact that there is no word approximating to 'mystical' in the Pali language or tradition is not decisive: it may reflect not the original events described but their later interpretation. Both the Buddha and, more than likely, some of his immediate followers, seem to have had experiences as a result of which they could only describe themselves as being 'like that' – they felt quite changed. On the other hand, what the tradition laid stress on was the understanding that resulted from this experience; and such evidence as we have from individuals other than the Buddha strongly suggests that they systematically cultivated a path to that experience and that understanding, so that the distinction between being on the path and reaching the goal became relatively unimportant.

If, then, the tradition valued the religious life more than the moments of mystical experience – and indeed the latter may well not have figured in the lives of many excellent monks and nuns – we may finally ask what was distinctively religious about Buddhist religious experience in this broader sense.

Conclusion: The Nature of Religious Experience

As I have mentioned above, the Buddha singled out certain things as being important and connected with a 'total reaction upon life'. This reminds us that to say that an experience is religious is an interpretation of that experience. But it is more than an interpretation in a purely intellectual sense, for it is also a feeling about the experience. One might say that it is a style of experiencing. Other possible examples of such styles or reactions would be the ironic or the cynical, both of which stand in contrast to the religious, in that they refuse to take the primary experiences seriously, whereas the religious style accords them a special seriousness.

Religion is a polythetic category, which means that it has several characteristics of which not all need be present in every instance. One could take a similar view of religious experience, and say that in most cases it will include behaviour based on a firm belief in what James calls 'the reality of the unseen'; and by emphasising this criterion one could certainly call something like the sensation of being outside one's own body or feeling an unseen presence 'religious experience'. However, I hope to have demonstrated that early Buddhist religious experience has a right to that title and yet seems in most cases to have nothing at all in common with encountering a poltergeist. Is my main conclusion thus negative?

I hope it is a little more. I have suggested that it may be helpful to view religious experience not as experience of a particular content or even a particular flavour, but rather as a way of reacting to one's own experience by setting it in a particular context, imparting to it a particular significance. Religious experience, in other words, is on this view a second-order experience.

I have mentioned the view that the value of an experience cannot be affected by, let alone reduced to, its origins. My view of religious experience moves even further in this direction. For if this is a way of experiencing one's experiences, it cannot be reduced to components in the way that James (1985, p. 27) suggests when he says that 'religious love is only man's natural emotion of love directed to a religious object'. If we shift attention from the object to the subject, the experiencer, religious love becomes rather an experience of loving which one endows with a certain kind of significance, an experience which one experiences as somehow self-authenticating and (at least temporarily) transformative. For me this makes better sense of erotic mysticism than does the distinction between a divine and a human object, and I feel no qualms about declaring that love for a human being may be a religious experience.

In sum, my main conclusions are these. First, while I agree with James that experience is 'the real backbone of the world's religious life', or at least its basis, I think that all experience is to a greater or lesser degree ineffable, and that mystical experience is not a special category characterised by ineffability, but simply a strong case of it. Second, James was too sanguine about the possibility of finding religious experience in its pure personal form, uncontaminated by social pressures, because he confused experience with its interpretation. Third, the Pali texts concerned with the earliest recorded Buddhist experiences refer to a great variety of experiences which are considered religious because of their context: a context set by the Buddha's teachings and experiences. Finally, this suggests that a religious experience may usefully be viewed not as a type of experience, like an erotic experience or a tragic experience or a hallucinatory experience, but rather as a way of experiencing one's experiences, a way which will involve attaching considerable significance to them; and this reaction is likely to have been learnt.

(First published as Occasional Paper No. 17, 1997)

Notes

1   He refers to it only four times in the book, and the longest of those references (James 1985, p. 401) contains some inaccuracies.

2   For more on the Buddha's refusal to philosophise and his pragmatism (see next paragraph), see Gombrich 1996, pp. 27–31.

3   1. Unifying vision, all things are one, part of a whole; 2. timeless and spaceless; 3. sense of reality, not subjective but a valid source of knowledge; 4. blessedness, joy, peace and happiness; 5. feeling of the holy, sacred, divine; 6. paradoxical, defies logic; 7. ineffable, can't be described in words; 8. loss of sense of self (Argyle 1997).

4   The first generations of Buddhists believed that with the inspiration of the Buddha before them they could attain nirvana. In Theravādin societies it came to be believed, a few centuries after the Buddha, that this was no longer possible, and that to attain nirvana one would have to await the arrival on earth of the next Buddha, Metteyya. In modern times this belief has again been superseded among educated people. No matter: all Buddhists believe that, even if perfection is out of reach, spiritual progress is possible during one's lifetime if one follows the Buddha's advice.

5   This text says nothing about applying the awareness of one's own physical states to other people, and I suspect that this move in the Satipaṭṭhāna account was prompted by doctrinal considerations rather than the fruit of meditative experience.

6   This is how yoga is defined at *Yoga-sūtra* 1,1.

Bibliography

Argyle, Michael 1997. 'The Psychological Perspective on Religious Experience', Occasional Paper No. 8 (2nd series), Oxford: Religious Experience Research Centre.

Carrithers, Michael 1983. *The Forest Monks of Sri Lanka*, Delhi: Oxford University Press.

Coulson, Michael 1976. *Teach Yourself Sanskrit*, London: English Universities Press.

Gombrich, Richard 1996. *How Buddhism Began: The Conditioned Genesis of the Early Teachings*, London: The Athlone Press.

Hamilton, Sue 1996. *Identity and Experience in Early Buddhism*, London: Luzac Oriental.

James, William 1985[1902]. *The Varieties of Religious Experience*, Harmondsworth: Penguin.

Marty, Martin E. 1985. 'Introduction' to W. James, *The Varieties of Religious Experience*.

Wilson, Bryan 1996. 'Religious Experience: a Sociological Perspective', Occasional Paper No. 2 (2nd series), Oxford: Religious Experience Research Centre.

Pali Canon

AN	Aṅguttara Nikāya
DN	Dīgha Nikāya
MN	Majjhima Nikāya
SN	Saṃyutta Nikāya
Snip	Sutta Nipāta
Thag	Theragāthā

CHAPTER 9

Women and Goddesses in the Celtic World

Miranda Aldhouse-Green

Introduction

This chapter concerns the evidence for the veneration of the female principle among the ancient Celtic peoples of Britain and Continental Europe during the period from about 500 BC–AD 400. One of the major problems in establishing contact with Celtic belief-systems lies in the virtual illiteracy of Iron Age communities; thus all our evidence is, to an extent, second-hand. There exist the written comments of Classical observers on their barbarian neighbours, but these contain inevitable bias or misunderstanding; significant matters are frequently omitted and unimportant things exaggerated. We possess also the writings of early post-Roman Ireland and Wales, but these present their own difficulties based on the lateness of their extant form. Whilst many of the vernacular stories do demonstrably contain important allusions to pagan Celtic religion, they were written down in the early Medieval Christian period and are thus somewhat removed from the context of the Iron Age (MacCana 1983, pp. 14–19). Finally, there is contemporary iconographic and epigraphic material, the evidence of archaeology, which is our most valuable resource. But even here, it is necessary to be aware of bias in terms of what has or has not survived and of interpretation from the viewpoint of the contemporary period. Of necessity, any attempt at interpreting the thought-processes and beliefs of past, illiterate societies will contain a subjective and circumstantial element.

We know from a study of material culture that women could attain a high rank in Iron Age barbarian Europe. In the fourth century BC, a lady of high status was buried at Reinheim in Germany with much ceremony, attesting her considerable prestige (Megaw 1970, nos. 73, 79–83). She was interred in a four-wheeled wooden cart, wearing sumptuous imported fabrics including silk, and with masses of solid gold jewellery. One item was a bracelet whose imagery is interesting, since on the terminal is depicted a goddess accompanied by a bird of prey and other animals, as if she is a divine mistress of beasts. This is a theme to which I shall return. Of even earlier date and more spectacular still was the burial, at Vix in Burgundy, of a princess with an enormous wine-mixing vessel or *krater*, imported over the Alps from Etruria: the container is 1 m 64 cm high and is of solid cast bronze, superbly decorated with figural designs. It was manufactured in about 500 BC (Megaw 1989, pp. 42, 45–6, 48).

If we investigate what contemporary Greek and Roman writers, like the Greek geographer Strabo (in his *Geography*, Book 4) or the Roman general and historian Julius Caesar (in *de Bello Gallico*), say of Celtic society in the first centuries BC–AD, the society which they describe is predominantly male-dominated, with a strict hierarchy of chiefs, knights, holy men and craftsmen, below whom were free men and serfs. But there are indications that women were not wholly in second place: Caesar mentions the practice of polyandry in Britain (Book 5, 14) and Dio Cassius alludes to the ferocity of womenfolk on the battlefield, describing them as nearly as large and formidable as their husbands (*Roman History*, Book 76, 2). More importantly, we know from other Mediterranean commentators that Celtic tribal queens reigned in their own right: Cartimandua of the great northern British confederation of the Brigantes is an example, but the most celebrated was Boudicca of the East Anglian Iceni:

> But above all the raising of the Britons, and the persuading of them to fight against the Romans, the winning of the leadership and the command throughout the war – this was the work of Boudicca, a woman of the British royal family who had uncommon intelligence for a woman ... she was very tall and her voice was harsh; she grew her long auburn hair to the hips and wore a large gold torc... (Dio Cassius *Roman History*, 62.2, 1–4)

There is another category of evidence for females of high status, capable of wielding power: this is the early Irish and Welsh literature, dating in its extant form to the Dark Ages and the early Medieval period, but full of pagan allusions which must relate to pre-Christianity. The Ulster Cycle of early prose tales provides us with some significant information about females and indeed goddesses – we will come to these presently. But the tales speak of sovereign queens, like Medb of Connaught who, like many female rulers of early Ireland, were more than queens and possessed superhuman, semi-divine status. Medb's husband Ailill was nothing more than a cipher, a passive consort whose character is not developed in the literature. It was Medb rather than her husband who mustered and led the Irish army to war against the Ulstermen (MacCana 1983, pp. 84–6).

From the concept of powerful Irish queens, we pass naturally to religion, since Medb herself was part-human, part-goddess She is an example of a tradition which runs through the vernacular legends of Ireland, whereby the land's fertility is blessed and the earth made fruitful by the ritual marriage between the goddess of territory and successive mortal kings. Thus 'mother-earth' is of prime importance and her union with the king is simply so that the land will flourish, though the male ruler also gains prestige and sovereignty by the marriage. Also of interest here is Irish literary information concerning the Druids. Whilst Classical writers speak at length of this priestly caste as being exclusively male, we know from the Ulster Cycle that female Druids existed: one named Scathach was responsible for instructing the young super-human hero Cú Chulainn (MacCana 1983, pp. 86, 102).

So it is possible to establish the presence of a tradition within Celtic society for powerful and influential females. If we now turn to religion *per se*, it is no suprise that, bearing the foregoing remarks in mind, many of the most important divinities we know from the archaeological evidence were female. An overview of these deities shows up several striking features: one is the close association between the goddesses and animals; another is the dualistic, ambiguous nature of their role (the same goddess may be in charge of war and fertility, or healing and death); a third feature is that a number of the goddesses have a direct or indirect link with fertility or prosperity, healing, renewal and rebirth after death; a fourth is the predominance of triplication in female religious imagery. Finally, we may note a predisposition for divine couples within Celtic cult-expression, embodying the male and female principle for particular divine concepts or themes.

The Warrior-Goddesses

> While Boudicca and her followers were committing these atrocities on the Romans, they performed sacrifices and feasted in the groves of Andraste – she was the goddess of Victory, and she enjoyed the Britons' especial reverence. (Dio Cassius, *Roman History*, 62.7, 1–3)

Andraste is the only female war-deity who is mentioned in Graeco-Roman sources. But triads of warrior-goddesses are well-documented in the early Irish literature. The Morrigna were the triple form of the Morrigan, a divinity who thrived an war and destruction, and who was at the same time a single and triple entity. Another bellicose triad were the three Machas, who were associated with horsemanship and who reflected the threefold aspect of the character of a single divine concept. Badb Catha was an Irish war-goddess who could turn into a monstrous raven on the battlefield and thus wreak havoc and panic among soldiers (MacCana 1983, pp. 86–9). In this connection, it is interesting that certain pre-Roman Celtic coins minted by Breton tribes bear images of horses ridden by huge crows or ravens. Certain scholars would see here a direct mythological link between the iconography of these coins and the Irish raven/war-goddesses mentioned in Insular literature (Duval 1987, p. 19 no. 1A). The raven occurs again in Celtic battle imagery: on the top of a Romanian Iron Age helmet is the figure of a raven with articulated wings, which would flap in an unnerving manner when the wearer charged his enemy (Cunliffe 1979, p. 59). One of the few pagan Celtic images of a war-goddess is a bronze statuette from Menez in Brittany: she wears a helmet on the top of which perches the figure of a goose, neck stretched out in aggression. This is of interest since geese were war-symbols in the Celtic world because they are aggressive creatures (Abbaye de Daoulais 1986, no. 80.01, pl. on p. 133).[1] Iron Age graves in Czechoslovakia contain the bodies of warriors accompanied by goose-bones, as if these birds were sacrificed during the funeral rites of the Celtic soldier (Megaw 1970, p.17); and on a Romano-Celtic inscribed stone at the fort of Risingham in Northumberland, images of a Celtic triple-headed god and figures of Mars and Victory are accompanied by a goose (Ross 1967, p. 272).

A number of pre-Roman Celtic coins carry the image of charioteers or riders on horseback: many of these, especially among the tribes of Brittany, are female. It is generally considered that the iconography of Celtic coins is frequently religious, at least in origin, and such figures as appear on the reverse may well represent divinities. These female warriors may brandish branches of trees, weapons or torcs (necklets which themselves are reflective of high status and sometimes of divinity; Duval 1987, pp. 44–50). Once again, these coins may be representing divine concepts which are recorded in the later vernacular literature; the Morrigan or Macha may be the war-goddess of the coins, and Medb is described as charioteer. What is interesting about these Irish deities is their ambiguous character: they were renowned for their sexual appetites, and presided over fertility as well as destruction. This combination of roles is repeated in the Romano-Celtic iconography of northern Britain where, on such carved stones as those from the Roman fort at Maryport in Cumbria (Green 1986, pl. 55), are crude Celtic sculptures of naked warrior-gods with shield and spear, horned and ithyphallic.

The Mistress of Animals

A number of Celtic goddesses known from both iconography and epigraphy during the Roman period in Gaul and Britain display a close affinity with the natural world and, in particular, with the imagery of animals. It is important to remember that beasts were crucial symbols in Celtic religion, which was itself close to animism (the recognition of a divine spirit in all living creatures and in the natural world as a whole, including forests, trees, rivers, springs and moutains).

One of the dominant goddesses was Epona, the horse-goddess, whose name is specifically associated with the Celtic word for horse. That she had an important place in the Celtic pantheon is demonstrated by the fact that she is one of the few Celtic goddesses mentioned in Classical literature (for example

Minucius Felix, *Octavianus* 27; Apuleius, *Metamorphosis* 3) and by her presence and worship in Rome itself. Her images, which appear frequently in Gaul and the Rhineland, are of a goddess clad in a long robe, either astride a mare or standing between two horses (Green 1989, pp. 16–24). The overwhelming message is one of gentle prosperity, fertility and well-being: on Burgundian carvings, the mare is sometimes accompanied by a sleeping or suckling foal; and Epona herself frequently carries fruit, bread or ears of corn. On a bronze statuette in the British Museum, unprovenanced except to Wiltshire (Johns 1971), Epona is seated on a throne or chair between two ponies who are, perhaps significantly, a male and a female. The goddess holds a yoke and a sheaf of corn-ears. Epona is probably to be seen as a goddess originally of the craft of horse-breeding, but who came to take on more general responsibility for fertility and prosperity. That she retained a specifically equine role is indicated by some of her dedicants, cavalry officers in the military frontier zones of the western Empire, who may have worshipped Epona as a protectress both of their horses and themselves (Linduff 1979; Oaks 1986). That the goddess had a profound symbolism connected with death and the life hereafter is suggested by some of her attributes and associations. She often carries a key, as on an image at Gannat (Allier); and this symbol may reflect her function as goddess of stables at one level, but her ability to unlock the gates of heaven at another. Epona's images sometimes occur in sepulchral contexts: many have been found, for instance, at the great cemetery of La Horgne au Sablon outside Metz, the ancient capital of the tribe of the Mediomatrici of eastern Gaul. On one relief from this site Epona rides on her mare, and behind them walks a human figure whom some have interpreted as the soul of a deceased believer being led to the otherworld[2]. Another interest in Epona's cult lies in the possible association with Rhiannon, a character from the Mabinogi, a Welsh set of tales dating from the eleventh or twelfth century AD, but once again incorporating elements of pagan mythology. Rhiannon appears in the First Branch of the Mabinogi as the wife of Pwyll, ruler of Dyfed. She is projected as a lady of supernatural status and associated with horses. When Pwyll first sets eyes on Rhiannon, she is riding slowly by on a dazzling white horse. He goes after her but however fast he or his followers ride, they cannot catch up with the horsewoman. Finally Pwyll calls to her to stop and she immediately obliges. The behaviour of the horse and its rider removes it from the purely mundane world of humanity and reality. But Rhiannon's equine association does not end there: later in the story she is (wrongly) suspected of murdering her baby son Pryderi and, as punishment, she is made to sit at the gate of the palace for seven years and offer to carry on her back to the palace any visitor to the court of Pwyll, like a beast of burden (Jones and Jones 1976, pp. 3–25).

Nehalennia was another important Romano-Celtic goddess: she differs from Epona in that she is known from only two temple-sites in the Netherlands, at

Domburg on the Island of Walcheren (Hondius-Crone 1955) and Colijnsplaat on the estuary of the East Schelde River (van Aartsen 1971). Both sanctuaries have been destroyed by incursions of the North Sea, but each is represented by a wealth of altars set up to Nehalennia by a rich and grateful clientèle. Nehalennia's images are idiosyncratic in that she is constantly accompanied by a large hound-like dog who sits by her side, gazing up at her in an attitude of protection and adoration. The goddess herself appears to have combined the roles of guardian of sea travellers, venturing across the North Sea mainly for trade-purposes, and that of a deity of prosperity. Thus, she was favoured by merchants in wine, fish, oil and salt, who required to be protected in their sometimes hazardous journeys, and at the same time wished for a blessing on their business transactions. So Nehalennia is depicted with large baskets of fruit and *cornucopiae*, but also marine symbols such as boats, oars and rudders.

The presence of the dog is something of an enigma. It is frequently interpreted as an underworld or chthonic emblem but it has none of the savagery of Cerberus, the three-headed guardian of Hades, the Classical other-world described by Virgil in book six of the *Aeneid*. So if the dog does have chthonic or death-symbolism, Nehalennia's companion may reflect an aspect of the goddess' role as a renewer of life after death, which is hinted at in some of her iconography. In both Classical and Celtic symbolism, dogs combined a chthonic with a healing/regenerative role, perhaps because of the legendary curative properties of their saliva. But equally the dog may be present as a guardian of hearth and home, just as Nehalennia herself is a protectress of sea-traders. Its large size but benign mien suggests this interpretation. In any event, the dog's constant presence with the goddess and the very close physical association between them (the dog's nose often touches Nehalennia's hand or the arms of her chair) argues for a very intimate connection between the divinity and her beast (Green 1989, pp. 25–6).

Many other goddesses projected in Romano-Celtic imagery reflect similar associations between animals and deities depicted in anthropomorphic form. We know of a bear-goddess, Artio, whose name reflects her ursine symbolism. She appears on a bronze group from Muri near Bern (Boucher 1976, fig. 291; Green 1989, fig. 10): here Artio, to whom there is an inscribed dedication on the base, is displayed seated, wearing a robe and diadem and with a vessel of fruit beside her; opposite and facing her is a large bear beneath a tree. The iconography of this goddess is equivocal: she may be a guardian of bears, but she may also protect humans against the injury or death an angry bear may inflict. A similar goddess is the topographical deity Arduinna of the Ardennes Forest: she appears as a bronze figurine, riding on the back of a boar (Boucher 1976, fig. 292). She is probably a Celtic version of the Roman huntress Diana; and again, she may perform the ambiguous role of guardian of and against the wild boars of her native woodland.

Two final animal-associations for the goddesses are sufficiently recurrent to be worthy of inclusion in the present discussion. First, it is possible to distinguish a group of nameless goddesses who have snakes as their consistent companions (Green 1989, pp. 25–6). Serpents in Celtic and many other religions possess a complicated symbolism based on a combination of the properties exhibited by such creatures. Snakes are (normally) earthbound reptiles who move effortlessly apparently without cause; they can insinuate themselves into the smallest crevice and are able to strike at speed. In addition, their physical appearance gives snakes phallic imagery, as does their long, involved coupling, the double penis of the male, and the multiple offspring which many snakes produce. The rippling movement also inspires water-imagery. Finally, the practice of sloughing their skins, which takes place several times a year, makes serpents an ideal allegory of rebirth and renewal of life after death.

The regeneration and fertility symbolism of the snake accounts for its frequent association with mother-goddesses: the Germanic triple mothers were often linked with the imagery of snakes who are represented twined within the branches of trees, perhaps reflective of the Tree of Life and the resurrection symbolism of deciduous trees which 'die' in the autumn and are 'reborn' in the spring with the new leaves. Snake-goddesses are not confined to any one area of Celtic Europe but they do cluster in the north east of Gaul. A rare British example is an image of a female deity at Ilkley (Yorkshire), who may be identified as Verbeia, the local spirit of the river Wharfe (Tufi 1983, no. 30, pl. 9). She appears as a schematic figure, with an oversized head and she grasps two snakes, depicted as rigid zig-zags. Here the imagery of the snake may have been chosen as a water- or specifically river-symbol. At the healing sanctuary of Mavilly in Burgundy, a goddess appears with snakes and torches (Ross 1967, p. 217). The snake may here reflect healing and regeneration, the sloughed skin perhaps representative of the god-assisted ability of humans to shed their illness. The light symbolised by the torch could be linked to Mavilly's special association with the curing of eye-disease and thus the restoration of sight.

Interestingly, goddesses may appear not only with snakes of normal type, but also with the specifically Celtic ram-horned serpent, itself a composite image reflecting the symbolism of the snake but enhanced by the fertility associations of horns. A goddess who was perhaps worshipped exclusively among the north-eastern Gaulish tribe of the Leuci appears at Xertigny and at Sommerécourt (both Haute-Marne), accompanied by ram-horned serpents (Green 1989, pp. 25–6; Esperandieu 1907–1966, nos. 4786, 4831). In the latter example, the deity sits cross-legged on the ground, a ram-horned snake entwined round her body, whom the goddess feeds from a large bowl of a porridge-like mash on her lap. That the goddess is herself primarily a fertility-divinity is indicated by her possession of a *cornucopiae*, fruits and a pomegranate – a potent symbol of regeneration in the Classical world.

Of all the species of bird associated with goddesses the most prominent is the crow or raven. We saw earlier that Irish war-goddesses could transmogrify to raven form. But the archaeological evidence provides us with complicated associations between ravens and female divinities. The sybolism of ravens is composite: as carrion-birds, with a reputation for cruelty (hence the collective 'an unkindness of ravens'), they possessed chthonic and death imagery, but all birds had symbolism linked to their power of flight, which caused people to perceive them as allegories of the soul flying to freedom after the release of death. Many anonymous Celtic goddesses appear on sculpture accompanied by ravens. But more interesting is the example of a deity to whom we can give a name, Nantosuelta, known from the inscription on an altar found near the Sarrebourg *mithraeum* in the land of the Mediomatrici around Metz (Espérandieu 1907–1966, no. 4568). Nantosuelta's name means 'winding river': on her images, she appear with the curious motif of a miniature house on a long pole and a large raven. On one Sarrebourg image, she also has a hive-like object; and on another, she appear with her consort Sucellus, the hammer-god. He is a well-documented and popular god, whose symbols and associations proclaim him as a god of prosperity but also with an underworld aspect. Nantosuelta appears to share this dualistic imagery: her house and hive suggest her role as a goddess of domestic well-being, whilst her raven may associate her with death. It is interesting that house and raven-symbols are again linked in the neighbouring land of the Treveri, where images of mother-goddesses are enclosed within house-shaped *aediculae* or miniature shrines (Green 1989, p. 27). It may be relevant to note that the raven is on occasions associated with healing cults, as at Mavilly, and it may be that these birds were linked with the symbolism of renewal or rebirth in the afterlife, in addition to the grim concept of death itself. At this point it is worth recalling the Rheinheim bracelet, with which I began this chapter, on which is depicted a goddess with a bird of prey on her head, but who appears to be a benefactress of animals.

The Healers and Water-Goddesses

All over Gaul and Britain in the early Celtic period, there grew up great healing cult-centres at the sites of springs, whose waters might possess the properties of heat, the presence of therapeutic minerals or simply the quality of purity. Unlike the situation in Classical Greece, which had important spring-sanctuaries (Ferguson 1989, pp. 80ff), most often the Celtic thermal deities were female. Their cults bore close affinities with those of the mother-goddesses, which are considered in a later section. In Britain, the best-known healer goddess was Sulis, the divinity who presided over the great healing shrine of *Aquae Sulis* at Bath. In the Roman period, she was equated with the Roman goddess Minerva whose name was adopted as a surname for the indigenous deity. Sulis Minerva ruled over a sanctuary which probably existed in some form for centuries before the Romans turned it into a richly-endowed and flourishing temple-precinct, with Classical buildings and sculptures of Graeco-Roman style. But the many inscriptions and the numerous, recently-discovered lead curse-tablets thrown into the spring, attest that Sulis remained first and foremost a Celtic goddess: her native name is always mentioned first in the epigraphic dedications, even though her cult-statue, of which only the gilded bronze head survives, presented the goddess in the guise of Minerva (Green 1986, pp. 154–5, figs. 69, 70). It is interesting that, etymologically, Sulis is a solar name and it may be that she was worshipped as a goddess of the sun because the quarter million gallons of water a day which gush from the springs are hot. The other important British water-goddess, who may also have had a curative role, was Coventina, who presided over the well and pool at the Roman fort of Carrawburgh in Northumberland (Allason-Jones and McKay 1985). Coventina's name is Celtic, and her images indicate that she was perceived by her followers as a nymph; on one stone relief she is betrayed in triple form, like the Three Mothers. Devotees visited her shrine and cast votive objects into the well, including jewellery, figurines and a number of bronze pins.

In Gaul, one of the most celebrated sacred healing establishments was at *Fontes Sequanae* at the springs of the source of the river Seine to the north of Dijon (Deyts 1985). The deity to whom the shrine was dedicated was Sequana, the personified spirit of the Seine. The only surviving image of the goddess herself is in the form of a bronze statuette of a draped woman, a diadem on her head, standing in a duck-prowed boat, her hand outstretched as if to welcome her suppliants. The site was visited both before and during the Roman period, and is rich in votive objects of both stone and wood: in 1963, a cache of over two hundred wooden (mainly oak heartwood) carvings was discovered in a water-logged deposit on the site of the springs. These consist of limbs, heads and other parts of human bodies, offered to Sequana, having been bought at a temple-shop by sick pilgrims in the hope that a gift to the goddess of the afflicted part of the body would result in a cure. When the Romans adopted the sanctuary, they erected more permanent temple buildings, and the offerings of the Romano-Celtic phase were of stone rather than wood. But the images were basically the same: arms, legs and heads, where the treatment of the eyes indicates the prevalence of eye-diseases and blindness, perhaps frequently brought about by malnutrition. Complete figures of pilgrims are also represented, sometimes carrying gifts in the form of a pet dog or bird, fruit or purses of money. Other disorders reflected by the votive objects of wood and stone include respiratory illnesses – asthma, bronchitis or pneumonia, perhaps, represented by images of the thoracic cavity. Sequana's devotees also suffered from goitre, and the occurrence of carved female breasts and male genitals are suggestive of milk-failure on the one hand and impotence on the other. The images of the pilgrims, usually dressed in heavy-weather hooded cloaks of the Celtic peasant, show us a community of ordinary, rural people who firmly believed that Sequana could help them in their physical distress. Some of the inscribed dedications tell us that their faith was justified (Green 1989, pp. 40–41, fig. 16; pp. 156–61, figs 69–72).

The Divine Marriage

One interesting divine manifestation in the Celtic world was the linking of gods and goddesses to form couples, each possessing a similar but not identical role (Green 1989, pp. 45ff). This is not a phenomenon which is confined to Celtic religion; we know of many Classical deities who were linked – Jupiter and his consort Juno, and the brother and sister Apollo and Artemis, are two examples. But in Celtic Gaul, there seems to have been a special predilection for the worship of two partners, male and female, who are of equal status. There is a discernible pattern here in that, very frequently, where we have inscribed names for these divinities, the male will be given a Roman name but the female invariably possesses a native Celtic name. Thus we have Apollo and Sirona who presided over the healing sanctuary at Hochscheid in the Rhineland (Dehn 1941, pp. 104ff) and Mercury and Rosmerta all over the Celtic world, including Britain; and there are many other more local examples. The imagery of Apollo and Sirona echoes this pattern: he is depicted in full Classical guise, as an elegant, rather effeminate, naked youth carrying his lyre, whilst Sirona, fully draped and wearing a diadem, carries three eggs and has a snake winding round her arm, attributes which do not find a parallel in that precise form in the Mediterranean world. These emblems signify that Sirona was a goddess of fertility and regeneration, appropriate symbols for a Celtic healer.

The cult of Mercury and Rosmerta is interesting. Since, in the iconography, Rosmerta generally adopts the caduceus of Mercury and frequently bears no other attribute, it was long considered that she was simply the female version of Mercury, without much individuality or identity of her own. But among the Aedui of Burgundy, Rosmerta was invoked on her own, without Mercury, and her cult was linked to that 'Numen' of the Emperor, giving her a particular prestige. This is exemplified by the site of Escolives-Sainte-Camille (Yonne) (Bémont 1969), the evidence of which indicates her independent existence, perhaps prior to the arrival of Roman influences which brought Mercury to Gaul. Rosmerta's name means 'The Great Provider' and her attributes sometimes endorse this prosperity symbolism: on British reliefs of the couple at Gloucester and Bath (Green 1989, pp. 45–73, fig 22), Rosmerta appears with a vat or wooden, iron-bound bucket, perhaps – like Celtic cauldrons – an emblem of abundance and constant replenishment.

But other divine couples may be of entirely indigenous Celtic character. This must be true of an important partnership, that of Sucellus and Nantosuelta (Green 1989, fig. 18). These are both Celtic names: Sucellus means 'The Good Striker'. We have met Nantosuelta before in the discussion of goddesses with ravens. Her house-on-pole and other such symbols of florescence as *cornucopiae*, proclaim her as primarily a goddess of domesticity, the raven perhaps present to express the chthonic aspect of her nature. Sucellus' main attribute is his hammer, an emblem which is alien to Classical iconography, and an implement which may signify power, noise, the hammering in of field boundary fences, or the striking of the earth in winter to bring about the reawakening of spring's fecundity.

In all these partnerships, the dominant imagery of the goddess is that of well-being, earthly productivity and prosperity. The male appears in many different guises: he may be a wine-god, a warrior or, like his partner, a god of abundance. The theme which is distinctive in all the evidence, especially that of the iconography, is that of a partnership, a true marriage of equals. This concept is crucial to their worship; dominance of one or the other cannot be demonstrated, and in the imagery it may be significant that, even allowing for the convention of sexual dimorphism, the deities are generally depicted as of equal size. Sometimes, we appear to have a god of Roman origin marrying a local goddess, in an allegory of the conflation of Roman and native culture. Or it may be that we are witnessing a universal goddess of the land, in varying form, consorting with many different and more localised deities, on the Irish pattern mentioned above. But whatever the precise origins of the partnership, what is important is the marriage itself. Whilst human fertility is not usually overtly expressed, there is nonetheless an implicit acknowledgement that in a good marriage there is fulfilment in every sense: the result of the union is success. The couples brought to their cult the strength of the mutual support which springs from the intimate relationship between male and female. The divine couples were very often represented on small, domestic, personal monuments, many being set up in private houses for family veneration, to bring blessing to the household. The couples provided comfort by their imagery of familiar, practical deities, easily identifiable with the ordinary families of peasant or artisan.

The Mother-Goddesses

Many types of so-called 'Mother-Goddess' were worshipped among the Celtic communities of Gaul, the Rhineland and Britain. Most distinctive, however, was the triadic form, which occurs in nearly all the regions of the Celtic world during the period of Roman influence. The Triple Mothers are a specific type, represented both epigraphically, as the *Deae Matres*, and iconographically. Their imagery owes a great deal to Roman art-forms and concepts: the Mothers are in origin a form of *Iunones* (the *Iuno* being the female spirit, just as the *Genius* was the essence of a man; von Petrikovits 1987). But the dominance of triplism is a manifestation of the adaptation of the mother-goddess to a Celtic milieu, so much so that the triple mother concept may be said to be an entirely Celtic phenomenon.

In Burgundy, especially among the tribes of the Aedui and the Lingones, the cult of the Triple Mothers displays a unique complexity. One specific group of Burgundian stone carvings is distinctive: the mothers appear to perform differing but interconnected functions which, at first glance, appear to be associated purely with human fertility but with, perhaps, a more profound significance. On a stone from the Roman settlement of *Vertillum* (modern Vertault) (Green 1989, fig. 84) comes a sculpture consisting of a triad of seated goddesses each with the right breast and shoulder bared as if in preparation for suckling a child. One deity holds a large swaddled baby on her lap; the central goddess unrolls a swathing-band or napkin; the third bears a basin and bath-sponge. Several Burgundian images show this apparently homely scene, but others call the simplicity of this imagery into question: a relief from Nuits-Saint-Georges shows the central goddess unrolling her napkin; the deity on the left has a *cornucopiae*; the goddess on the right nurses a swaddled infant but she also grips a balance-beam. To the right of the central mother is the prow of a boat and a steering-oar, to the left is a globe. The napkin and balance-beam combination is repeated at Saint-Boil in the same region. The more complicated imagery of these stones has led some scholars (Thevenot 1968, pp. 173–6), and rightly in my opinion, to reinterpret the napkin as a parchment or scroll, the Book of Life. So the goddesses may not simply reflect human fecundity but also the passage of life and death. The balance belongs to the Roman Fates and the rudder and globe to Fortuna. So the idea may be that the mothers watch over the newborn baby and protect it; the *cornucopiae* symbolises success on earth; the scroll shows the inevitable one-way journey towards death – when the parchment comes to the end, the boat carries the soul to the otherworld. I think it is unnecessary and simplistic to have to choose between napkin and scroll; they are not mutually exclusive as motifs. Instead, this motif may be an instance of deliberate ambiguity: napkin and scroll are similar visual images, and the iconography is probably interpretable at a number of levels; human fertility at one, the message of life and death at another (Green 1989, pp. 191–3).

The imagery of the triadic mother-goddesses of the German Rhineland forms a distinct group which, unlike the Burgundian stones, does not allude overtly to human reproduction. In Germany the mothers are referred to as *Matronae* rather than *Matres*; their epithets or surnames proclaim them as goddesses of individual localities and the deities were called by a bewildering variety of Celto-Germanic names. An example is the cult of the *Matronae Vacallinehae* at the sanctuary of Pesch (Lehner 1918, pp. 74ff). But, by contrast, their imagery varies little. Many monuments are the result of first-rate craftsmanship, and dedicants were frequently high officials within the Roman provincial administration or senior army officers. In all the Germanic triadic images, the pattern consists of the depiction of a young central goddess with long flowing hair, often smaller than her companions, flanked by two older women wearing huge circular bonnets or headdresses, seemingly made of stiffened linen and fastened in place by knotted willow-twigs. All three goddesses carry fruit or bread and there is sometimes associated faunal and floral symbolism. It may be that the age difference discernible in the goddesses reflects the varying virtues of womanhood; nubile, attractive youth, representative of fertility and renewal, flanked by experienced and mature middle age. These goddesses must have been more than simple domestic guardians: in order to attract devotees of high status and intelligence, the cult must have offered deep satisfaction and comfort in both this world and the unknown paths of the afterlife (von Petrokovits 1987; Green 1989, p. 198).

The cult of the mothers in Britain is relatively poorly represented. The most interesting group of sculptures comes from Cirencester, the tribal capital of the Dobunni, which has produced a rich and varied cult iconography including a number of triplistic forms. Three triple mother reliefs come from the town, in addition to several depictions of single mothers, unaccompanied or with other deities (Green 1986, fig. 34; Green 1989, fig. 87, pp. 198–202). One shows the three goddesses, sprawling in relaxed attitude on a semi-circular bench. Each is accompanied by a male infant, one of whom reaches up towards his mother's breast. The central goddess holds a lap-dog. Here the symbolism is apparently simply that of fecundity, but the presence of the dog may introduce an otherworld element, and rebirth after death may be reflected. The other two sculptures are more formalised: one shows the goddesses in long pleated robes, the central one with an infant in arms, the other two bearing trays of fruit. That three separate entities are depicted is suggested by the slighly different hairstyles of all three. The central female is larger than her companions and this, and her possesion of a baby may suggest her higher status, as does the fact that the other goddesses incline towards her. The final carving from Cirencester portrays three matrons, again each with a different hairstyle, indicating their individuality. Abundance and the earth's bounty is expressed by baskets of fruit and loaves, but again the overt symbolism may conceal a deeper meaning: the lower folds of the goddesses' clothing form the shape of dolphins, and it is possible that here is a reference to death and the protection of the mothers in the sea journey to the Blessed Isles – the main Classical symbolism of the dolphin.

The cult of the Triple Mothers was undeniably a widespread, popular and successful cult, which may have developed from a simple fertility religion to a much deeper concept of protection and well-being in all aspects of life and death. The mothers were often associated with curative spring shrines: healing, regeneration and fertility are closely intertwined themes.

Finally, we should examine triplism itself: sometimes the mothers are identical, true triplets, but often they carry different attributes, have varying coiffures or are of different ages. One major function of triplication must have been to intensify the potency of the symbolism. But triplism may have had a separate significance based on number, and this may be why so many Celtic deities, apart from the mothers, were triadic. But we must ask the question as to whether we are seeing one goddess with three facets or three. The varying emblems the goddesses may bear could simply refer to the possesion by one entity of several sets of symbols, but, on the other hand, care is frequently taken to make marked differences between the physical forms of the goddesses. Like much Celtic symbolism, the interpretation of triple imagery may embrace many concepts and involve fluidity, ambiguity and personal choice on the part of the spectator/devotee. We may have three deities, one mother with three aspects or three intensifying images. We may have the embodiment of triadic concepts like sky, earth, underworld; before, behind, here; earth, air, water; past, present and future. Or all these ideas may together be reflected by the Mothers' triple form.

Conclusion

The imagery and symbolism of the Celtic goddesses expresses the wide range of functions they were perceived to possess. The iconographic and epigraphic evidence is suggestive of an underlying complexity and a dynamic mythology, perhaps we may go so far as to say theology. Many of the goddesses were local, topographically defined entities, presiding over a single healing spring-shrine – like Sulis at Bath, or Sequana in Burgundy. But others were worshipped over a wide area and achieved intertribal or even pan-tribal status – like Epona or the Triple Mothers. By far the majority of the goddesses were involved with the fundamental concerns of humankind: prosperity, fertility, health, success and death. The war-goddesses of the free Celtic (that is pre-Roman) world which are present on the coins, and those ferocious female divinities of the vernacular literature are not present in the Romano-Celtic iconography, though a peaceful goddess of well-being may be married to a war-god. But what is interesting is that these goddesses were worshipped as much by men as by women and that some of their holy places achieved great importance, drawing pilgrims from far afield. Few of the sanctuaries which are known to have been dedicated to a masculine deity have produced the wealth of cult-material of either *Aquae Sulis* or *Fontes*

Seouanae. Study of the evidence reveals that, as far as religion was concerned, the female principle achieved more than mere equality in Celtic Europe.

(First published as Occasional Paper No. 1, 1991)

Notes

1   Musée de Bretagne, Rennes.
2   Musée Archélogique de Metz.

Bibliography

van Aartsen, J. 1971. *Deae Nehalennriae*, Rijksmuseum van Oudheden, Leiden, Middelburg.
Abbaye de Daoulais 1986. *Au Temps de Celtes: Ve-Ier siècle JC*, Musée Archéologique Breton de Quimper: Association Abbaye de Daoulais.
Allason-Jones, L. and McKay, B. 1985. *Coventina's Well*, Trustees of the Clayton Collection, Chesters Museum, Chesters.
Bémont, C. 1969. 'A propos d'un nouveau monument de Rosmerta', *Gallia* **27**, pp. 23–44.
Boucher, S. 1976. *Recherches sur les bronzes figurés de Gaule pré-romaine et romaine*, École Française de Rome, Paris and Rome.
Cunliffe, B.W. 1979. *The Celtic World*, London: Bodley Head.
Dehn, W. 1941. 'Ein Quelheiligtum des Apollo und der Sirona bei Hochscheid', *Germania* **25**, pp. 104ff.
Deyts, S. 1985. *Le sanctuaire des Sources de la Seine*, Dijon: Musée Archéologique.
Duval, P.-M. 1987. *Monnaies Gauloises et Mythes Celtiques*, Paris: Hermann.
Espérandieu, E. 1907–1966. *Recueil Général des Bas-Reliefs de la Gaule romaine et pré-romaine*, Ernest Leroux, Paris.
Ferguson, J. 1989. *Among the Gods*, London: Routledge.
Green, M.J. 1986. *The Gods of the Celts*, Gloucester: Alan Sutton.
—— M.J. 1989, *Symbol and Image in Celtic Religious Art*, London: Routledge.
Hondius-Crone, A. 1955. *The Temple of Nehalennia at Domburg*, Amsterdam: Meulenhoff.
Johns, C.M. 1971. 'A Roman bronze statuette of Epona', *British Museum Quarterly*, **36** (1–2), pp. 37–41.
Jones, G. and Jones, T. (trans. & introd.) 1976. *The Mabinogion*, London: Dent.
Lehner, H. 1918. 'Der Tempelbezirk der Matronae Vacallinehae bei Pesch', *Bonner Jahrbücher*, vols. 125–126.
Linduff, K. 1979. 'Epona: a Celt among the Romans', *Collections Latomus*, **38**, fasc. 4, pp. 817–837.
MacCana, P. 1983. *Celtic Mythology*, London: Newnes.
Megaw, J.V.S. 1970. *Art of the European Iron Age*, New York: Harper & Row.
Megaw, J.V.S. and Megaw, R. 1989. *Celtic Art: From its Beginnings to the Book of Kells*, London: Thames and Hudson.
Oaks, L.S. 1986. 'The goddess Epona: concepts of sovereignty in a changing landscape', in M. Henig and A. King (eds), *Pagan Gods and Shrines of the Roman Empire*, Oxford University Committee for Archaeology, monograph no. 8, 1986, pp. 77–84.
von Petrikovits, H. 1987. 'Matronen und verwandte Gottheiten', *Ergebnisse eines Kolloquiums veranstaltet von der Göttinger Akademiekommission für die Altertumskunde Mittel- und Nordeuropas*, Beihafte der *Bonner Jahrbücher*, Köln/Bonn: Bans 44, pp. 241–254.

Ross, A. 1967. *Pagan Celtic Britain*, London: Routledge & Kegan Paul.

Thevenot, E. 1968. *Divinités et sanctuaires de la Gaule*, Paris: Fayard.

Tufi, S.R. 1983. *Corpus Signorum Imperii Romani: Great Britain vol. 1, fasc. 3, Yorkshire*, London and Oxford: British Academy and Oxford University Press.

CHAPTER 10

Religion, Gender and *Dharma*:
The Case of the Widow-Ascetic

Julia Leslie

Introduction

'Suttee' is the term coined by the British to denote the practice whereby a woman burns herself alive on her husband's death. The word in its original Sanskrit is *satī*, meaning 'good woman'; it is the feminine form of *sat*, meaning 'that which is real or true or good'. The most common Sanskrit terms for the practice are *sahagamana* ('going with'), *anugamana* ('going after'), and *anumaraṇa* ('dying after'). With the British entry into India, therefore, the Sanskrit term denoting the person (*satī*) became the Anglo-Indian term denoting the practice ('suttee'). With this change of terms came a change of emphasis. The Sanskrit word carries wholly positive associations: the woman who refuses the dishonour of widowhood is glorified as a heroic goddess. The Anglicized version carries highly negative associations: the practice is condemned as an atrocity perpetrated by Indian men (or, at the very least, by Indian culture) on defenceless Indian widows. Victor becomes victim.[1] In order to avoid confusion, the discussion in this chapter will alternate between the two Sanskrit terms: *satī* for the person and *sahagamana* for the act.

One question is obvious. Why would any woman choose to take her own life in such a way? While force was certainly used in a minority of ugly cases, at its 'best' *sahagamana* was performed as a glorious, self-elevating and totally voluntary act.[2] As a *satī*, a 'truly virtuous woman', a wife not only refuses to become a widow; she ceases to be a woman at all. She becomes a goddess, empowered to bring salvation to her family. Even today, while this powerful ideology is rejected vehemently by many Indian women, it is accepted without hesitation by others.[3] But there is another, equally important question. Why would any woman choose to live in hardship and poverty, which was the traditional life of the widow? As in the case of the *satī*, it is easy for an outsider to see the widow as the victim of her culture. Many are indeed so victimized. In its ideal form, however, widowhood may be seen as an equally valid (and equally demanding) religious path for women: the path of the widow-ascetic. By this path too, *karma* may be reversed; husbands and families may be brought to salvation. Again, while increasing numbers of women reject this model, it is still largely unquestioned in traditional India.

In the world of *dharmaśāstra* (Sanskrit religious law) what we have here is a religious progression culminating in a choice: from woman to wife, and from wife to either heroic *satī* or widow-ascetic. In such a world, the concept 'woman' (*strī* as in *strī-svabhāva*, 'the inherent nature of women') is always negative. The concept 'wife' (*strī* as in *strīdharma*) denotes the woman who has taken the religious path of devotion to her husband.[4] When her husband dies, the wife does not automatically become a widow. Only when her husband's body is consumed in flames (that is, with or without his wife) is she deemed to have made her choice: the heroic path of the *satī* (*sahagamana*) or the ascetic path of the widow (*vidhavādharma*).

Here I want to examine some of the tensions between these two religious paths as they are revealed in the traditional arguments put forward in their favour by pandits trained in Sanskrit religious law. In the process, I wish to draw attention to two Sanskrit treatises: Tryambakayajvan's *Strīdharmapaddhati* or *Guide to the Dharma of Women*; and Vāsudevāśrama's *Yatidharmaprakāśa* or *Explanation of the Dharma of Ascetics*.[5]

Tryambakayajvan's *Strīdharmapaddhati* or *Guide to the Dharma of Women*

The *Strīdharmapaddhati* was written between 1720 and 1750 by Tryambakayajvan, an orthodox pandit and minister at the Haratha court of Thanjavur in southern India. It was written in Sanskrit, arising from and intended for an elite. It thus encapsulates for its place and time the opinions of an influential group. In more general terms, it teaches us something of the fascinating, if often obscure, reasoning of *dharmaśāstra* relating to women, reasoning that still shapes ideas about gender in India today. For Tryambaka's aim was to summarize the views of Sanskrit religious law relating to women, including the rulings relating to widowhood and *sahagamana*. Tryambaka is a traditionalist, seeking to reinforce the ideals of Hindu *dharma* (and Hindu womanhood) at a time of political insecurity, since he was writing in a world dominated by Muslims who did not encourage *sahagamana*. From 1691, the Maratha Rajas of Thanjavur owed allegiance to the Mughal Empire centred in Delhi. They were cut off from their Maratha origins and from the hallowed region of Sanskrit culture in the north.[6] To a man like Tryambaka, Hindu *dharma* must have seemed at risk.

The *Strīdharmapaddhati* addresses this challenge. Thus Tryambaka portrays women not as individuals but as parts that fit into and strengthen the whole (that is, *dharma*). For the assumption of *dharmaśāstra* is that every individual must perform his or her allotted role (allotted, that is, by the precepts of *svadharma* and *strīdharma*) in order that universal harmony may result. By reinforcing the proper role of women, therefore, Tryambaka is both recreating Hindu *dharma* and, by extension, establishing the perfect world. For him, as for so many previous exponents of *dharmaśāstra*, the proper role of women embraces both *sahagamana* and widowhood. Tryambaka's views on these two interrelated topics are to be found among the nine 'duties common to all women'. The arguments relating to dying with one's husband are discussed first, the lifestyle of the widow-ascetic second. For when a man dies, his wife is faced with a choice: not simply life or death as some might see it, but a choice between two religious paths. This is how Tryambaka describes it. His argument is geared to deciding which of these two religious paths she should take. As we shall see, either path may be recommended on positive grounds. For both demonstrate the essential power of the good woman for the salvation of husband and family.

My concern here is to draw a parallel between the male ascetic's choice between ritual suicide and a life of renunciation, and the startlingly similar choice facing the woman whose husband has died. This parallel is implicit in Tryambaka's work. My intention is to demonstrate that, at least in the ideal terms of *dharmaśāstra*, widowhood may be deemed as positive a path for women as the life of the renouncer is for men. Tryambaka gives us our first clue to this interpretation in his response to the traditional objection that *sahagamana* is a form of suicide, and therefore prohibited. Two quotations support the objection; both from the sacred source of revealed truth (śruti) and both therefore authoritative. The *Śatapatha-brāhmaṇa* (X.2.6.7) insists that one should live out one's allotted span of life. The *Īśopaniṣad* proclaims that 'those who kill themselves' will go to hell (3.3).[7] Tryambaka's response is that this prohibition on suicide does not constitute an absolute ruling. It is a general rule (*sāmānyavacana*) open to modification by supplementary rules that specify exceptions. He argues by analogy with other general rules: the prohibition on killing living beings, for example, is modified by supplementary rules relating to specific animal sacrifices. In the same way, the prohibition on suicide allows for exceptions. Tryambaka names three such exceptions: the ritual suicide of the ascetic in a sacred place; the warrior's deliberate courting of death in battle; and the self-sacrifice of the *satī*.

This link between the ascetic, the warrior and the *satī* in the heroism of their chosen death is instructive. For the religious heroism they share becomes differentiated at the level of class (or *varṇa*) and gender: one expression for the male brahmin, another for the male *kṣatriya*, a third for women. The question of whether the heroism of women should be further differentiated by *varṇa* is raised later. Tryambaka concludes that it should be: the brahmin woman (ideally, the chief wife, the *patnī*) should have the honour of dying on her husband's pyre, alongside his corpse (hence the term *sahagamana*); wives of lower *varṇa* should burn on separate pyres (hence the term *anugamana*). Equally instructive is the unspoken link between warrior, ascetic and widow when they survive. The religious path they share now is one of spiritual purpose, dedication and self-denial. The warrior will risk his life repeatedly, ready each time to lose all for the sake of others. The ascetic or renouncer consciously abandons all and steps forward into death, turning back only at the brink. The wife whose husband has died faces death beside him; only when she turns back from the place of the *satī* may she be called a widow. These three paths suggest a prior custom common to them all: that of renouncing the world when at the point of death, which in time became renunciation as an alternative to death.

Another clue to this interpretation is provided by Tryambaka's response to the objection that *sahagamana* is prohibited to brahmin women. Before arguing against the objection, he produces several quotations in support of it. For example:

> ... following one's husband when he has died is not (appropriate) for brahmin women; but, for the other *varṇas*, this is held to be the supreme duty for women.
>
> Whatever good that the brahmin woman can do for her husband when she lives (after his death), that she cannot do for him when she dies (with him); grieving for her husband for a long time is better.
>
> She should follow her husband when he is alive and not follow him when he is dead. For by living (after he dies), she does good (for him); but by dying (with him) she becomes one who has committed suicide.
>
> Any woman belonging to a brahmin caste who follows her dead husband (onto his funeral pyre) will take neither herself nor her husband to heaven on account of (the sin of) suicide.
>
> The brahmin woman who does not die with her husband (even though she is) distracted by grief, obtains the goal of renunciation; (whereas) by dying, she becomes one who has committed (the sin of) suicide.

Each of these quotations culminates in the assertion that a brahmin woman who insists on joining her husband in death must be deemed guilty of the crime of suicide. As I have indicated, Tryambaka disagrees. My concern here, however, is to draw attention to several subsidiary but important points: first, that the woman whose husband has died is faced with a choice between two paths, suicide (whether as ritual or crime) and survival; second, that the heroic path, ritual suicide, is generally considered more appropriate to the warrior class; third, that survival, seen as the ascetic path, is thought by some to be appropriate for brahmins; and fourth, that the debate concerning which path is more effective in religious terms is a lively one.

The link between the male renouncer and the widow, implicit in Tryambaka's views, is at its clearest here. For the path of the widow is explicitly described as the path of 'renunciation' (*pravrajyā*). Tryambaka glosses *pravrajyā* as *brahmacaryam* (the life of the celibate ascetic), a term which in the context of *strīdharma* is synonymous with *vidhavādharma* (the duties or lifestyle of the widow).

Tryambaka and Traditional Views of Renunciation: Vāsudevāśrama's *Yatidharmaprakāśa*

In order to demonstrate the similarities between the path of the male renouncer and that of the widow-ascetic, I shall now present a brief comparison between Tryambaka's views on *sahagamana* and widowhood, and some of the traditional views on renunciation as expressed in Vāsudevāśrama's *Yatidharmaprakāśa*.

First, as Olivelle (1977) explains, renunciation according to Vāsudeva's definition is a negative state: 'an abandonment of one life-style, not the adoption of another', defined 'not by what it is but by what it is not'. The actual practices of the renouncer are significant not in themselves but in the fact that 'they constitute the negation of other practices typical of life-in-society'. If we place these statements in the context of Tryambaka's discussion of *strīdharma*, we find remarkable echoes. For the lifestyle of the widow is repeatedly and deliberately described in terms that contrast it with the life of the married woman. For example, while the wife should devote considerable time and energy to her physical appearance (as the outward sign of marital happiness and good fortune), the widow must not. Instead, she should wear undyed garments, no bodice, no perfumes or ointments and no jewellery. While the wife should dress her hair with flowers and ornaments, the widow's hair is unadorned or trimmed, or her head is shaved. While the wife may partake of any dish she has prepared for her husband and family, the widow's diet is sparse. While the wife may sleep on a 'high bed', the widow must sleep on the floor. The renunciation of the widow is precisely the negation of the lifestyle of the wife.

Second, the procedure of renunciation as described by Vāsudeva culminates in ritual suicide. He explains: 'Thereupon he should undertake (one of the following courses): entering water, entering fire, the path of heroes, the Great Journey, or dwelling in a cave'. These are all methods of taking one's life: by drowning oneself in a stream or river; by entering a forest fire in order to burn to death; by seeking a hero's death in an honourable war; by walking towards the Himalayas without food or drink until one drops; or by fasting to death in a mountain cave. Suicide was the ideal. But, as Olivelle suggests, the option of survival for the purpose of pursuing an ascetic life was increasingly accepted until it became the norm. The parallel for the wife whose husband has died is clear.

Third, the daily practices of the renouncer as described by Vāsudeva reveal many similarities with the lifestyle of the widow as described by Tryambaka.

For example, the rules relating to begging, as formulated by Vāsudeva, indicate that food is simply a means of subsistence, of staying alive, not a source of pleasure. Similarly, according to Tryambaka, the widow 'should allow her life to continue' only 'as long as her life-breath continues of itself'. Like the renouncer, she should eat only once a day but, in addition, she is expected to perform severe fasts. She should 'willingly mortify her body', living on flowers, roots and fruits; or, alternatively, on fruits, vegetables, barley or milk. Elsewhere, Tryambaka intones that food cooked by a widow is impure, the implication being that neither she nor anyone else should eat it. The chewing of betel is among the pleasures prohibited to both renouncer and widow. As Tryambaka intones:

> The ascetic, the celibate student, and the widow – each of these should avoid (chewing) betel, massaging oil (into the body), and also eating out of a brass (or copper) vessel.

The question of shaving the head at the onset of renunciation is discussed by both authors. The two models do not coincide exactly: for the renouncer, the stress is on begging and the abandonment of fire; in the case of the widow, it rests on a simplicity of diet and appearance and the absence of the qualification to cook. But the similarities are striking.

Fourth, the ambivalence in attitude towards the renouncer as demonstrated by Vāsudeva's text is matched by a surprisingly similar ambivalence towards the widow in Tryambaka's treatise.[8] In the case of the renouncer, while some authorities place him beyond the category of the pure and the impure, others in varying contexts ascribe to him impurity as well as extreme purity. For example, the renouncer's food is compared to cow's meat, his water to alcoholic drink. Such views are apparently so common-place that Vāsudeva feels it necessary to devote a section of his work to proclaiming the high status and essential dignity of the renouncer from the point of view of the householder. His section on purification rituals, on the other hand, presents a modified version of the rules normally applied to householders, modified precisely to indicate the higher status and purity of the renouncer. On the principle that the purer the individual the more stringent the purification necessary, the requirements made of the renouncer are four times those made of the householder.

While the details of these discussions are not mirrored exactly in Tryambaka's description of the widow, there are some interesting parallels. For example, impurity and inauspiciousness are traditionally ascribed to widows. The sight of a married woman first thing in the morning is auspicious; the sight of a widow is not. The cooking of a married woman is pure; that of a widow is not. In Tryambaka's discussion of purification rituals, the measures allotted to women depend on whether she is being compared with men or other women. For example, after urinating the male householder should purify his penis, his left hand. and then both hands, by applying one, three and two lumps of earth respectively; after defecating, twice as many; but in the case of women and the low-caste *śūdra*, only half the quantity is required for each equivalent action. On the principle that the purer the individual the more stringent the purification required, one would expect twice as many applications to be stipulated for Vedic students as for householders, three times as many for hermits, four times as many for ascetics; but only half as many for women. For the normal scale of purity places the ascetic at the top and women at the bottom. But when the discussion is restricted to the world of *strīdharma*, the measures are allotted in reverse: the menstruating woman requires sixty lumps of earth to cleanse herself on the fourth day; the menstruating widow twice as many. The implication here is not that menstruating wives and widows stand higher on the scale of purity than ordinary women, but that their extreme impurity requires more drastic measures.

Like Vāsudeva, Tryambaka feels it necessary in view of such statements to devote some space to proclaiming the essential dignity and auspiciousness of widows. He begins with a crushing quotation that summarizes the traditionally negative attitude towards widows:

> Just as the body, bereft of life, in that moment becomes impure, so the woman bereft of her husband is always impure, even if she has bathed properly.
> Of all inauspicious things, the widow is the most inauspicious; there can never be any success after seeing a widow.
> The wise man should avoid even her blessing – excepting only that of his mother – for it is devoid of all auspiciousness, like the poison of a snake.

But this is not Tryambaka's point. On the contrary, he dismisses such remarks as applying only to the widow who does not behave in the appropriate ascetic manner. For the *pativratā* (the devoted wife) who truly follows the path of widowhood earns a triple reward: she is both happy and auspicious in this life; she goes to heaven when she dies, the same heaven as her husband; and she will marry the same husband in her next life. According to Tryambaka, the inauspiciousness traditionally attributed to the widow is no more than a threat intended to keep her on her narrow ascetic path. Although not very convincing in its application in the real world, this interpretation is especially interesting in the context of our discussion, for it recalls the dire threats levelled in Vāsudeva's work at the fallen renouncer. Viewed in this light, Vāsudeva might argue that the attribution of impurity to the renouncer applies only to the failure or the fraud.

Fifth and last, the question of the rulings relevant to the *kali* age is raised by both authors, with similar conclusions. This is the notion that the cycle of time moves from the first or Golden Age through progressively more degenerate

Ages until it reaches the fourth or worst Age (*kali*), at which point the universe disintegrates. After a long period of quiescence, the whole process begins again. Another image is of the 'cow of *dharma*': at first, it stands on four legs, then three, then two, then one. All of recorded history belongs to the precarious one-legged era, the *kali* or modern age.[9] The point here is that some practices, of which people are considered capable in the Golden Age, are no longer acceptable (or indeed attainable) in a degenerate world. This is the theory of *kaliyugavarjya* (literally, the things 'to be avoided in the modern age'). According to this theory, both renunciation and ritual suicide (including *sahagamana*) are prohibited in the *kali* age.

The question of renunciation is tackled by Vāsudeva, that of *sahagamana* by Tryambaka. In each case, the prohibitions are given first, and then the problem is neatly sidestepped. Both authors conclude that such controversial issues cannot be resolved by an appeal to scripture. For Vāsudeva, the 'conduct of good men' is the best authority for allowing renunciation. For Tryambaka, the question of *sahagamana* in the *kali* age is best left to 'great men' to decide. Having said that, however, he proceeds to demonstrate that the safest course of action for the less-than-perfect wife remains that of joining her husband on the pyre. Despite the rulings regarding the *kali* age, it is clear that neither author has any doubt that the religious path he is discussing *works*.

Problems in the Parallel between Widow-ascetic and Renouncer

Finally, we must ask where this instructive parallel between the ideal life of the widow and that of the renouncer breaks down. Several points need to be made here.

First, while the male renouncer is expected to be a homeless wanderer, it is traditionally believed that a woman may not sever her family ties. As Vāsudeva explains, when the student has completed his year with a teacher, he should take his leave and wander the earth without transgressing *dharma*, rejoicing in solitude (*ekārāmaḥ*). Vāsudeva glosses *ekārāmaḥ* to mean not associating with other renouncers, whether male or female. In the process, and in parenthesis, he cites and appears to support a text ascribed to Baudhāyana allowing women to renounce. According to this view, it is possible to be a homeless wanderer and not transgress *dharma*, not even the *dharma* of women. Within the confines of *dharmaśāstra*, however, this is a controversial point. The wanderer's life and the notion of *strīdharma* are more commonly seen as incompatible. For most writers on *dharmaśāstra* agree with Tryambaka that the widow may never leave home as a true renunciate. For example:

> A widow who is devoted to her husband should not do anything without (first) asking her sons.

Forsaking sons, brothers and other (male relatives) after her husband (dies), and living independently, incurs condemnation.

A woman without a husband should not be deprived of father, mother, son, brother, mother-in-law and maternal uncle; otherwise she is to be condemned.

Nothing should be done independently by a woman, either as a child, a young girl, or an old woman, even in her (own) home.

Her dependence is simply transferred from husband to sons. It is clear from such rulings, and from repeated derogatory references to female ascetics throughout the *Strīdharmapaddhati*, that Tryambaka deems the path of the independent ascetic or renouncer closed to women. One example will suffice to indicate Tryambaka's position on this point. In his section in praise of the *pativratā*, he quotes at length from Bhīṣma's conversation with Yudhiṣṭhira on the behaviour of good women, taken from the *Anuśāsanaparvan* of the *Mahābhārata*. In particular, he recalls the dialogue between Sumanā and Śāṇḍilī when the two women meet in heaven. In answer to Sumanā's prompting, Śāṇḍilī describes the meritorious behaviour that brought her there:

I am not a wearer of the ochre robe (of the renunciate), nor one who dons the bark garments (of the hermit). It was not by shaving my head (like a religious mendicant), nor by wearing matted locks (like an ascetic) that I came to be a deity.

As Śāṇḍilī explains, she simply followed the dictates of her religious duty to her husband. According to this view, the only ascetic path open to women is that of the widow: a life of austerity conducted at the proper time, without display, and under the protection of male relatives.

Second, what are the qualifications necessary for the renouncer? According to Vāsudeva, they fall into two categories: the appropriate external circumstances (by which he means *varṇa* or social class) and the proper internal disposition (by which he means detachment). According to some authorities, the former excludes all but brahmin men; according to Vāsudeva and others, includes all twice-born men; while a minority view, apparently also supported by Vāsudeva, allows even women to renounce. But is clear that the more important qualification is the internal one: detachment (*vairāgyam*) as 'the cause of renunciation'.

If we compare these rulings with Tryambaka's views on widowhood, we find only the most superficial similarities. For the primary qualification for any woman to take up the ascetic path is neither social class nor inner disposition; it is the death of her husband, and the consequent need to preserve her virtue. While it is evident that Tryambaka considers the path of the widow-ascetic more appropriate to brahmins, he does not disqualify other women from it. More important, the question of a woman's natural disposition towards renunciation is only important once her husband is dead. While he lives, the good wife should have nothing to do with female ascetics, let alone emulate them. Indeed, while listing the women with whom the good wife should never associate, Tryambaka places the female renouncer (*pravrajitā*) alongside the courtesan, the female gambler, the woman who meets her lover in secret, the female juggler or magician, and the woman of bad character. Another such list bars the good woman from contact with the female religious mendicant (*śramaṇā*) along with the washerwoman, the female sceptic, and the woman who hates her husband. When her husband is dead, she is still not entitled to embark upon the life of the independent renunciate. For while a man may choose to renounce family life and devote himself to his religion, a woman may not: for a woman, religion *is* her family life. Hence Tryambaka's ruling that renunciation (*pravrajyā*) is to be avoided; it is one of the six things that cause women and *śūdras* to fall.[10] Instead, she should pursue the path of the widow-ascetic with single-mindedness (a path which, in another context, he himself terms 'renunciation'). The implication is clear: if she cannot trust herself to do this, she would be well advised to take the path of the *satī*.

Third, strictly speaking, while widowhood is certainly an ascetic path, it is not renunciation. The important dichotomy here is that between *nivṛtti* and *pravṛtti*; that is, the difference between non-action that promotes the cessation of *saṃsāra* (the cycle of rebirth); and actions that bring rewards (whether in this world, heaven or the next life) and thereby promote the continuation of *saṃsāra*. When Vásudeva describes the practices of the renouncer as the negation of life in society, *nivṛtti* is what is meant. When Tryambaka describes the activities of the widow as a negation of the lifestyle of the wife, *nivṛtti* could not be further from his mind. In fact, both the paths facing the woman whose husband has died are described in terms of worldly goals. *Sahagamana*, for example, is discussed as an optional (or *kāmya*) ritual: a woman need only perform it if she wants the rewards accruing to it; in this case, rewards relating to heaven and the next life. The alternative of widow-hood is discussed in similar terms.[11]

For Tryambaka, the key point of *strīdharma* – devotion to one's husband – remains the constant and primary theme for wife, widow and *satī*. The rulings regarding the widow are especially graphic. For example:

> She may worship Viṣṇu if (as she does so) she thinks of her husband, not otherwise. She should always meditate on her husband alone; that is, (on her husband) in the auspicious guise of (the god) Viṣṇu.
> She who takes refuge in the *dharma* of the virtuous wife should always worship her husband, bringing him to mind by means of a portrait or a clay model.

The wife, the widow and the *sati* all operate in the world of *strīdharma*, within the contextual framework of *dharma* and *saṃsāra*, and thus within the sphere of *pravṛtti*.

Conclusion

I conclude with the most striking difference between the path of the renouncer and that of the widow-ascetic. For what I began by presenting as a 'problem of choice' proves in this revealing context to be a *lack* of choice. This conclusion is already implied by the discussion of the rulings for the *kali* age. For, if (unlike Vāsudeva and Tryambaka) we take these rulings at face value, renunciation and ritual suicide (including *sahagamana*) are prohibited in the *kali* age. The man in question is left with a return to ordinary life; the woman with the ascetic path of widowhood. For the man has three options to choose from: ritual suicide, renunciation – or neither. His decision neither to take his own life nor to renounce leaves him no worse off than before. But the woman in the parallel position described by Tryambaka has only two options: *sahagamana* or widowhood. If she decides not to become a *sati*, she faces the hardships of life as a widow, regardless of her natural disposition for the ascetic life. Tryambaka puts so much feeling into the debate concerning which of these two paths a woman should take precisely because there is no third alternative. We may even have some sympathy for him when he implies that a woman faced with such a choice should prefer the certain glory of the heroic path. For it may well be safer and easier to die as a *sati* than to risk the possibility of failure on the widow's path.

The angry lament of Kannaki in the Tamil classic *Cilappati-kāram* says it all:

> And must I die of sorrow, like the wretched women who take fearful oaths upon the pyres of their beloved husbands?
>
> Must I die of despair, like the lonely women who carry their grief from pilgrimage to pilgrimage, and bathe in holy rivers, after the death of husbands who wore fragrant flower-garlands on their broad chests?
>
> Must I languish in loneliness, like the forlorn women who, after their tender husbands have vanished in the funeral pyre's smoke, remain, half alive, in abject widowhood? (tr. Danielou 1965)

Kannaki speaks for all women (whatever their preferred language, whether of North or South India) who seek to live by the exacting brāhmaṇical code; and her lament is justified. For *dharmaśāstra* provides no sanction for a third, non-heroic and non-ascetic path. There is no room for ordinary survival, let alone for a merry widow.[12]

(First published as Occasional Paper No. 4, 1991)

Notes

1   An earlier paper (Leslie 1987/88) explores this contrast in more detail, juxtaposing textual views on *sahagamana* with opinions on the widely publicized death of Roop Kanwar in Rajasthan in September 1987 (Badhwar et al. 1987). In the process, it attempts to confront the ethical issues embedded in cross-cultural work of this kind. Further on *satī* and *sahagamana*, see *Manushi* 1988 and *Seminar* 1988.

2   For the reservations that must be voiced here, I refer to my earlier paper: see note 1 above.

3   There has always been a faction for whom *sahagamana* is abhorrent; hence the debates on the subject in Sanskrit and vernacular texts. The controversy continues today, in private and in public. A good example was the confrontation in the late 1980s between Niranjan Dev Teerth, the powerful pro-*satī* Shankaracharya of Puri, and Swami Agnivesh, the maverick leader of the Hindu reform movement, the Arya Samaj; see Dutt (1988) and Singh (1988).

4   See Leslie (1986, 1989) for explorations of this contrast between 'wicked woman' and 'perfect wife'. This distinction between 'bad woman' and 'good wife' is also to be found in the vernacular: in Hindi, for example, *strī* has a generally sexual connotation while *aurat* is more neutral; in Urdu, *mahilā* means 'a lady', *zanānā* 'a female'.

5   For the former, see my own analysis and partial translation of the *Strīdharmapaddhati* (Leslie 1989); for the latter, see Patrick Olivelle's edition and translation of the *Yatidharmaprakāśa* (Olivelle 1976, 1977).

6   *Brahmāvarta*; Manu II.17–18.

7   Most translators of the *Upaniṣads* take this phrase not as a literal reference to suicide but as a metaphorical allusion to ignorance of the 'true self' (*ātman*). The *Bṛhadāraṇyakopaniṣad* (see Limaye and Vadekar 1958) has a similar verse in which the phrase is replaced by 'those who are ignorant and unawake'. Like many traditional commentators, however, Tryambaka takes the *Īśopaniṣad* verse (see Limaye and Vadekar 1958) literally; see also Sharma and Young (forthcoming).

8   This ambivalence is less suprising when viewed in the context of ritual suicide. For, strictly speaking, neither individual should still be alive: both have in some sense evaded the call to suicide.

9   By 'recorded history' I mean documentation that is generally agreed to be based on historical fact. I do not include legendary material in this category; the *Rāmāyaṇa*, for example, is traditionally placed in the *tretāyuga* or Third Age.

10   *Japas tapas tīrthayātrā pravrajyā mantrasādhanam/devatārādhanaṃ ceti strīśūdrapatanāni ṣat* (Sdhp. 25 v. 1).

11   Of course, the asceticism and ritual suicide of the male may also be 'reward-oriented'. Hence the importance of the *nivṛtti/pravṛtti* framework. Dharma is contextual, true renunciation contextless.

12   A version of this chapter with additional footnotes and complete references was published under the title 'A Problem of Choice: The Heroic *Satī* or the widow-Ascetic', in Leslie (ed., 1991).

Bibliography

Badhwar, Inderjit, with Pratap, Anita, Ahmed, Farzand, Awasthi, Dilip and Rattan, Kamaljit, 1987 'Widows: Wrecks of Humanity', *India Today* (15 November 1987).

Danielou, Alain (tr.) 1965. *Shilappadikaram (The Ankle Bracelet) by Prince Ilango Adigal*, New York: New Directions.

Dutt, Anuradha, 1988. 'The Weekly Debate: Niranjan Dev Teerth and Swami Agnivesh', *The Illustrated Weekly of India*, 1 May 1988.

Goldman, Robert P. (tr.), 1984 *The Rāmāyana of Vālmīki: An Epic of Ancient India, Vol. I: Bālākaṇḍa*, Princeton: Princeton University Press.

Leslie, Julia 1986. 'Strīsvabhava: The Inherent Nature of Women', in N.J. Allen, R.F. Gombrich, T. Raychaudhuri and G. Rizvi (eds), *Oxford University Papers on India*, Vol. I, Part 1, Delhi: Oxford University Press.

————— 1987/88. 'Suttee or Satī: Victim or Victor?', *Bulletin of the Center for the Study of World Religions* **14** (2), pp. 5–23.

————— 1989. *The Perfect Wife: The Orthodox Hindu Woman according to the Strīdharmapaddhati of Tryambakayajvan*, Delhi: Oxford University Press.

————— (ed.) 1991. *Rules and Remedies in Classical Indian Law*, Leiden: E.J. Brill.

Limaye, V.P. and Vadekar, R.D. (eds) 1958. *Eighteen Principal Upaniṣads*, Pune.

Manushi 1988. **42–3** (double issue devoted to *satī*), Delhi.

Olivelle, Patrick 1976 and 1977. *Vāsudevāśrama Yatidharmaprakāśa: A Treatise on World Renunciation*, Part I: critical edition (1976), Part II: English translation (1977), Vienna: De Nobili Research Foundation.

Seminar 1988. **342** (issue entitled 'Satī: A Symposium on Widow Immolation and its Social Context'), Delhi.

Sharma, Arvind and Young, Katherine K. (forthcoming), 'The Meaning of *ātmahano janāḥ* in *Īśa Upaniṣad* 3.3'.

Singh, Ramindar 1988. 'Polemics Postponed: Agnivesh's Showdown with Shankaracharya Prevented', *India Today*, 30 April 1988.

CHAPTER 11

A Buddhist-Christian Encounter in Sri Lanka: The Pānadura *Vāda*

Ria Kloppenborg

adau vāda isit[1].

Introduction: Background to the Debate

After the British took control of the coastal areas of Sri Lanka in 1796 from the Dutch, it soon became clear that they, contrary to the Portuguese and Dutch colonial powers which preceded them, were after complete political control of the island. In 1815 they took Kandy and from that moment Buddhism and the Buddhist *sangha* gradually lost their dominant place in Ceylonese politics. Being deprived of the traditional protection of the rulers, the *sangha* entered a period of serious decline which eventually led to a series of reforms in the 19th century. This development can be considered crucial in the history of modern Buddhism and started a definite 'change of character' (Gombrich 1988, p. 173), leading to what has later been called 'Buddhist Modernism' (Bechert) or 'Protestant Buddhism' (Obeyesekere and Malalgoda). It originated as a protest against Christian missionary activities and at the same time incorporated typically middle-class, Victorian, Protestant values (Kloppenborg 1992).

The main missionary organizations came to Sri Lanka in the being of the 19th century: the Wesleyans in 1814 and a few years later the Church of England's Church Missionary Society. According to Malalgoda (1976, pp. 172ff)[2] the Wesleyans were far more energetic and held the three main positions of Colombo, Galle and Matare. Although the Wesleyan missionary Daniel John Gogerly was one of the first to learn Sinhala and Pali, to study Buddhism seriously and to advocate the use of the vernacular in missionary schools and for native clergymen (de Silva 1965, pp. 157ff), this was merely done out of missionary policy. The majority of the missionaries looked upon the traditional religion of the Sinhalese 'as a massive evil structure that had to be destroyed before conversion proper could begin' (Malalgoda 1976, p. 204). Since the missionary societies had their own printing presses, these were used for propaganda and polemics. In 1831 Gogerly wrote: 'At present it is by means of the press that our main attacks must be made upon this wretched

system ... We must direct our efforts to pull down this stronghold of Satan.'
(*ibid*, pp. 204–5).

The Buddhist attitude towards non-Buddhist beliefs and practices has
always been one of tolerance; accepting one idea did not mean to them
rejecting another idea. They 'had no urge to regard two religions as violently
opposed to each other, to regard one as the "Truth" and the other as "Error"'
(*ibid*, p. 206). So when they were invited for discussions and debates, they really
did not see the use of that. They offered the missionaries hospitality in their
temples, monasteries and preaching halls, regarding them as colleagues.

The harsh words and insults in the Christian propaganda changed their
attitude. First they felt injured and sent petitions to the government (beginning
in the 1820s), with little result (*ibid*, p. 204). The petitions did, however, make
the government aware of the possibilities of religious strife. The government
was faced by a strong and well-organized missionary effort and, having ignored
the Kandyan Convention of 1815, had financially supported Christianity.
Therefore a much more cautious attitude seemed to be required to prevent an
eventual increase of religious antagonism (de Silva 1965, pp. 118ff).

Then in the 1830s attempts were made to reply to the missionaries in order to
find their own, Buddhist, position in the 'encounter'. When Gogerly published
his 'Kristiyāni Prajñapti' (Evidences and Doctrines of the Christian Religion)
in 1849 (reprinted in 1853), including an introduction entitled 'Proofs that
Buddhism is Not a True Religion', the Buddhists were willing to accept the
challenge. They started two printing presses, one in Galle in 1862, financed by
King Mongkut, and one in Colombo in 1855, an old press taken over from the
Christians. The main authors whose works were published by these presses
were Mohoṭṭivatte Guṇānanda (1823–1890) in Colombo and Hikkaduve
Sumangala in Galle. Guṇānanda's first publication was a reply to Gogerly's
book. He also started a Society for the Propagation of Buddhism, and these
developments slowly made the Buddhists more self-confident, and made the
conditions for a more equal encounter.

The Opponents and their Backgrounds

After Gogerly's death in 1862, he was succeeded by Spence Hardy, who
continued the study of Pali and Buddhism and ran the Wesleyan presses till his
return to England in 1865. Christian leadership in the confrontation then fell
on the Sinhalese Wesleyan minister David de Silva, a former protégé of
Gogerly. The encounter of de Silva and Guṇānanda had been going on already
for a number of years through publications when they met face to face in the
Pānadura debate.

In the long tradition of Buddhism, public debating has always been one
important way to convey the message and to attract converts. The Buddha's

debates and debating techniques, practices and conventions are clear from many passages in the Dīgha Nikāya (Manne 1992). It is obvious that most of these debates, even when they did actually take place, have been revised and standardized by later reciters and redactors. It seems probable that the early Buddhist practice of debating can be traced back to debates in the Vedic tradition (Witzel 1987). It eventually led to a specific literary form, even in the early Buddhist canonical texts, where a hypothetical opponent or opponents are employed.

It is interesting for our subject to point to the renewed popularity of this literary type of debate in the period of Sri Lankan history under discussion (Sarathchandra 1950). Guṇānanda, the Buddhist participant at the Pānadura debate, used this literary form of *vāda* in most of his publications since 1865. And the most impressive report of a public debate in Pali, the *Milindapañha* – discussions between the Buddhist monk Nāgasena and a Greek-Bactrian ruler by the name of Menander – had Guṇānanda's special attention. He published a Sinhala translation of that debate in 1878, a volume of nearly 650 pages, the largest volume issued by the Buddhist press. In his preface Guṇānanda calls the book priceless for the way in which it may suppress erroneous opinions.

Guṇānanda had earlier been challenged to a debate in 1865, but because of disagreements on the procedure, this debate took the form of an exchange in letters (Malalgoda 1976, p. 225). After that, a few minor debates took place: in three of them (Vāragoda 1865, Liyangēmulle 1866 and Gampala 1871), Guṇānanda was the Buddhist champion. As a member of the Amarapura Nikāya, which was established in 1800 as a result of the upward mobility of the low castes under colonial rule (especially the Dutch rule) and as a result of the refusal of the dominant Siyam Nikāya to give higher ordination to low caste monks, Guṇānanda certainly was a worthy opponent of the Methodist de Silva. Perhaps they had more in common than they realized. In any case, by character and experience Guṇānanda was the first choice amongst his Buddhist colleagues for the final and historical encounter that took place in Pānadura.

Analysis of the Pānadura Debate

The *vāda* took place on 26 and the 27 of August 1873. In total eight lectures were delivered by the parties, four on each day. The lectures were reported by John Capper, editor of the *Ceylon Times*. This report was revised by the disputants, and later published, together with an introduction and annotations by J.M. Peebles, an American Methodist. His annotations were partly based on the observations on the debate made by the *Ceylon Times* special correspondent John Perera, a Sinhalese Christian.

My analysis is based on the reprint of Peebles's report, published by the Maha Bodhi Press in Colombo in 1955, entitled *The Great Debate: Buddhism and Christianity Face to Face* (Peebles 1955). The foreword clearly states the editor's position as favourable to the Buddhist cause: 'Buddhism in Ceylon was in great danger. About the year 1860 the eminent Ven. Migettuwatte Guṇānanda Thero, the silver-tongued orator of the age, emerged like a noble Knight of old'.[3] Peebles also anticipates some of the critiques made of Buddhist views, for example 'that it has been charged with atheism'. This charge, Peebles continues, 'is rank injustice. It is true that Buddhists do not believe in a personal, human-shaped God, the subject of limitations, and even of such passions as anger and jealousy but they *do* believe in a supreme Power' (*ibid*, pp. 6–7). This of course is an opinion that is clearly not in agreement with Theravāda Buddhist teaching and shows the apologetic standpoint of the editor. Peebles also alludes to the discussion on the concept of *nirvana* as an impersonal state, and here too we find an interesting apology: 'By *nirvana* we all understand a final reunion with God ... It is the very opposite of personal annihilation' (*ibid*, p. 11). Regarding comparative ethics we find the following position:

> The tone of morality is higher, and the practice of charitable deeds far more prevalent in Buddhist than in Christian countries. It is sad to write, though true, that bull-fights, dog-fights and men-fights – the latter under the name of *war* – indicate the status of Christian morals. (*ibid*, p. 13)

In sum, his views on Christian missionary involvement are mixed:

> So far as missionaries teach the people of the East the English language; so far as they instruct them in the arts and sciences, and encourage secular education generally, they do great good; but in matters of religion they have nothing *new* to teach the Orientals that is *true*. (*ibid*, p. 7)

The Discussions at Pānadura

It is recorded that on the first day approximately five thousand people attended the debate, and on the second day, more than ten thousand. Each district had sent a fixed number of Buddhist attendants, while the Protestants sent catechists and clergymen from every denomination. In the centre of the field where the debate was held a raised platform was decorated on the Buddhist side with flags and colourful draperies; on the Christian side it was all in white. Each speaker was allowed one hour and there were four lectures each day, from 8 to 10 in the morning and from 3 to 5 in the afternoon. Since David de Silva started the debate, Guṇānanda had the advantage of the final and closing speech.

The Great Debate also mentions strengths and weaknesses of the opponents. De Silva was learned and fluent, knowing Pali and quoting from the Pali texts, although the latter seems to have been lost on this audience. Guṇānanda spoke on the level of his public, trying to avoid difficult words or giving long quotations in a language the audience did not understand. He also used western (that is British) oratory styles like standing and gesticulating, as well as the traditional Buddhist technique of answering a question with another question. 'Of all the weak points in Protestantism, he only touches upon those which will excite the ridicule of the people and evoke a smile of derisive contempt' (Peebles 1955, p. 37).

De Silva's first speech starts with a topic that has been discussed since the time of the Buddha: if Buddhism teaches that a person has no soul, how can that person experience the results of good or bad actions (*karma*) in another life? De Silva quotes extensively from various Nikāyas, showing that Buddhist philosophy describes a person as consisting of only impermanent and material groups of elements (*khandha*), with the Buddha defining death as the breaking up of these groups. His conclusion is that 'there is no *Ātma* or soul which survives the body'; therefore 'any being which would exist hereafter and suffer punishment or reap the rewards for the actions committed in this world … must be a different being' (*ibid*, p. 49). Since 'this surely is contrary to all principles of justice', it follows that 'no religion ever held out greater inducements to the unrighteous than Buddhism did' (*ibid*, pp. 53–4).

Guṇānanda's reply starts with an attack on de Silva's lecture, describing it as 'a very desultory and rambling speech, which … nobody understood' (*ibid*, p. 55). Coming to de Silva's critique, he explains the Buddhist idea that the person in a new life is neither the same nor a different being (*na ca so, na ca añño*); no part of the five *khandha* would be transferred to another existence, while at the same time the person in a next life was not a different being. Then Guṇānanda discusses the Christian idea of a soul, concluding that, since according to the Christian a soul goes to a state of misery or bliss without any change, it must be the case that a human soul goes to heaven with all its imperfections. A second argument in defence of the Buddhist teaching of *anatta* (no-abiding-self) is then given when he emphasizes the transitoriness or impermanence of all phenomena, including the five *khandha*. 'But yet the being who is produced simultaneously [*sic*] with the extinction of *Pañcaskhandha* was not a different being' (*ibid*, p. 59). And then he offers his audience this comparison:

> The much revered Bible of the Christians was not the original Bible written by Moses and others, and in use amongst the primitive believers of Christ; and yet they could not say it was a different Bible. The substance in both was the same, though it was *not* the identical book; so it was with *Ātma*. (*ibid*)

Hence Guṇānanda's conclusion on *anatta* is that 'it was as incorrect to say that it was a different being who suffered for the good or evil committed here, as to assert that it was the *identical* doer with all his environments who thus suffered' (*ibid*).

In a second argument Guṇānanda analyses the process of dying, by which the desires and expectations of a dying person are seen as causes for the origination of a 'new' being to whom these desires and expectations are transferred. Another traditional point of controversy is then brought forward by the Buddhist: the Christian concept of God. Is not the idea of a jealous or envious God in the Old Testament, who is eager even for human sacrifices, hard to reconcile with the image of the omniscient Creator? And is it not a contradiction for a Creator who was declared omniscient to repent any actions and to grieve, as in Genesis 6:6? And he provides his audience with a number of other examples from the Old Testament which lead him to the conclusion that the Creator was not omniscient.

The third lecture gives de Silva's reply. By now the crowd had increased threefold. De Silva seems rather worried and instead of using his previous, polite, way of address, uses the word 'opponent' when referring to Guṇānanda. His reaction to Guṇānanda's remarks on the Christian concept of God seems weak: he points at a symbolic meaning of the Old Testament images, and continues with a vague attack on the Buddhist teaching of *paṭiccasamuppāda* ('conditioned genesis') in which he makes some errors, for example regarding the interpretation of *viññana* consciousness, the third component of the *paṭiccasamuppāda*, which he actually takes as *āyatana-viññana*, the consciousness of the sense organs. Thereby he believes to have proven the absurdity of the whole series, since the sense-organs thus preceed *nāma-rūpa*, *phassa* and *vedanā* ('name and form', 'contact' and 'sensation'). In consequence, asks de Silva, is this 'not an absurdity, and a confusion of thought. Is it not like saying the son is begotten by the father, and the father is begotten by the son, and both have one origin, ignorance?' (*ibid*, p. 79).

The fourth lecture, Guṇānanda's last speech of the first day, starts with a remark on de Silva's use of the word *viruddhakāraya*, 'opponent'. Although Guṇānanda believed there was no personal enmity between them, 'he regretted to say that he had no alternative but to do the same' (*ibid*, p. 80). Coming back to the concept of God, Guṇānanda argues that his 'opponent' did not explain the jealousy assigned to the Creator in relation to his other attributes. De Silva's explanation, in which the passages from the Old Testament previously quoted by Guṇānanda are said to be symbolic, is regarded by the latter as 'explaining away'. Guṇānanda continues his attack with this question: 'How did Christians get over the difficulty arising out of God's injunction to circumcise Moses' son, thereby betraying His fondness of human blood in common with evil spirits having similar tastes?' (*ibid*, p. 84). He then discusses another instance which he believed showed God's fondness of human sacrifices: the case of Jephthah's daughter. Although the Protestants said that sacrifice was not literally carried out, the Roman Catholics stated that it was. Therefore he ends this part of his speech by complimenting the Roman Catholics, who, he claimed, in contrast with the Protestants did not 'alter their Bibles whenever it suited them' (*ibid*, p. 91). Another topic which must have been attractive to his audience concerned the significance of good or ill omens. He compares the omens that are said to have occurred at the time of the birth of the Buddha and of the Christ, respectively: the thirty-two good and cheerful omens at the birth of the Buddha, and the massacre of innocent children. This brings him, as expected, to some unpleasant remarks about the Christian saviour. He is reported as ending with the declamation that 'if his opponents are in a position to show that even an ant had died in consequence of Buddha's birth, he ... would renounce Buddhism as speedily as possible' (*ibid*, p. 94).

Two days later the debate continued. The Christian party now thought it wiser to use a more popular speaker, who would understand the public's interests better. Hence the third speech from the Christian side was by a catechist of the Church Missionary Society, F.S. Sirimanne, who appears to have had a better understanding of these kinds of public debates. He starts by emphasizing that he had not heard one argument against his religion that could not be met by a school boy. Then he returns to the issue of *anatta* and *karma* and accuses Guṇānanda of distorting the facts on Christianity, either through ignorance or deliberately; for example, he argues that Jephthah's daughter was not killed, and that the story was symbolic and had to do with the girl's virginity. Furthermore the massacre of the innocent children did not take place at the birth of Christ but two years later, whereas if we look carefully at the circumstances surrounding the Buddha's birth, many people did die, first of all his own mother 'seven days after giving birth to this extraordinary baby, who is said to have been able to walk and speak very plainly at the moment of his birth. The wonder is that the mother of such a gigantic monster should have lived even for seven days' (*ibid*, p. 104).

Later in his speech he returns to this issue by pointing at the *bodhisattva*'s ten *pāramitās*, which he describes as 'sacrifices', and especially at *dāna-paramitās* 'or almsgiving, which, besides others, consisted of the extraordinary offering of his eyes, head, flesh, blood, wives and children' (*ibid*, p. 107), thereby referring to the *Jātaka* stories, and especially to the *Vessantara-jātaka*. He continues describing the model happy family of husband and wife, loving their children and living in perfect harmony. 'What will they think of a father, living in such happiness, giving up his children without any hesitation or sorrow to a wandering hermit, amidst the cries and lamentations of his wife and ... children' (*ibid*, p. 108). And this did not happen just once. According to the Buddhist scriptures, claims Sirimanne, if the ropes and strings with which the wives and children of Buddha who were sacrificed by him were tied, were collected in a heap its height would be a million times greater than that of Mahāmeru ... This will give them a tolerably good idea of the number of wives and children sacrificed. (*ibid*, p. 109)

'So, Guṇānanda', he continues, 'what about your promise to renounce Buddhism?' He ends with an attack on the immorality of Buddhist monks, which at this time, following recent developments in the *sangha*, must have been painful for his Buddhist colleagues to hear. Regarding the three refuges, he seriously doubts the effectiveness of the third, which he calls 'the refuge in Priests'. He points at the controversy between the Amarapura (Guṇānanda's Nikāya) and Siyam Nikāya, which both refuse to accept each other's ordination. As he puts it:

the immorality of the priests was well known; and was it not like the blind leading the blind for the Buddhist priests, men full of lust, envy, and ignorance as they were, to attempt to guide the people who foolishly took refuge in the *Sangha*, or the priesthood? (*ibid*, p. 112)

In his reply Guṇānanda addresses all the issues that have been discussed, clarifying the Buddhist position in a serious, less rhetorical manner. He tries to explain the *paṭiccasamuppāda* with some examples, basing himself strongly on the *Visuddhimagga*, and concluding that *viññana* comes into existence simultaneously with *nāma-rūpa*, thereby refuting his opponent's erroneous interpretation. For the first time in the debate he then quotes extensively from the New Testament, trying to expose another contradiction. This concerns a passage in I Corinthians 15, verses 22–8, that by believing in Christ all 'shall escape the punishment of eternal hell-fire and obtain everlasting happiness' (*ibid*, p. 119). On the other hand he points to Matthew 25, verses 41–6, where the verses read 'Then shall he say also unto them on the left hand, depart from me, ye cursed, into everlasting fire ... for I was hungered, and ye gave me no meat'. Guṇānanda claims that the latter passage refutes the former: 'If words have any meaning, this clearly shows that men's salvation does not depend upon belief in Christ alone, but to attain happiness hereafter it was necessary to perform righteous or good actions' (*ibid*, p. 120).

David de Silva returned to give his third and last speech. He emphasizes Sirimanne's point on the inhuman actions described in the *Jātakas*, and then raises a different question: where can we find the mountain Meru or Mahāmeru, which is according to Buddhist cosmology the centre of the world? He even shows his audience a globe of the world, explaining that

the circumference of the earth is 25,000 miles. This is admitted by all civilized nations of the world ... Therefore a mountain with such dimensions (as given in the Buddhist texts) could not exist on this earth'. (*ibid*, p. 140)

Rather pitifully he concludes with the demand that 'Mahāmeru ... must be placed on the earth; if not, Buddhism must be rejected at once' (*ibid*, p. 143). As a reaction to the Buddhist critique of the Christian God's omniscience, de Silva points out that one can find contradictions in the Buddhist texts too. For example, he points out that it is stated that the Buddha had the power of knowing everything, while at the same time he was unaware of the fact that his precepts, for instance the precept of celibacy, were being misunderstood or transgressed by his monks: 'one priest had connection with a female monkey, another priest with his own mother, and another with his own sister' (*ibid*, p. 143).

Guṇānanda's closing speech starts with a list of counter-arguments. Here is his predictable reaction on the matter of Mount Meru: 'The little globe which the Reverend gentleman produced was one made on Newton's principle; but even amongst Englishmen there were serious doubts about ... that theory' (*ibid*, p. 153). For did not the Bible state that the sun moved and the earth stood still? And where would the Reverend place the garden of Eden? Regarding the immorality of Buddhist monks, he argued that 'no blame could be attached to Buddhism, or any other religion, because of the immorality of some of its preachers' (*ibid*, p. 157). Missionaries did not prove to be moral either, for 'who would dream of adducing the argument that Christianity was false because the wife of a well-known Protestant clergyman, when she got ill, had gone to a distant village, and with the connivance of her husband, performed a *devil ceremony*, though he knew well of such an instance' (*ibid*, p. 157). Regarding the attack on the Buddha's omniscience, Guṇānanda claimed that he was indeed omniscient 'but his omniscience was not of such an unpleasant nature as that ascribed to Jehovah' who is said to see and know everything, at all times, and is therefore forced to witness all misery continuously, whereas the Buddha only 'saw what he wanted to by directing his power to it' (*ibid*, p. 160).

As Guṇānanda had the final word, it was expected that he would use his last half hour for a serious critique of several Christian ideas and concepts. For example, there was the unsatisfactory story of the bodily resurrection: who would believe the words of Mary Magdalene, who at one time was possessed by devils and who could therefore be considered to be mentally unstable? And what about the removal of the body by the disciples, while there were no guards? There was also the issue of the Christian theory of a Creator: when the Bible states that the spirit of God moved over the waters, might we not in fact conclude that water was the cause of all animal and vegetable life, as is clear if we observe the natural phenomena around us? Also to be considered is the question: three Gods or One? Guṇānanda ends his presentation by expressing his satisfaction that he had proved the truth of Buddhism and the falsity of Christianity.

Consequences of the Debate

The text of the debate as published by Peebles was also published in the United States of America, where it caused enthusiastic reactions. Colonel H.S. Olcott, for example, who founded the Theosophical Society together with Madame Blavatsky in 1875, was first attracted to Buddhism by this report. Soon after the foundation of the Theosophical Society, Olcott had established contact with Indian as well as Ceylonese leaders such as Dayanand Saraswati, Sumangala and Guṇānanda. In 1879 Madame Blavatsky sent her book *Isis Unveiled* (1877) to Guṇānanda, who later would publish abstracts from this work.

In 1880 Olcott and Blavatsky arrived in Sri Lanka and founded the Buddhist Theosophical Society. Olcott started to organize the Buddhist revival and became its major fundraiser. The Buddhist Theosophical Society seems to have been 'theosophical' in name only, due to influences we will discuss later; in fact it exemplified a 'modernist' or 'Protestant' Buddhism (Malalgoda 1976, pp. 242–6). In the coming years the relationship between Olcott and Guṇānanda became less friendly and even hostile, and after 1887 they parted over the issue of the involvement of lay persons, which was promoted by the Theosophists but was greatly resented by the Buddhist monks, who felt themselves the custodians and leaders of the Sri Lankan Buddhist civilization.

Another point of controversy may be found in the way many Sinhalese regarded Olcott, Blavatsky and the Theosophical Society. Olcott was regarded by many as a 'Mr. Facing Bothways' (Wickremeratne 1993, p. 2) and there were serious doubts regarding his credentials as a Buddhist, so that a 'public examination' was asked for to test his knowledge of Buddhism. Also Madame Blavatsky was criticized for her alleged psychic powers. Of course, Sumangala as well as Guṇānanda must have been aware of the fact that, in the end, Theosophy and Buddhism would not be able to reconcile their theories. What bound them principally was their anti-Christian attitudes (*ibid*, p. 4).

After his first visit to Sri Lanka, Olcott took with him to the headquarters of the Theosophical Society at Adyar, India, a young pupil, Don David Hewavitarane, later known as the *anagārika* ('homeless') Dharmapāla, born in 1864 in Colombo in an upper middle class family and educated in Christian mission schools. He had attended the Pānadura *vāda* and in 1878 came into contact with Guṇānanda, who, with other leading monks, had a decisive influence on him. He became the 'organizer' of Guṇānanda's ideals: the anti-Buddhist sphere of Dharmapāla's missionary education had evoked strong reactions in him. Back in Sri Lanka, the influence of Guṇānanda and

Sumangala – including their rejection of the Theosophical Society's involvement in the Buddhist renaissance – made Dharmapāla, who was then the main ideologist of the Buddhist Theosophical Society, opt for a change in emphasis in the Society's standpoint, which from then on became purely Buddhist and 'modernist'.

It was then that he adopted the *anagārika* role, in which renunciation and worldly involvement were combined. Although following the rules of Buddhist novices, he remained in the secular world to perform political and social action as well as missionary activities. In order to symbolize his chosen this-worldly involvement, he did not shave his hair and beard like the Buddhist monks, and in order to symbolize his asceticism he wore special white robes. In his views he established a strong link between nationalistic feelings and Buddhist renewal and revival, a link that provided the basis for contemporary so-called 'Buddhist chauvinism' in Sri Lanka.

His oratory style was obviously copied both from Guṇānanda and from the propagandism of the Christian missionaries, as encapsulated in the Pānadura *vāda*. In 1902, in a pamphlet entitled 'History of an Ancient Civilization' published in the United States, Dharmapāla wrote:

> The bright, beautiful Island of Ceylon is under the barbaric imperialism of England ... The sweet, tender, gentle Aryan children of an ancient, historic race are sacrificed at the altar of the whisky-drinking, beef-eating belly-god of Heathenism. (Guruge 1965)

However, while sharply criticizing western cultural and political domination, he admired science and technology, as did Guṇānanda. For example, on 9 October 1909, in his newspaper *Sinhala Bauddhaya*, he speaks of the British as 'the most enlightened, the most philanthropic, the most cultured of all European races'. 'England', he writes, 'gives us arts, sciences'.

However, although admitting that he admired the ethical doctrines of Christ, especially the Sermon on the Mount in Matthew's Gospel, he rejected historical Christianity which he felt had failed in Europe. While science and technology had brought progress and reduced poverty and ignorance, Christianity and Christian theology had failed to provide a moral basis for daily life:

> In Christian countries scientists are at work to elevate the masses by scientific methods, while the missionaries that go to Asia are utterly deficient in scientific knowledge, and all that they can offer are the myths of Canaan and Galilee which had their origin in the backwash of Arabia. (Guruge 1965, p. 25)

In this and other instances, Dharmapāla's influence on the development of modern Sri Lankan Buddhism cannot be stressed enough.

Returning to the issue of 'encounter' or 'dialogue' in more recent times, it is striking how often, on Buddhist as well as on Christian sides, references are made to the Pānadura *vāda*. For example, in 1974 Gunapala Dharmasiri published his thesis, which had been presented at the University of Lancaster, in Sri Lanka. This work, *A Buddhist Critique of the Christian Concept of God* (Dharmasiri 1974), led to new and long discussions and debates in Sri Lanka, in public as well as in print, all in a more friendly atmosphere (although it had its sharp edges). That the historical influence of the Pānadura *vāda* was still setting the tone for debate is acknowledged by the Roman Catholic interfaith theologian, Aloysius Pieris, who in an issue of the journal *Dialogue* entirely devoted to Dharmasiri's book, wrote that 'one consequence of [the *vāda*] is that the Buddhists took their turn to challenge the Christians and put them on the defense' (Pieris 1975, pp. 83ff). Pieris describes Dharmasiri's recent publication as 'a critique, and a ruthless one at that!'. He continues:

> Its tone is polemical, its language provocative and its purpose apologetical ... The more cynical (among the Christians) have recognized it is a distant echo of the theological manuals of a bygone era wherein the Buddhists tenets, uprooted from their contexts with tools borrowed from Aristotle, were dismissed as so many bundles of contradictions. (*ibid*)

The rather nervous and apologetic reaction from the Christian side led to another *vāda*. Dharmasiri and 'Buddhist colleagues of his own choice' were asked for a 'frank exchange' and the encounter took place on 26 October 1975. It was, in fact, one of the public signs of the change of attitude of Christians towards dialogue with Buddhism, and resulted in a new openness and understanding to challenge the fundamentalist attitude of the Christians and the triumphalistic attitude of the Buddhists that had been the legacy of the Pānadura *vāda*.

(First published as Occasional Paper No. 9, 1994)

Notes

1 'In the beginning was the Word (*vāda*).' First line of the Gospel of John in its Sanskrit translation by the Bible Society of India.

2 As also acknowledged by Gombrich (1988, pp.172ff), Malalgoda's work is the most important source of information on this period.

3 Cf. Wickremeratne (1993, p. 2, n.6): 'Of these two famous Buddhist monks of the period the great Buddhist figure was Guṇānanda, whose oratorical skill even the missionaries could scarce forbear to admire. His antipathy to Christianity was so great that his criticisms were considered intemperate and even scurrilous. His genius was that of a propagandist rather than that of an organizer.'

Bibliography

Dharmasiri, Gunapal, 1974. *A Buddhist Critique of the Christian Concept of God*, Colombo.

Gombrich, Richard 1988. *Theravada Buddhism: A Social History from Ancient Benares to Modern Colombo*, London and New York: Routledge.

Guruge, A. 1965. *Return to Righteousness: A Collection of Speeches, Essays and Letters of the Anagārika Dharmapāla*, Colombo.

Kloppenborg, Ria, 1992. 'The Anagārika Dharmapāla (1864–1933) and the Puritan Pattern', in *Nederlands Theologisch Tijdschrift*, **46** (4), pp. 277–284.

Malalgoda, Kitsiri 1976. *Buddhism in Sinhalese Society 1750–1900*, Berkeley: University of California Press.

Manne, Joy 1992. 'The Dīgha Nikāya Debates,' *Buddhist Studies Review* **9** (2), pp. 117ff.

Peebles, J.M. (intr. and annotations) 1955. *The Great Debate: Buddhism and Christianity Face to Face*, Colombo: Maha Bodhi Press.

Pieris, Aloysius 1975. 'God. A Buddhist Critique and a Christian Response', *Dialogue* (New Series) **II** (3), November-December 1975.

Sarathchandra, E.R. 1950. *The Sinhalese Novel*, Colombo.

de Silva, K.M. 1965. *Social Policy and Missionary Organizations in Ceylon 1840–1855*, London: Longmans for the Royal Commonwealth Society.

Wickremeratne, L.A. 1993 [1970]. 'Religion, Nationalism and Social Change in Ceylon, 1865–1885', *Studies in Society and Culture: Sri Lanka Past and Present*, Colombo (first published in *Comparative Studies in Society and History* **12**, pp. 434–443, 1970).

Witzel, M. 1987. 'The Case of the Shattered Head', *Studien zur Indologie und Iranistik* **13–14**, pp. 363–415.

CHAPTER 12

Religion and Community in Indigenous Contexts

Armin W. Geertz

Introduction: What is Community?

Communities are wonderful things. They provide standards for human behaviour and human relations. They regulate relations between individuals and groups. They decide on important issues like what constitutes a man, what constitutes a woman, and how relations between them ought to be. They create contexts for identity, meaning, morality and politics. They decide what is good and what is evil. They are, in sociologist Emile Durkheim's words, ultimate authorities, forces that raise individuals above themselves. A community is a consciousness of consciousnesses and the highest form of human mind (Durkheim 1995, pp. 16–17, 211–16, 445, 447–8).

Indigenous peoples are good examples to choose when exploring the relationship between religion and community, because they demonstrate the variety and creativity of humanity. But it should be noted here that I am not suggesting that indigenous peoples are communalistic with no individualism, as some Western social philosophers have claimed. There are enough examples of individualism and dissidence in indigenous societies to dissuade from this point of view.[1]

I will formulate a few characteristics of community before moving on to my main points. In my opening eulogy I claimed that community is the source of just about everything and is a wonderful thing. Well, I take that back. Community is only wonderful half the time. I have chosen for this chapter some 'hairy' examples of the downside of community in order to drive the point home. Community is not just a social or institutional context. It is the creator of meanings, worlds, hermeneutical strategies and many other things that help individual humans to make it through existence in a fairly meaningful way. Sociologists have been quite taken up with the term: for example, G.A. Hillery (1955, p. 119) reviewed 94 definitions of community and concluded that 'beyond the concept that people are involved in community, there is no complete agreement as to the nature of community'. The term is often used as a synonym for society, group, social system, and social organization. There have also been a number of efforts at typology, for instance Joachim Wach's and Milton Yinger's typologies of religious communities (Wach 1962[1944]; Yinger 1965[1957] and 1970).[2]

Some authors use community in a more limited context. Gideon Sjoberg suggested a modification of Talcott Parson's (1951, p. 91) definition:

> A community is a collectivity of actors sharing a limited territorial area as the base for carrying out the greatest share of their daily activities. This definition implies that persons interact within a *local* institutional complex which provides a wide range of basic services, yet it also takes into consideration the fact that the community is not necessarily a self-sufficient unit. (Sjoberg 1959)

This definition would apply to indigenous contexts, which normally are restricted in terms of size and territoriality, but this definition is perhaps too narrow. At any rate, community today has grown exponentially so that we often speak about the global village, the global community and the international community. It is not necessarily size, or even location, that determines the convergence of individuals in communities. Thus it might seem more appropriate to choose communication and meaning construction as defining characteristics of community. Reformulating Sjoberg, we might define community as a *collectivity of actors sharing meanings and activities in the context of a common worldview.* Such a definition draws heavily on Clifford Geertz's hermeneutic and semiotic concept of culture. This focus on meaning and on community as a moral body neither negates nor neglects day-to-day living in the world, as will become clear later in this paper. Communities practise and produce a whole series of human universals ranging from language and communication, naming and taxonomy, notions of person, kinship, gender and age, as well as laws, customs, etiquette, aesthetics, worldviews and religion, to the more mundane concerns of shelter, tool-making, subsistence activities and sexual reproduction (cf. Brown 1991).

Religious communities, on the other hand, are more specifically focused. In many societies, communities are both religious and secular, depending on the time and context. In this sense, communities mark entrances into (initiation), changes during (transition rituals) and exits from (funerals) the community. Ritual and pageant mark important community activities and are integral to maintaining and shaping community norms and identity. The community consists as well of differentiation in the group based on function and merit. Religious validation adorns social markings such as gender, family, and clan and integrates these in terms of the natural and sacred world. In fact, community is often conceived as a sacred or semi-sacred entity in itself (Weckman 1987).

Cognition and Community

Let us change perspective for a moment and see what community does to the individual. It may strike some readers that approaching community through the individual is like putting the horse on the saddle. But humour me for a moment. I hope that you will see the wisdom of this strategy.

Long ago, Emile Durkheim presented significant insights on religion, community and society. Although I am not a Durkheimian, I think that his insights on a number of matters are just as relevant today as they were at the turn of the twentieth century. Durkheim (1995, p. 15) promoted the insight that all humans are inherently dual beings, namely, an individual being with its basis in the body and a social being representing the highest reality in the intellectual and moral realm. Reading Durkheim today, we are struck by how psychologized his social theory was. Society for him is the collective consciousness of individuals coming together under common aims, truths, and sensibilities. Individuals and communities presuppose each other, nurture each other, and express themselves through each other. Thus, said Durkheim (*ibid*, p. 447), 'there is something impersonal in us because there is something social in us, and since social life embraces both representations and practices, that impersonality extends quite naturally to ideas as well as to actions.'

These were interesting ideas at the time. They have since then become more commonplace in various guises in psychological and cognitive theory. One of Durkheim's contemporaries, the pragmatist and founding father of social psychology in the United States, George Herbert Mead, was working along similar lines. Let us briefly dwell on a few of his main concepts and theories.

Mead was not interested in individualistic psychology but more in the role of society in the development of the mind. He focused on the dynamics of social action and postulated that both meaning and mind have their origins in the social act through reflexiveness. To Mead the self is constructed through role taking, during which the social attitudes of the 'generalized other' exert influence on the conduct of the individual and on the development of the self. Thus the 'I' becomes aware of the social 'me', or, a telling phrase, 'the mind as the individual importation of the social process' (Mead 1962[1934], p. 186). As he wrote concerning the mind:

> Mind arises in the social process only when that process as a whole enters into, or is present in, the experience of any one of the given individuals involved in that process. When this occurs the individual becomes self-conscious and has a mind; he becomes aware of his relations to that process as a whole, and to the other individuals participating in it with him; he becomes aware of that process as modified by the reactions and interactions of the individuals – including himself – who are carrying it on … . It is by means of reflexiveness – the turning-back of the experience of the individual upon himself – that the whole social process is thus brought into the

experience of the individuals involved in it; it is by such means, which enable the individual to take the attitude of the other toward himself, that the individual is able consciously to adjust himself to that process, and to modify the resultant of that process in any given social act in terms of his adjustment to it. Reflexiveness, then, is the essential condition, within the social process, for the development of mind. (Mead 1962[1934], p. 134)

The same with intelligence:

It is generally recognized that the specifically social expressions of intelligence, or the exercise of what is often called 'social intelligence', depend upon the given individual's ability to take the roles of, or 'put himself in the place of', the other individuals implicated with him in given social situations; and upon his consequent sensitivity to their attitudes toward himself and toward one another. These specifically social expressions of intelligence, of course, acquire unique significance in terms of our view that the whole nature of intelligence is social to the very core – that this putting of one's self in the places of others, this taking by one's self of their roles or attitudes, is not merely one of the various aspects or expressions of intelligence or of intelligent behavior, but is the very essence of its character. (*ibid*, p. 141, n. 3)

And, even more importantly, the same with the self. It is the social process that is responsible for the appearance of the self: we are one thing to one person and another thing to another. We discuss politics with one, religion with another. We are lovers for one and enemies for another. And there are parts of the self that exist only in relationship to itself (*ibid*, p. 142). The integration of these various selves into a unified whole occurs through reflexiveness:

The reflexive character of self-consciousness enables the individual to contemplate himself as a whole; his ability to take the social attitudes of other individuals and also of the generalized other toward himself, within the given organized society of which he is a member, makes possible his bringing himself, as an objective whole, within his own experiential purview; and thus he can consciously integrate and unify the various aspects of his self, to form a single consistent and coherent and organized personality. Moreover, by the same means, he can undertake and effect intelligent reconstructions of that self or personality in terms of its relations to the given social order, whenever the exigencies of adaptation to his social environment demand such reconstructions. (*ibid*, p. 309, n. 19)

There is, thus, a dialectic between the individual self, the individual mind and society. Society stamps the pattern of its organized social behavior on its individual members and gives the individual a mind that allows conscious conversation with his or her self 'in terms of the social attitudes which constitute the structure of his self and which embody the pattern of human society's organised behavior as reflected in that structure'. On the other hand, this mind makes it possible for the individual to set the stamp of its 'further developing self' upon the structure and organization of human society, thus being able to reconstruct or modify the patterns of group behavior (*ibid*, p. 263, n. 10).

I have dwelt at some length on Mead in order to help us understand the dynamics of community and individual. But how much of this is still scientifically viable in light of recent insights drawn from developmental psychology and cognitive psychology? Perhaps one of the most significant discoveries in cognitive science that may give us a clue to the significance and function of religion is the emerging understanding of consciousness. One of the main proponents of the so-called 'Multiple Drafts Model', Daniel Dennett (1991, p. 111), explained this model as follows:

> According to the Multiple Drafts model, all varieties of perception – indeed, all varieties of thought or mental activity – are accomplished in the brain by parallel, multitrack processes of interpretation and elaboration of sensory inputs. Information entering the nervous system is under continuous 'editorial revision' ... .

These editorial processes occur in various parts of the brain. The novel feature of the Multiple Drafts model is that 'feature detections or discriminations *only have to be made once*', which means that:

> ... once a particular 'observation' of some feature has been made, by a specialized, localized portion of the brain, the information content thus fixed does not have to be sent somewhere else to be *re*discriminated by some 'master' discriminator. In other words, discrimination does not lead to a re*presentation* of the already discriminated feature for the benefit of the audience in the Cartesian Theater – for there is no Cartesian Theater ....

These various discriminations occur over the course of time as:

> ... something *rather like* a narrative stream or sequence, which can be thought of as subject to continual editing by many processes distributed around in the brain, and continuing indefinitely into the future. This stream of contents is only rather like a narrative because of its multiplicity; at any point in time there are multiple 'drafts' of narrative fragments at various stages of editing in various places in the brain ... . (*ibid*, pp. 112–13)

Dennett's main hypothesis is that the conscious subject is a *virtual* subject. This virtual person is like a virtual machine. In supposing that there is a stream-of-consciousness virtual machine in the memosphere, even though there is no shared machine language between brains, methods of transmission throughout the culture must be 'social, highly context-sensitive, and to some degree self-organizing and self-correcting'. Furthermore, the fact that human beings can share this 'software' must mean that the shared systems have a 'high degree of lability and format tolerance'. The methods of transfer, however, are limited to socialization. In answer to what problems this virtual machine is supposed to solve, Dennett invokes the psychologist Julian Jaynes, who argued in 1976 that:

> ... its capacities for self-exhortation and self-reminding are a prerequisite for the sorts of elaborated and long-term bouts of self-control without which agriculture, building projects, and other civilized and civilizing activities could not be organized. (*ibid*, pp. 221–2)

It is my hypothesis that community and religion, in terms of Dennett's thesis, could then be conceived of as handy instruments to shape and control virtual persons and selves, and thereby to reinforce and re-construct culture and civilization from brain to brain and generation to generation (Geertz 1999). The community, in Mead's terms, consists of individuals busily contributing to the process of communal generalization through the dual activity of systematizing and reformulating their multiple selves in terms of the values and attitudes of the generalized other. In Dennett's perspective, as I understand him, this process could then be understood as the communal maintenance of consciousness and identity both for itself and its constituents.

Dennett's theory is not uncontested. One of his more formidable critics, philosopher John Searle, dismisses the theory because it ignores in his words the subjective feel of experience, which he calls 'qualia'. Pain, for instance, besides being a neuro-physiological exchange of impulses is also a specific internal qualitative feeling. Consciousness does not have bodily sensation comparable to pain, but it has the quality of 'ontological subjectivity'. In Searle's opinion, Dennett's theory ignores the subjective feelings that are the data that a theory of consciousness should explain (Searle 1997, pp. 98–9). Searle believes that the brain causes conscious experiences that are inner, qualitative, and subjective states (*ibid*, p. 110). Dennett dismisses Searle's criticism because it sides with the traditionalist assumption that 'intuitions we all have about consciousness' are bedrock and time-tested.[3] Unfortunately the two have been arguing for decades, so it is difficult for non-specialists to figure out what is going on.

Another way of approaching this crucial problem has been formulated by the neuroscientists Gerald M. Edelman and Giulio Tononi. They are well known, among other things, for their experiments with NOMAD (Neurally Organized Mobile Adaptive Device) the thinking robot.[4] Concerning 'qualia', they emphatically state that no theory or description can ever substitute an individual's experience of a 'quale', no matter how correct the theory is in describing underlying mechanisms. They posit that each quale corresponds to different states of the dynamic core:

... which can be differentiated from billions of other states within a neural space comprising a large number of dimensions. The relevant dimensions are given by the number of neuronal groups whose activities, integrated through re-entrant interactions, constitute a dynamic core of high complexity. Qualia are therefore high-dimensional discriminations. (Edelman and Tononi 2000, p. 157)

These discriminations are multimodel and body-centred and are carried out:

... by the proprioceptive, kinesthetic, and autonomic systems that are present in the embryo and infant's brain, particularly in the brain stem. All subsequent qualia can be referable to this initial set of discriminations, which constitute the basis of the most primitive self. (*ibid*)

The key to their theory is what they call the 'dynamic core'. This is the subset of the neuronal groups in our brain which contributes directly to conscious experience. It is dynamic because it is an ever-changing ongoing integration of neurons mostly within the thalamo-cortical system. The general properties of conscious experience are emitted 'by linking these properties to the specific neural processes that can give rise to them' (*ibid*, p. 140). In other words, they confirm William James' insight at the turn of the twentieth century that consciousness is a process and not a thing. It is, in the words of Edelman and Tononi, a dynamic core based on neural interactions 'rather than just on a structure, a property of some neurons, or their location' (*ibid*, p. 146). Conscious experience is integrated, private, coherent, differentiated, and informative. It depends on the distribution of information from many parts of our brain, and it is context-dependent. It is flexible and adaptive, thus being able to respond to and learn from unexpected associations. Even though we can differentiate among billions of different conscious states within a fraction of a second, there are limits to 'how many partially independent sub-processes can be sustained within the core without interfering with its integration and coherence' (*ibid*, p. 150). Because the dynamic core is unified and integrated, it moves from one 'global state' to another and thus has a serial nature, like a series of scenes that follow one after the other. Thus consciousness is a process that is both continuous and continually changing at a rate of about 100 milliseconds. The dynamic core, then, 'can maintain its unity over time even if its composition may be constantly changing' (*ibid*, p. 152).

Getting back to my main point, Edelman and Tononi (2000, p. *xii*) emphasize that consciousness 'in its full range' does not arise solely in the brain, because according to their theory, the 'higher brain functions require interactions both with the world and with other persons'. They summarize their findings as follows:

[W]e argue that neural changes that lead to language are behind the emergence of higher-order consciousness ... Once higher-order consciousness begins to emerge, a self can be constructed from social and affective relationships. This self (entailing the development of a self-conscious agent, a subject) goes far beyond the biologically based individuality of an animal with primary consciousness. The emergence of the self leads to a refinement of phenomenological experience, tying feelings to thoughts, to culture, and to beliefs. It liberates imagination and opens thought to the vast domains of metaphor. It can even lead to a temporary escape, while still remaining conscious, from the temporal shackles of the remembered present. (*ibid*, p. 193)

This insight coincides well with the whole realm of narrative theory in developmental psychology and in anthropological psychology. The basic idea, according to Edelman and Tononi, is that the child develops the 'true subject' by constructing scenes via primary consciousness. These scenes rapidly develop with the help of concepts refurbished through gesture, speech, and language (*ibid*, p. 198). This process continues throughout life and is clearly dependent on social interaction.

This fascinating topic of 'transactional selves', 'narrative selves', etc, deserves more mention,[5] but I must move on to the social side of community. A cardinal point that most psychologists have noted is that humans are extraordinarily transparent to each other. The intersubjectivity regularly referred to in this paper assumes, in Jerome Bruner's words, that we have easy access into each other's minds, an access that cannot be explained simply by empathy (Bruner 1986, p. 57). Human beings, he noted:

... must come equipped with the means not only to calibrate the workings of their minds against one another, but to calibrate the worlds in which they live through the subtle means of reference. In effect, then, this is the means whereby we know Other Minds and their possible worlds. (*ibid*, p. 64)

The Construction of Community

As any sensible teenager will tell you, community norms are somewhat – if not completely – arbitrary and restrictive. This is because they are consensual. Constructivist theories have been around for quite a while. Durkheim, once again, can serve as a starting point. He noted that the categories that societies provide are based on a minimal moral as well as logical consensus (Durkheim 1995, p. 16). These two elements prefigure the famous analytical categories introduced by Clifford Geertz during the 1960s, namely 'ethos' and 'world-view'. The two confirm each other in an effective tautology: the world is made intelligible by the logic of a community's worldview, and this logic is inevitably felt to be right as sensed by the community's ethos.

The Austrian phenomenological sociologist Alfred Schutz argued that social realities organize the principles of our *Lebenswelt*, and that the meaning of the experience of living in a certain way and its interpretation are always retrospective. The two conditions in the construction of meaningful worlds are, according to Schutz (1932, 1971), a stock of knowledge about the world organized into features and horizons, and the interpretive procedures themselves. Peter Berger and Thomas Luckmann helped revive Schutz's phenomenological sociology in their programmatic sociology of knowledge, which concerns itself with all that passes as knowledge in a society and the consequent social construction of reality (Berger and Luckmann 1987[1966]; see also Searle 1995). Their primary focus is on the processes of institutionalization and socialization which ensure the persistence of typifica-tory schemes. They developed the idea of 'sedimentation', which posits that human experiences congeal in recollection as sediment. This sediment becomes social when objectivated in a sign system. They argued that its transformation into a generally available object of knowledge allows it to be incorporated into a larger body of tradition. The argument runs further that this aggregate of collective sedimentations can be acquired monothetically, that is, as cohesive wholes, 'without reconstructing their original process of formation' as 'knowledge' by specified 'knowers' to others in the social network. All three instances – knowledge, knowers, and non-knowers – are defined in terms of what is socially defined as reality. It is especially in the realm of the definition, transmission, and maintenance of social meaning that control and legitimation procedures become paramount (Berger and Luckmann 1987[1966], p. 134).[6]

The socially objectivated meanings become systematized or at least encompassed by a community's symbolic universe. The symbolic universe is conceived, according to Berger and Luckmann, 'as the matrix of *all* socially objectivated and subjectively real meanings; the entire historic society and the entire biography of the individual are seen as events taking place *within* this universe'. Furthermore, a point that is relevant here is that the meaning-bestowing capacity of a symbolic universe, although constructed by social objectivations, 'far exceeds the domain of social life, so that the individual may "locate" himself within it even in his most solitary experiences' (*ibid*, p. 114.)

I will refrain from addressing the ongoing critical discussion inside and outside constructionist theory during the last decades, not least from realist camps, and move on to my examples instead (cf. Miller and Holstein 1993a and b). In an earlier paper (Geertz 1990) I demonstrated how two situations recorded during fieldwork among the Hopi Indians of northeastern Arizona could be described and understood in terms of social psychology. I showed how public confession served as the reaffirmation of community values through shame, and how guilt served a similar function in private situations. Similar examples will now be presented.

Community as Control

Communities control the maintenance of their symbolic universes and the applications of generalized identity by many means. One of the efficient means is the use of ritual and pageantry. In rituals and pageants we not only find expressions of community values and sensitivities but we also find their veritable construction and maintenance.

The Hopi Indians are well known for their colourful ceremonial pageants. In former times they could last up to 16 days at a time, sometimes more, but with the exception of one or two towns, the ceremonial calendar has become greatly reduced. About 10,000 Hopis are situated in 10 pueblo villages on or just below the southwestern mesa fingers of the Colorado Plateau near the edge of the Painted Desert of northeastern Arizona. One village lies outside the Hopi Reservation right next to Tuba City. Hopi society consists of loosely organized matriclans, each with their own religious traditions, sacred paraphernalia, housing and land holdings. The clan mother owns clan material and spiritual property, and her brother uses them on her behalf. The rights and possessions of each clan are legitimated in their oral traditions, and these rights are based on knowledge and cultic power. Hopi religion is a good example of the legitimation and maintenance of each clan's symbolic universe, and it would make sense that much time and effort is given to this legitimation and maintenance, even more so because of the simple fact that other clans are continually vying for power and legitimation in the face of conflicting claims and conflicting traditions. Thus, Hopis spend a lot of time narrating their clan traditions, or at least the relevant edited and re-edited portions of those traditions, to each other. In my study of Hopi prophecies (Geertz 1994[1992]), I demonstrated to what extremes Hopis will go in maintaining their interests, even to the point of constructing new prophecies in the guise of ancient traditions.

One of the most puzzling aspects of Hopi culture and religion is the initiation of young children of both genders aged 8–10 into the masked Katsina cult. Katsinas are conceived to be gods and spirits with close ties to the flora, fauna and other natural, especially meteorological, phenomena. This initiation is prerequisite for further mobility in the Hopi system of prestige and authority. Consequently, the children and their parents are put under enormous social pressure to go through with the ritual. The initiation occurs during the great spring ceremony called Powamuya during the month of February. The themes of the ceremony are the invocation of warmth, germination and growth and the initiation of children, and the main actor is the god of fertility, Muy'ingwa.[7]

The ceremony marks the first half of the Katsina cycle when the Powamuy Fraternity turns over responsibility for the rest of the season to the other fraternity responsible for the Katsina cult, namely the Katsina Fraternity. Initiations into both fraternities occur during this ceremony, but, whereas the initiates of the Powamuy Fraternity are not subjected to violence, the initiates of the Katsina Fraternity are ritually whipped with yucca under great tumult, screaming and intimidation (witnessed also by the Powamuy initiates). The Katsina Fraternity wears the masks during the Katsina dances and requires therefore a special initiation. But why the violence?

First of all, it is clear that communal values and sensitivities are imparted during the ceremony both through the pageantry, song and dance itself, but especially through the instructions given by none other than Muy'ingwa himself, as well as by the elders of the two fraternities. Muy'ingwa arrives from the centre of the symbolic world. He poetically describes in an archaic and repetitive language the cosmic regions and says that the children must learn the ceremonies. Finally, he breaks the mesmeric spell and announces that the children must be whipped in order to 'enlighten their hearts' (Voth 1901, p. 101.) Suddenly several deities with frightening masks descend on the children and whip them one at a time while grunting, howling, rattling, trampling and brandishing their whips. One Hopi man, the famous Don Talayesva, never forgot his initiation. Because of disciplinary problems, he was whipped twice the normal amount of four strikes, so that blood ran down his backside (Simmons 1974[1942], p. 83).

Two days later, the children are exposed to a shocking revelation during a midnight dance held in the secret ceremonial chambers. The dancing Katsinas, the gods that they have known, loved and feared all the years of their tender childhood, take off their masks and reveal that they are humans, that they are the uncles, fathers and older brothers of the initiates. Don Talayesva wrote in his autobiography:

> They were not spirits, but human beings. I recognized nearly every one of them and felt very unhappy, because I had been told all my life that the Katcinas were gods. I was especially shocked and angry when I saw all my uncles, fathers, and clan brothers dancing as Katcinas. I felt the worst when I saw my own father – and whenever he glanced at me I turned my face away. When the dances were over the head man told us with a stern face that we now knew who the Katcinas really were and that if we ever talked about this to uninitiated children we would get a thrashing even worse than the one we had received the night before. 'A long time ago,' said he, 'a child was whipped to death for telling the secret.' I felt sure that I would never tell. (*ibid*, p. 84)

Needless to say, Don became a responsible, model citizen, or at least he tried to anyway.

Scholars have debated on why this seemingly peaceful people apply such violent measures to young children. It is clear that in order to ensure a continual supply of dancers to don the masks, sing the songs and dance the dances, the children have to learn the truth one way or other. It is also clear that the initiation legitimizes communal values and norms and allows the neophyte to accrue further knowledge of Hopi cosmology and theology. But not only knowledge is at stake. The use and control of clan masks cannot be had without initiation. Furthermore, initiation is the doorway to all later social engagement.

Social psychologist Dorothy Eggan (1956) argued that emotional commitment was at stake in Hopi socialization processes. In the continual process of deliberate instruction in kinship and community obligations, clan history and mythology, work and social roles, she argued, the Hopis used fear 'as a means of personal and social control and for the purposes of personal and group protection'. She further claimed that the children were taught 'techniques for the displacement of anxiety, as well as procedures which the adults believed would prolong life'. She continued:

> Constantly one heard during work or play, running through all activity like a connecting thread: 'Listen to the old people – they are wise'; or, 'Our old uncles taught us that way – it is the *right* way'. Around the communal bowl, in the kiva, everywhere this instruction went on; stories, dream adventures, and actual experiences such as journeys away from the reservation were told and retold. And children, in the warmth and security of this intimate extended family and clan group, with no intruding outside experiences to modify the impact until they were forced to go to an alien school, learned what it meant to be a good Hopi from a wide variety of determined teachers who had very definite – and *mutually consistent* – ideas of what a good Hopi is. (Eggan 1956, p. 351)

Eggan argued that in the accounts she had collected about the initiation and subsequent revelation, it was evident that a process of reorganizing the emotions held towards the Katsinas is thereby triggered. She claimed that the disillusion was held more firmly in adult memories than the actual physical ordeal. A shock like that, she added, can operate in both negative and positive ways. It can and does, in this example, lead at first to religious disenchantment, resentment, and anger. But it can also lead to the mobilization of an individual's dormant potentialities. In Mead's terms, it would constitute the mobilization of certain values of the generalized other. In this case, Eggan claimed, it is the reinforcement of the individual's need to belong:

> He had the satisfaction of increased status along with the burden of increasing responsibility, as the adults continued to teach him 'the important things,' and conformity gradually became a value in itself ...
> It was both the means *and* the goal. Conformity surrounded the Hopi –

child or adult – with everything he could hope to have or to be; outside it there was only the feeling tone of rejection. Since there were no bewildering choices presented (as in the case in our socialization process), the 'maturation drive' could only function to produce an ego-ideal in accord with the cultural ideal, however wide the discrepancy between ideal and reality on both levels. (Eggan 1956, p. 364)

Another Hopi man, Emory Sekaquaptewa, recounted how the initiation strengthened him and helped him realize the true nature of the Katsinas:

> When it is revealed to him that the kachina is just an impersonation, an impersonation which possesses a spiritual essence, the child's security is not destroyed. Instead the experience strengthens the individual in another phase of his life in the community. (Sekaquaptewa 1976, p. 38)

Sekaquaptewa claimed that the initiation helped him to learn that his childlike fantasizing concerning the Katsinas could, in fact, be continued in adult life on another level. From now on, the adult must learn to project himself into the spirit world in order to achieve spiritual experience. For him, the Katsina dance is more than aesthetic:

> I feel that what happens to a man when he is performer is that if he understands the essence of the kachina, when he dons the mask he loses his identity and actually becomes what he is representing ... . The spiritual fulfillment of a man depends on how he is able to project himself into the spiritual world as he performs. He really doesn't perform for the third parties who form the audience. Rather the audience becomes his personal self. He tries to express to himself his own conceptions about the spiritual ideals that he sees in the kachina. He is able to do so behind the mask because he has lost his personal identity ... . The idea of performing to yourself is a rather difficult one for me to describe in terms of a theory ... . But the essence of the kachina ceremony for me as a participant has to do with the ability to project oneself into the make-believe world, the world of ideas and images which sustain that particular representation. (Sekaquaptewa 1976, p. 39)

G.H. Mead could not have said it better! A quote from Durkheim is relevant at this point:

> The force of the collectivity is not wholly external; it does not move us entirely from outside. Indeed, because society can exist only in and by means of individual minds, it must enter into us and become organized within us. That force thus becomes an integral part of our being and, by the same stroke, uplifts it and brings it to maturity. (Durkheim 1995[1912], p. 211)

The great shock for Hopi initiates is not so much the whipping as it is the revelation. Even many years later, the revelation maintains its hold in memory.

Anthropologist Harvey Whitehouse introduced a distinction that may throw some light on how this occurs. He distinguishes between two divergent modes of religiosity dubbed 'doctrinal' and 'imagistic'. The latter mode is especially relevant in the context of Hopi initiation. Whitehouse (2000, p. 1) writes:

> The imagistic mode consists of the tendency, within certain small-scale or regionally fragmented ritual traditions and cults, for revelations to be transmitted through sporadic collective action, evoking multivocal iconic imagery, encoded in memory as distinct episodes, and producing highly cohesive and particularistic social ties.

Whitehouse's understanding of the imagistic mode was developed among other things on the basis of Brown and Kulik's (1982) theory of 'flashbulb memory', which was further developed by Wright and Gaskell (1992). The theory proposes that surprising, intense, and emotionally arousing circumstances stimulate long-term memory, so that they not only are remembered quite clearly but they become even more vivid over the years (Whitehouse 1995, p. 195; 2000, pp. 7–9). When confronted by circumstances that violate existing cognitive schemas, the mind evidently searches frantically for relevant schemas, and failing this, a unique schema is encoded. An important point is that the emotional excitation that accompanies the encoding is crucial to the whole process:

> Such memories of distinct episodes may endure a lifetime, both because repetition of the surprising event is unlikely and because, even if a substantially similar event is experienced, the traces left by the first will have been so strongly reinforced by excessive emissions from the brain's emotional centres that the original set of representations will retain much of its salience, detail, and uniqueness. (Whitehouse 2000, p. 9)

This certainly is the case with Hopi Katsina initiation. Even though it would be a misrepresentation to characterize Hopi religion as imagistic, or even that the Katsina initiation is devoid of doctrinal techniques, it is nevertheless the case that the initiation is highly emotional and physically emphatic, and the revelation is undeniably imagistic. It is not so much a matter of what Hopi initiates are told; rather it is what they see and feel emotionally and corporeally that creates a life-long impact on them.

The Communal Construction of Good and Evil

There is one further point that needs to be made before moving on to other examples. The crux of Hopi identity is in their concept of the heart. This complex issue is central to Hopi ideas of good and evil and, ultimately, of ideal society. The evidence indicates that the Hopi ritual person is the ideal person. He or she embodies all of the qualities of what it means to be Hopi. The word *hopi* means 'well behaved, well mannered', and it indicates that the person is humble, hospitable, good humoured, helpful, peaceful, diligent, and so on.[8] Of such a person it is said, *pam loma'unangway'ta*, 'he has a good heart'. A good and pure heart is essential to a proper lifestyle and is of supreme importance in ritual activity.

Dorothy Eggan (1956, pp. 360–61) captures the essence of this idea:

> A good heart is a positive thing, something which is never out of a Hopi's mind. It means a heart at peace with itself and one's fellows. There is no worry, unhappiness, envy, malice, nor any other disturbing emotion in a good heart. In this state, cooperation, whether in the extended household or in the fields and ceremonies, was selfless and easy. Unfortunately, such a conception of a good heart is also impossible of attainment. Yet if a Hopi did not keep a good heart he might fall ill and die, or the ceremonies – and thus the vital crops – might fail, for ... only those with good hearts were effective in prayer. Thus we see that the Hopi concept of a good heart included conformity to all rules of Hopi good conduct, both external and internal. To the extent that it was internalized – and all Hopi biographical material known to the writer suggests strongly that it was effectively internalized – it might reasonably be called a quite universal culturally patterned and culturally consistent Hopi 'super-ego'.[9]

This 'super-ego' is clearly evident by the continuous probing of one's heart, the constant anguish about whether the illness or death of a family member was due to one's bad heart, the constant examination of the hearts of their neighbours, and so on. A commonly heard statement, noted by Eggan, is, 'It is those NN clan people who ruined this ceremony! They have bad hearts and they quarrel too much. That bad wind came up and now we will get no rain' (*ibid*, p. 361).

People say about those who are well behaved that 'they have followed the right path', *puma put pöhutwat angya*. My analysis of various statements and sources has led me to postulate that this path refers to a Hopi causal chain:

> The Hopi conceive of human life as an integral part of a chain reaction. It is a logical sequence of givens: proper attitude and the careful completing of ceremonials bring the clouds, which drop their moisture and nourish their children (the corn and vegetation). The crops are harvested and human life is regenerated, the stages of life continue and the Hopi ideal is reached: to become old and die in one's sleep. (Geertz 1986, p. 48)

The causal chain is dependent on the morals of each individual – especially the chiefs – and on the proper completion of the ceremonies. In order to complete the ceremonies properly, one must be initiated into clan knowledge and tradition. Ritual persons are spoken of as *pam qatsit aw hintsaki*, 'he/she works for life'; in other words, human life is equated with ritual life.

The main psychological activity during all ritual contexts (ceremonial as well as non-ceremonial) is that of nurturing the state of mind which can maintain the holistic image of reality mentioned above. It is a matter of concentration or *tunatya*, 'intention'. The sponsor of a ceremonial or a dance is called *tunatyay'taqa*, 'he who has an intention, that is, a sponsor'. Proper intention is integral to the above-mentioned causal chain. An old Hopi maxim is: 'When one carefully pays heed, and always concentrates on it, then he will be the one to have influence on these clouds, this is what they say'.[10] If a host, or anyone for that matter, breaks a link anywhere in the chain, it affects the rest of the chain. Thus, a host who is unknowledgeable, immoral or evil fails to entice the gods and spirits to participate in the ceremonial, and the rain clouds therefore stay away from the area and do not nourish the crops. Without crops, irreparable damage is done to the whole fabric of life, and the people starve, become ill and die. Thus, this concentration is a communal matter. Everyone must concentrate and do it wholeheartedly. Not only the men, but the women as well. As one woman told me:

> We have in our hearts only to see the crops. And these women probably do not have any bad thoughts within themselves when they prepared food for the performers and took it to the kiva. Through their hard work they will earn a (good) harvest, and they have this in mind as they do it.[11]

It is instructive to recall Mead's social psychological perspective on ritual:

> Thus, for example, the cult, in its primitive form, is merely the social embodiment of the relation between the given social group or community and its physical environment – an organized social means, adopted by the individual members of that group or community, of entering into social relations with that environment, or (in a sense) of carrying on conversations with it; and in this way that environment becomes part of the total generalized other for each of the individual members of the given social group or community. (Mead 1962[1934], p. 154, n. 7)

The easiest way for a witch or evil-hearted person to make life difficult for his or her fellows is to destroy that collective concentration by sowing discontent, doubt and criticism, as well as actively fighting it with evil ritual concentration. One does not, however, have to be evil in order to ruin things. One can have egoistic intentions when sponsoring a dance or one can simply sponsor a dance carelessly. Hence the downside of Hopi ethics is the role of witchcraft and gossip. I will attend to witchcraft in a moment. On gossip, Dorothy Eggan correctly noted:

> In this situation, where belonging was so important, and a good heart so vital to the feeling of belonging, gossip is the potential and actual 'social cancer' of the Hopi tribe. It is devastating to individual security and is often senselessly false and cruel, but in a country where cooperation was the only hope of survival, it was the *servant* as well as the policeman of the tribe. Not lightly would any Hopi voluntarily acquire the title Kahopi – '*not* Hopi', and therefore not good. Throughout the Hopi life span the word kahopi . . . was heard, until it penetrated to the very core of one's mind. It was said softly and gently at first to tiny offenders, through 'Kahopi tiyo' or 'Kahopi mana' to older children, still quietly but with stern intent, until the word sometimes assumed a crescendo of feeling as a whole clan or even a whole community might condemn an individual as *Kahopi*. (Eggan 1956, pp. 362–3)[12]

Gossip can be seen as a social cancer, but it is important to realize its potential as one of the major expressions of social identity in traditional Hopi contexts. I have argued elsewhere that gossip defines the identity of self and redefines the roles and identities of others. It is an on-going dialogue about oneself and others and, therefore for better or for worse, it is a kind of narrated ethics. It serves as a social conscience judging everyday behavior in relation to cultural and ethical ideals (Geertz 1994[1992], pp. 211–12, 213). I was told by one of my consultants after a long oratory on the importance of pure thoughts and concentration on the causal chain and how people unfortunately perform ceremonials today for selfish gain or to impress others, that 'really, those who wish to do evil with or to the katsinas can actually do it.' He also referred to the fact that some katsina dancers are not beneath practising love magic on unresponsive girls.[13]

There are only a few studies on Hopi witchcraft and sorcery; the best are Titiev (1943), Malotki (1993) and Malotki and Gary (2001).[14] This material gives an intimidating impression of powerlessness and abject fear of occult attack by witches or sorcerers. Those who deliberately commit evil can come from one's own matrilineage or one's closest family members, with the result that suspicion, gossip and spite often pollute family and interpersonal relations. During my stays among the Hopi, a significant amount of time was spent listening to gossip about whether this or that person was a witch or sorcerer. My analysis of the evidence revealed a causal chain of the evil life which mirrors the above-mentioned causal chain of the good life. Whereas the latter is meant to ensure *suyanisqatsi*, 'a harmonious and tranquil life', the former ensures *koyaanisqatsi*, 'a corrupt life, a life out of balance'. These two lives reveal an opposition between the good religious life and the evil magic one. Magic and sorcery are purportedly practised by people who need to increase their own life expectancy – which is shortened because of their pact with evil – through the occult murder of close relatives. They are initiated into the sorcerers' society just like the good people are initiated into the religious fraternities, and like them they are organized along the same hierarchical lines and perform the same kinds of rituals. Their activities are motivated by evil intentions, in other words, in opposition to the host of a religious ceremonial, the sorcerer is a *nukustunatyay'taqa*, 'he who has an evil intention'.

Once again, Dorothy Eggan demonstrated how the insidious idea of evil is inculcated in Hopi individuals:

> It is true that we, too, are told we should keep good hearts and love our neighbors as ourselves. But we are not told that, if we do not, our babies will die, *now, this year!* Some children are told that if they do not obey the various 'commandments' they learn in different churches they will eventually burn in a lake of hell fire, but they usually know that many of their world doubt this. In contrast, Hopi children constantly *saw* babies die because a parent's heart was not right; they *saw* evil winds come up and crops fail for the same reason; they *saw* adults sicken and die because of bad thoughts or witchcraft (to which bad thoughts rendered a person more vulnerable). Thus they learned to *fear* the results of a bad heart whether it belonged to themselves or to others. There were witches, bogey Kachinas, and in objective reality famine and thirst to fear. Along with these fears were taught mechanisms for the displacement of anxiety, including the services of medicine men, confession and exorcism to get rid of bad thoughts, and cooperative nonaggression with one's fellows, even those who were known to be witches. But the best technique was that which included all the values in the positive process of keeping a good heart, and of 'uniting our hearts' in family, clan, and fraternal society – in short, the best protection was to be *Hopi* rather than *Kahopi*. (Eggan 1956, p. 363)

There are a whole range of topics in this quote that deserve closer attention, but for lack of space, I will restrict myself to one interesting example of this socially imposed, internalized hermeneutic (Geertz 1994[1992], pp. 63ff; Geertz 1992, pp. 18ff) that was related to me by one of my consultants. He was participating in a Katsina dance when suddenly his mask began choking him. Keeping his problem hidden from the other participants, he succumbed to the mask and admitted his guilt to it. He then pleaded with the mask to forgive him:

> As we were about to go, I put my mask on. But it suddenly cut my breath short! It felt like someone had tied my throat .... I tried to pull it off, but I could not at first. Then it finally came loose and I got my mask off real fast. I waited until I was ready to step on the cornmeal path. Then I prayed to my mask, 'Please don't do this to me! Please don't!' I prayed for his forgiveness. For him not to bother me so that I could enjoy myself. I wanted to perform the dance well. This is what I thought to myself, what I thought to my mask, as I put it back on. (Geertz 1990, pp. 321–2)

After that he could breathe easily, see clearly, dance all day without getting tired and sing loudly without losing his voice. As he said, 'my friend had punished me for neglecting him', that is he had not followed the proper ritual procedure and had thus failed the causal chain of the good life.

The situation illustrates, as you may have guessed by now, the voice of the 'generalized other' assuming the organized social attitudes of the group, and in this manner the community exercises control over the conduct of its members. As Mead said:

> And only through the taking by individuals of the attitude or attitudes of the generalized other toward themselves is the existence of a universe of discourse, as that system of common or social meanings which thinking presupposes as its context, rendered possible. (Mead 1962[1934], p. 156)

Thus, when my consultant punishes himself and has an intense internal dialogue with his leather mask, this strikes me as an example of the field of mind being co-extensive with and including all the components of 'the field of the social process of experience and behaviour'. As Mead wrote: 'If mind is socially constituted, then the field or locus of any given individual mind must extend as far as the social activity or apparatus of social relations which constitutes it' (Mead 1962[1934], p. 223, n. 25.) My consultant, on the other hand, believed that he was carrying on a true inner dialogue with both the spirit of the mask and the ancestors:

> And my grandfathers used to tell me, even though the mask is made of leather, it will become a spirit, so you can pray to it. It is spirit even though it does not look like much. It is nothing but leather, but the spirit takes over. They [the katsinas] are the ones that help you along your life path. If you really believe in it, it will help you throughout your life. (Geertz 1990, p. 322)

But it can also be interpreted as a result of the role that human communication plays in constructing the self and internalizing the values, attitudes and sentiments of the community.

Conclusion

Much more could be said, but I think my points have been made. I have tried in this chapter to show the continuity between early sociologists and social psychologists and recent cognitive theory, and to demonstrate their viability in interpreting evidence concerning Hopi Indian religion. Briefly, communities are active causal factors in the construction of virtual selves. These selves are cognitively embodied but develop through the dialectics of external and internal techniques for imparting communal values, sentiments, and world-views. The external techniques are socialization, instruction, affect, ritual, and other mechanisms of universe maintenance. The internal techniques consist of internalization, the continual narrative with the social other, self-exhortation by the communal super-ego and the communal maintenance of consciousness. The community consists of individuals busily contributing to the process of communal generalization through the dual activity of systematizing and reformulating – literally narrating – their multiple selves in terms of the values and attitudes of the generalized other.

Postscript

On first presenting this chapter in oral form,[15] a question was raised from the floor concerning the nature/nurture problem as well as the problem of 'free will': that is, that people are born with talents and proclivities which social psychology cannot account for, nor can it account for the individual's 'free will'. I could only agree that cognitive research is based on materialist, behaviourist, and mechanical theories and that social psychology is based on behaviour.

It is interesting that the question of 'free will' plays little or no part in cognitive research. One can read the hesitancy in Francis Crick's account, *The Astonishing Hypothesis* (Crick 1995), where several of the main cognitive scientists were still on virgin ground concerning free will. Crick's hypothesis on this question assumes that there is a part of the brain that is concerned with planning future actions. The individual is not conscious of the complicated computations that occur in this region of the brain, only of the decisions it makes. These computations as well as the decision to act on a certain plan are subject to the structure of the brain and to inputs from its various parts, but the brain will in such instances appear to itself to have free will. Sometimes the brain makes choices that cannot be explained. In such circumstances, the brain:

> ... can attempt to explain to itself why it made a certain choice (by using introspection). Sometimes it may reach the correct conclusion. At other times it will either not know or, more likely, will confabulate, because it has no conscious knowledge of the 'reason' for the choice. This implies that there must be a mechanism for confabulation, meaning that given a certain amount of evidence, which may or may not be misleading, part of the brain will jump to the simplest conclusion. (Crick 1995, p. 266)

Further neurological studies seem to confirm that this 'free will' is located in a region called the *anterior cingulate sulcus*, next to Brodmann's area 24, a region that receives a large amount of inputs from the higher sensory regions and is located at or near the higher levels of the motor system (*ibid*, pp. 267–8). Such a notion of 'free will' is so alien to what we in the human sciences associate with the term that I am at a loss about what to do with it. On the one hand, this view of it fits in well with the descriptions and claims made in this paper. On the other hand, it raises fundamental challenges concerning the nature of human beings to philosophers and theologians as well as to scholars in religious studies, anthropology, sociology and psychology. It seems that the more we learn about humans, the more alien they/we become.

(First published as Occasional Paper No. 23, 2001)

Notes

1 Many anthropologists concur: for example, Lienhardt (1991[1985]).

2 See Robertson's (1970) discussion of these typologies.

3 Dennett's response is reprinted in Searle (1997, p. 115).

4 See the website of the Neurosciences Institute in La Jolla, California: http://www.nsi.edu/public/index2.asp.

5 See for example Bruner (1986), Sarbin (ed., 1986) and Goldschmidt (1990).

6 See my application of these insights in Geertz (1994[1992]).

7 cf. Geertz (1987, p. 3), Geertz and Lomatuway'ma (1987, pp. 59ff), Voth (1901) and Bradfield (1973).

8 On Hopi ethics see Brandt (1954), Voegelin and Voegelin (1960), Geertz and Lomatuway'ma (1987, p. 47) and Geertz (1986).

9 By 'super-ego' Eggan is referring to the Freudian idea of the internalization of the punishing, restrictive aspects of parental images, real or projected: cf. Eggan (1956, p. 361, n. 43).

10 *Pu' pay pas antsaniiqa, pas put sutsep aw tunatyawtaqa, pam hapi pu' paasat imuy oo'omawtuy amumi tuyqawiy'taniqat pay yan pi lavayta* (Geertz and Lomatuway'ma 1987, p. 320).

11 *Pay itam putsa' natwanit aw yoyrikyaniqey, tunatyawyungwa. Pu' ima momoyam son hiita nukushiita angqe' tunatyawkyaakyang, itamungem piw pangso kivami naakwayit tumaltotangwu. Maqsoni'am piw hiita natwanit aasataniqat oovi, piw sonqe tuwat yan wuuwankyaakyangw pantotingwu* (Geertz and Lomatuway'ma 1987, p. 292).

12 See also my chapter on gossip and information management in Geertz (1994[1992], pp. 210–214).

13 Geertz and Lomatuway'ma (1987, p. 236): *Pay pas antsa piw pumuy katsinmuy akw nunukpanninik pay piw sonqe patsaki.*

14 I have also collected interview material, some of which is published in Greetz and Lomatuway'ma (1987) and Greetz (1994[1992]).

15 At the joint BASR/EASR conference at the University of Cambridge, September 2001.

Bibliography

Berger, Peter L. and Luckmann, Thomas 1987[1966]. *The Social Construction of Reality: A Treatise in the Sociology of Knowledge*, Garden City: Doubleday.

Bradfield, Richard M. 1973. *A Natural History of Associations: A Study in the Meaning of Community*, London: Gerald Duckworth and Company.

Brandt, R.B. 1954. *Hopi Ethics: A Theoretical Analysis*, Chicago: University of Chicago Press.

Brown, Donald E. 1991. *Human Universals*, New York: McGraw-Hill, Inc.

Brown, R. and Kulik, J. 1982. 'Flashbulb Memory', in U. Neisser (ed.), *Memory Observed: Remembering in Natural Contexts*, San Francisco: W.H. Freeman.

Bruner, Jerome 1986. *Actual Minds, Possible Worlds*, Cambridge: Harvard University Press.

Crick, Francis 1995. *The Astonishing Hypothesis: the Scientific Search for the Soul*, New York: Touchstone.

Dennett, Daniel C. 1991. *Consciousness Explained*, Boston: Little, Brown and Co.

Durkheim, Emile 1995[1912]. *Les Formes élémentaires de la vie religieuse: Le système totémique en Australie*, [Paris: F. Alcan 1912], Eng. trans. by Karen E. Fields, New York: The Free Press.

Edelman, Gerald M. and Tononi, Giulio 2000. *Consciousness: How Matter Becomes Imagination*, Harmondsworth: Penguin.

Eggan, Dorothy 1956. 'Instruction and Affect in Hopi Cultural Continuity', *Southwestern Journal of Anthropology* **12** (4), pp. 347–370.

Geertz, Armin W. 1986. 'A Typology of Hopi Indian Ritual', *Temenos* **22**, pp. 41–56.

——— 1987. *Hopi Indian Altar Iconography*, Leiden: E.J. Brill.

——— 1990. 'Hopi Hermeneutics: Ritual Person among the Hopi Indians of Arizona', in Hans G. Kippenberg, Yme B. Kuiper and Andy F. Sanders (eds), *Concepts of Person in Religion and Thought*, Berlin: Mouton de Gruyter, pp. 309–335.

——— 1992. *The Invention of Prophecy: Continuity and Meaning in Hopi Indian Religion.*

——— 1994[1992]. *The Invention of Prophecy: Continuity and Meaning in Hopi Indian Religion* (edited and abridged version of the 1992 edition, published in Aarhus by Brunbakke Publications), Los Angeles: University of California Press.

——— 1999. 'Definition as Analytical Strategy in the Study of Religion', *Historical Reflections/ Reflexions Historiques* **25** (3), pp. 445–475.

Geertz, Armin W. and Lomatuway'ma, Michael 1987. *Children of Cottonwood: Piety and Ceremonialism in Hopi Indian Puppetry*, Lincoln and London: University of Nebraska Press.

Goldschmidt, Walter 1990. *The Human Career: the Self in the Symbolic World*, Oxford: Basil Blackwell.

Hillery, G.A. 1955. 'Definitions of Community: Areas of Agreement', *Rural Sociology* **20**.

Lienhardt, Godfrey 1991[1985]. 'Self: Public, Private. Some African Representations', in M. Carrithers, S. Collins and S. Lukes (eds), *The Category of the Person: Anthropology, Philosophy, History*, Cambridge: Cambridge University Press, pp. 141–155.

Malotki, Ekkehart (ed. and trans.) 1993. *Hopi Ruin legends, Kiqötutuwutsi, narrated by Michael Lomatuway'ama, Lorena Lomatuway'ama and Sidney Namingha, Jnr.*, Lincoln and London: University of Nebraska Press.

Malotki, Ekkehart and Gary, Ken 2001. *Hopi Stories of Witchcraft, Shamanism and Magic*, Lincoln and London: University of Nebraska Press.

Mead, George Herbert 1962[1934]. *Mind, Self and Society: From the Standpoint of a Social Behaviorist*, (ed. and intro. by C.W. Morris) Chicago: University of Chicago Press.

Miller, Gale and Holstein, James A. 1993a. *Constructionist Controversies: Issues in Social Problems Theory*, New York: Aldine de Gruyter.

——— 1993b. *Reconsidering Social Constructionism: Debates in Social Problems Theory*, New York: Aldine de Gruyter.

Parsons, Talcott 1951. *The Social System*, Glencoe: The Free Press.

Robertson, Roland 1970. *The Sociological Interpretation of Religion*, New York: Schocken Books.

Sarbin, Theodore R. (ed.) 1986. *Narrative Psychology: the Storied Nature of Human Conduct*, New York: Praeger Publishers.

Schutz, Alfred 1932. *Der Sinnhafte Aufbau der sozialen Welt*, Wien: J. Springer.

——— 1971. *Collected Papers I-III*, The Hague: Martinus Nijhoff.

Searle, John R. 1995. *The Construction of Social Reality*, New York: Simon and Schuster.

——— 1997. *The Mystery of Consciousness*, New York: The New York Review of Books.

Sekaquaptewa, Emory 1976. 'Hopi Indian Ceremonies', in Walter H. Capps (ed.), assisted by E.F. Tonsing, *Seeing with a Native Eye: Essays on Native American Religion*, New York: Harper and Row.

Simmons, Leo W. (ed.) 1974[1942]. *Sun Chief: the Autobiography of a Hopi Indian*, New Haven: Yale University Press.

Sjoberg, Gideon 1959. 'Community', in J. Gould and W.L. Kolb (eds), *A Dictionary of the Social Sciences*, London: Tavistock Publications, pp. 114–115.

Titiev, Mischa 1943. 'Notes on Hopi Witchcraft', *Papers of the Michigan Academy of Science, Arts and Letters* **28**, pp. 549–557.

Voegelin, C.F. and Voegelin, F.M. 1960. 'Selection in Hopi Ethics, Linguistics and Translation', *Anthropological Linguistics* **2**, pp. 48–78.

Voth, Henry R. 1901. 'The Oraibi Powamu Ceremony', Field Columbian Museum Publication 83, Anthropological Series **3** (2), pp. 60–158.

Wach, Joachim 1962[1944]. *Sociology of Religion*, Chicago: Chicago University Press.

Weckman, George 1987. 'Community', in Mircea Eliade (ed.), *The Encyclopedia of Religion*, New York: Macmillan, Vol. 3, pp. 566–571.

Whitehouse, Harvey 1995. *Inside the Cult: Religious Innovation and Transmission in Papua New Guinea*, Oxford: Oxford University Press.

——— 2000. *Arguments and Icons: Divergent Modes of Religiosity*, Oxford: Oxford University Press.

Wright, D. and and Gaskell, G.D. 1992. 'The Construction and Function of Vivid Memories', in M.A. Conway, D.C. Rubin, H. Spinnler and W.A. Wagenaar (eds), *Theoretical Perspectives on Autobiographical Memory*, Netherlands: Kluwer Academic Publishers.

Yinger, J. Milton 1965[1957]. *Religion, Society and the Individual*, New York: Macmillan.

——— 1970. *The Scientific Study of Religion*, New York: Macmillan.

CHAPTER 13

African Spirituality, Religion and Innovation

Elizabeth Amoah

Introduction

As someone who comes from the African continent, which displays complex and diverse realities that are going through constant and rapid changes, I find the theme of religion and innovation appropriate and challenging. It is appropriate because, first, the rapid changes in the social institutions in Africa affect in one way or the other the religious traditions on the continent. This demonstrates that religion and other aspects of culture sometimes do critique and change each other and that the process of innovation in religion is, in a way, a response to changing historical systems. By saying this, I am not ignoring the fact that religious innovators go through genuine religious and spiritual experiences. However, the fact that the existing cultural and social contexts give clarity and meaning to such experiences cannot be totally ignored.

Second, the reality of religious plurality can be seen everywhere in Africa and consequently complex religious realities have emerged from the encounter between the various religious traditions. For example, the encounter between the indigenous African religions and Christianity in particular continues to result in the emergence of new religious movements that are not just 'Christian', not just 'traditional', but more nuanced and intricate religious realities. That is to say that African people have changed Christianity as presented to them by Europeans. They have set their own priorities and have interpreted the Gospel in a way that is relevant to their own realities. Similarly, the indigenous religions have gone through changes and modifications.

This is not to say, however, that the process of exchange between different religious traditions is unique to the African continent. Africans did (and are doing) what everyone has done. Indeed, Christianity in its historical development has gone through similar processes in whichever cultural situation it has been introduced. In this regard, John Pobee (1979, p. 56) writes:

> Both Christianity and African religion, as they are today, are alloys of things. Christianity, as it came to West Africa, is a composite of the teaching of Jesus, Semitic culture, Greco-Roman culture, and European culture.

The point I am trying to make is that any religion that is 'dissolved in the solvent' of the existing culture, in this case the culture of pluralism, will surely go through the process of innovation. Depending on the prevailing situation, some aspects of that religion will inevitably be rejected, adapted or modified.

Since plurality and change are global phenomena, it is apt to argue that innovation in religion is a universal situation. Therefore, the theme is not only appropriate to my context alone but to other contexts as well. Who would have thought, for example, that an opening worship of the recent Lambeth Conference of the Anglican Communion would incorporate Afro-Brazilian dance, African music and drums, Swahili and Arabic languages as prominent media of expression in an ancient Anglican cathedral in Britain? Or that Anglican Bishops would be asked to visit disco bars and clubs in the attempt to reach out to the youth? This is surely evidence of the global nature of innovation in religion. Our changing world is becoming increasingly complex and pluralistic and this makes innovation in religion inevitable.

Again, the complicated and fluid nature of the realities in our world today makes the theme challenging. It poses fundamental issues. For example, there is the tendency to generalize and oversimplify any discussion on the varying religious realities in Africa. Also, given the vast array of data, the choice as to which theory or model is appropriate for analysing the process of religious innovation in Africa becomes problematic. So it is expedient to briefly declare my interests as well as the theoretical frame for the discussion. For the past years, I have been researching into and teaching phenomenology of religion, African traditional religion and the history of the Church in Africa, particularly West Africa. My researches have taken me to visit shrines and churches, including my own Methodist church in Ghana. I have participated in various activities organized by a number of the African Instituted churches – activities that range from healing services, 'all night' prayer and deliverance services, to rolling on the beach.[1] In the traditional shrines, I have also observed the performance of different rituals such as *munnsuyi*, a ritual performed in Akan traditional religion to drive away evil spirits or to avert an impending misfortune for individuals and the community at large. Again, my research on women and religion in Ghana has taken me to some Ghanaian Muslims who are popularly, but inappropriately, called *mallams*.[2] In their role as Muslim 'medicine men', they sometimes write versions from the Qur'an on slates, wash these passages away with water, and bottle the concoctions as love potions for their clients.

The context of my research is basically Ghana, but my findings would seem to be true of many African societies. From my research, I have come to realize that, first, the process of Christian and Islamic mission in Africa has been a phenomenon of exchange whose focus has been between non-African and African thought-forms. More importantly, however, within the minds of African persons, traditional African realities have continued to exist in exchange with Christian and Islamic expressions. Second, some African Christians and Muslims continue to practise, even if in modified forms, some of the resilient cultural practices that are intertwined with indigenous religions. I have in mind *rites de passage* at such times as birth, death and puberty, as well as marriage. Again, it has also been observed that some of the essential Christian and Islamic symbols such as the Bible and the Qur'an are found in the traditional shrines and they have become part and parcel of the existing traditional religious symbols.

A crucial implication from these observations is that African persons did not simply embrace these two foreign religions passively. Religions in Africa are not in watertight compartments. Rather, they influence each other to some degree. More so, these religions and cultures have a strong grip on African persons, despite the strong influence of modernity. I agree therefore with Professor Assimeng when he says:

> Given the rapidity of change in Africa, it has often become difficult to examine where tradition ends, and where modernity begins for Africans. This is because while their aspirations are essentially modern, the cultural orientation from which Africans behave appears to be traditional. (Assimeng 1989, p. 1)

In other words, traditional African culture, though not static, is crucial in shaping life's pursuits and priorities. It is precisely in support of the fact of continuity, particularly in religion, that Eugene Nida argues that when persons adopt a new religion 'they give new meaning to old traits or they attach old meanings to new events' (Nida 1963, p. 241). That is to say, there will always be what is described as a 'carry-over' from the former to the new religion. In my opinion, this observation is a true picture of the African situation where many African persons move from one religion to another. A related question to this observation – a question that has occupied the minds of scholars of religion for some years – is: what is religion to the African? In other words, what do Africans want in religion? I submit that in any discussion on innovation in religion, the correlation between the desires and aspiration or the wanting and the practice of religion is a very crucial issue that needs to be critically examined.

Having said this, I shall now discuss the thrust of this chapter. From the short résumé of my research interest, it is obvious that my approach is phenomenological. Thus, I am quite aware that my claims as an outsider may be different from that of the religious innovators. The main thesis of this chapter is that in the course of changes that have beset African societies, the resilient aspects of the traditional African religious heritage have often shown themselves to be very much alive in the Christian renewal movements on the continent. The rest of the chapter thus is set out in two main sections plus a brief conclusion. The first section deals with terminology and clarifies the use of pertinent terms such as 'indigenous spirituality', 'religion' and 'innovation'. The second section deals with charismatic renewal movements in Ghana, in which I discuss some of the elements of indigenous African religions that have been 'carried over' to these movements. The conclusion revisits pertinent questions and issues posed by the process of innovation in religion.

The Use of Terminology

The complex nature of religion has resulted in corresponding varied theories and models. These include historical, philosophical, theological and anthropological perspectives. For me, the varied nature of these theories is an indication that all the component features emphasized by the proponents of such theories are very crucial to what religion is. It is, therefore, difficult to arrive at an all-embracing model or theory for a comprehensive analysis. And yet, there is the need for a theory of religion that will facilitate a sound discussion on the theme of religious innovation. In her seminal work, *Innovation and Tradition in Religion: Towards an Institutional Theory*, Claire Disbrey (1994) identifies 'the features of standard forms of religion'. She argues that many religious people see their faith as a product of human ideas and the intervention in human history of something that is beyond it. However, she also views this process as being inseparably linked with reason and experience (Disbrey 1994, p. 86). Even though such an institutional theory of religion seems to overshadow the importance of the religious and spiritual experiences of religious innovators, it is nonetheless crucial to any discussion on innovation in religion.

Disbrey further argues that there is a correlation between the process of innovation in religion and changing historical situations. She asserts in this regard that:

> systems of beliefs and action including criteria of authority, 'bedrock propositions', and 'world pictures' are discarded and new ones created, that can be seen as intelligibly related to both what preceded them and to the historical changes that precipitated them. (Disbrey 1994, p. 87)

For Disbrey, innovation in religion entails discarding unsuitable old systems and creating new and suitable ones in a changing situation. I share Disbrey's view, a view maintained also by many scholars, that innovation is a process of renewing and altering existing systems into something new to suit new conditions. The emphasis here is renewing or altering but it does not necessarily imply throwing away or completely discarding the old. With regard to this, Nida (1963, p. 231) argues that:

Cultural processes include inertia (the stabilization and preservation of existing patterns) and momentum (growth and change), which expresses itself in additions, losses and displacements. The changes which take place are often so slow as to be almost imperceptible.

By saying this, Nida does not overlook the fact that the introduction of Christianity in other cultures has resulted in some radical changes in those cultures.

As a process, innovation has several variants. First, there is the process of borrowing. In this process, elements in one religious tradition are taken over into another religious tradition. We have already seen how the Bible, the Christian cross and some Muslim elements have found their way into traditional African shrines. The celebration of Christmas and Easter eggs demonstrate, among other things, how Christianity has borrowed from other religious traditions. It has also been observed that 'borrowing does not imply that the "debtor" culture will use the new cultural feature in the same way as the "creditor" culture did' (Nida 1963, p. 234). For example, many African Christians use traditional African drums, music and dance in the church, but they publicly, though not perhaps privately, reject the belief in the powers of the gods and the ancestors to influence their lives. We need to emphasize here that in some ways the African experience is different. In Africa, a new religion was imposed more or less *in toto* and it was those most meaningful elements of their own traditional religion that were retained (not borrowed). Of course, the traditionalists did borrow Christian and Muslim symbols.

The borrowed elements may be combined with the existing religious structures. This brings us to the second variable in innovation in religion, namely, combination, adaptation or coalition. In this process, the transferred elements are creatively combined into a new synthesis. In some instances, elements from the old religion are completely discarded because they are seen as not conducive to the new situation. For example, in Ghana all efforts are being made by human rights activists and feminist groups to abolish some elements of the *Trokosi*, a traditional religious system of the Anlos of the Volta Region. In the *Trokosi* system, both old and young women are taken into shrines as payment of evil done by relations. Similarly, the traditional Akan religious practice of burying people alive, especially favourite wives with dead chiefs, has been abolished.

Before I discuss the question of why some elements and not others are carried over in religious innovation, I shall first examine some of the salient features of indigenous African spirituality. 'Spirituality' connotes attitudes, beliefs and practices that mould people's lives and help them to be in harmony with themselves, with nature and with the supernatural. In this sense, spirituality is about an orientation and a journey, which expresses itself in community and fellowship. 'African spirituality', with its several ramifications, is rather a broad concept. It is not the intention of this chapter to engage in any discussion on the differences between the two words 'spirituality' and 'religion'. Suffice to say that, in African cultural heritage, religion permeates almost all aspects of life. Thus, the words 'spirituality' and 'religion', as used in the African context, overlap.

In the traditional African world view, religion connotes beliefs and experiences of what is conceived to be a community of spirit powers. Appropriate communicative mechanisms have been devised to establish continual and reciprocal relationships between persons and the spirit powers (Platvoet, 1993; Parrinder, 1974). The diverse spirits range from the creator god, gods/goddesses and ancestors to several other spirits that harmoniously exist for the total well-being of humanity.

The belief in the existence of the community of spirits is demonstrated in a typical African traditional prayer in which there is a roll-call of as many spirits as can be remembered. For example, a typical traditional Akan prayer for the success of the conference[3] would be as follows:

> *Nana Nyame, kokrobeti a yensan ho mmo pow, nsa, Asase Yaa, nsa, abosom a mo wo ha nsa, Nanaom nsaamanfo, nsa, yesere mo se momeka yen ho efise mo na monim adeko nti a yehiamu ha. Yyesere mo, moma yen nyasa, odo ne nteasea ama dwumadi a esi yen anim ye akoso.*

This is translated as:

> Grandparent Nyame, the thumb without which we cannot tie a knot, here is drink. The earth deity Yaa, here is drink. All the numerous gods and goddesses, this is your drink. Our grandparents who have gone before us, this is your drink. We beseech you to be with us, for you know why we are here today. We ask you for wisdom, we ask you for love and understanding so that the task before us now is successfully accomplished.

This short, but typical, Akan prayer illustrates the strong belief in a community of spirits that is capable of influencing the lives of people and the belief that in any successful venture, there is the need to solicit the help of as many spirits as possible.

In African societies, there is a demonstrable cultural disposition that emphasizes the spiritual dimension of total human life. This finds expression in a certain specific conception of nature, of humanity and god's relations with the creatures of various types. It also finds expression in the relationships between persons and their physical environment and in the ways in which explanations are sought for the major problems of life: the problem of meaning of life, the problem of suffering and the problem of evil. Specifically, for example, Evans-Pritchard's study of the Nuer (1969) shows that the central theme of *Kwoth* (spirit) is the key understanding of their religion. There are 'spirits of the above' and 'spirits below'. There are also spirits attached to, or linked with, a specific lineage or sections of a society that has the lineage as its basic framework. At every level of the social structure then, there are spirits. Thus Evans-Pritchard concludes that spirits are a refraction of the Nuer social order. Similarly, Busia (1954) says that the universe of the Ashanti of Ghana is full of spirits. There is the 'great god' who is recognized as the creator, and a number of other deities and the ancestors. These ancestral spirits form the subject of the daily prayers for those requests that ensure the survival of their living relations. Thus, as Busia says, the ancestral spirits constitute the link between the living and spiritual resources of the lineage. Fortes (1983) also demonstrates the linkage between the ancestral spirits and the living members of Ashanti patrilineal communities. Specifically, he demonstrates how the moral obligation of the elder child to the father carries on after the father has died. Thus, misfortunes that befall the elder child are often seen as punitive actions by the deceased father in order to remind the child of his or her filial and religious duty of remembrance and loyalty.

In all these instances, the centrality of the spirits in the religious thinking of African persons is clearly apparent. This further reinforces an awareness of the spiritual dimension of life. In this regard, misfortunes or mishaps are similarly interpreted in some cases as arising from the activities of malevolent spirits, a typical example of which is reflected in witchcraft.[4] This established feature of African indigenous religion should be taken together with the fact that the religion has a more practical rather than a meditative or 'philosophical' slant.[5] Thus, religion is perceived as a tool for survival and for enhancing life in its broad sense. 'Being religious' in this way implies active participation in rituals such as praying, sacrificing, consulting diviners and seeking esoteric knowledge and power from the spirits, as well as maintaining good relationships with people. In summary, it implies: 1) enlisting the support of as many spirits as possible: god, the deities and the ancestors, and 2) overcoming evil spirits believed to exist in witchcraft. It also implies the continual maintenance of harmony between humanity, nature and the spirits. I submit that this is the essence of the religious life of many Africans who are traditionally oriented. The goal of this orientation is to achieve total well-being or enhanced life, the signs of which are the following: prosperity, fertility, virility, children, good health, a long and peaceful life, and total protection from any malignant spirit. Again, life is seen as a continuous struggle. It is a journey requiring the support of the spirits and the equipping of oneself with spiritual power appropriate to such a journey. The quest for the holistic life is such an obsession that any religious tradition that promises life will be embraced.

This brings us to another significant feature of traditional African religion: the strong belief that life's contingencies are so many and varied that several different avenues may be needed for their solution. This pragmatic attitude to religion is thus an observed feature of traditional religious life in which there is a marked degree of restlessness and movement from one religious tradition to another or the practice of more than one religious tradition at the same time. Therefore, in the indigenous African religious system, it is not irreligious to borrow from or combine several religious traditions. Religion in such a worldview becomes a sort of insurance policy. The more one has, the richer one is likely to be. The more cults one consults, the better equipped one is for life.

Charismatic Renewal Movements in Ghana

There is the need to emphasize again that in the course of the changes that have beset African societies, many aspects of the religious heritage discussed earlier in this paper are very much alive. Religious innovators in Africa seek to adapt them and use them to address new issues related to the changing society in various ways. The various processes of innovation in religion have given rise to a large number of new religious movements on the continent. These have attracted scholarly research and volumes of articles and books have been written on them. I shall not, therefore, go into details of the new religious movements in Africa.

The charismatic renewal movements that have become very popular since the 1970s are part of renewal processes that the churches in Africa have been going through. As with the study of new religious movements, much work has been done since their inception. Some of the established and major features of the charismatic movements are as follows:

1　They put great emphasis on the baptism of the Holy Spirit and on speaking in tongues.
2　They believe strongly that a crucial element of salvation is deliverance from malignant and satanic powers. Thus they devote much time to prayers, fasting and deliverance sessions. The ultimate goal of these spiritual exercises is to deliver people from witchcraft and diseases.
3　They have a large, youthful membership.
4　They resort to the use of modern media for communicating their message. In this regard, American style of preaching is noticeably a common feature in the charismatic movements.
5　What is popularly known as the 'prosperity gospel' is very typical of many of these movements. The theological basis of the prosperity gospel is that God, through the Holy Spirit and the blood of Jesus, is able to change any human situation. Wealth and spiritual well-being are attainable by obeying God's laws and through rigorous spiritual discipline, as well as giving generously to God's work (Hackett 1995).
6　There is an observed feature of successive movements from one charismatic group to another, as well as the practice of belonging to more than one

charismatic group at the same time, since many of these movements appear to be non-denominational. It is thus common to find in Ghana, for example, an individual who simultaneously belongs to different charismatic groups such as the Women Aglow, the Central Gospel International Church and a charismatic Bible study and prayer group in a Presbyterian church.

Many scholars have also stressed the social, economic and political dimension of the causes of these movements. Some have even shown how external factors have influenced their emergence (Hackett 1995; Omenyo 1994; Gifford 1990). These and other factors are crucial to the emergence and the nature of religious cultures with new languages, symbols and message.

In all these, however, the fact remains that indigenous African spirituality plays a major role in the emergence of the African instituted churches or the renewal movements. It is not surprising, therefore, that the common feature in all the varying types of these movements is the emphasis on the pervasive presence and the power of the spirit and the spirit world, as well as the need to spiritually equip oneself for life's contingencies. Again, these movements stress the belief that misfortunes and natural disasters arise from the activities of spirits. Thus, for example, one of the several criticisms by the charismatic movements of the mainline churches is that the dynamic presence and the power of the spirit are lacking in the old churches (Omenyo 1994).

It is no wonder that a marked feature of the charismatic renewal movements in general is the emphasis on spirit baptism, with speaking in tongues as the accompanying feature. If one closely observes the mode of behaviour that accompanies the experience of speaking in tongues in some of these movements, one may not be totally wrong in saying that there is an observed similarity between this and spirit possession in the traditional shrines. Some of those who go through the baptism of the Holy Spirit dance, jump up and down, as well as contort their bodies in all sorts of shapes and make unintelligible sounds, in much the same way as those possessed by the deities in the traditional shrines. The basic difference, though, is that in the Christian renewal movements, the spirit is understood as being the Holy Spirit, the spirit of God, while in the traditional shrines, the spirits are varied and many.

How then do these charismatic movements in Ghana differ from similar movements elsewhere, and what makes them African? There are surely several answers to this simple but probing question. I shall attempt to answer this question by briefly saying that these renewal movements clearly exhibit some of the prominent features of the indigenous African religious heritage such as:

1 The pervasive presence and power of the spirit and the need to constantly equip oneself spiritually for life's contingencies.

2   The tendency to emphasize the spiritual dimension of experiences that occur in social life. A related feature to this is the tendency to stress misfortunes as arising from the activities of malevolent spirits.

3   The tendency to view religion as a means for survival and for enhancing holistic life.

4   The practice whereby members move freely from one religious group to another, as well as belonging to more than one religious tradition at the same time.

These and several other features make these charismatic movements truly African.

Again, I have said that, in the African cultural heritage, religion is a means for survival in any situation. Therefore, the fact that these new religious movements address daily and practical issues is not a novelty. It is part and parcel of the African religious heritage. Thus, the charismatic movements are, in a sense, addressing needs and functions that were customarily or traditionally performed by the traditional cults. The thinking here is that these movements have retained from the traditional African religious system the tendency to emphasize the spiritual dimensions of experiences that occur in social life, experiences that relate to meaning, suffering and evil in human life. For example, after the earth tremor in Accra in March 1997, some of the members of the charismatic movements, particularly the Reverend Bishop Dr Duncan-Williams, publicly declared that the tremor was caused by exorcised demons. Rosalind Hackett (1995, p. 203) quotes the same Bishop Duncan-Williams as saying:

> You see, Satan knows that if he keeps the saints in the hole-ridden shoes, in rented houses, with unpaid bundles of bills and hardly enough to eat, then he can effectively stop the spreading of the gospel through books, equipment, international crusades and by satellite, radio, television and other means.

Without going into much detail, a brief look at the sort of prayer requests that are represented in these movements in Africa shows that they span a wide range of daily and practical issues. These are issues such as infertility or barrenness, promotion in jobs, self-advancement, success in examinations, success in marriage, obtaining and retaining lucrative business contracts, protection from 'new' ailments such as hypertension, strokes and even AIDS, and protection from malevolent spirits. All these, and many more, are presented for solution through varying media by these movements.

Such requests are clearly related to the stresses and strains arising from the changing economic, political, religious and social structures. In this regard, many of the charismatic movements in Ghana, for example the Full Gospel

Businessmen's Fellowship International, Women Aglow, Christian Faith Action Ministry and the International Central Gospel Church, clearly reflect essential features of indigenous African spirituality (Atiemo 1993).

It must be emphasized again, however, that the members of these movements have a strong aversion to traditional religious beliefs and practices. They do not reject the pervasive power of the deities and the ancestors. However, they now accept that these spirits are satanic and that acknowledging their power, instead of the power of God through Jesus Christ and the Holy Spirit, is at the root of many of the social problems and personal problems in life. This is obviously a case of the modification of traditional African religion. The traditional belief in the deities and ancestors as powers that are capable of enhancing life has given way to a belief in an all-powerful God who is manifested through Jesus Christ and the Holy Spirit. The traditional deities exist, but they have become demonic and satanic. Even though to the outsider, there is clear evidence of carry-over from the indigenous African religious heritage into the charismatic movements, this is something that insiders vehemently deny. They claim that the innovations in their movements are solely biblically based. Without denying the biblical basis for these movements, one may add that there seems to be a great deal of similarity between, for example, some aspects of ancient Jewish religious beliefs and indigenous African beliefs (Dickson 1984; Oduyoye 1995).

So far, I have argued that some of the indigenous religious features that are fundamental and most meaningful to Africans are demonstrably present in the new Christian movements. The crucial question we need to ask at this stage, then, is 'why have these specific features been taken over by the Christian renewal movements in Africa?' A simplistic way of answering this question is by saying that religious innovators in Africa have a sound business sense and know what their customers want. The fact still remains that in the context of social realities that are characterized by crisis upon crisis, people want to be reassured (as it has been the custom) that several avenues are needed in adjusting to such realities in contemporary Africa. The features that have been carried over from the indigenous African religions to the renewal movements are definitely important and meaningful to Africans.

Conclusion

The underlying question that runs through the process of innovation in religion in Africa is as follows: 'If some of the fundamentals of traditional African religion are still relevant in adjusting to contemporary situations and are not absolutely contradictory to the biblical teachings, why not retain them?' The emphasis here is on the relevancy of the resilient religious elements. In saying this, I am not forgetting the fact that it is necessary that the borrowed (or retrieved) elements from the old religious traditions are wisely selected and creatively blended into the new religious tradition to serve the purpose for which they are meant.

Earlier on in this chapter, it was pointed out that it is usually the superficial structures from the existing system that are carried over to the new system. In Ghana, for example, Presbyterians who become traditional chiefs at Abokobi, an old missionary centre, are installed by Presbyterian clergy in an attempt to modify the traditional ritual of installing chiefs to suit the church's teachings. But the fact remains that such chiefs continue to perform the political and religious roles as intermediaries between the ancestors and the community at large (Busia 1951). In performing such duties, these Christians – who are now also traditional chiefs – are obliged by custom to pour libation to the ancestors and the gods of the community, thus acknowledging the power of these spirits. In such a situation, it is very difficult to separate the surface structure from the deep structure in the attempt to modify a traditional ritual into a Christian ritual. Conflicts in religious beliefs may occur.

The point I am trying to make is that the issue of syncretism, which is seen by some as being problematic in other contexts (Oduyoye 1995), is a crucial issue here, since it is an inevitable occurrence in every society where new and old religions meet. To see syncretism as problematic in other cultures is to see those cultures themselves as being problematic. In other words, if syncretism – an integral element in the process of innovation in religion – in any situation is problematic, it should be problematic in all situations.

By way of a final summary, I would like to stress again the following points:

1 The complex and fluid nature of realities today makes us question our methodologies and theories on religion constantly.
2 The cultural heritage (including the religious heritage) and the changing situations in any given context are relevant to the process and the variants of innovation in religion.
3 The reality of religious plurality that is now the case everywhere makes innovation in religion inevitable.

The process of innovation in religion – an inevitable process in our complex and changing world – should challenge us to adopt a new and critical look at ourselves, our own religious histories and traditions, as well as those religious traditions that are easily dismissed by us. This requires an attitude of openness to, and respect for, all faith traditions. All, in varying ways, embody the ultimate goal of religion, namely the enhancement of life, which entails peace, justice and reconciliation.

(First published as Occasional Paper No. 19, 1998).

Notes

1 It has been observed that many of these renewal movements in Ghana at times engage in praying and healing activities throughout the night: hence the popular expression 'all night'. Others, too, engage in healing, praying and other religious activities on the beaches. In a particular activity in which I participated, members of the group who had the strong desire to have the 'spirit' were asked to roll on the beach amidst drumming, singing and dancing till the 'spirit' descended on them.

2 The word *mallam* is the Ghanaian corruption of the Arabic word *mu'allim* which means 'a teacher of the Islamic faith'. In the popular sense, *mallam* is used to describe a Muslim who practises as a traditional healer and a diviner.

3 The conference in question was the 1998 BASR annual conference at the University of Wales, Lampeter, at which this chapter was first presented in oral form.

4 In my view, the spirit reflected in witchcraft is a morally neutral spirit. That is, it is neither good nor bad. It is the purpose for which it is used that determines its moral nature.

5 The word 'philosophical' is used here in the Western sense in which empirical justification and validity are sought to explain reality.

Bibliography

Assimeng, J.M. 1989. 'Historical Legacy, Political Realities and Tensions in Africa', in *Encounter of Religions in African Cultures*. Report and papers of a consultation sponsored by the Lutheran World Federation and the World Council of Churches, University of Malawi.

Atiemo, A.O. 1993. *The Rise of the Charismatic Movements in the Mainline Churches in Ghana*, Accra: Asempa Press.

Busia, K.A. 1951. *The Position of the Chief in the Modern Political System of Ashanti*, Oxford: Oxford University Press for the International African Institute.

——— 1954. 'The Ashanti', in D. Forde (ed.), *African Worlds: Studies in the Cosmological Ideas and Social Values of African Peoples*, Oxford: Oxford University Press for the International African Institute.

Dickson, K. 1984. *Theology in Africa*, London: Darton, Longman and Todd.

Disbrey, C. 1994. *Innovation and Tradition in Religion: Towards an Institutional Theory*, Aldershot: Avebury.

Evans-Pritchard, E.E. 1969. *The Nuer: A Description of the Modes of Livelihood and the Political Institutions of a Nilotic People*, Oxford: Oxford University Press.

Fortes, M. 1983. *Oedipus and Job in West Africa*, Cambridge: Cambridge University Press.

Gifford, P. 1990. *Christianity: To Save or Enslave?* Harare: EDICESA.

Hackett, R.I.J. 1995. 'The Gospel of Prosperity in West Africa', in R. Roberts (ed.), *Religion and the Transformation of Capitalism*, London: Routledge, pp. 199–214.

Nida, E. 1963. *Customs, Culture and Christianity*, London: Tyndale.

Oduyoye, M. 1995. 'Christianity and African Culture', *International Review of Mission* **84** (332/333), pp. 77–90.

Omenyo, C. 1994. 'The Charismatic Movement in Ghana', *Pneuma* **16**, pp. 169–185.

Parrinder, E.G. 1974. *African Traditional Religion*, London: Sheldon Press.

Platvoet, J.G. 1993. 'African Traditional Religions in the Religious History of Humankind', *Journal for the Study of Religion* **6** (2), pp. 29–48.

Pobee, J.S. 1979. *Toward an African Theology*, Nashville: Abingdon Press.

CHAPTER 14

Unificationism: A Study in Religious Syncretism

George D. Chryssides

Introduction

This chapter seeks to explore the subject of religious syncretism, with particular reference to the Unification Church, popularly known as 'the Moonies' and renamed the Family Federation for World Peace and Unification (FFWPU) in 1996. How is it possible for a set of beliefs and practices, so radically different from those of mainstream Christianity, to arise; and how is it possible for those who subscribe to them to insist that they constitute a legitimate version – indeed a superior version – of Christian faith?

The anti-cult lobby (on which, see below) claims that the answer is perfectly straightforward: the Reverend Sun Myung Moon is an authoritarian leader whose teachings must be unquestioningly accepted by his brainwashed followers; he himself is a megalomaniac with aspirations of grandeur which lead him to proclaim himself as the Lord of the Second Advent who has done what Jesus Christ could not accomplish. Followers of the Rev Moon equally insist that the answer is a perfectly straightforward one: the young Sun Myung Moon received a vision of Jesus Christ on Easter Morning, 1935, which was subsequently complemented by various revelations received through prayer and journeyings into the spirit world.

I do not believe that either of these explanations is correct, and in what follows I intend to show how Unificationism has emerged as a syncretic blend of Protestant Christianity and Korean folk shamanism. In my discussion I shall outline some of the methods of evangelism that were used by the Christian missions, arguing that the boundaries between apparently competing religions (in this case Christianity and shamanism) are inevitably far from clear, and that this blurring of boundaries leaves ample scope for ambiguity and synthesis. Methodologically, my approach draws on field work undertaken in the late 1980s as well as on Unificationist publications, some them publicly available, others only available to members. Additionally, I draw on material on the history of Korean religion together with accounts of Christian missionary activity to build up a picture of how a number of small messianic-apocalyptic

Korean groups took their rise drawing on both sets of ideas, Protestant Christian and folk shamanic. In addition to participant-observer work in Unificationist seminars, much has been gained from informal conversations, both with members and ex-members, sympathisers and critics.

In just over a decade since the original paper was written,[1] the Unification Church has undergone more change than simply a change of name to FFWPU. As I hope to show, syncretism does not always entail a harmonious blend of ideas; on the contrary, important tensions have emerged within the FFWPU, particularly in connection with a recent renewed and explicit emphasis on shamanism. Indeed, some of my informants, who were members in the 1980s and 1990s, have now become ex-members; formerly believing that they had espoused a religion that could unite Christianity, as well as the other world's religious traditions, they have now told me that the FFWPU's shamanic practices have proved divisive, and alienated them from the organisation. It is worth pointing out too that, from the mid-1990s, the advent of the computer internet has to some degree simultaneously changed the Unification Church and those who research it. The church, including its shamanic practices, is now clearly visible by anyone who cares to visit an FFWPU web site, and the World Wide Web reciprocally provides an important new resource for the researcher. Texts that were once regarded as esoteric, such as *The Tradition — Book One* (there was never a Book Two), a liturgical manual which sets out the Church's ritual practices and methods of observing its distinctive festivals, is now publicly available in its totality through Internet access.

Brainwashing or Revelation?

I turn now to the competing hypotheses of 'brainwashing' and 'revelation' as explanations for the origins of new religious movements (NRMs), and in particular the Unification Church. The 'brainwashing' theory is espoused by the anti-cult movement (ACM) and the counter-cult movement (CCM).[2] Thus the Vatican Report, *New Religious Movements: A Challenge to the Church* accuses NRMs of 'highly sophisticated recruitment methods' including 'unconditional surrender to a guide or leader', isolation strategies, and 'bombarding the recruit with talks and lectures, slogans and clichés, designed to dull the mind and stop him thinking for himself' (Catholic Truth Society 1986, p. 10). Similarly, FAIR (Family Action Information and Resource), the most prominent British cult-watching organisation, warns of indoctrination techniques and characterises leaders as those who 'demand absolute and unquestioning obedience' (FAIR, 1994).

This view of the 'cult' originating through the teachings of the messianic leader is not without its academic pedigree. Max Weber is renowned for his 'institutionalisation' thesis, in which he claimed that religions progress from origins in a charismatic leader, through 'routinisation', to a more formal organised structure, particularly after the leader's death. I have elsewhere argued that Weber's analysis does not reflect what normally happens within NRMs, claiming that presumed charisma comes as much from the group as from the leader, and that Weber's three stages are not sequential (Chryssides, 2001). Even more damaging to the thesis that NRMs arise from brainwashing by a charismatic leader is the important study by Eileen Barker (1986). As a result of extended empirical study, Barker demonstrated that, out of those who commenced a Unificationist 2-day workshop, only 8 per cent joined the organisation as full-time members for a week or more. Only a minute 0.005 per cent had associated with the Unification Church after two years (Barker 1986, pp. 146–147). If a university had such appalling drop-out figures, it would be in very serious difficulties, to say the least!

From the standpoint of the believer, of course, the leader's message is accepted, not because of indoctrination, but because it is a genuine revelation. In my book *The Advent of Sun Myung Moon* (Chryssides 1991) I discussed the Rev Sun Myung Moon's claim to have obtained a special divine revelation. As a scholar of religion, one must remain neutral on the question of the authenticity of revelatory claims. Theoretically, it is possible that at least one movement studied by scholars possesses a uniquely true revelation, although, if I were a seeker, I think I would take the view that, since there were so many such claimants, the odds against my alighting on the real one were not in my favour! Be that as it may, however, the important point to note in this context is that divine revelations (whether real or imagined) do not occur in a vacuum: their very recognition depends on their contextualisation within a previously known religious context. For example, anyone who is afforded a vision of the Virgin Mary can recognise her as such only if they are already acquainted with the Christian tradition and Mary as an object of devotion. Thus, even if Moon's alleged meetings in the spirit world with Confucius, Jesus and the Buddha were genuine, such claims already presuppose a coming together of a variety of religious traditions, and the task of explaining how they come together remains a genuine one. My task in this essay is therefore to explain how Unificationism, like a number of new religions in Korea, was able to arise as part of a broader phenomenon of religious syncretism. My argument will relate primarily to the evolution of the Unification Church, but much of what I have to say will shed light on syncretism more widely.

It will be helpful at the outset to identify some of the main differences between Unificationism and mainstream Christianity, to which the former's detractors, mainly Christian evangelicals, are keen to draw attention. Most attendees will no doubt be familiar with the counter-cult literature which pairs off 'Moonie' beliefs with those of Christian orthodoxy, sometimes using a double column parallel text (for example Bjornstad, 1976; Davies, 1990;

Brooks and Robertson, 1985). The details vary, but the pairs generally go something like this.

'Moonie'	Mainstream Christian
Moonies preach a new revelation in *Divine Principle*.	The Bible is the word of God which contains all that is necessary for salvation.
God manifests dual prime qualities: male and female, yin and yang.	God is a Trinity of Father, Son and Holy Spirit.
Adam and Eve fell as a consequence of Eve's fornication with Lucifer.	Adam and Eve fell through disobedience: they ate of the Tree of Knowledge.
Men and women must pay 'indemnity' as repayment for sin.	'By grace are ye saved, not by works, lest any man should boast.' (Ephesians 2:8)
Jesus did not fully accomplish his mission.	Jesus Christ paid the price for humankind's sin.
Jesus' mission involved marrying and begetting sinless children.	Jesus came to die on the cross.
Jesus' death accomplished 'spiritual salvation' only, not 'physical salvation'.	Jesus' death and resurrection are the assurance of bodily resurrection.
Jesus opened Paradise to spirits who remained at the 'form spirit' stage.	Jesus Christ offers full salvation.
A second messiah is needed to complete Jesus' mission.	'Neither is there salvation found in any other.' (Acts 4:12).
The Rev Moon is the Lord of the Second Advent, the 'returning resurrection' of Jesus Christ.	Jesus Christ will return on the clouds of heaven at the Second Coming.

How Christianity was Propagated

How is it possible for such apparently enormous divergencies to arise? I wish to examine a number of different factors at work in Korea, which resulted in the formation of various 'New Christian' groups, as I have labelled them.[3]

The first factor was the method by which Christianity was propagated in Korea. Where communications are good and political power centralised, it is relatively easy to pounce on the heretics and to ensure that a (supposedly) 'pure' form of Christianity is maintained. Military conquests ensured that the Christianity of the Romans prevailed and was enforced. Emperors could call Councils and Synods together and cause the official hierarchy of the Christian faith to anathematise the heretics and to define orthodoxy. Offenders could be brought to trial and formally excommunicated. By contrast, in Korea, the Christian message was propagated in a 'lower key' way. It relied on the creeping infiltration of the missionaries, and was carried out in a more piecemeal and haphazard fashion. Not only was there no centralised power or authority to enforce the 'true' version of Christianity on its converts, but the missionaries themselves lacked complete control over what was propagated and how it was understood.

In *The Advent of Sun Myung Moon* I refer in particular to two practices which the missionaries employed. One was the use of pedlars or colporteurs, itinerant distributors of Christian literature, such as tracts or copies of Luke's gospel, who would distribute their wares and promptly depart to continue their mission of literature distribution elsewhere in the country. The colporteurs did not employ the principle now usually associated with mission, namely that mission should be carried out 'in dialogue' (World Council of Churches, 1980); that is, there was no opportunity for their enquirers to ask them questions, or for the literature distributors to check that their propaganda had been understood in an acceptable way.

The second strategy to ensure the greater propagation of the Christian message was the practice of requiring that each convert, before gaining admission to the church, must have preached the gospel to at least one other person. This 'pyramid selling' approach may well have been good for business in terms of maximising numbers, but it had the obvious drawback that the raw recruit, having only recently discovered the Christian faith, was probably unable to distinguish between 'authentic' Christianity (as preached by the western missionaries) and indigenous folk shamanism. Although it is alleged that catechumens were subjected to a formal examination before acceptance by the churches, the questions put to them did not demand any kind of theological sophistication. The missionaries Blair and Hunt, for example, report that the questions put to baptismal candidates were: 'How long have you been a Christian?', 'Who is Jesus?', 'Why do you believe in Him?', 'Have you kept the sabbath faithfully?', 'Do you have daily family prayers?' and 'Have you brought anyone to Christ?' (Blair and Hunt 1977, p. 48).

Furthermore the Christian Churches adopted the practice of ensuring that those who sought ordination were not too remote from the indigenous people. Not only did this mean that they were obliged to enjoy no more than a modest life style, but that they should not become intellectually too far above the level of the average Korean. Again, while this may have achieved success for Christianity (about 17 per cent of South Korea's population are Christian), its price was a very low level of theological sophistication, and lack of control of what was propagated in the name of the Christian religion. It is therefore not surprising that the minority of the population who found Christianity attractive continued to espouse ideas and practices which derived from the folk shamanism which was rife in Korea.

Exclusivism and Inclusivism

It was not only the methods of the missionaries but the religious climate of Korea itself which furthered religious syncretism. The Semitic religions (Judaism, Christianity and Islam) have always insisted on exclusive allegiance: from the time of Moses' revelation at Mount Sinai, God has affirmed that 'I the Lord your God am a jealous God' (Exodus 20:4). By contrast, eastern religions tend to be pursued simultaneously, the practitioner using whichever one of a variety is best suited to his or her immediate purpose. One missionary, the Rev George Hebert Jones stated:

> [The Korean husband] personally takes his own education from Confucius; he sends his wife to Buddha to pray for offspring; and in the ills of life he willingly pays toll to Shamanite Mu-dang and Pansu. The average Korean is thus a follower of all three systems, in the hope that by their united help he may reach a happy destiny. (Jones 1902, p. 39)

Westerners often find difficulty with the notion of embracing a plurality of religions simultaneously; but the notion that one might use a variety of religions for their own distinctive purposes is rather like the notion that we use different shops for different purposes. To many Koreans, the Christian missionaries' insistence that they may follow one and only one religion was like informing citizens that they may only make their domestic purchases at the baker's!

Some brief explanation of the ideas and practices of Korean folk shamanism are appropriate at this juncture. Although it is sometimes said that Sun Myung Moon is effectively a shaman, any such identification must be treated with caution, for Moon himself does not fit the normal mould of Korean shaman.

The Korean shaman (*mudang*) is almost invariably female rather than male, and has a social role consisting in *yonghom* (spiritual power) and *nunchi'i* (social sensitivity) (see Choi 2003). The *mudang*'s role is to accept commissions by the living to perform rituals on behalf of the dead. Spirits may need to be placated, or a deceased person – especially someone who has not died naturally – may not have been able to receive the appropriate rites of passage: in such cases the *mudang* can cause the spirit to be at rest. The shaman's activities also include healing as an important element. It is evident that Moon does not fit this role: he is the wrong gender, he does not accept commissions, he does not undertake healings (although several followers have claimed that ailments disappeared once they committed themselves to him), and he tends to be visited by spirits rather than engage in active travel in the spirit world. Further, as Nansook Hong (1998, p. 70) reveals, Moon has his own personal *mudang*. Nonetheless, Unificationism's keen interest in spirits, their alleged contact with members, and the shamanic rites that form part of the organisation have a much greater affinity with indigenous Korean folk religion than with the Christianity that the missionaries present.

Given that Christianity developed in Korea alongside a relatively unchecked espousal of folk shamanism, it is not surprising that the ideas from both religions inter-mingled under the name of Christianity. As one Korean informant said to me: 'Missionary activity enabled the propagation of shamanism in Christian guise.' For many converts Christianity was something which was legitimated by shamanism in the first place. Before taking a major decision, it is quite customary for a Korean to consult a shaman, and hence, faced with the question of whether or not to accept the Christian faith and way of life, many Koreans would seek a shamanic consultation before proceeding.

Indeed, it is noteworthy that the Rev Moon himself is said to have taken the *Divine Principle* to the world of the dead for authentication. (This story is a rare example of Moon actively journeying amongst spirits, rather than receiving visitations.) Unification members believe that he journeyed into the spirit world with what he took to be the answer to the only remaining question about the *Principle* for which he sought confirmation. The question was about how the Fall took place. After much study and prayer, Sun Myung Moon had finally concluded that it was through sexual misconduct on the part of Lucifer. He took this explanation to God, Jesus and Lucifer amongst other spirits. At first, God rejected it; a second attempt on Moon's part brought a subsequent denial; however, on a third attempt God vindicated Sun Myung Moon, and Lucifer hid his head in shame. (This story also has a Buddhist component: it is held within Buddhism that if one asks a Buddha a question three times, he is obliged to answer.)

The notion of the Fall as a sexual sin was in fact already implicit in Korean thought. A well known Korean legend (the 'Namwon legend') tells of a man committing adultery in heaven and falling down to earth as a serpent. The serpent, the story continues, became a young woman who tried to seduce a scholar. Suddenly becoming aware that her sexual advances constituted misconduct, she ascended back into heaven again (Kyn 1981, p. 89).

Similarities between myths afford a further, and fairly obvious, way in which syncretism gains momentum. Hearing the Christian missionaries preach about the Fall, this could well be taken as confirmation of the famous Namwon legend, particularly in a situation where the Korean mind, unlike that of the missionaries, did not necessarily see the two faiths as competing but as potentially co-existing. The missionary story of the Fall seemed like corroboration of the Namwon story. Where the missionary account lacked certain details – for example, the information that the serpent seduced Eve rather than simply offered advice to her – such details could easily, and understandably, be inferred from other elements of the biblical narrative: for example, did not Adam and Eve cover their genital areas when God found them in the Garden? (Indeed the missionaries themselves may have imported sexual allusions into the story as a result of centuries of Christian tradition, whose artists had depicted the Fall with obvious sexual overtones.) This process of theological addition was scarcely a Korean invention, but something which the Church had practised almost from its inception: for example, it is not actually stated in the Genesis narrative that the serpent, Lucifer and Satan are to be equated, but the writer of Revelation is obliging enough to make this identification (Revelation 12:9). If one Christian scripture can supplement another in detail, why should not Korean religious consciousness shed light on apparently missing details in the missionary message?

The Korean world view, which populated the universe with spirits, was not difficult to reconcile with the new Christian message. Although the resurrection of the dead tends to be couched in terms of heaven and hell, the indigenous population may not have heard sufficient of the Christian message to make any inferences about whether or not the existence of a spirit world formed an important part of Christian cosmology. Remember that many enquirers were likely to have read little more than the colporteurs' tracts, and that there had been a very high illiteracy rate in Korea. (As late as 1945, only 22 per cent of Koreans could read, although it should be noted that South Korea has now one of the highest literacy rates in the world.) The full text of the Bible in Korean did not become available until 1911.

Sun Myung Moon himself, however, did not rely on imaginatively reconstructing the Christian message from a few tracts. It is a popular misconception of Unificationism, and indeed many new religious movements, that they 'know only a few texts' and ignore the rest. It is said that Moon studied the Bible very closely, comparing English, Korean and Japanese translations, thus indicating the meticulousness of his study. Such accounts must be treated with some caution, however: most people who have heard Moon address an audience in English are not at all impressed by his mastery of the language. Nonetheless, *Divine Principle* demonstrates a very intimate knowledge of scriptural detail, explaining quite obscure passages of which most Christians remain ignorant.

A 'full Bible' approach to the Christian message, of course, reveals that there are references to a more shadowy spirit world, even if at times communication with it is discouraged: for example, King Saul's consultation with the witch at Endor (1 Samuel 28). Mention is made of after-death states which are not obviously to be identified with the joys of heaven or the fires of hell: for example, the Hebrew concept of *sheol*, Jesus' rather cryptic remark to the dying thief about being with him 'in Paradise', and the descent into *Hades* (1 Peter 3:19) which the writer of Revelation quite deliberately distinguishes from hell in one significant verse (Revelation 20:14).

Abandoning the Indigenous Religions?

The pronouncement that Christianity brooked no rivals was not necessarily an injunction which weeded out those elements of the Korean world view which proved unacceptable to the Christian missionaries. Missionaries have often evangelised on the assumption that it is obvious what Christianity is and what is incompatible with it, but a little reflection will show that such an assumption is fraught with difficulties. Consider what might happen if missionaries representing some new faith attempted to persuade European Christians to abandon Christianity in favour of this new religion which, they tell us, supersedes it. At first appearance this might seem straightforward enough, but exactly what would the instruction to give up Christianity amount to?

This instruction would probably mean denying that Jesus Christ is the sole means of salvation; it would probably involve ceasing to participate in Christian liturgical acts, and discontinuing practices such as reciting the creed and receiving the sacraments. But would giving up Christianity also mean no longer loving one's neighbour, following the teachings of the Sermon on the Mount, or regarding Jesus as a great ethical teacher and example? And what about those areas which are arguably more cultural than religious, but yet which draw on the Christian basis of much western culture? For example, would abandoning Christianity mean the abolition of Easter holidays, giving Christmas presents, observing Sunday as the traditional day of rest, or abandoning the Protestant work ethic – whatever that would mean?

Of course, what is allowed to continue and what must be jettisoned depends on the attitude of the proselytisers. Being thoroughly familiar with their own incoming religion, they are in a good position to determine what is likely to be acceptable and what is not, although even so they may misunderstand the nature of certain customs which prevail amongst the indigenous population. The indigenous population, however, knowing little about the new missionary religion, will find it difficult (certainly at first) to determine which practices may be continued and which must be abandoned. What then was or was not compatible with Christianity? Was ancestor veneration (construed as 'ancestor worship' by many missionaries) such an example? What about the quest for the political unification of Korea? Or how about consultations with the shamans to make contact with the dead? Or the Confucian ethic of 'right and harmonious relationships'? Surely the missionaries did not want to deny that there should be harmonious relationships between king and subject, father and son, husband and wife, elder brother and younger brother, friend and friend? On the one hand, such ideas are key concepts in Confucianism and Korean shamanism, and thus, from the missionaries' standpoint, belonged to the 'foreign religions'. On the other hand, they have plain affinities with the biblical narrative: relationships between king and people, between younger and elder brothers, and so on.

Content and Method: the 'What' and the 'How' of Thinking

There is another important factor which contributes to syncretism. A missionary enterprise can be capable of changing *what* people think. What is much more difficult, and perhaps impossible, is changing *how* people think. What I mean is this. It is easy enough to bring people to believe something which they do not already know: for instance, a non-Christian who has never heard of the existence of Jesus Christ can fairly readily be brought to a belief that Jesus of Nazareth lived, taught and died in first-century Palestine. What is more difficult to erase is the whole set of preconceptions, associations and inferences which accompany certain types of belief.

Let me give one example which lies outside Unificationism. Western converts to Buddhism will typically assume that Buddhism entails vegetarianism. After all, they reason, one fundamental Buddhist precept forbids the taking of life (human or animal); hence this must avoid the eating of dead animals. Although this line of reasoning is valid enough within western thought categories, this is actually a very un-Buddhist way of reasoning. For the traditional eastern Buddhist, the precept which prohibits killing means exactly what it says, no more and no less. To eat a dead animal is not to kill it, and if a Buddhist monk is offered meat or fish in his alms bowl then he is obliged to accept it. Of course a westerner can try to convince the traditional Buddhist that buying meat is placing a vote in favour of animal slaughter, but again this is a very western and un-Buddhist way of reasoning: it assumes a teleological view of ethics which is foreign to the ethical absolutism which is enshrined in the Precepts. The Precepts are not undertaken to achieve a societal 'this worldly' goal, but to enable the aspirant to make progress on the path to *nirvana*. (If one tries to insist that surely a Buddhist *must* accept that non-violence entails the avoidance of financially supporting animal slaughter, then this only reinforces the point that the westerner finds it difficult to absorb the *method* – the 'how' – of thinking which characterises Buddhism.)

Similar cultural differences can result in a markedly different concept of a religious hero. The missionaries preached Jesus as the ideal man (as well as the Son of God), and it would therefore be natural for some Koreans to equate this 'ideal man' with the neo-Confucian concept of the 'perfect man'. The perfect man, to the Confucian, is the husband of the family, the one who comes from a pure 'blood lineage', the one who achieves success; certainly not the celibate teacher who meets with a judicial death. Someone who experiences an unnatural and untimely death becomes a wandering wraith, confined to the lower realms of the spirit world. Consequently, a Korean might well reason, if salvation is to be attained for humankind, some new dispensation is needed which will ensure the advancement of those spirits whose state falls short of perfection. And since marriage is the hallmark of the ideal person, provision must be made to ensure the marriage of spirits where this is appropriate, including Jesus Christ himself.

There is one final ingredient which facilitates religious syncretism, and it is this. Those supposedly 'new' elements must also (generally) be able to be discovered as 'lost elements' in the original religion. The Book of Genesis states that Adam and Eve covered their genitals after the Fall, thus giving impetus to the notion that the Fall was a sexual misdeed. Jesus as a Jew would have been brought up to value family life, hence it would be surprising if his parents had not intended him to marry and have children: indeed Jesus refers to himself as the bridegroom on several occasions. Not only can the 'new' elements often be found to be present in Christian scripture, but problematical teachings on which missionaries have insisted can, conversely, be found to lack biblical support. Obvious examples are the divinity of Christ and the doctrine of the Trinity.

Conclusion: The Tensions of Syncretism

Syncretism, however, does not necessarily mean harmony, and it is a common feature of religious syncretism that in its attempt at achieving unity it divides more than it unites. Not only has Unificationism attracted hostile criticism from mainstream Christians, but its reliance on a very specific and relatively unfamiliar form of shamanism has undoubtedly limited its global appeal. The recent interest in shamanism in the West has largely drawn on the teaching of Michael Harner, who has championed a 'core shamanism' that purportedly transcends its specific cultural expressions, and of Carlos Castaneda, whose writings aroused interest in Native American indigenous religion through their interaction with the psychedelic counter-cultural revolution of the 1960s. By contrast, Korean shamanism is little known to the western public, who have little, if any, interest in undertaking rites for spirits, ensuring that the dead have the opportunity to receive posthumous marital blessings, or receiving messages from a few deceased Unificationist founder-leaders who channel their supposed experiences in the spirit work through selected mediums. It is therefore unsurprising that the Unification Church has not succeeded in effecting a unification of Christian denominations, as it set out to do, let alone the unification of the world's religions.

My argument, I believe, has shown several things about religious syncretism. It need not occur through divine revelation, nor through eclectic amalgamations of doctrines by controversial religious leaders such as Sun Myung Moon. It is a natural, even logical process, by which indigenous and missionary faiths do not sharply contrast, a process which relies on the incoming religion to define – often retrospectively – what is or is not acceptable, and indeed which continues unchecked if this does not happen. It is a process whereby the new theoretical content is assimilated within the old indigenous method of reasoning, an aspect of culture which is hard for the native even to recognise, let alone alter. Finally, the process of syncretism often relates back to the missionary faith, recognising that what appear to be new elements constitute no more than a return to the original teachings from which the missionary religion has developed through the course of time.

Postscript

As is characteristic of NRMs, affairs in the Unification Church have developed rapidly, and much has changed since this chapter was first published in 1993. Events have tended to confirm my original contention that the very localised form of shamanism that underlies Unificationist belief and practice is a barrier to gaining universal acceptance. After the late 1980s the drive of the Unification Church for increased numbers declined, and membership achieved a steady state. The Church's theological rationale was that the kingdom of heaven was not to be gained through membership, but through the Blessing (marriage) ceremony, and the criteria for eligibility were relaxed, enabling non-members as well as members to join. This development in thinking was marked by the name change in 1996 to the Family Federation for World Peace and Unification. Much work has been done by way of organising seminars to promote traditional family values, and many of the seminars entail participants' affirmation of such values, as defined by the FFWPU. Affirmation of these is effectively an undergoing of the Blessing, but without the necessity of affirming the shamanistic worldview that the old-style 'mass weddings' entailed.

At the same time the core FFWPU membership has been steered in a direction that involves a greater emphasis on shamanistic ideas. Sun Myung's mother-in-law, Hyo Nam Kim, who died in 1989, is now believed to deliver guidance to members from the spirit world, through a medium, Hoon Mo Nim. A sacred shrine has been set up at Chung Pyung in Korea, and members are periodically instructed to go there to attend seminars. Sang Hun Lee, a senior Church leader, died in 1997, and purportedly relayed messages from the spirit world, some of which were collected in his *Life in the Spirit World and on Earth* (Lee 1998), and some of which have been published on the Internet. Lee has apparently met numerous deceased religious and political leaders, including Confucius, the Buddha, Jesus, and Muhammad, all of whom acknowledged Sun Myung Moon as the messiah. Not only have such happenings served to impede the FFWPU's interfaith work and to distance mainstream religious leaders from its activities, but they have proved too much for some of their own members, a number of whom have now left the movement.

Moon himself, of course, is now in old age, being 83 at the time of writing, and when he dies his own presumed entry in the spirit world will inevitably be attended with new revelations, mediumistic activities and theological speculations. There is little likelihood of Unificationism becoming more mainstream, and it seems probable that the shamanic features within the movement will become even more pronounced as time passes.

(First published as Occasional Paper No. 7, 1993)

Notes

1   This chapter is an expanded version of BASR Occasional Paper No. 7 (1993), which in turn developed material in my (then) recently published monograph, *The Advent of Sun Myung Moon* (Chryssides 1991).

2   The usual distinction between the ACM and CCM is that the former is secular, while the latter is religious, normally Christian. The CCM seeks to 'counter' NRMs by presenting a religious alternative, whereas the ACM tends to aim to 'rescue' members from 'cults' and to impede the latter's progress. On the anti-cult movement in the UK, see Chryssides (1999b).

3   For an explanation of the term 'New Christian' see Chryssides (1991, p 88), and for an account of the Unification Church in the context of other 'new Christian' movements, see Chryssides (1999a, chapter 4, pp. 120–163).

Bibliography

Barker, E. 1986. *The Making of a Moonie: Brainwashing or Choice?* Oxford: Blackwell.

Bjornstad, James 1976. *The Moon Is Not the Son*, Minneapolis: Bethany Fellowship Inc.

Blair W.N. and Hunt, Bruce F. 1977. *The Korean Pentecost and the Sufferings which Followed*, Edinburgh: Banner of Truth Trust.

Brooks, Keith L. and Robertson, Irvine 1985. *The Spirit of Truth and the Spirit of Error*, Chicago, Moody Press.

Catholic Truth Society 1986. 'Sects: The Pastoral Challenge', in *Briefing 86*, 6 June 1986, pp. 142–152 (republished as *New Religious Movements: A Challenge to the Church*, London: The Incorporated Catholic Truth Society).

Chryssides, George D. 1991, *The Advent of Sun Myung Moon: The Origins, Beliefs and Practices of the Unification Church*. London: Macmillan.

—— 1999a. *Exploring New Religions*, London: Cassell.

—— 1999b. 'Britain's Anti-Cult Movement', in B. Wilson and J. Cresswell (eds), *New Religious Movements: Challenge and Response*, London: Routledge, pp. 257–273.

—— 2001. 'Unrecognized Charisma: A Study of Four Charismatic Leaders – Charles Taze Russell, Joseph Smith, L. Ron Hubbard and Swami Prabhupada', *CESNUR Library Texts and Documents*; web version of revised conference paper, London School of Economics, April 2001. Located at URL: http://www.cesnur.org/2001/london2001/chryssides.htm.

Choi, Chungmoo 2003. 'The Artistry and Ritual Aesthetic of Urban Korean Shamans', in G. Harvey (ed.), *Shamanism: A Reader*, London: Routledge pp. 170–185.

Davies, Eryl 1990. *Truth under Attack: Cults and Contemporary Religions*, Darlington: Evangelical Press.

FAIR (Family Action Information and Rescue), n.d. [c.1994]. 'Cults: Are you vulnerable' (leaflet), London: FAIR.

Hong, Nansook 1998. *In the Shadow of the Moons: My Life in the Reverend Sun Myung Moon's Family*, Boston: Little, Brown and Company.

Jones, G.H. 1902. 'The Spirit Worship of the Koreans', *Transactions of the Korea Branch of the Royal Asiatic Society*, **2**, pp. 37–58.

Kyn, Chang Ki 1981. 'The Unification Principle and Oriental Thought', in Lee Nyong Hang (ed.), *Research on the Unification Principle*, Seoul: Song Hwa Press.

Lee, San Hun 1998. *Life in the Spirit World and on Earth*. New York: Family Federation for World Peace and Unification.

Nyong, Lee Hang (ed.), 1981. *Research on the Unification Principle*. Seoul: Song Hwa Press.

World Council of Churches 1980. *Recommended Guidelines to the Churches*, in *With People of Other Faiths in Britain: A Study Handbook for Christians*, London: United Reformed Church.

CHAPTER 15

Multiculturalism, Muslims and the British State

Tariq Modood

Introduction

The large presence of Muslims in Britain today (between 1.5 and 2 million, more than half of South Asian, primarily Pakistani, origins) is a result of Commonwealth immigration from the 1950s onwards. This was initially male labour from rural small farm owning and artisan backgrounds, seeking to meet the demand for unskilled and semi-skilled industrial workers in the British economy, with wives and children arriving from around the 1970s. The proportion of urban professionals among South Asian Muslim immigrants was small, though it increased with the arrival of political refugees from East Africa in the late 1960s and 1970s (although the majority of this group were Hindus and Sikhs). Britain, especially London as a cosmopolitan centre, has been very attractive to some of the rich and professional classes from the Middle East, especially from the 1970s onwards, with many investing in property in the city. There have, during recent times, also been waves of political refugees from other parts of the Muslim world, Somalia and Bosnia being two notable cases.

The relation between Muslims and the wider British society and British state has to be seen in terms of a development, and rising agendas, of racial equality and multiculturalism. Muslims, indeed, have become central to these agendas even while they have contested important aspects – especially the primacy of racial identities, narrow definitions of racism and equality and the secular bias of the discourse and policies of multiculturalism. While there are now emergent Muslim discourses of equality, of difference and of (to use the title of the newsletter of the Muslim Council of Britain) 'the common good', they have to be understood as appropriations and modulations of contemporary discourses and initiatives whose provenance lies in anti-racism and feminism. While one result of this has been at times to throw advocates of multiculturalism into theoretical and practical disarray, another has been to stimulate accusations of cultural separatism and revive a discourse of 'integration'. While we should not ignore the critics of Muslim activism, we need to recognise that at least some of the latter is a politics of 'catching-up' with racial equality and feminism. In this way religion in Britain is assuming a renewed political importance. After a long period of hegemony, political secularism can no longer be taken for granted. Rather, it is having to answer its critics as there is a growing understanding that the incorporation of Muslims has become the most important challenge of egalitarian multiculturalism.

Racial Equality Movements

The presence of new population groups such as these has made manifest certain kinds of racism in Britain, and anti-discrimination laws and policies began to be put into place from the 1960s onwards. These laws and policies, initially influenced by contemporary thinking and practice in relation to anti-black racism in the USA, assume that the grounds of discrimination are 'colour' and ethnicity. Not only is it in the last decade or so that Muslim assertiveness has become a feature of majority-minority relations, but indeed prior to this racial equality discourse and politics was dominated by the idea that the prevailing post-immigration issue was 'colour-racism' (Rex and Moore 1967; CCCS 1982; Sivanandan 1985; Gilroy 1987). This perspective was epigrammatically expressed twenty years ago by the writer, Salman Rushdie: 'Britain is now two entirely different worlds and the one you inherit is determined by the colour of your skin' (Rushdie 1982). He, together with most anti-racists, has come to adopt a more pluralistic perspective, and one in which the Muslim presence is seen as a fact to be ignored at one's peril. Nevertheless, in a pure or mixed form, the US-derived racial dualism continues to be an influential force in British social science and radical politics (Luthra 1997). One consequence of this is that the legal and political framework still reflects the conceptualisation and priorities of racial dualism.

At the present time, it is lawful to discriminate against Muslims *qua* Muslims because the courts do not accept that Muslims are an ethnic group (though oddly, Jews and Sikhs are recognised as ethnic groups within the meaning of the law). While initially not remarked upon, this exclusive focus on race and ethnicity, and the exclusion of Muslims but not Jews and Sikhs, has become a source of resentment amongst Muslims. Muslims do, however, enjoy some limited indirect legal protection *qua* members of ethnic groups such as Pakistanis, Arabs and so on. Over time, groups like Pakistanis have become an active constituency within British 'race relations' (Middle Easterners tend to classify themselves as 'white' and on the whole have not been prominent in political activism of this sort, nor in domestic politics generally). One of the effects of this politics is to highlight the 'racial' dimension of the newly settled populations and as an issue of concern in various policy areas.

A key measure and indicator of racial discrimination and inequality has been numerical under-representation in prestigious jobs, public offices, etc. Hence, people have had to be (self)classified and counted, so that group labels, and arguments about which labels are authentic, have become a common feature of certain political discourses. Over the years, it has also become apparent that by these measures of inequality it is Asian Muslims, and not Afro-Caribbeans, as policy-makers had originally expected, who have emerged as the most disadvantaged and poorest groups in the country (Modood 1992, Modood *et al.* 1997). To many Muslim activists the misplacing of Muslims into 'race' categories and the belatedness with which the severe disadvantages of the Pakistanis and Bangladeshis has come to be recognised by policy-makers means, at best, that race relations are an inappropriate policy niche for Muslims (UKACIA 1993). At worst, the activists perceive a conspiracy to prevent the emergence of a specifically Muslim socio-political formation (Muslim Parliament 1992). To see how such thinking has emerged we need to consider the career of the concept of 'racial equality'.

The initial development of anti-racism in Britain followed the American pattern, and indeed was directly influenced by American personalities and events. Just as in the USA, the colour-blind humanism of Martin Luther King, Jnr, came to be mixed with an emphasis on black pride, black autonomy and black nationalism as typified by Malcolm X (both of these inspirational leaders visited Britain). Indeed, it is better to view this development of projecting racial 'difference' and positive blackness as part of a wider socio-political climate which is not confined to issues of race and culture, nor to non-white minorities. Feminism, gay pride, Quebecois nationalism and the revival of Scottishness are some prominent examples of these new identity movements which have become an important feature in many countries, especially those in which class politics has declined.

In fact, it would be fair to say that what is often claimed today in the name of racial equality, especially in the English-speaking world, is more than would have been recognised as such in the 1960s. Iris Young expresses well the new political climate when she describes the emergence of an ideal of equality based not just on allowing excluded groups to assimilate and live by the norms of dominant groups, but based on the view that 'a positive self-definition of group difference is in fact more liberatory' (Young 1990, p. 157).

The shift is from an understanding of 'equality' in terms of individualism and cultural assimilation to a politics of recognition, to 'equality' as encompassing public ethnicity. 'Equality' is not having to hide or apologise for one's origins, family or community but requires others to show respect for them and adapt public attitudes and arrangements so that the heritage they represent is encouraged rather than contemptuously expected to wither away. There seem, then, to be two distinct conceptions of equal citizenship, each based on a different view of what is 'public' and 'private'. These two conceptions of equality may be stated as follows:

1   The right to assimilate to the majority/dominant culture in the public sphere; and toleration of 'difference' in the private sphere.
2   The right to have one's 'difference' (minority ethnicity, etc.) recognised and supported in the public *and* the private spheres.

While the former represents a liberal response to 'difference', the latter reflects the 'take' of radical identity politics. The two are not, however, alternative conceptions of equality in the sense that to hold one, the other must be rejected. Multiculturalism, properly construed, requires support for both conceptions. For the assumption behind the first is that participation in the public or national culture is necessary for the effective exercise of citizenship, the only obstacle to which are the exclusionary processes preventing gradual assimilation. The second conception, too, assumes that groups excluded from the national culture have their citizenship diminished as a result, and sees the remedy not in rejecting the right to assimilate, but in adding the right to widen and adapt the national culture and the public symbols of national membership to include the relevant minority ethnicities.

It can be seen, then, that the public-private distinction is crucial to the contemporary discussion of equal citizenship, and particularly to the challenge to an earlier liberal position. In a complete reversal of the liberal position, it has been argued that the assumption that difference must be privatised works as a 'gag-rule' to exclude matters of concern to marginalised and subordinated groups, such as women, who want erstwhile private gender relations to be the subject of collective deliberation and reform (Benhabib 1992; Fraser 1992). By extension, the same might be said of the religious practice of minorities; their political integration in terms of equality inevitably involves their challenging the existing boundaries of publicity. Integration flows from the process of discursive engagement as marginal groups begin to confidently assert themselves in the public space, and others begin to argue with and reach some agreement with them, as well as with the enactment of new laws, policies and so on. So the focus becomes participation in a discursive public space (Arendt 1963 and 1968; Habermas 1983 and 1987) and equality becomes defined as inclusion within a political community, not in terms of accepting the rules of the existing polity and its hallowed public-private boundaries, but the opposite. It is in this political-intellectual climate that Muslim assertiveness has emerged as a domestic political phenomenon; what would earlier have been called 'private' matters have become bases of the struggle for equality. In this respect, the advances achieved by anti-racism and feminism (with its slogan, 'the personal is the political') have acted as benchmarks for subsequent political group entrants, such as Muslims. As I will show, while Muslims raise distinctive concerns, the logic of their demands often mirrors those of other equality-seeking groups.

Muslim Identity Politics

The battle over *The Satanic Verses* that broke out in 1988–89 was seen by all concerned in terms of a battle between Islam and The West. On the Muslim side, it generated a far more impassioned activism and mobilisation than any previous campaign against racism (Modood 1990a). Many 'lapsed' or 'passive' Muslims – by which I mean Muslims, especially the non-religious, for whom hitherto their Muslim background was not particularly important – (re)dis-covered a new community solidarity. What was striking was that when the public rage against Muslims was at its most intense, Muslims neither sought nor were offered any special solidarity by any other non-white minority. The political embrace of a common 'black' identity by all non-whites – seen up to then as the key formation in the politics of post-immigration ethnicity – was seen as irrelevant to an issue which many Muslims insisted was fundamental to defining the kind of 'respect' or 'civility' appropriate to a peaceful multicultural society, that is to say, to the political constitution of 'difference' in Britain (Modood 1994). It was in fact white liberal Anglicans who tried to moderate the hostility against the angry Muslims, and it was inter-faith groups rather than Christians active in anti-racism, let alone political 'black' organisations, that tried to create space where Muslims could state their case without being vilified.

Why some identities are asserted rather than others is of course a contextual matter. Part of the answer as to which identity will emerge as important to a group at a particular time, however, lies in the nature of the minority group in question (Modood 1990b). Pakistanis were 'black' when it meant a job in a racial equality bureaucracy, 'Asian' when a community centre was in the offing, 'Muslim' when the Prophet was being ridiculed, 'Kashmiris' when a nationalist movement back home had taken off and blood was being spilt. That the Caribbeans have mobilised around a colour identity and the South Asians around religious and related identities is neither down to chance nor just a 'construction', but based on something deeper about these groups. That Muslims in their anger against *The Satanic Verses* found a depth of indignation, a 'voice' of their own, in a way that most had not found in relation to events and in mobilisation in the previous decades cannot be explained merely in terms of political leaderships, rivalries, tactics, etc. Certainly, some individuals and organisations exploited the situation, but they could not have done so if there was not a 'situation' to exploit.

Religious Equality

I have given some account of what terms like 'equality', 'inclusion' and 'recognition' mean in contemporary discourses, but what do they mean in practical terms? What kinds of specific policy demands are being made by or on behalf of religious groups and Muslim identity politics in particular, when these kinds of terms are being deployed? I suggest that these demands have three dimensions, which get progressively 'thicker' and which are progressively less acceptable to radical secularists.

The first and very basic demand is for no religious discrimination: that is, that religious people, no less than people defined by 'race' or gender, should not suffer discrimination in job and other opportunities. So, for example, a person who is trying to dress in accordance with their religion or who projects a religious identity, such as a Muslim woman wearing a headscarf (*hijab*), should not be discriminated against in employment. At the moment in Britain there is no legal ban on such discrimination and the government has said that the case for it is not proven. The legal system leaves Muslims particularly vulnerable because while discrimination against *yarmulke*-wearing Jews and turban-wearing Sikhs is deemed to be unlawful *racial* discrimination, Muslims, unlike these other faith communities, are not deemed to be a racial or ethnic group. Nor are they protected by the legislation against religious discrimination that does exist in the UK, for this, being explicitly designed to protect Roman Catholics, only applies to Northern Ireland. The best that Muslims are able to achieve is to prove that the discrimination against them is indirectly against their ethnic characteristics, that they suffered an indirect discrimination by virtue of being, say, a Pakistani or an Iraqi. While it is indeed the case that the discrimination against Muslims is mixed up with forms of colour-racism and cultural-racism (Modood 1997), the charge of indirect discrimination is a much weaker offence in law, carrying with it no compensatory requirements for the victim. Moreover, some Muslims are white and so do not enjoy this second-class protection. Indeed, many Muslim activists argue that religious freedom, being a fundamental right, should not be legally and politically dependent upon dubious concepts of race and ethnicity (UKACIA 1993). Campaigning for religious discrimination legislation in Britain has an importance for Muslims that is greater than for other minority faiths. The same applies to the demand for a law in Britain as a whole (again, it already exists in Northern Ireland) to curb and punish incitement to religious hatred to parallel the law against incitement to racial hatred (which extends to certain forms of anti-Semitic literature) (CRE 1990; Modood 1993a). After some years of arguing that there was no evidence of religious discrimination in Britain, the hand of the British government has been forced by the European Union's Article 13 of the Amsterdam Treaty (1999), which includes religious discrimination in the list of forms of discrimination that all member states are expected to eliminate. Accordingly, the UK government recently announced its intention to implement a European Commission directive to outlaw religious discrimination in employment in 2003 (Cabinet Office et al. 2001).[1] A Muslim organisation concerned with these issues is the Forum Against Islamophobia and Racism (FAIR), set up in 2000 'for the purpose of raising awareness of and combating Islamophobia and racism, monitoring specific incidents of Islamophobia and racism, working towards eliminating religious and racial discrimination, campaigning and lobbying on issues relevant to Muslim and other multi-ethnic communities in Britain' (publicity materials).

The second demand is for parity with native religions. Many minority faith advocates interpret equality to mean that minority religions should get at least some of the support from the state that older established religions do. Muslims have led the way on this argument too and have made two particular issues politically contentious, namely, the state funding of schools and the law of blasphemy. After some political battle, the government has in the last few years agreed to fund four Muslim schools, as well as a Sikh and a Seventh Day Adventist school, on the same basis enjoyed by thousands of Anglican and Catholic schools and some Methodist and Jewish schools. (In England and Wales, over a third of state-maintained primary and a sixth of secondary schools are run by a religious group.) Some secularists are unhappy about this. They say they accept the argument for parity but believe this should be achieved by the state withdrawing its funding from all religious schools. It has even been argued – though in the name of integration rather than multiculturalism – that this should be done expressly to prevent state-funded Muslim schools. Most Muslims reject this form of equality, by which the privileged lose something but the under-privileged gain nothing (except perhaps the resentment of the newly dispossessed). More specifically, the issue of 'equalising upwards' versus 'equalising downwards' is about the legitimacy of religion as a public institutional presence.

Muslims have failed to get the courts to interpret the existing statute on blasphemy to cover offences beyond what Christians hold as sacred, but some political support exists for an incitement to religious hatred offence, mirroring the existing offence of incitement to racial hatred. Indeed, the government inserted such a clause in the post-11 September 2001 security legislation, in order to conciliate Muslims who, amongst others, were strongly opposed to the new powers of surveillance, arrest and detention that were being proposed. As it transpired, most of the latter was made law, but the incitement to religious hatred offence was defeated in Parliament, though the new legislation affords protection against harassment, violence and criminal damage to property motivated by religious hatred.

The third demand is for positive inclusion of religious groups: that is, that religion in general, or at least the category of 'Muslim' in particular, should be a category by which the inclusiveness of social institutions should be judged in the same way that anti-racists use 'black' and feminists use 'female'. This would mean, for example, that employers would have to demonstrate that they do not discriminate against Muslims by explicit monitoring backed up by appropriate policies, targets, managerial responsibilities, work environments, staff training, advertisements, outreach and so on (FAIR 2002; CBMI 2002). Similarly, according to this model, local authorities should provide appropriately sensitive policies and staff, especially in relation to (non-Muslim) schools, social and health services and, say, fund Muslim community centres or Muslim youth workers in addition to the existing Asian and Caribbean community centres and the existing Asian and Black youth workers (Muslim Parliament 1992; UKACIA 1993). To take another case: an organisation like the BBC currently believes it is of political importance to review and improve its personnel practices and its output of programmes, including its on-screen 'representation' of the British population, by providing for, and winning the confidence of, say, women, ethnic groups and young people. Why should it not also use religious groups as a criterion of inclusivity and have to demonstrate that it is doing the same for viewers and staff defined by religious community membership? In short, Muslims should be treated as a legitimate group in their own right (not only because they are, say, Asians), whose presence in British society ought to be explicitly reflected in all walks of life and in all institutions; and whether they are so included would then become one of the criteria for judging Britain as an egalitarian, inclusive, multicultural society. A potentially significant victory along these lines was made when the government agreed to include a religion question in the 2001 Census. This was the first time such a question had been included since 1851 and its re-incorporation was largely unpopular outside the politically active religionists, amongst whom Muslims were foremost. However, this initiative has the potential to pave the way for widespread 'religious monitoring' in the way that the inclusion of an ethnic question in 1991 led to the routinisation of 'ethnic monitoring'.

These policy demands no doubt seem odd within the terms of the French or US 'wall of separation' between the state and religion and may make secularists uncomfortable in Britain too. But it is clear that they virtually mirror existing anti-discrimination policy provisions in the UK. In an analysis of some Muslim organisations' responses to a CRE consultation on the reform of the Race Relations Act in the early 1990s, following the activism stimulated by the Rushdie affair, I argued that the main lines of argument could be captured in the following three positions:

(i)   a 'colour-blind' human rights and human dignity approach;
(ii) an approach based on an extension of the concepts of racial discrimina-
      tion and racial equality to include anti-Muslim racism;
(iii) a Muslim-power approach.

I concluded that these 'reflect not so much obscurantist Islamic interventions into a modern secular discourse, but typical minority options in contemporary Anglo-American equality politics, and employ the rhetorical, conceptual and institutional resources available in that politics' (Modood 1993b, p. 518).

All three approaches are in evidence today, though some high-profile radicals have made a Muslim-power approach more prominent, not dissimilar to the rise of black power activism after the height of the civil rights period in the USA. This approach is nourished by despair at the victimisation and humiliation of Muslims in places such as Palestine, Iraq, Bosnia, Chechnya, Kashmir, Kosovo and Afghanistan. For many British Muslims, such military disasters and humanitarian horrors evoke a strong desire to express solidarity with oppressed Muslims through the political idea of the *Ummah*, the global community of Muslims, which must defend and restore itself as a global player. To take the analogy with US Black Power a bit further, one can say that as black nationalism and Afrocentrism developed as one ideological expression of black power, so similarly, political Islamism has emerged as a search for Muslim dignity and power.

Muslim assertiveness, then, though triggered and intensified by what are seen as attacks on Muslims, is not primarily derived from Islam or Islamism but from contemporary western ideas about equality and multiculturalism. It is, however, increasingly being joined by Islamic evocations and Islamists, especially as there is a sense that Muslim populations across the world are repeatedly suffering at the hands of their neighbours, aided and abetted by the US and its allies, and Muslims must come together to defend themselves. Politically active Muslims in Britain, however, are likely to be part of domestic multicultural and equality currents, emphasising discrimination (direct, indirect and institutional) in relation to educational and economic opportunities, political representation, the media and 'Muslim-blindness' in the provision of health-care and social services, for example. They are arguing for remedies which mirror existing legislation and policies in relation to sexual and racial equality (Modood 2002).

A Panicky Retreat to a Liberal Public-Private Distinction

If the emergence of a politics of difference out of and alongside a liberal assimilationist equality created a dissonance, as indeed it did, the emergence of a British Muslim identity out of and alongside ethno-racial identities has created an even greater dissonance. Philosophically speaking, it should create a lesser dissonance for it seems to me that a move from the idea of equality as sameness to equality as difference is a more profound conceptual movement than the creation of a new identity in a field already crowded with minority identities. But this is to ignore the hegemonic power of secularism in British political culture, especially on the centre-left. While black and related ethno-racial identities were welcomed by, indeed were intrinsic to, the rainbow coalition of identity politics, this coalition is deeply unhappy with Muslim consciousness. While for some, this suspicion is specific to Islam, for many the ostensible reason relates to a religious identity generally, which, it is held, should be confined to the private sphere. What is most interesting is that in this latter objection, if it is taken at its face value, the difference theorists, activists and paid professionals revert to a public-private distinction that they have spent two or three decades demolishing. The unacceptability of Muslim identity is no doubt partly to do with the conservative views on gender and sexuality professed by Muslim spokespersons, not to mention issues to do with freedom of expression, as arose in the Rushdie affair (Modood 1993b). But these are objections to specific views, and as such they can be argued with on a point-by-point basis – they are not objections to an identity. The radical secularist objection to Muslim identity as a politicised religious identity is, of course, incompatible with the politics of difference perspective on the essentially contested nature of the public-private distinction described earlier. It is therefore in contradiction with a thoroughgoing conception of multi-culturalism, which should allow the political expression of religion to enter public discourse (Modood 1998; Parekh 2000). We thus have a mixed-up situation where secular multiculturalists argue that the sex lives of individuals – traditionally, a core area of liberal privacy – are a legitimate feature of political identities and public discourse, and seem to generally welcome the sexualisa-tion of culture, if not the prurient interest in the sexual activity of public characters, while on the other hand, religion – a key source of communal identity in traditional, non-liberal societies – is to be regarded as a private matter, perhaps as a uniquely private matter. Most specifically, Muslim identity is seen as the illegitimate child of British multiculturalism.

Indeed, the Rushdie affair made evident that the group in British society most politically opposed to Muslims, or at least to Muslim identity politics, were not Christians, or even right-wing nationalists, but the secular, liberal intelligentsia. Muslims are frequently criticised by columnists in the respectable press in a way that few, if any, other minority groups are. Muslims often remark that if in such articles the words 'Jews' or 'blacks' were substituted for 'Muslims', the newspapers in question would be attacked as racist and indeed risk legal proceedings (Runnymede Trust report on Islamophobia 1997). Just as the hostility against Jews, in various times and places, has been a varying blend of anti-Judaism (hostility to a religion) and anti-Semitism (hostility to a racialised group), so it is difficult to gauge to what extent contemporary British Islamophobia is 'religious' and to what extent 'racial'. Even before the aftermath of 11 September, it was generally becoming acknowledged that, of all groups, Asians face the greatest hostility, and Asians themselves feel this is because of hostility directed specifically at Muslims (Modood et al. 1997). In the summer of 2001, the racist British National Party began explicitly to distinguish between good, law-abiding Asians and Asian Muslims (see BNP website). Much low-level harassment (abuse, spitting, name-calling, pulling off a headscarf and so on) continues to go unreported, even though the number of reported attacks since 11 September has been four times higher than usual (in the US it has increased thirteen-fold, including two deaths) (Herbert and Burrell 2002).

The confused retreat from multiculturalism has of course been given an enormous impetus by the events of 11 September. They led to widespread questioning, once again echoing the Rushdie affair, about whether Muslims can be and are willing to be integrated into British society and its political values. This has ranged from anxiety about terrorist cells and networks, recruitment of alienated young Muslims for mischief abroad and as a 'fifth column' at home; to whether Muslims are willing to give loyalty to the British state rather than to transnational Muslim leaders and causes; and to whether Muslims are committed to what are taken to be the core British values of freedom, tolerance, democracy, sexual equality and secularism. Many politicians, commentators, letter-writers and phone-callers to the media, from across the political spectrum, not to mention the Home Secretary, have blamed the fact that these questions have had to be asked on the cultural separatism and self-imposed segregation of Muslim migrants and on a 'politically correct' multiculturalism that has fostered fragmentation rather than integration and Britishness. The New Labour government of Prime Minister Tony Blair has been at the forefront of this, as have been many others who are prominent on the Centre-Left and have long-standing anti-racist credentials. For example, the Commission for Racial Equality published an article by the left-wing author, Kenan Malik, arguing that 'multiculturalism has helped to segregate communities far more effectively than racism' (Malik 2001). Hugo Young, the leading liberal columnist of the Centre-Left newspaper, *The Guardian*, went further and wrote that multiculturalism 'can now be seen as a useful bible for any Muslim who insists that his religio-cultural priorities, including the defence of jihad against America, overrides his civic duties of loyalty, tolerance, justice and respect for democracy' (Young 2001). More extreme again, Farrukh Dhondy, an Asian who has pioneered multicultural broadcasting on British television, writes of a 'multicultural fifth column' which must be rooted out and state funding of multiculturalism redirected into a defence of the values of freedom and democracy (Dhondy 2001).

One of the issues that has come to be central to this debate is that of 'faith schools', that is to say, state-funded schools run by religious organisations rather than by local authorities. While they must teach the national curriculum and are inspected by the central government they can allocate some space to religious instruction, though not all do so. They are popular with parents for their ethos, discipline and academic achievements and so can select their pupils, often giving priority to children whose parents can demonstrate a degree of religious observance. Violent disturbances in some Northern English cities in the summer of 2001, in which Asian Muslim men were amongst the central protagonists, were officially blamed on the fact of segregated communities and segregated schools (Cantle 2001; Ritchie 2001). Some of these were church-run schools and were more than 90 per cent Christian and white. Others were amongst the most under-resourced and under-achieving in the country and had rolls of more than 90 per cent Muslims. Although some parties, including several official reports (Ouseley 2001), dubbed these 'Muslim schools', in fact, they were nothing of the sort. They were local, bottom-of-the-pile comprehensive schools which had suffered from decades of under-investment and 'white-flight' but which were run by white teachers according to a secular national curriculum. 'Muslim schools' then came to be seen as the source of the problem of divided cities, cultural backwardness, riots, lack of Britishness and a breeding ground for militant Islam. Muslim-run schools were lumped into this category of 'Muslim schools', even though all the evidence suggested that their pupils (mainly juniors and girls) did not engage in riots and terrorism and, despite limited resources, achieved better exam results than local authority 'secular' schools. On the basis of these constructions – of 'Muslim schools' and 'faith schools' alike – tirades by prominent columnists in the broadsheets were launched, arguing against the allowance of state-funding to any more Muslim-run schools, or even to a church-run school. Once again, demands were made to make the British state entirely secular. For example, Polly Toynbee argued in *The Guardian* that a pre-condition of tackling racial segregation was that 'religion should be kept at home, in the private sphere' (Toynbee 2001).

Conclusion

In conclusion, I would suggest that the emergence of Muslim political agency has thrown British multiculturalism into theoretical and practical disarray. This is worrying because on any objective reading there cannot be what one might call a race relations settlement in Britain without the Muslims, because nearly half of all non-whites are Muslims. On the other hand, Muslims cannot prosper without political allies and without the goodwill of the educated classes, both of which are denied to them at the moment. What is true of Britain is true of other countries too. A hundred years ago, the African-American theorist, W.E.B. duBois, predicted that 'the problem of the twentieth century is the problem of the colour line' (DuBois 1995); today, we seem to be set for a century of the Islam-West line. The political integration or incorporation of Muslims (there are more Muslims in the European Union than the combined populations of Finland, Ireland and Denmark) has not only become the most important goal of egalitarian multiculturalism but is now pivotal in shaping the security, nay, the destiny of many peoples across the globe.

(First published as Occasional Paper No. 25, 2002)

Notes

1 See 'Employment Equality (Religion or Belief) Regulations 2003', operative from 2.12.03.

Bibliography

Arendt, H. 1963. *On Revolution*, New York: Viking Press.

Arendt, H. 1968. *Human Condition*, London: University of Chicago Press.

Benhabib, S. 1992. *Situating the Self*, New York: Routledge.

British National Party (BNP) [online] Available at http://www.bnp.org.uk [accessed 15 May 2001].

Cabinet Office et al. 2001. *Towards Equality and Diversity: Implementing the Employment and Race Directives*, London: UK Government.

Cantle, T. 2001. *Community Cohesion: A Report of the Independent Review Team*, London: The UK Home Office.

CBMI (Commission on British Muslims and Islamophobia) 2002. *Response To the Commion on Racial Equality's Code of Practice*, February, London: CBMI.

CCCS (Centre for Contemporary Cultural Studies) 1982. *The Empire Strikes Back*, London: Hutchinson.

CRE (Commission for Racial Equality) 1990. *Free Speech: Report of a Seminar*, London: CRE.

CMEB (Commission on Multi-Ethnic Britain) 2000. *The Future of Multi-Ethnic Britain*, London: Profile Books.

Dhondy, F. 2001. 'Our Islamic Fifth Column', in *City Journals*, **11** (4). Available from http://www.city-journal.org/html/11_4_our_islamic.html [accessed 5th November, 2001].

DuBois, W.E.B. 1995. *The Souls of Blacks*, New York: Signet.

FAIR (Forum Against Islamophobia and Racism) 2002. *A Response To The Government Consultation Paper, 'Towards Equality and Diversity: Implementing the Employment and Race Directives'*. London: FAIR.

Fraser, N. 1992. 'Rethinking the Public Sphere', in G. Calhoun (ed.) *Habermas and the Public Sphere*, Cambridge, Mass.: MIT Press, pp. 109–142.

Gilroy, P. 1987. *There Ain't No Black in the Union Jack*, London: Routledge.

Habermas, J. 1983. *The Theory of Communicative Competence, vol 1: Reason and the Rationalisation of Society*, Boston: Beacon.

Habermas, J. 1987. *The Theory of Communicative Competence, vol 2: Lifeworld and System*, Boston: Beacon.

Herbert, I. and Burrell, I. 2002. 'Dossier Reveals a Massive Rise in Attacks on British Muslims', *The Independent* (London), 4 January.

Luthra, M. 1997. *Britain's Black Population: Social Change, Public Policy and Agenda*, Aldershot: Ashgate.

Malik, K. 2001. 'The Real Value of Diversity', *Connections*, Winter 2001–2002, London: Commission for Racial Equality.

Modood, T. 1990a. 'British Asian Muslims and the Rushdie affair', *Political Quarterly*, **61** (2), pp. 143–160. (Reproduced in J. Donald and A. Rattansi (eds), 1992, *'Race', Culture and Difference*, London: Sage).

—— 1990b. 'Catching up with Jesse Jackson: Being Oppressed and Being Somebody', *New Community*, **17** (1), pp. 87–98. (Reproduced in T. Modood, 1992.)

—— 1992. *Not Easy Being British: Colour, Culture and Citizenship*, London: Runnymede Trust.

—— 1993a. 'Muslims, Incitement to Hatred and the Law', in J. Horton (ed.) *Liberalism, Multiculturalism and Toleration*, London: Macmillan, pp. 139–156. (Reproduced in UKACIA, 1993.)

———— 1993b. 'Muslim Views on Religious Identity and Racial Equality', *New Community* **19** (3), pp. 513–519.

———— 1994. 'Political Blackness and British Asians', *Sociology*, **28** (3), pp. 859–876.

———— 1997. 'Difference, Cultural Racism and Anti-racism', in P. Werbner and T. Modood (eds), *Debating Cultural Identity*, London: Zed Books, pp. 154–172.

———— 1998. 'Anti-essentialism, Multiculturalism and the "Recognition" of Religious Minorities', in *Journal of Political Philosophy*, **6** (4), pp. 378–399. (Reproduced in W. Kymlicka and W. Norman (eds), 2000, *Citizenship in Diverse Societies*, Oxford: Oxford University Press).

———— 2002. 'The Place of Muslims in British Secular Multiculturalism', in N. Alsayyad and M. Castells (eds), *Muslim Europe or Euro-Islam: Politics, Culture and Citizenship in the Age of Globalisation*, New York: Lexington Books, pp. 113–130.

Modood, T., Berthoud, R., Lakey, J., Nazroo, J., Smith, P., Virdee, S. and Beishon, S., 1997. *Ethnic Minorities in Britain: Diversity and Disadvantage*, London: Policy Studies Institute.

Modood, T. et al., 1997. *Britain's Ethnic Minorities: Diversity and Disadvantage*, London: Policy Studies Institute.

Muslim Parliament of Great Britain 1992. *Race Relations and Muslims in Great Britain: A Discussion Paper*, London: The Muslim Parliament.

Ouseley, H. 2001. *Community Pride, Not Prejudice: Making Diversity Work in Bradford*, Bradford: Bradford Vision, Bradford City Council.

Parekh, B. 2000. *Rethinking Multiculturalism: Political Theory and Cultural Diversity*, London: Palgrave.

Rex, J. and Moore, R. 1967. *Race, Community and Conflict*, Oxford: Oxford University Press.

Ritchie, D. 2001. *Oldham Panel: one Oldham one Future*, Oldham Independent Review Team.

Runnymede Trust Commission on British Muslims and Islamophobia 1997. *Islamophobia: A Challenge To Us All*, London: The Runnymede Trust.

Rushdie, S. 1982. 'The New Empire Within Britain', *New Society*, 9 December 1982, pp. 417–421.

Sivanandan, A. 1985. 'RAT and the Degradation of the Black Struggle', in *Race and Class*, **XXVI** (4), pp. 1–34.

Toynbee, P. 2001. 'Religion must be Removed from all Functions of State', in *The Guardian*, 12 December 2001. Available from: http://www.guardian.co.uk.

UKACIA 1993. *Muslims and the Law in Multi-faith Britain: Need for Reform*, London: UK Action Committee on Islamic Affairs.

Young, H.A. 2001. 'Corrosive National Danger in our Multiculturalism Model', *The Guardian*, 6 November 2001. Available from: http://www.guardian.co.uk.

Young, I. 1990. *Justice and the Politics of Difference*, Princeton: Princeton University Press.

Separating Religion from the 'Sacred': Methodological Agnosticism and the Future of Religious Studies

James L. Cox

I am grateful to the editor of this volume for giving me the opportunity to have the 'last word' amongst such rich and varied contributions to the Occasional Papers Series of the British Association for the Study of Religions. I intend to use this 'afterword' as a way of looking 'forward', particularly in response to what I see as the present crisis confronting scholars who seek to employ methodologies that are in some sense unique to Religious Studies.

Especially since the publication of Ninian Smart's *The Science of Religion and the Sociology of Knowledge* (1973), the academic study of religions has been dominated by the concept that the scholar of religions, for methodological purposes, makes no comment on the truth, reality or value of the religious communities under study. In traditional phenomenology of religion, this has been associated with the idea of *epoché*, whereby scholars suspend their personal judgements about any religion whilst they are engaged in their academic work. Smart called this 'methodological agnosticism', by which he meant simply that 'we neither affirm nor deny the existence of the gods' (Smart 1973, p. 54). In his reader exploring the insider/outsider problem in the study of religion, Russell McCutcheon (1999, pp. 216–217) characterises 'methodological agnosticism' in the following way: 'Not knowing how the universe really is organized – not knowing if it is organized at all – the scholar of religion seeks not to establish a position in response to this question but to describe, analyse, and compare the positions taken by others'. The idea that academics must adopt a neutral, value-free position with respect to the study of religions, which is endorsed at least implicitly by many of the papers in this volume and, in my view, still constitutes mainstream thinking amongst scholars of religion, stands at the root of the current crisis confronting Religious Studies in Britain, both ideologically and institutionally.

Methodological Agnosticism as a Surreptitious Theology

In his controversial book, *The Ideology of Religious Studies* (2000), Timothy Fitzgerald of the University of Stirling argues forcefully that, by insisting on 'methodological agnosticism', scholars within the academic study of religions have adopted, either unwittingly or surreptitiously, a form of liberal theology, where the universal transcendent becomes the defining focus for the study of religion. 'Methodological agnosticism', according to Fitzgerald, has been used to support the claim that religion comprises a distinct category for study, *sui generis*, in a classification of its own, requiring its own peculiar methodologies. But, he asks, what makes religion somehow distinct, *sui generis*, and unique? The only available answer must be its transcendental referent, variously called God, the sacred or the ultimate. This is because, by definition, methodological agnosticism, although ostensibly refusing to investigate the transcendent, bases its claim to methodological uniqueness precisely on its agnostic position in relation to the transcendent. When this becomes the defining focus for its methodology, we are no longer in the realm of the social sciences, but theology, which also bases its methodologies in relation to the study of that which is entirely non-falsifiable.

Nowhere can this be seen better than in the writings of Ninian Smart (Fitzgerald 2000, pp. 54–70), whom Fitzgerald associates with the movement to make the study of religion non-reductive to other disciplines in the social sciences while retaining a non-theological approach. Fitzgerald contends that, rather than somehow bridging the gap between social scientific reductionism and theology, Smart actually becomes entangled in a massive contradiction. Throughout his many writings, Smart maintains, according to Fitzgerald, an essentialist, reified concept of religion, but soon runs into difficulties and is forced to identify 'religion-like' characteristics in non-religious ideologies such as nationalism, Marxism, Freudianism and sport.

Smart is well known for his division of religion into what he calls its 'dimensions': ritual or practical, doctrinal or philosophical, mythic or narrative, experiential or emotional, ethical or legal, organisational or social, and material or artistic (Smart 1997, pp. 10–12). Religious manifestations vary from culture to culture, but an essence, called 'religion', transforms itself into particular cultural and social expressions. Fitzgerald (2000, p. 56) calls this an imagery 'of a primary substance, an essence, taking on some of the secondary properties of the institutional media through which it manifests itself'. 'Religion-like' ideologies thus possess many of the dimensions of religion, including ritual, myth, beliefs and community, but they lack the dimension of the sacred. This is why they only resemble religions. For Fitzgerald, this means that Smart, despite his attempt to develop an approach to the study of religions which can be reduced neither to the social sciences nor to theology, fails precisely because he retains a theological perspective by insisting that the 'sacred' comprises the unique focus of religion.

Fitzgerald contends that, as non-theological scholars of religion, the object of our inquiry is not a transcendental referent, since that cannot be investigated using methods that are open to the natural and human sciences. The object of our study is 'culture, understood as the study of values, and the interpretation of symbolic systems, including the ritualization of everyday life' and 'the legitimation of power' (2000, pp. 20–21). If the object of our study is culture, then the methods employed in scholarly research belong largely within the social sciences. Methods unique to religion do not exist, unless scholars of religion either surreptitiously or unwittingly smuggle into their agenda theological motives. Fitzgerald's analysis thus creates a 'crisis' within the academic study of religions by forcing scholars of religion either to embrace theology quite transparently, or to admit that they actually study cultural practices. University departments of Religious Studies, as a result, should either be collapsed into theology programmes or subsumed within schools of social and cultural studies. This conclusion seems inevitable, unless we can uncouple the sacred, God or Fitzgerald's transcendental referent from 'religion'.

Separating the Sacred from Religion

The French sociologist, Danièle Hervieu-Léger has attempted to do just that in a book first published in French in 1993, with the English version appearing in 2000 under the title *Religion as a Chain of Memory* (see also Hervieu-Léger 1999). Hervieu-Léger agrees with Fitzgerald that most scholars have defined religion substantively, that is by identifying its essence with the contents of belief, such as 'mysterious power, total separation between a sacred and profane world and an ambivalence which renders the sacred an object at once of fascination and revulsion' (Hervieu-Léger 2000, p. 49). This way of defining religion transforms the concept of 'sacredness' from an adjective into a noun, and thereby quite narrowly renders 'the sacred' the unique subject matter of all religions. Functional definitions of religion, by contrast, are so broad as to include almost anything. Usually, they depict religion as a quest for meaning, or an attempt to make sense of the world, or a way to overcome the fear of death. Functional definitions thus see religion, in Hervieu-Léger's words, 'as the mechanism of meaning which enables humanity to transcend the deceptions, uncertainties and frustrations of everyday life' (*ibid*, p. 34).

Hervieu-Léger argues that by turning the act of defining religion towards the social context which necessitates it, the deficiencies found in both substantive and functional definitions can be overcome. Thus, scholars will no longer seek to isolate the 'essence' of religion, but instead will analyse the transformations occurring in the socio-historical manifestations of religion. This leads to Hervieu-Léger's central contention: religion exists when 'the authority of tradition' has been invoked 'in support of the act of believing' (*ibid*, p. 76). She explains:

> *As our fathers believed, and because they believed, we too believe ...* Seen thus, one would describe any form of believing as religious which sees its commitment to a chain of belief it adopts as all-absorbing. (emphasis hers) (*ibid*, p. 81)

Since no religion subsists without the invocation of the authority of a tradition, neither substantive nor functional definitions refer necessarily to religious phenomena. Rather, they imply a concept that confers on objects, symbols or values that which results in a feeling of radical dependence 'experienced, individually and/or collectively, in emotional contact with an external force' (*ibid*, p. 106–107). This suggests that although people who experience 'the sacred' testify to encountering a force or a power that is greater than themselves, this does not provide evidence for the existence of religion.

The example of sport helps elucidate Hervieu-Léger's point. She characterises sport as producing instantaneously collective meaning for the participants and spectators. Sporting events provide rituals and they fulfil expectations. Spectator sports in contemporary society, in Hervieu-Léger's words, foster 'access to an experience of the sacred (an immediate, emotional realization of meaning)' (*ibid*, p. 104). This experience, however, is not religious because it is instantaneous, spontaneous and does not result from the authority transmitted through a chain of belief. Hervieu-Léger concludes: 'What sport (and other domains) well exemplify is that, in modern society, the form of experience that is known by the term "sacred" may occur outside any religion' (*ibid*, p. 107). Scholars of religion thus need to develop methods that investigate the key elements of religion, which, for Hervieu-Léger include expressions of believing, memory of continuity and the legitimating reference to an authorised version of such memory (*ibid*, p. 97).

Hervieu-Leger's thesis has been well documented in many contexts. In my own experience of the Shona-speaking people of Zimbabwe, for example, it soon became evident to me in field studies that the order of the spirit world corresponds closely to the hierarchical order of society. The myths, rituals and rules of Shona religion transmit the authority of the ancestors, and by extension the chiefs and elders, and are legitimated by them. The Shona are religious, on this view, not because they believe in the ultimate power either of Mwari (the high God) or in *mhondoro* (senior ancestral spirits), but so long as such beliefs maintain the chain of tradition, or, under various internal or external influences on society, find the authority disrupted and substitute appropriate alternatives. Where authority is challenged, as has been done by government agencies in Zimbabwe recently, problems occur in the society until a resolution to the interrupted chain of memory is achieved.

If Hervieu-Léger is right, therefore, Smart's error has resulted from his identification of religion with the sacred. If this connection is uncoupled, it will be clear that there is no need to identify 'real' religion as focusing on a transcendental object and 'quasi-religion' as that which lacks such a focus. Nationalism, Marxism, Freudianism and sport all lead participants into an experience of that which is greater than themselves and thus induce feelings of sacredness. As a result, they cannot be distinguished from conventional religions, like Christianity, Buddhism, or Islam, on grounds that they lack a focus on the sacred or a transcendental referent, but because they lack an authoritatively transmitted collective memory.

Conclusions for the Academic Study of Religions

Fitzgerald's critique of Smart and the resolution to the problem of the sacred provided by Hervieu-Léger suggest important directions for the future of Religious Studies. In the first instance, it now seems clear that scholars of religion cannot avoid the conclusions put forward by Fitzgerald that religions must be studied as social and cultural expressions within specific historical, geographical, political and economic contexts. Smart's dimensions can be employed, but without carrying forward his essentialist idea of religion as transcendentally focused. We can also endorse his polymethodical approach by drawing on the full range of human sciences to understand how traditions have been transmitted authoritatively in various societies and how these have been re-enforced in myths, rituals, doctrines, legal institutions, artistic expressions and in testimonies of believers. Following Hervieu-Léger, moreover, we can study religion in its social and historical manifestations as a chain of memory, passed on authoritatively from generation to generation, whilst at the same time adapting to changing local and global contexts. Rather than leading to the demise of Religious Studies, therefore, by separating the sacred from religion a methodological middle ground between theology and culture is restored. If Fitzgerald's argument can be countered, in a way suggested by Hervieu-Léger, the field known as Religious Studies can be expanded to encompass within it a rich variety of cultural practices whilst eliminating once and for all any illicit association with confessional theology.

Bibliography

Fitzgerald, Timothy 2000. *The Ideology of Religious Studies*, New York and Oxford: Oxford University Press.

Hervieu-Léger, Danièle 2000. *Religion as a Chain of Memory*, Cambridge: Polity Press.

Hervieu-Léger, Danièle 1999. 'Religion as Memory: Reference to Tradition and the Constitution of a Heritage of Belief in Modern Societies', in Jan G. Platvoet and Arie L. Molendijk (eds), *The Pragmatics of Defining Religion: Contexts, Concepts and Contests*, Leiden: Brill, pp. 73–92.

McCutcheon, Russell (ed.) 1999. *The Insider/Outsider Problem in the Study of Religion: A Reader*, London and New York: Cassell.

Smart, Ninian 1973. *The Science of Religion and the Sociology of Knowledge*, Princeton: Princeton University Press.

Smart, Ninian 1997. *Dimensions of the Sacred. An Anatomy of the World's Beliefs*, London: Fontana Press.

Index

Abraham, 34, 43
academic departments, xxi–xxii, 14
academics, xxi, 15, 59, 61, 114–117
  see also scholars
actors, 194, 195
Adam and Eve, 234, 238, 241
Aedui, 158, 160
Africa
  adaptation, 221, 224, 228
  change, 218, 219, 224, 226, 227, 228
  history, 103–104
  independent churches, 99
  modernity, 219
  moving between religions, 224, 226
  new religions, 217, 219, 225, 228
  return to, 101–103
  spirituality, 221–223, 225
  see also African traditional religion
African-Americans, 94–95, 97, 98, 102
African Christians, 219
  in Europe, 91–92, 98, 99, 100, 101, 102
  identity, 99, 100, 101
African diaspora, 94–104
African Instituted churches, 218, 225
African traditional religion
  and Christianity, 217
  modification of, 227, 228
  and other religions, 218–219, 221, 224, 225
  spirits, 222–223, 224, 225, 226
afterlife, 153, 154, 156, 161, 183, 239
Ahmed, Akbar, 28
Akan, 218, 221, 222
Albrow, Martin, 74, 75
altered states, 135, 142
Amaterasu, 111–112
ambiguity, 151, 162, 231
Amsterdam, xiv
analysis, xxviii, xxxv, 104, 124
anatta, 183, 184, 185
ancestors, 211, 221, 223
Andraste, 151

animals, 151, 152–156, 157, 240
anthropology, 15, 33
anti-cult movement (ACM), 231, 232
anti-racism, 245, 246–248
anti-semitism, 250, 254
anxiety, 204
Apollo, 158
apophatic experience, 143
Appadurai, A., 74, 75
apperception, 135, 142
archaeology, 21, 149, 151, 156
archetypes, 40
architecture, 16
Argyle, Michael, 125, 127
Ark, 48–49
arts, 20
asceticism, 189; *see also* widow-ascetic
Ashanti, 223
Asian Muslims, 247
Assimeng, Professor, 219
assimilation, 248, 253
atheism, 182
Augustine, 43–44
authority, 14, 262–263
awareness, 133, 135, 138
awe, 126

Babin, Pierre, 26–27
Badb Catha, 151
Baetke, W., 65
Bailey, Edward, 4
Bangladeshis, 73, 74, 247
baptism, 225
Barker, Eileen, 233
Bath, 157
Bath College of Higher Education, 3
Bauman, Z., 67, 69, 70, 77, 78
Baumann, Gerd, 72–73, 743, 80, 93, 99, 100
Baumann, M., 100, 104
bear symbol, 154
behaviour, 6, 7, 15, 34, 36